Maria Martin's World

Maria Martin's

The University of Alabama Press *Tuscaloosa*

World

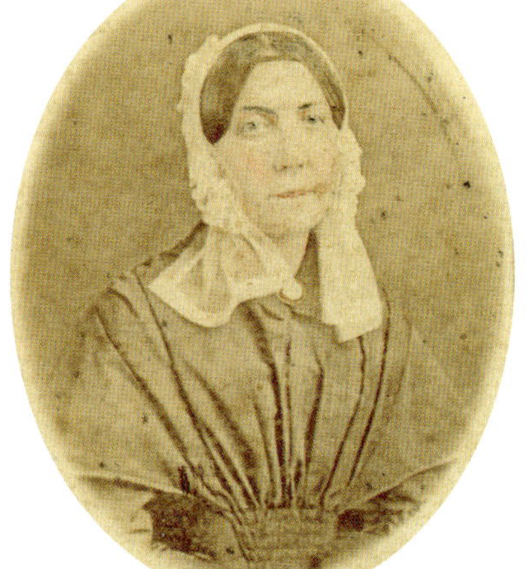

ART &
SCIENCE,
FAITH &
FAMILY *in*
AUDUBON'S
AMERICA

DEBRA J. LINDSAY

The University of Alabama Press
Tuscaloosa, Alabama 35487-0380
uapress.ua.edu

Typeface: Adobe Caslon and Bembo

Frontispiece: Maria Martin (1796–1863), c.1855 carte-de-visite. This is the only known image of Maria Martin. Given the touches of color added to the image, it was likely prepared by William Hunt. Known for his "photographic paintings," he joined George Cook in his Charleston shop in 1855 (Teal, 2001). Courtesy of the Charleston Museum.

Cover image: Loblolly bay (*Gordonia lasianthus*) by Maria Martin, June 1832. Study for Havell edition, *Birds of America*, plate 168, fork-tailed flycatcher (*Tyrannus savana*). Watercolor, graphite, black ink; 54.8 x 35.9 cm (21⁹⁄₁₆ x 14⅛ in). 1863.17.168. Purchased by public subscription from Mrs. John J. Audubon. Collection of the New-York Historical Society. Digital image created by Oppenheimer Edition.

Cover design: Michele Myatt Quinn

Publication made possible in part by generous contributions from Dr. Cameron and Judge J. Scott Vowell, Beverley Hart and William E. Smith Jr., and Sandra Irving.

Library of Congress Cataloging-in-Publication Data

Names: Lindsay, Debra, author.

Title: Maria Martin's world: art and science, faith and family in Audubon's America / Debra J. Lindsay.

Description: Tuscaloosa: The University of Alabama Press, [2018] | Includes bibliographical references and index.

Identifiers: LCCN 2017007058 | ISBN 9780817319519 (cloth) | ISBN 9780817391218 (ebook)

Subjects: LCSH: Martin, Maria, 1796–1863. | Audubon, John James, 1785–1851. | Women painters—South Carolina—Charleston—Biography. | Botanical artists—South Carolina—Charleston—Biography. | Charleston (S.C.)—Biography.

Classification: LCC F273.M38 L56 2018 | DDC 759.13 [B] —dc23

LC record available at https://lccn.loc.gov/2017007058

CONTENTS

LIST OF ILLUSTRATIONS

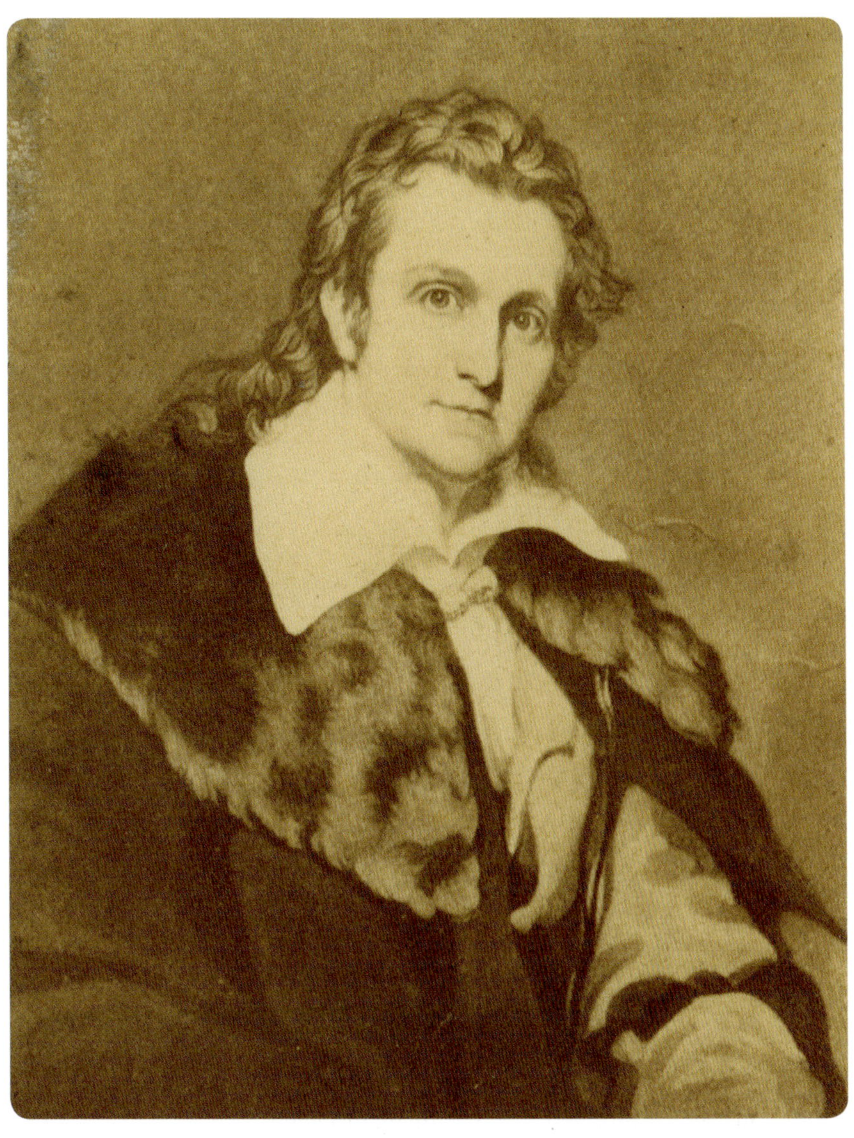

FIGURE 1. John James Audubon (1785–1851), 1831. Photographic reproduction of carte-de-visite on paper, laid on card (after a miniature by Frederick Cruickshank [1800–1868]) by Horton & Allen Photographers, Boston, c. 1861–1862. 10.5 x 6 cm (4⅛ x 2 3/8 in). Department of Prints, Photographs, and Architectural Collections, PR011, Box 1. Collection of the New-York Historical Society. Digital image created by Oppenheimer Edition.

PREFACE

Maria Martin's World is about a deliberately private woman whose artistic talents were deployed for a very public purpose. Maria Martin painted botanicals and insects for John James Audubon's *Birds of America,* and was acknowledged for doing so.

Ironically, the anonymity most artists and illustrators could usually expect when working for natural scientists eluded the one person who would have appreciated it most: Maria Martin was acknowledged more frequently than any of Audubon's other assistants, including his sons, John Woodhouse and Victor Gifford.[1] Although many acquainted with Maria Martin's work in *Birds of America* have claimed she expected no less and deserved much more, this pious, self-effacing woman neither sought nor desired such recognition. The modern sensibilities behind suggestions that she had aspirations as an artist or that she sought personal acclaim were antithetical to the ideals that shaped her: evangelical Lutheranism and Southern culture.

An ordinary woman who sometimes found herself in the kinds of extraordinary circumstances associated with public accolades, Maria Martin saw such attention as notorious rather than noteworthy and, in this regard, she reflected her time and place. A lifelong resident of antebellum Charleston with its bell-tolling curfews for enslaved inhabitants and rigid social rules for men and women of the free classes, neither she nor her family would engage in behavior that might jeopardize their place in that world. When Maria Martin met Audubon in October 1831, she was living with her sister Harriet, and her brother-in-law, the reverend John Bachman, in a mansion in a suburban neighborhood inhabited by professionals, businessmen, and gentlemen planters.

Childhood years spent in the artisanal district, where she and her sisters lived above the mantua-making shop owned by her mother, were but a memory. With a modicum of middle-class respectability inherited from her father, the son of a Lutheran pastor, and financial security provided by her mother's entrepreneurial skills, Maria grew up in a household where hard-earned capital and cachet were protected. Maria and her sisters did not disappoint. Raised according to the doctrines and dictates of the Lutheran church, not least of which was the responsibility to serve God and man with humility and forbearance, words and deeds reflected place and position as well as piety. It is

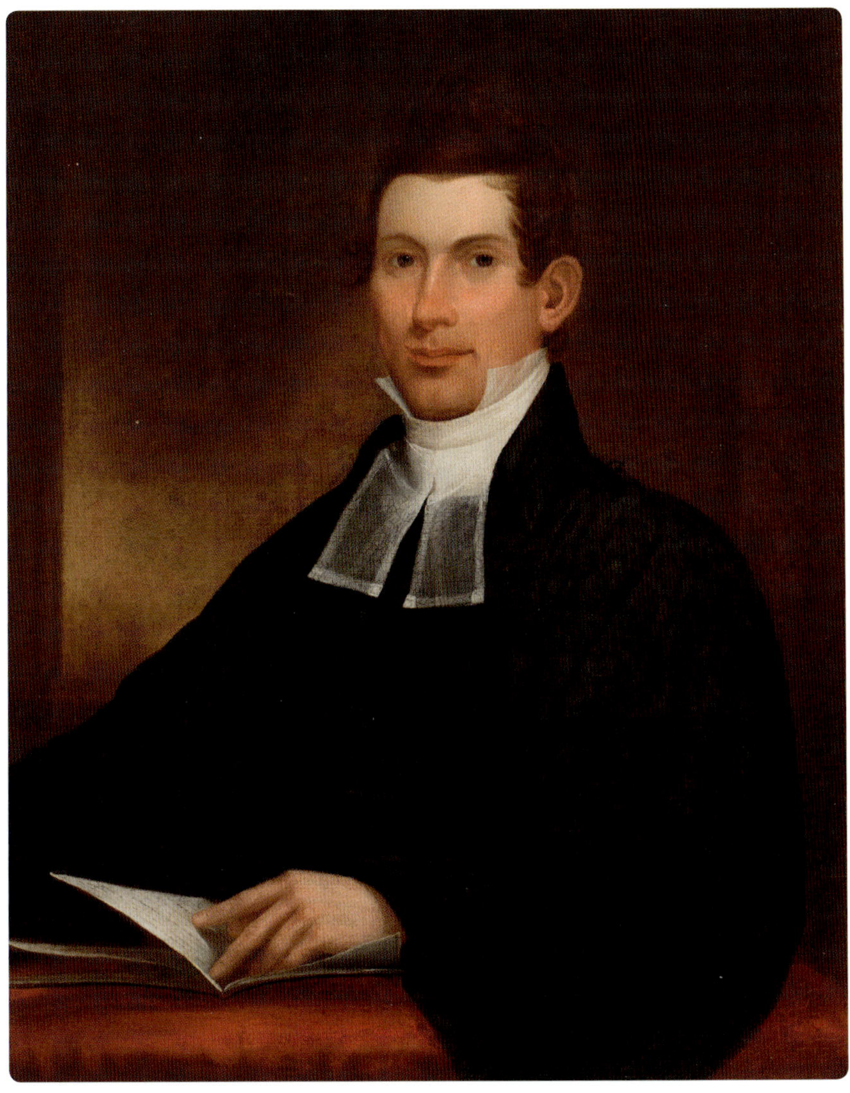

FIGURE 2. John Bachman (1790–1874), 1821–1822. Photographic reproduction of an oil painting by A[lvan] Fisher (1792–1863). Courtesy of Haskell Grimball Carr.

thus unsurprising that Maria Martin did not expect recognition for the beautiful botanicals and insects she painted. She was as unaccustomed to receiving praise for talents divinely given, as she was accustomed to discharging duties faithfully and without fuss.

On route to Florida, where he hoped to find species for volumes two and three of *Birds*, Audubon stopped in Charleston and met John Bachman. The reverend insisted that the artist-naturalist and his companions relocate from rented rooms to his home, and from that day forward Audubon assumed an important place within the household where Maria Martin lived. Likewise, she came to assume an important role in creating *Birds of America*. An amateur artist, by the time Audubon and his companions left a few weeks later, Maria Martin had familiarized herself with what Audubon called his "style of drawing" and, six months after that, she was painting botanicals good enough for *Birds*. A few months after that she was painting insects and, as a result, her entomological and botanical paintings appeared in all but the first volume, already published, and in the volume devoted to water birds. So ubiquitous were her additions to the volume completed during the winter of 1836–1837 in Charleston that Audubon simply stated that Maria Martin "assisted in the finishing of the plants, branches of trees, and flowers" for an undisclosed number of the seventy birds painted that season.[2] For a woman whose first thirty-five years of life were defined entirely by faith and family, the day Audubon arrived on the doorstep of her sister's home was nothing less than transformational.

At the same time, much about Maria Martin's existence remained the same. A dutiful sister, daughter, and wife, she spent the better part of her adult life assisting others. As the youngest of four siblings, she was expected to care for her mother, and she did. She was also devoted to an older sister Harriet, who married John Bachman soon after he arrived in Charleston. She was devoted to their children, her young nieces and nephews, who looked to her as a second mother when their biological mother was indisposed by illness. She was also dedicated to John Bachman, first as the sister-in-law who stepped in as helpmeet from time to time, and then after her sister died, as his wife. Indeed, family responsibilities always took precedence. Even as she painted for Audubon, she led a very private life, largely within the walls of her sister's home; it is therefore unsurprising, perhaps even fitting, that this gifted artist and able student of natural history remained almost completely anonymous. For example, while anyone familiar with *Birds of America* might have noted her efforts, Maria's botanicals were not mentioned by Sarah Josepha Hale, the editor of *Godey's Lady's Book* and author of *Flora's Interpreter* (1853) and the *Women's Record* (1853), by Elizabeth F. Ellet, whose *Women Artists in All Ages and Countries* (1859) was a standard for decades, or by Phebe A. Hanaford, an ardent abolitionist who listed just six Carolinians as "artists of worth" in *Women of the Century* (1877).[3] In fact, Maria Martin's privacy was so well protected that she was not even mentioned in books and articles on Audubon until 1917, when Francis Hobart Herrick, a carcinologist with an aptitude for scientific illustration and ornithology, published *Audubon, The Naturalist*.[4] With access to family papers, Herrick produced a germinal study in which Maria Martin appeared a half dozen times.[5]

Before Herrick, only one publication mentioned Maria Martin: *John Bachman: The Pastor of St. John's Lutheran Church, Charleston* (1888), compiled by Catherine Lindauer Bachman (1832–1908). As Bachman's second wife, Maria Martin has a presence in the story of his life that is hardly surprising; nonetheless, she was far from a main character in a volume published, at least in part, to rectify the fact that John Bachman was almost completely invisible in two previously published biographies of his friend and collaborator. Both Robert Buchanan (1841–1901) and Lucy Audubon (1787–1874) had but two brief paragraphs describing the men's collaboration in 1833 and 1836, a paltry few lines describing their work on *Quadrupeds*, and not a single word about their momentous meeting in 1831.[6] Based on a manuscript prepared by Lucy Audubon, these two publications had obvious omissions, and Catherine Bachman attempted to correct them. As a result, her life and letters volume offers a glimpse into how a world based on family and faith could be conducive to science, and documents illustrative of her father's contributions also shed light on Maria Martin. Indeed, evidence of her role as a dutiful friend, "sister," and (second) wife of John Bachman, as well as letters describing her work as Audubon's assistant contained within *The Pastor of St. John's Lutheran*, have been augmented by further investigation, and as Catherine Bachman intimated, some of the most beautiful paintings in *Birds of America* were completed in the Bachman household. Likewise, work on *The Quadrupeds of North America* (1846–1854), a groundbreaking publication in mammalogy, emerged via the convergence of family, faith, and science that occurred periodically in the home where Catherine was born just weeks after Audubon's first visit there.[7] Although seldom in the foreground, like the botanicals that formed the backgrounds to Audubon's birds, Maria Martin occupies an important place in *The Pastor of St. John's Lutheran.*

It would nonetheless be misleading to suggest that any but the most astute students of natural history and a few family members were aware of Maria Martin's work in *Birds of America*, at least until the 1950s. As Annie Roulhac Coffin (1892–1978), a fourth-generation descendant of the Bachman family, drafted what she hoped would be a beautifully illustrated biography of her ancestor, an Audubon enthusiast named Alice Ford (1906–1997) met with her to learn what she could about Audubon's Charleston collaborators. As a result, Ford devoted a few pages in the first of four books she published on Audubon—*Audubon's Butterflies, Moths and other Studies* (1952)—to his only female background painter.[8] Five years later, an entry on Maria Martin appeared in *The New-York Historical Society's Dictionary of Artists in America, 1564–1860* (1957), a project begun in 1939 under the auspices of the Works Progress Administration.[9] Brief, but no better or worse than many of the some ten thousand individuals profiled, Maria Martin was noted for having assisted "John James Audubon by painting backgrounds for many of his series of American birds."[10] More dramatically inclined, Ford claimed that Maria Martin "may well have been the most influential woman on the American nineteenth century natural history horizon,"[11] and her views influenced E. Buckner Hollingsworth, a popular author on horticulture. As Hollingsworth was preparing a manuscript on women and gardens, Donald Peattie, a naturalist who had published a book on Audubon in 1935, suggested that Maria Martin was an appropriate subject for *Her Garden Was Her Delight* (1962), and she devoted a chapter to her. For the most part, Hollingsworth adapted materials from *Audubon's Butterflies* to her purposes; however, she ignored Ford's prefatory comments acknowledging assistance from Coffin and others. Instead, she claimed that with "the exception of three pages in Alice Ford's highly specialized little book nothing whatever has been written about Maria Martin."[12] In fact, Coffin's first article on her talented ancestor had appeared in *Art Quarterly* two years earlier.

Not long after, Coffin's second article, "Audubon's Friend—Maria Martin," was published in the *New-York Historical Society Quarterly*.[13] Through her efforts, Maria Martin was also included in *Notable American Women* (1971), a project spearheaded by scholars at Radcliffe College determined to record and publicize women's achievements.[14] Well timed to influence celebratory plans for Audubon sesquicentennials, Coffin's early articles on Maria Martin reminded curators like Marshall B. Davidson (1907–1989) of her work. Although there had been several Audubon exhibitions since the 1930s, Coffin's ancestor was mentioned specifically in two catalogues.[15] In 1966, the New-York Historical Society reproduced the original paintings for *Birds of America* from its collection in a volume edited by Davidson, a former curator at the Metropolitan Museum of Art and one of the experts consulted when *The New York Historical Society's Dictionary of Artists in America* was prepared two decades earlier, and twenty-two plates were noted as containing Maria Martin's botanicals or insects. Additionally, Davidson mentioned her twice in his introduction to *The Original Water-color Paintings by John James Audubon for Birds of America*.[16] One year earlier, a catalogue prepared by Edward Dwight (1919–1981), director of the Munson-Williams-Proctor Institute (Utica, NY), for a jointly sponsored exhibition with the Pierpont Morgan Library noted that Maria Martin painted birds, specifically the tricolored heron and the great egret, and that she also replicated the houses and other elements in the backgrounds.[17] Perhaps most significantly, with Annie Coffin's assistance, the museum community of Maria Martin's home state exhibited her work, some paintings still in private hands, at the Gibbes Museum of Art in Charleston and at the Columbia Museum of Art in 1964.[18]

Like other artists, Maria Martin learned to paint by copying the masters. In this case, she copied the unrivalled nature paintings of John James Audubon, an aspect of her work noted in *Audubon Watercolors and Drawings*, the catalogue for the jointly sponsored exhibition in 1965. Twenty years later, curators at the Charleston Museum went further when they exhibited her replicas of Audubon's tricolored heron and great egret as part of a retrospective on the making of *Birds of America*. In the accompanying catalogue, authors Albert Sanders and Warren Ripley ensured that Maria Martin received her due. They positioned her tricolored heron and great egret opposite those painted by Audubon, and they also displayed botanicals and insects from her sketchbooks. With access to family heirlooms, and the documentary and visual artifacts deposited in the museum archives, original volumes of Audubon's elephant folio edition of *Birds of America*, and recent publications on the business and production of these magnificent volumes (Waldemar Fries [1889–1985], *The Double Elephant Folio: The Story of Audubon's Birds of America*, 1973; Lois Elmer Bannon and Taylor Clark, *Handbook of Audubon Prints*, 1980), Sanders and Ripley mounted an impressive tribute to Maria Martin in *Audubon: The Charleston Connection*.

They also benefited from the expertise of Annie Coffin and Edward Dwight: more than a decade earlier, these two experts met in Charleston to determine whether paintings believed to have been executed by Maria Martin were indeed her work.[19] In the end, Sanders and Ripley produced a lavishly illustrated catalogue with sixteen color plates, including several of Maria's paintings. Her paintings of the fever tree (*Pinckneya pubens*, plate 165), the Franklinia tree (*Franklinia alatamaha*, plate 185), the flame azalea (*Rhododendron calendulaceum*, plate 198), the zephyr anglewing (*Polygonia gracilis zephyrus*, plate 373), and two views of the white peacock butterfly (*Anartia jatrophae*)—one from her sketchbook as well as those added to plate 355—were in the catalogue, as was the rare Florida atala hairstreak (*Eumaeus alata*) and a watercolor of Schwartzia sp. from her sketchbooks. Beyond assisting Audubon, Maria Martin painted snakes for John Edwards Holbrook, and the black racer (*Coluber constrictor*) she contributed to *North American Herpetology* was reproduced in the catalogue, as was a reticule decorated with lace and florals.

So impressed were Sanders and Ripley with their local artist that, like Alice Ford before them, they made claims going well beyond anything Maria's stalwart promoter, Annie Coffin, dared suggest. Maria Martin was, they asserted, "the only well-known South Carolina female artist of the 19th century."[20] Whether they deduced her import from materials at hand or arrived at it in conversation with Coffin's daughter, Anne Coffin Hanson (1921–2004), a professionally trained painter and professor of art history at Yale University who inherited her mother's artifacts in 1978, they were not timid in their assessment.[21] In any event, the exhibition mounted five years after Coffin's death would have gratified the woman who devoted herself to moving Maria Martin from background to foreground in Audubon's story. It is, however, less clear that this effort would have been considered sufficient to "right the record." As Coffin faced her ninth and final decade, she still believed that Maria Martin deserved a full-scale biography, and she continued searching—unsuccessfully—for an academic publisher for "The Amiable Miss Martin: A Record of a Woman and Her Times."[22]

It is tempting, although incorrect, to see Coffin's failure to find a publisher as an indictment of the times in which she lived. Biographies by women and about women were certainly undervalued in a genre traditionally written by men and about men, but that was not her problem. It was not that her subject was problematic; it was her approach. While midcentury scholars were using concepts such as gender, class, and race,[23] Coffin was nostalgic rather than critical, evocative rather than evaluative. Marred by a tendency to borrow heavily and uncritically from *The Pastor of St. John's Lutheran*, a romanticized nineteenth-century depiction of antebellum life characterized by a palpable yearning for a time before the Civil War, in Coffin's retelling, Maria Martin was a woman from a bygone and beloved era. As hagiographic as the biography from which she borrowed, Coffin's manuscript evinced a determination to secure her ancestor's rightful place in the making of *Birds of America* that was fueled by an unshakeable conviction that Audubon was responsible for Maria Martin's anonymity.[24] She was simply unable to undertake the kind of detached analysis expected in the second half of the twentieth century. As a result, Coffin was also incapable of capitalizing on the information preserved in *The Pastor of St. John's Lutheran*.

Although relegated to the background in a story about an important man in a man's world, the women of the Bachman household were nonetheless present in a book where they could have been excluded entirely. Indeed, the potential of this life-and-letters biography was only realized several years later by James B. "Jay" Shuler (1926–1997) in *"Had I the Wings": The Friendship of Bachman and Audubon* (1995). Because Bachman's sixty-year career as a cleric and scientist is grounded in the domestic world where his friendship with Audubon began and flourished, Shuler provides Audubon scholars and enthusiasts with a deeper understanding of both the Charleston community of naturalists and the role of the Bachman family in making *Birds of America* and *The Quadrupeds of North America*. Indebted to Coffin and, like her, inspired by *The Pastor of St. John's Lutheran*, this National Parks naturalist (and expert on Bachman's warbler) devoted years to reconstructing the friendship between Bachman and Audubon. In fact, the time expended nearly matched the twenty-year friendship he examined, and so when Shuler's book finally appeared, it was one of many new publications on Audubon.[25]

Of those published in the 1980s and 1990s, only one, *Audubon: Life and Art in the American Wilderness* (1993) by Shirley Streshinsky, makes more than passing reference to Maria Martin; however, in 2000, Lester Stephens mentions her in relation to *Birds of America*, *The Quadrupeds of America*, and *North American Herpetology* in *Science, Race and Religion in the American South: John Bachman and the Charleston Circle of Naturalists, 1815–1895*.[26] More obviously dedicated to "righting the record," *Women in the Field: America's Pioneering Women Naturalists* (1991) contains a short chapter on Maria Martin. More significantly, Maria Martin's contributions to Audubon's paintings of birds are acknowledged in *Audubon's Aviary: The Original Watercolors for* The Birds of America, by Roberta J. M. Olson. Published in 2012 as part of a three-year exhibition of the original watercolors in the New-York Historical Society collections, Olson's book and the three exhibitions she mounted as curator of the Audubon collection provide the first comprehensive inventory of the contributions made by Audubon's assistants. Confident that Martin contributed to "around thirty" of the paintings used for *Birds*, the inventory compiled with the assistance of Alexandra Mazzitelli identifies specifically twenty studies and one unpublished painting containing botanicals or insects by Maria Martin.[27] This talented woman has thus been acknowledged with greater frequency and consequence since Coffin's first articles, and yet the full extent of her artistic and scientific contribution awaits analysis.

Recent publications have done much to secure Maria Martin's rightful place as a botanical artist, but we know little more about the woman behind these paintings than we did some fifty years ago. Until *Maria Martin's World*, this remarkable woman remained as obscure as the other women, both free and slave, with whom she lived in her sister's household. In the pages that follow, kinship, faith, and community are more than merely backdrop to Maria Martin's work in science and art. Her story has been contextualized and repositioned in order to reveal the full complexity of her life as an affluent slave-owning Southerner whose German ancestry and Lutheran faith are no less important than her work in natural history. Typically cast as a supporting character in books that focus on the better-known men she assisted, *Maria Martin's World* tells her story.

Although *Maria Martin's World* was initially envisioned as a traditional biography, it did not take long to discover that conventional approaches would not work. I had what might be referred to as a documentary deficit: Maria Martin never published a single document in her name—not an article, not a poem, not a story—and just twenty-seven letters, only four addressed to Audubon, and one very brief diary have survived. Although the paucity of sources is often attributed to the Civil War, it is more likely that her letters perished because of modesty rather than wartime depredations. After all, scores of letters written by Bachman and Audubon survived and, in fact, it is in their correspondence where references to the missing Martin documents may be found. Among a select group of women eminently able to communicate in writing, the very church doctrine that demanded literacy also shaped behavior and Maria Martin, no less than other women of her generation, would not invite censure for unseemliness. She would not deviate from a well defined, if unarticulated, set of rules governing male-to-female friendships. In the early nineteenth century, only familial relationships were entirely safe when it came to male-female friendships: all others risked allegations of romantic love, or worse, unless conducted through an intermediary or some other mutually acceptable arrangement.[28] It can hardly be coincidental that archival collections contain considerably more letters written after Maria Martin's family was joined to the Audubon family through marriage than they do from the preceding period. In any event, Maria Martin did not leave much for a biographer to work with, and while she is far from the "edge of history" occupied by people known only through church registers, census records, or plantation ledgers, her story sometimes veers toward the format described by medievalist Robin Fleming as "more 'times' than 'life.'"[29]

Less a traditional marshaling of documentary evidence left by a public figure than an account of a daughter, an aunt, a wife, a (step-)mother, and a grandmother who became an accomplished natural history painter, *Maria*

Martin's World examines work performed for a very public purpose by a very private woman and situates all within the domestic sphere she seldom left.[30] To do so often required analysis of what biographer Robert Rotberg calls a "conjunction of circumstances," that is, making inferences and establishing linkages between and among political, religious, cultural, scientific and personal attitudes and actions.[31] As he acknowledges improvements to biographical writing that have arisen through scholarship on women whose public contributions are inexplicable except in reference to their private lives, Rotberg draws on insights offered by Susan Ware. The coeditor of volume five of *Notable American Women* (2004), the dictionary in which Maria Martin was one of thirteen hundred entries in 1971,[32] Ware recognizes the special demands associated with writing a biography of women whose contributions are intellectual or artistic. Like the editors of earlier volumes of *Notable American Women* who came to appreciate that women's accomplishments could only be understood by considering them within the complex world in which they lived, their "upbringing and social environment," and by taking into account factors such as circumstance, coercion, and "chance,"[33] Ware believes the rewards of trying to reconstruct lives of those who are intensely private and thus often hidden from view are commensurate with the challenge. If men and women in public offer an opportunity to "seamlessly weave their subjects into the wider exterior world," those of interest for their private lives provide, Ware states, "a window on a wider vista."[34] Maria Martin is a case in point. She was a gifted artist known for having contributed to a natural history *tour de force*, but she was also a Lutheran, a Southerner of German ancestry, a slave owner and a woman of means in a city where class rivaled race as an identifier, and she lived during a time that has long fascinated historians. Her life began as Charleston was emerging as one of the most important economic and political centers of the slave states, and it ended as the Confederacy defended the principles she embraced as a citizen of the Old South. Known to posterity through science and art, the time and place in which she lived were fundamental to who she was and what she did, and *Maria Martin's World* attempts to convey how these interconnected complexities both impeded and facilitated the accomplishments acknowledged by Audubon.

ACKNOWLEDGMENTS

This book has taken an inordinately long time to materialize by current standards in academia. I first became acquainted with Maria Martin between 1991 and 1993, when I was researching the wives of nineteenth-century scientists as a SSHRCC postdoctoral fellow at St. John's College, University of Manitoba, and more than twenty-five years later I am pleased to offer her story in print. I am grateful to the Social Sciences and Humanities Research Council of Canada for funding that allowed me to transition from doctoral research focusing on fur traders and indigenous trappers who collected for the Smithsonian Institution to the history of women whose efforts were indispensable to the scientific careers of husbands and fathers, and I would also like to thank the institution that provided me a home. There I discussed my work with colleagues, especially Jack Bumsted, who provided encouragement and advice. Librarians, archivists, and curators also figure prominently among those to whom I am indebted, particularly individuals from the following institutions: the Charleston Museum; the Charleston Library Society; the American Philosophical Society Library; the Beinecke Rare Book and Manuscript Library, Yale University; the Caroliniana Library, University of South Carolina, Columbia; the Houghton Library, Harvard University; the James R. Crumley Jr. Archives of the Lineberger Memorial Library, Lutheran Theological Southern Seminary, Lenoir-Rhyne University; the Marlene and Nathan Addlestone Library, College of Charleston; the New-York Historical Society; the Pennsylvania Historical Society; the Manuscripts Division of Rare Books and Special Collections, Princeton University; the South Carolina Department of Archives and History; the South Carolina Historical Society; the Stark Museum of Art; and the Joseph Downs Collection and Archives, Winterthur Library. I would specifically like to thank Harlan Greene, who allowed me to examine (and copy) a daybook kept by one of Maria Martin's nieces now in his personal collection; Jennifer Scheetz and Jennifer McCormick, archivists at the Charleston Museum; and Roberta Olson, curator at the New-York Historical Society. Their observations and suggestions were invaluable as *Maria Martin's World* took shape.

Without doubt, my greatest debt of gratitude goes to Jane Grimball Greely, Haskell Grimball Carr, Anne Carr, and Blaine Garson. Their treasured paintings, sketchbooks, and scrapbooks were indispensable as I attempted to reconstruct the life of a woman who lived in the shadow of the men she assisted. Their artifacts reveal much about Maria Martin's expertise as a natural history artist, and a number have been reproduced in this volume with their permission and through the photographic and technical skills of Richard Rhodes (Rick Rhodes Photography & Imaging, Charleston), Jim Gipe (Pivot Media Inc., Amherst Connecticut), Sean Money (Charleston Museum), Kelli Babcock, (Digital Initiatives Librarian, University of Toronto), and David J. Holbert and Erin Rushing (Smithsonian Institution Libraries). I would also like to acknowledge the New Brunswick Museum for permission to reproduce an image of Lucy Audubon in their collection. Without these materials a difficult task would have been all but impossible and, at one point, I was resigned to forging ahead without these artifacts even though I knew they existed somewhere.

It was with great regret that I conceded defeat in my efforts to find Maria's beautiful paintings; however, in 2011, a chance meeting affected my work profoundly. It was my good fortune to meet Lucile MacLennan. She knew long before I did that Maria Martin deserved her place in history, and when we parted company she was determined to locate the descendants I could not find. Within days, she succeeded where I had failed, and I am deeply appreciative of her efforts on behalf of *Maria Martin's World*. Beth Motherwell, senior acquisitions editor for the natural sciences, was equally convinced that Maria Martin's story was worth telling, and her support has been unflagging. I would also like to acknowledge Christine Robson: from transcribing documents to searching entomological databases as we identified unnamed illustrations, her efforts have been invaluable. Last, but not least, I would like to thank my husband, Larry Gagnon. He cheered me on when the work was slowgoing or stalled—and this is no small feat when more than two decades elapse from start to finish. As *Maria Martin's World* moved from conception to completion, I benefited from the comments and suggestions of many, especially the anonymous reviewers selected by the University of Alabama Press, and I am most appreciative. Of course, any errors or omissions are mine.

Maria Martin's World

INTRODUCTION

Maria Martin, an unmarried thirty-five-year-old evangelical Lutheran from Charleston, South Carolina, became an accomplished painter within months of meeting John James Audubon, and her botanicals, insects, and amphibians appeared in volumes two and four of *The Birds of America* (1830–1838). Over the next two decades, she acquired further expertise in natural history. She painted snakes for John Edwards Holbrook's *North American Herpetology* (1842), and assisted in drafting the descriptive taxonomies prepared by John Bachman, her brother-in-law (and husband from 1848) for *The Viviparous Quadrupeds of North America* (1846–1854), a collaborative project with the Audubon family. Until then, she lived quietly, devoting herself to family, living in anonymity in a deeply religious household, and her circumstances changed little as a result of her work in natural history: her contributions were unknown to all but the most astute students of natural history and a close circle of family and friends. Uncharacteristically healthy in a household devastated all too frequently by disease and death, she was able to devote time and energy to natural history even as she nursed family members, including three nieces and a sister who died of consumption, only thwarted by an injury sustained in 1840.[1] While traveling to Cuba with one of her consumptive nieces, she fell. Initially, she was little troubled by what she described as a "dislocated" elbow, but the arm flared up periodically until 1856, when it became swollen, rigid, and "perfectly helpless." By then, the pain was "incessant," and she could no longer paint, write, or do fancy work.

Before her tragic accident, Maria Martin lived to serve. Whether it was her family or naturalists such as Audubon and Holbrook, she was unstinting in her efforts. The pain was difficult to bear, but the fact that debility meant she was "no longer useful" was a source of great sorrow.[2] She missed being able to paint and write, seeing her infirmity as a "great deprivation." How could it have been otherwise? Just two years earlier she had assisted John Bachman, by then her husband, complete the descriptive taxonomies to accompany Audubon's paintings in *Quadrupeds.* During the 1840s, she cared for her dying mother (Rebecca Martin) and sister (Harriet Martin Bachman), as well as three nieces who died of consumption. Death was a common occurrence in the home where she lived, and it could not but have affected her greatly, especially the deaths of her nine nieces and nephews—Cordelia (1820–1821), John Edward (1822–1822), Henry (1824–1824), twins Ellen and Clara (1827–1828), Maria Rebecca (1816–1840), Mary Eliza (1818–1841), Julia (1825–1847), and Harriet (1823–1858). She lent aid and comfort to all but one, Harriet, who died after Maria Martin was too unwell to do so. Indeed, Maria Martin was an indispensable member of her sister's household, and it was Audubon's good fortune that he made her acquaintance during a decade of relative health. Had it been otherwise, she would have been too occupied with her caregiving duties to indulge her interests in painting and natural history.

Exactly how many of Maria Martin's illustrations appeared in *Birds* is difficult to determine; however, given Audubon's idiosyncratic approach to acknowledging assistance it is more than likely that her contributions exceeded those estimated thus far.[3] Additionally, Maria Martin's assistance went beyond her beautifully rendered botanicals and insects. Not long after meeting Audubon, she also played a role in supplying information for his *Ornithological Biography,* acquiring skills and knowledge in taxonomy and systematics that proved useful as she worked alongside her brother-in-law the following decade as he prepared the text for *Quadrupeds.* Moreover, Bachman benefited from her artistic talents. As she was completing her last paintings for Audubon in the late 1830s, she provided line drawings for the articles on lagomorphs, rodents, and soricomorphs that solidified Bachman's reputation as a mammalogist. But with the completion of *Birds* and these few sketches, Maria Martin did little in natural history until the end of the 1840s. Family demands prevented her from pursuing these interests and, when she did return to natural history, she focused on textual description rather than scientific illustration.

To some extent, her shift from painting to research and writing reflected the fact that Audubon's sons assumed increasing responsibility for painting backgrounds during the 1840s. Indeed, they painted many of the figures of the species depicted in *Quadrupeds.* At the same time, it is clear that Maria Martin's transition from painter to researcher was also indicative of broader shifts in the scientific world. As Audubon's assistant, she participated in a tradition in which textual description supported visual imagery rather than the other way around, and Audubon's efforts to produce a visual record of North American birds that was more accurate and aesthetically superior to those of his predecessors—especially *American Ornithology; or, the Natural History of the Birds of the United States* (1808–1814) by Alexander Wilson—epitomized that approach. As she assisted Bachman with *Quadrupeds*, Maria Martin focused on describing specimens rather than on painting them, and her efforts reflected a transformation in the natural sciences in which the newest methods being developed in taxonomy and systematics were rigorously applied so as to understand the natural world. In other words, Maria Martin's artistic and scholarly contributions are clearly sufficient to secure her place in the history of ornithology and mammalogy, but they also exemplify a more profound change taking place in the sciences.

As an illustrator and a researcher, Maria Martin participated in what has been described as a defining moment in the natural sciences. In *Picturing Nature*, Ann Shelby Blum traces how text replaced image as professional scientists moved into the natural sciences, and 1830 to 1850—the years during which Maria Martin was most active—was an important transitional period. Field naturalist-artists like Audubon still believed they represented the best way to learn about nature and that they were the experts who should determine how that knowledge was to be conveyed, but they were not alone in advancing such claims.[4] At the same time, university-educated scientists who spent more time in the laboratory than in the field believed they offered a better way to acquire and disseminate knowledge. If subsequent developments have been interpreted as text's inevitable victory over illustration, Blum shows that midcentury participants were by no means so sure. Neither artist-naturalists nor descriptive taxonomists were able to discern that a written discourse characterized by close study of specimens and an encyclopedic knowledge of published research would replace visual imagery based on observation and illustration of living species in their natural environment, but by the end of the nineteenth century, text trumped art as illustrators were hired to supply drawings for publications written by men whose authority did not depend upon their ability to draw. The stakes were high, and Maria Martin's efforts as an artist and as a researcher are useful to our understanding of the transition from image to text.

Unlike the important people, developments, and ideas central to Blum's analysis, Maria Martin is a less visible participant who straddled the two approaches and whose efforts in creating scientific images and scientific text reveal how ordinary individuals participated in this transition and to what effect. Maria Martin, for example, often played a mediating role as she worked alongside men who disagreed over whether text or image was best suited to convey information about natural history, and while working on the *Viviparous Quadrupeds of North America* Maria did what she could to smooth over differences between John Bachman and John James Audubon. Bachman insisted that accurate field notes and thorough research in the taxonomic literature were essential to producing a credible monograph on mammals, while Audubon refused to record important taxonomic details while painting the species Bachman was attempting to describe. Foreshadowed by Bachman's earlier criticism that Audubon carelessly recorded the anatomical and physiological details of species found in the *Ornithological Biography*, the difficulties that plagued their second project were far more serious. No matter how deep the friendship established almost twenty years earlier, by the late 1830s Bachman had no qualms about criticizing Audubon, and the woman who strove for amicability could intervene unobtrusively so as to restore collegiality. Less invested in either discourse, she assisted one and then the other, exercising tact and diplomacy when clashes occurred. If she had a bias, it was to the man not the method. Maria Martin spent her entire adult life assisting John Bachman. She joined his household after he married her sister Harriet, and until 1848, she was the dutiful aunt who helped raise the Bachman children. Then, two years after her sister died, she married Bachman and became, in his words, his "beloved wife—the companion of all my thoughts & studies [and] my emanuensis [*sic*] who has held the pen whilst I dictated 1,400 sermons."[5]

Over some three decades, Maria and Harriet became used to impromptu guests. Their home was frequented by church officials, parishioners, and neighbors; however, both could have been nothing less than flabbergasted when the reverend announced that Audubon and his companions, taxidermist Henry Ward (1812–1878) and artist George Lehman (d. 1870), would be joining them for an extended period.[6] On route to Florida to do fieldwork, the three men would hardly have resembled the clerics and professors or family and friends who typically occupied guest rooms at the Bachman residence, but the parson and the painter were immediately drawn to one another despite their differences.

Bachman, the straightlaced Lutheran pastor from New York who went to Charleston in 1815 to minister to the evangelical German community was, in most ways, the exact opposite of the risk-taking French émigré he had befriended. Audubon's business ventures had failed repeatedly until the 1820s, when he decided to abandon a fairly conventional life as a merchant and make his mark as an authority on birds, ironically devoting much of his time and energy to convincing wealthy people to invest in one of the riskiest projects of his life: a costly book containing reproductions of his paintings of American birds. On yet another "ramble" in search of birds, the iconoclastic naturalist standing in the foyer of the Bachman home had just spent the better part of two months traveling from New York by steamboat and wagon and was undoubtedly more "American Woodsman" than gentleman as he entered the stylish mansion on the edge of Charleston, but his welcome suggests that the characteristics that served him so well when petitioning patrons or meeting Fellows of the London Royal Society endeared him to his Charleston host.[7] Whether the rest of the household embraced him so eagerly is unclear.

The women and children, both free and enslaved, could hardly have been prepared for what transpired over the next three weeks in the ground floor rooms of their home: Audubon and his assistants skinned and mounted nearly three hundred specimens in space set aside for taxidermy.[8] Provided with private quarters and workspace, Audubon occupied a guest room normally reserved for more fastidious visitors—friends and family whose impositions did not involve depositing carcasses in a heap at the back of the garden—and a ground-floor breakfast room was converted into a studio.[9] Recalled affectionately by children who watched in amazement as the room where they congregated daily for their first meal and prayers with their father was repurposed and filled with mounted specimens and painting paraphernalia, but the changes associated with Audubon's visit were surely not viewed positively by all. If changes to the breakfast routine were welcomed by the children, they were most certainly less well received by the enslaved women who had to carry yet another meal up a flight of stairs rather than serving it in the usual place which was just steps away from the kitchen located in one of the outbuildings behind the main house. Likewise, the constant parade of dead birds in and out of a room previously dedicated to dining went beyond simple inconvenience for the men and women who cleaned the makeshift taxidermy room. Had Audubon thought for a moment that he was to become a long-term guest, he would have surely considered the impact that "painting from nature" would have on his Southern benefactors: the activities taking place down the hall from the pastor's study in rooms formerly dedicated to family gatherings or accommodations for out-of-town guests on church business were at odds with the well-appointed residence of an affluent Southern family.[10]

A modest version of the very finest homes of antebellum Charleston, the fifteen-room mansion with piazzas running the full length of both first and second floors could not but have conveyed the impression that comportment

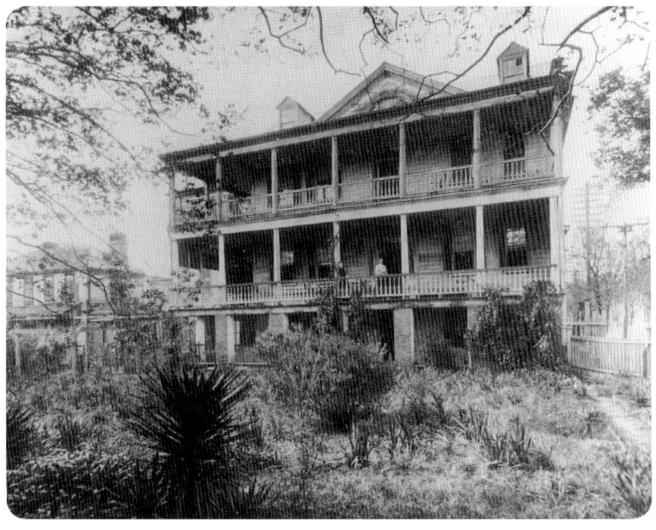

FIGURE 3. Bachman residence, 7 (149) Rutledge Avenue, Cannonsborough, c. 1920. The original photograph no longer exists. St. John's Lutheran Church and the Charleston Museum have copies. Courtesy of the Charleston Museum.

rather different from Audubon's alleged preference for living off the land among his feathered friends was required. As Audubon entered through narrow double doors with "tiny diamond-form[ed] panes of glass," he saw refinement all around: from the ornate mahogany chiffonier just inside the door, to the clock standing on the landing of the staircase leading to private quarters above, he could only assume that this home was occupied by genteel folk—and confirmation came quickly. As he scanned his surroundings, he saw formal parlors with "panelled walls, garlanded in delicate stucco" designed and decorated in the Federal style. Appointed with "high wainscoting [*sic*] and tall mantels," mirrors and collectibles such as Dresden figurines and Bohemian glassware were illuminated by a "glittering crystal chandelier,"[11] and a vignette reminiscent of those encountered while seeking subscribers for *Birds of America* in the British Isles took shape. Euphoric over finding accommodations and an enthusiastic new friend, he seemed to forget how his routine and requirements might impose upon those around him. He instead focused on his utter good fortune in finding himself comfortably situated. In his first letter home, he wrote: "Mr Bachman would have us all stay at his house—he would have us to make free there as if we were at our own encampment . . . he would not suffer us to proceed farther South for 3 weeks . . . Could I have refused this kind invitation? No!"[12]

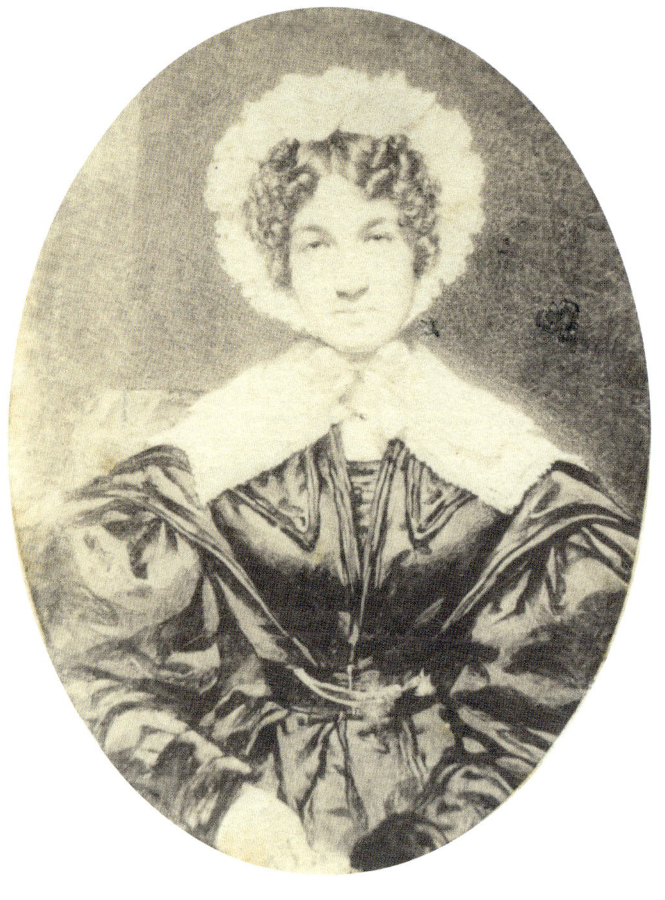

FIGURE 4. Lucy Bakewell Audubon (1787–1874), albumen print carte-de-visite, c. 1860, after a miniature by Frederick Cruickshank (c. 1831), by Charles D. Fredricks & Company, New York. 10.3 x 6.4 cm. Accession no. 4907. Courtesy of New Brunswick Museum.

Only a week later, he again wrote his wife, Lucy, of his extraordinary reception, stating: "Here I am the very pet of every body and had I time or Inclination to visit the great folk I might be in dinner parties from now untill Jany next."[13] Three weeks later, he elaborated in a report on their progress. They had skinned over two hundred specimens representing some sixty different species and had drawn fifteen figures. They had also been on numerous outings in search of birds, and there was a steady stream of onlookers in the workrooms.[14] But one of the most interesting pieces of information was the one he failed to mention: Bachman had placed at his disposal a deeply religious and largely female household.

Had Lucy Audubon speculated about Charleston or the Bachman family based on what she learned from her husband's letters, she would have had half the story at best. Bachman's generosity, as well as the scale and luxury of his home, belied the reality of life under his roof. While the Bachman residence may have resembled those occupied by the wealthy and powerful, aside from a shared conviction that the institution of slavery was the special responsibility of Southerners, there was little common ground between this pietistic Lutheran household and the Charleston elite. While Bachman's prowess as a hunter made him a welcome guest in the upcountry homes of the planter class, he had a dim view of what he described as their predilection toward "laziness [and] extravagance," and his family did not mingle with the wives and children of his hunting partners.[15] The Bachman women socialized with relatives, close neighbors, and members of their church. The parties and balls, races and gambling enjoyed by elite families were verboten. Even sporting events were discouraged. Their gatherings evinced none of the frivolity of the well to do. Their amusements were more useful. As Bachman warned Audubon, "clergymen ought not to be frolicsome," and the same dictum applied to his largely female family. He claimed he had no "bad habits" other than "telling a long yarn," and his family was "as plain as a pikestaff." The women and girls amused themselves with fancywork and sewing, painting and music, reading and writing.[16] That birds were skinned by the dozens down the hall from the reverend's office would have elicited less surprise among his parishioners and hunting friends than if the Bachman children were spotted partying alongside the sons and daughters of the planter elite during the social season. Under the reverend's watchful eye, an austere regimen prevailed.

As second in command, Maria Martin ensured compliance. Unequivocal when it came to religious matters, she had no compunction about assuming responsibility for the "catechetical and moral instruction" of her nieces and nephews, and John Bachman appreciated her efforts. In a letter lamenting the death of his beloved wife Harriet, Bachman noted that although ill health interfered with her maternal responsibilities, his children had turned out well because Maria "kept the family together [and] has complete control of the children so that they have not given me a moments pain."[17] Had Harriet not been invalided for some twenty years, her motherly duty to oversee the religious instruction of their children would have occupied much of her time. However, her health was precarious, and Maria Martin assumed responsibility for ensuring that the Bachman children were raised according to Lutheran practices and principles. In a pietistic household, this was an especially demanding commitment as her nieces and nephews were expected to become good Christian men and women who were well schooled in Biblical studies and completely dedicated to serving God selflessly, humbly, and cheerfully. Moreover, when Harriet was unable to supervise domestic affairs, Maria stepped in. Although slaves tended gardens, cleaned house, cooked meals and more, slave-owning women were not idle, especially in a household that often exceeded two dozen people.[18] As a slave owner herself, Maria Martin was familiar with how to ensure that enslaved men and women carried out their tasks, and so the responsibilities of a surrogate mistress were different in degree rather than in kind. Nonetheless, this was no small matter: more than a dozen men, women, and children—including Thomas the cook and gardener, William the carpenter, Venus the "washerwoman," Tony the butler, nursemaids Pussy and Diana—worked under her watchful eye.[19] Aside from Thomas, who became proficient at skinning birds, the responsibilities of the enslaved men and women were largely domestic; however, with three extra people and a "home laboratory" that was unsanitary, unsightly, malodorous, and messy, even domestic duties expanded. Additionally, once it became clear that Thomas had an aptitude for natural history, others had to assume responsibility for tasks he had done previously. At the same time, whether enslaved men and women performed work directly related to natural history or their labor allowed others to indulge their interests in science, ultimately they were part of the collaborative effort that produced *Birds of America* as well as *The Quadrupeds of North America.*

That slavery allowed Maria Martin to pursue natural history and devote hours to painting is unsurprising; many of her contemporaries were spared the drudgery of day-to-day life through the labor of others. What is perhaps more remarkable is that she would spend her leisure hours in activities denied most women of her generation.[20] Although botany became fashionable among women in the nineteenth century, Maria Martin's participation preceded that development, and it occurred in a place where science was dominated by men who could not contemplate a role for women in their organizations.[21] And yet, in many ways, this Southern evangelical Lutheran woman, who lived in a world in which patriarchy dictated place and position, found herself in a world inhabited by men. Most obviously, she worked alongside Audubon, spending hours at the easel painting native flowers, shrubs, and branches, as well as butterflies, beetles, and more. She worked unstintingly, without complaint, approaching this work much as she did any other: she believed it was a duty and a privilege to assist if asked.[22] She saw efforts that some might consider individual accomplishment in terms of how they served others. She willingly accepted the role of Bachman's helpmeet in her invalided sister's stead, and she was equally obliging to Audubon's demands. As she assisted Bachman prepare sermons, answer correspondence, and tend to the many administrative and pastoral obligations of St. John's Lutheran, she agreed to help Audubon in the painting room set up just down the hall from Bachman's office, or the room she referred to as "our little study."[23] There, she substituted one typically masculine space for another as she spent hours improving her skills and aesthetic by emulating Audubon's unique "method of drawing." Whenever called upon, she responded willingly as an artist, as a researcher, or even as an assistant in the taxidermy room. Ironically, it was precisely because she subscribed to the ideology of female submissiveness that she was able to accomplish so much in a sphere that was still hostile to women.

Motivated, disciplined, and talented, she produced botanicals that were good enough for *Birds* within months of meeting Audubon, and it is tempting to see her contributions as exceptional. In some ways, they were. Hardly a dabbler, Maria Martin's work was published in one of the most beautiful natural history books produced in the last two centuries. However, Maria Martin was one of several gifted artists recruited to work on *Birds*. As has often been noted, Audubon had a knack for finding and cultivating talent—male and female, beginner and veteran—that manifested as early as 1820, when he decided to make *Birds of America* his life's work.[24] Then, he employed Joseph Mason (1802–1842), a former student, to paint plants as they traveled from Cincinnati to New Orleans. Only thirteen, Mason completed more than fifty botanicals. A few years later, Audubon established an important relationship with Robert Havell Jr. (1793–1878), son of the (second) engraver to whom he entrusted his project. Although Audubon's correspondence gives the impression that he expected the engraver to provide exact replicas of his original paintings, Havell's technical and creative wizardry was fundamental to the success of *Birds of America*. He supplied foliage, flowers, and other indicators of natural habitat on the color plates he was engraving, and he even composed a number of plates when figures arrived in London without backgrounds.[25] In 1824, Audubon engaged another talented assistant, George Lehman, a Swiss-born landscape painter. Hired to assist in finishing paintings needed to show Britons whom Audubon hoped to convince to subscribe to *Birds,* Lehman's services were temporarily terminated while his employer was overseas, but he was rehired in 1829 and employed periodically until 1832. Lehman painted some three dozen backgrounds, considered comparable to those by Audubon himself. However, Lehman's services were no longer needed once Audubon had two new assistants: Maria Martin and his son, John Woodhouse. By then, Audubon believed his youngest son was mature enough and talented enough to serve as his companion and assistant on a field trip to Labrador. As usual, he was correct. John Woodhouse developed into a fine artist, contributing to at least thirteen plates in *Birds* and drawing half of the one hundred and fifty figures in *The Quadrupeds of North America*.[26]

Always important, collaboration became increasingly so as Audubon's conception of *Birds of America* became more comprehensive, and Maria Martin was as perfect an assistant as could be found. An unmarried, mature God-fearing woman of independent means, she sought neither remuneration nor commendation. In helping Audubon, she was doing work that was both useful and appropriate, and as she found purpose and meaning in assisting him, she placed no demands on his purse or prestige. Such was not the case with paid employees. Sometimes, as in January 1832 when Audubon found himself in St. Augustine, Florida, ahead of the migrating birds, his employees were a costly burden. Departing Charleston in December, Audubon's assistant Lehman sat idle for most of January.[27] Equally irritating situations arose when assistants expected formal recognition. While naturalists had long taken credit for work done by anonymous artists, Audubon's first protégé, Joseph Mason, expected to see his name engraved on the paintings they had worked on together, and he was sufficiently disgruntled by Audubon's failure to credit him that he aired his complaints in Philadelphia at the very moment Audubon was trying to convince ornithologists and publishers there of the value of *Birds*.[28] That Philadelphia scientists did not support Audubon in 1824 has been linked to his dispute with Mason, and such pitfalls could be avoided if he relied on friends or family. Paper, paints, and brushes were all Maria Martin ever needed.

Although Mason was perhaps more vocal than other aggrieved artist-employees, his experience with Audubon was hardly unique. Conceit and context dovetailed to ensure that Audubon's acknowledgments were scant. Experts estimate that approximately one-third of the painting in *Birds* was done by others, but Audubon seldom admitted his debts and never did so fully.[29] Moreover, as his reliance on others grew, he became correspondingly indifferent to their efforts. He largely ignored the artists and artisans, researchers and writers who helped. When he did express gratitude publicly, he could be both calculating and disingenuous. Almost ten years after the unpleasantness with Mason, for example, he described him as "a young man who was for some time employed by me, and who has drawn plants to some of my birds, although not so successfully as my amiable friend Miss Martin, or George Lehman, who finish those they draw as beautifully as my learned and valued friend William MacGillivray of Edinburgh does his faithful drawings of birds."[30] Such feigned flattery surely did not impress Maria Martin. She could not help but see that Mason's botanicals were beautifully rendered, and she neither expected nor needed compliments—real or fake. Whether drawing plants and animals for Audubon's plates was an attractive activity because it meant artistic abilities previously deployed on frivolous fancywork were put to better use, whether she picked up the paintbrush to please Audubon or Bachman or both, or whether she participated due to a combination of factors, ultimately, she served *Birds* as she served family: unreservedly, humbly, and faithfully.[31]

Maria Martin worked diligently to transform herself from a skilled fancy worker who painted flowers on handicrafts to an accomplished botanical artist; and, in an astonishingly short period, she learned to paint aesthetically pleasing and scientifically accurate plants. She did so by devoting an incalculable number of hours to copying Audubon's technique and his images, but she also copied background painters employed by Audubon, especially George Lehman. She became so proficient so quickly that many have assumed she was painting like a professional even before meeting Audubon, but this was not the case. Though her apprenticeship with him was short and sporadic, paintings of flowers preceding his arrival attest to his role in the transformation of her skills and aesthetic. Maria Martin practiced what she learned while he was in residence for one month in the autumn of 1831, and for shorter periods in March and April 1832 as he as he made his way home from Florida. In 1833–1834, Audubon spent five months in Charleston when he, Lucy, and John Woodhouse lived there from October to March, and she worked alongside him and John Woodhouse in 1836–1837, when they returned to complete paintings needed for the last volume of *Birds*.[32] But Maria Martin also honed her skills by copying natural history publications. She copied plates from volume one of *Birds,* but she also copied the botanicals from publications by Pierre-Joseph Redouté (1759–1840). And her efforts garnered recognition denied other collaborators, even Audubon's sons, Victor Gifford and John Woodhouse. They were woefully underacknowledged for their contributions. They, like Joseph Mason, should have fared better; however, it would serve no purpose to diminish Maria's accomplishments because others, equally crucial to completing *Birds*, were not credited appropriately. The accolades received were well deserved. Under Audubon's guidance, she went from being a talented crafter who decorated female accouterments to a credible artist.[33]

From the outset, Maria Martin had no trouble accepting that *Birds* was

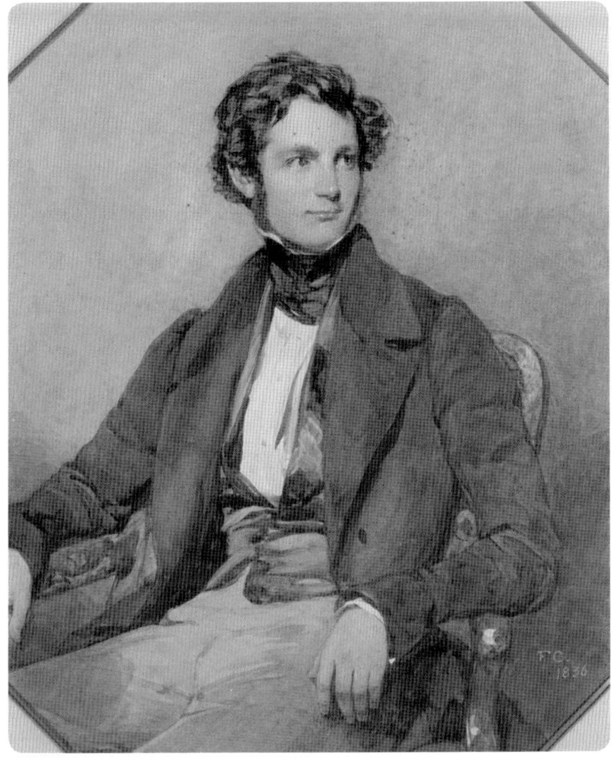

FIGURE 5. John Woodhouse Audubon (1812–1862), 1836. Photographic reproduction of watercolor by Frederick Cruikshank. 24.1 x 20.3 cm (9½ x 8 in) Frick Art Reference Library Photoarchive, Digital image, 50823. Courtesy of the Frick Art Reference Library.

an important project. Taking Audubon's lead, she could not have felt otherwise. With volume one already published and volumes two and three in progress, Audubon's only major concern was ensuring sufficient capital to finance *Birds*. Although securing funding for his project could be a serious distraction (as it competed with the actual work of painting), if Audubon had any doubts about the prospects of completing his project, they would have been dispelled before leaving Charleston. Free room and board, special workrooms, and two new collaborators—one completely unable to contain his excitement over his newfound friend—provided ample proof. Bachman, a normally circumspect clergyman, veered dangerously close to hyperbole in trying to convey his enthusiasm as he claimed that Audubon's visit gave him "new life," and that it rekindled his interest in ornithology.[34] No doubt exaggerating the enthusiasm of his family, Bachman persisted in believing that everyone was equally keen, and he reiterated their alleged interest two years later, with emphasis, when he

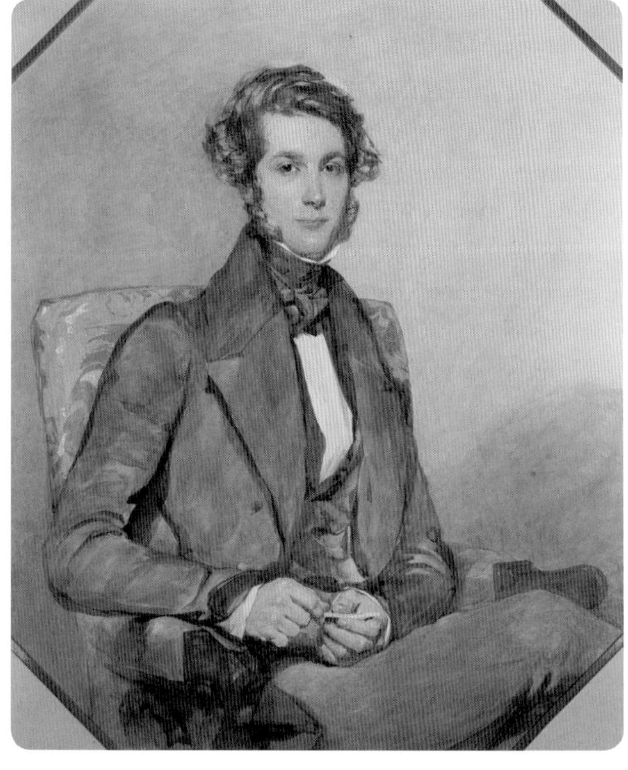

FIGURE 6. Victor Gifford Audubon (1809–1860), 1836. Photographic reproduction of watercolor by Frederick Cruikshank. 26.7 x 21.6 cm (10½ x 8½ in) Frick Art Reference Library Photoarchive, Digital image, 50822. Courtesy of the Frick Art Reference Library.

invited Audubon to return to Charleston. Writing in a style reserved for his new friend, he was uncharacteristically expressive as he mustered his powers of persuasion to convince Audubon that, in 1833, everyone awaited his return with anticipation. Although he had extended a personal invitation when he was in New York in May, he felt compelled to restate his case in September.[35] Assuming the bird-wintering grounds that first drew Audubon south in 1831 would again prove enticing, he sent a letter that began grandly: "Hail! My old friend, all hail! Health, success and happiness attend you—the winds, the waves, the heavens and fortune, have all smiled on you. Welcome, thrice welcome, to the homes and hearts of your friends! Long may you be spared to be the honored instrument of giving to the world the figures and the biography of that beautiful feathered race, that seem to acknowledge you alone as worthy of commemorating their forms and their histories."[36] So anxious was Bachman to see his new friend that he was surprisingly sensitive to Audubon's jaded views of established religion, refashioning a Biblical reference to the "starry host of heaven" ever so slightly as he extended the hospitality of his home.[37] He also clearly overstated the extent to which his nine children—six of whom were aged seven or younger—his wife, never robust, and the elders of his household, shared his passion for natural history. He claimed that "all rejoiced" when told of Audubon's rambles, and stated that "even my old mother was much interested" in his work.

While it was more likely that his mother and his mother-in-law were only mildly curious about what was going in the ground-floor rooms set aside for painting and taxidermy, John Bachman's eagerness to renew his acquaintance with Audubon was boundless. He could not conceive that others might feel differently or, as in the case of his youngest children, be utterly indifferent to the activities taking place beneath them. Certainly Maria Martin's life as a botanical painter was a direct result of Audubon's visit, and Bachman's long interest in natural history was stimulated by Audubon's visit; indeed, even those with scant interest in natural history could not escape the impact of Bachman's increased involvement in the scientific community or his research in the natural sciences.[38] Whether Bachman sensed that others might be drawn in regardless of the extent to which they shared his passion for natural history, after 1831 everyone in his home—young and old, indisposed and healthy, enslaved and exploited—lived in a world shaped by science as well as by religion. After all, neither complicity nor enthusiasm is prerequisite to life-altering experiences, and children too young to do little more than look on with macabre fascination as visiting bird men went about their business eventually accepted such activities as the norm. By the late 1830s, when Bachman turned his attention to mammalogy and the two families discussed the possibility of a project on quadrupeds, science was as much a part of daily routines as religion. The Bachman children studied drawing and botany among stuffed animals "posed as in life" and surrounded by bottles and jugs containing "two-headed or five-legged freaks of nature" as well as other "gruesome yet alluring" organisms preserved in alcohol.[39] Living in a house where books and scientific artifacts vied for shelf space with imported curios, the children transcribed notes and helped with research. They also collected natural curiosities and preserved specimens. Indeed, many could be collected in their garden, an intriguing place where native plants, vegetables, and herbs, as well as imported ornamentals and trees collected by friends, family, and acquaintances served as a home for the wild animals caged and tethered there. Whether the children found such activities as alluring or idyllic as they appear in retrospect is unclear. Others in the household would have had a more accurate view as daily routines for enslaved men, women, and children became more burdensome with each new endeavor. In addition to preparing meals and keeping house for extra people, rooms where specimens were skinned and staged required special attention. Because decay set in quickly in the Carolina climate, when Audubon was in residence putrid carcasses had to be removed regularly to the back of the garden where they formed a fetid pile.[40] Additionally, the beasts and birds Bachman acquired had to be cared for, and slaves risked life and limb looking after animals such as the lynx and black bear.[41]

If not quite transformed, Audubon was affected by his Charleston friendships. Watching the Bachman family pull together on his behalf, he could not help but be impressed. During a few short weeks, much was accomplished with the assistance of strangers who, from his perspective, treated him more like family than his own family had when he needed help with volume one. Although both Victor Gifford and John Woodhouse were trained as youngsters to prepare and paint specimens, father and sons had become estranged between 1826 and 1829 while Audubon was in Britain, and Victor was especially unreceptive to requests from afar.[42] Filial affection was supposed to ensure the kind of loyalty that money could not buy, but Victor was skeptical that the father who had failed at business so many times would be successful in a venture as implausible as an expensive publication depicting the birds of America, and he resisted overtures of any kind until November 1829. Although Victor was thereafter more favorably disposed toward his father, neither he nor his brother worked on *Birds* before Audubon's Charleston visit.

In December 1831, having observed what could be accomplished when the resources of an entire household were at his disposal, John James proposed his family join him when he returned to England to oversee the printing of *Birds*. He was well aware of his dependency on Lucy—she had rescued him from penury time and time again—but the idea that his sons could play an even larger role in the realization of his project became apparent as Audubon witnessed just how productive domestic labor could be, and he wrote Lucy suggesting that they all work together in "an established Partnership for Life consisting of Husband Wife and Children."[43] Working in an environment where male and female, old and young, free and slave pulled together to assist him, he completed fifteen illustrations and five plates; he recruited Maria Martin, a budding artist whose innate ability, intellect, and interest in learning how to improve her skills produced plants and insects that quickly became good enough to embellish his figures for *Birds*; and he obtained the confidence and cooperation of John Bachman, a man who was to become his staunchest ally and collaborator.

Capitalizing on the generosity of his Charleston acquaintances, Audubon set aside any qualms he might have had about imposing on his new friends. Caught up in the excitement, John Bachman was equally unconcerned that his new friendship might affect his family. Even as *Birds* became an increasingly important activity, or as *The Quadrupeds of North America*, a three-volume work containing one hundred and fifty drawings, was planned in the late 1830s, he saw no reason to worry about unintended consequences. If, for example, those living under his roof had to endure an unpleasant, unsanitary disorderliness as birds were gutted and stuffed in bug-infested rooms before being deposited in the garden to decompose under a Southern sun, their discomfort was a small sacrifice as he and his friends endeavored to learn more about God's creatures. Likewise, the possibility that natural history might alter the evangelical beliefs or pietistic practices of this devout home caused little worry. In an age when studying the natural world was synonymous with studying God's creation, hours devoted to ornithology or botany were just as meaningful as hours spent helping the poor and needy. Nonetheless, these activities did have an effect. Over time, subtle changes occurred in how scientific pursuits were viewed.

It is highly unlikely, for example, that Bachman's youngest daughter, Catherine, would have produced a biography of her father that emphasized his scientific activities, important though they may have been, had there not been a significant shift in thinking between Audubon's first visit and the publication of *John Bachman: Pastor of St. John's Lutheran Church, Charleston* (1888). Bachman was a distinguished pastor, president of the Synod of South Carolina (1824–1834), a founder of the Southern seminary, and author of numerous theological tracts, but when Catherine assembled his correspondence to let her father "speak for himself," she painted a detailed picture of domesticity, science, and religion in a narrative that privileged science. Intending to glorify her father, she focused disproportionately on his scientific work, overshadowing the accomplishments of almost sixty years devoted to pastoral and missionary work, to administrative and educational work, and to doctrinal disputation.[44]

In her own understated way, Catherine Bachman also attempted to ensure credit for her beloved Aunt Maria. Born in January 1832, not long after Audubon departed for the Florida wintering grounds, Catherine went from babe in arms to toddler and school girl watching her Aunt Maria (and others) work on *Birds*. Initially oblivious to specimens being eviscerated, stuffed, positioned, and painted, as she passed through adolescence to womanhood most of her father's scientific publications appeared with Maria Martin's assistance, and Catherine did not ignore her efforts. In Maria's hands, science was as important as religion, and *The Pastor of St. John's Lutheran Church* offered a romanticized view of his accomplishments. While her contemporaries glossed over the ugliness of institutionalized slavery as they romanticized antebellum life, Catherine glossed over the unpleasant parts of natural history. In a chapter devoted to extolling her father's pastoral work among African American slaves and injured soldiers, she recalled wistfully how the lower level of her home, converted into a Confederate infirmary during the Civil War, had once hosted scientists and artists.[45] She did not, however, mention how her family endured the revolting smell of rotting flesh that enveloped home and garden periodically or how staging and painting hundreds of birds as they turned putrid triggered vermin infestations.

Maria Martin was, of course, one of the artists alluded to in *The Pastor of St. John's Lutheran Church.* Typically appearing as an author of addenda to correspondence by others, especially John Bachman, her presence is palpable if amorphous on almost every page in this volume. And she is there because her favorite niece, Catherine, made it so. Influenced by the aunt who raised her, Catherine's life unfolded in much the same way as that of the aunt she admired. Like Maria Martin, Catherine watched her older sisters marry, move out, and start families of their own while she remained behind, serving those who raised her. She also became her father's assistant and caregiver after the death of her beloved Aunt Maria (who technically became her mother in 1848 when she married John Bachman) on December 27, 1863.[46]

As she chronicled her father's achievements, biographer Catherine Bachman reconstructed the world in which she and her female forebears lived, and Maria Martin appears as the self-sacrificing helpmeet she was. Consequently, her contributions to *The Birds of America* are glossed over in the biography of John Bachman. But the woman who avoided public life as she devoted herself to family and friends is nonetheless present, and Catherine provides a lens through which a different view of Maria Martin's world may be seen. In her narrative, Maria transcends the liminality associated with anonymity and apprenticeship and emerges as an indispensable participant and facilitator in scientific collaboration. Indeed, it was largely because of her efforts that Jay Shuler could describe the Bachman residence as "Audubon's American home where he was always welcomed, where he stored his treasures, where a studio awaited him, and where he frequently returned to work" in his perceptive book on the friendship between Audubon and Bachman.[47] If the peripatetic naturalist, something of an *esprit libre* with an expressive temperament described as "mercurial," could work productively in a household where expectations and behaviors were far different from life in the field or in the courts and clubs where well-heeled subscribers found his eccentricities fascinating, it was because Maria Martin realized the promise of Bachman's invitation.[48] In a household that was intensely private, predominantly female, and deeply religious, she made Audubon, his assistants, and his family welcome in a way that the reverend could not.

As mediatrix between the world inhabited by men and that inhabited by women and children, free and slave, Maria Martin ensured that both Audubon and Bachman had the freedom to do as they wished and that the expertise and labor needed for *Birds*, *Quadrupeds*, and more were at their disposal. As science and art were incorporated into daily routines, Maria reoriented the activities over those whom she controlled. For her nieces and nephews, that reorientation meant tutoring in the relevant academics, as well as in drawing and painting. For the enslaved men, women, and children she supervised, that reorientation meant ensuring their labor allowed everyone else to focus on Audubon's magnificent work. And for Maria Martin herself, that reorientation meant transformational change. As art and science were added to domestic responsibilities just months after her thirty-fifth birthday, a world scarcely imagined was created.

1

FAMILY

Born July 6, 1796, Maria Martin's safe arrival was cause for thanks. In addition to the usual worries associated with pregnancy and childbirth, her family home was just beyond the area leveled by the "great fire of 1796." Some three hundred families lost everything in the conflagration that consumed several blocks in the heart of Charleston just two and a half weeks earlier. Living on the east side of Meeting Street, about 600 feet north of the last building to go up in smoke before firefighters extinguished the flames, if Maria's parents agreed with neighbors who were secretly "relieved" that the beef market—or the malodorous eyesore identifiable from afar by the flock of buzzards perpetually encircling the area looking for scraps—had succumbed, other thoughts were paramount. As Jacob and Rebecca watched the market, the Huguenot Church, and at least 250 dwellings go up in smoke, they would have been more concerned about their home, their business, and their three young children: Eliza (1790–1851), Harriet (1791–1846), and Jane (1793–1825).[1] After taking stock, they could not but have been relieved that the expectant Rebecca had not given birth prematurely.

For much of her young life, Maria Martin grew up in a noisy, dangerous neighborhood. The devastation caused by the fire added to that of the Revolutionary War, and both stimulated construction.[2] When George Washington visited Charleston in 1791, he noted that there were approximately 1,600 dwellings; a decade later, another one thousand had been added.[3] In Maria's neighborhood, renewal and rehabilitation had an added dimension: as buildings damaged by fire or by the British occupation of 1780–1782 were replaced, several important public buildings were erected as well. Between 1800 and 1804, a City Hall was built on the site of the old beef market, the South Carolina Meeting Hall went up a little farther south along Meeting Street, and construction on the Circular Congregational Church, a magnificent structure capable of holding two thousand worshippers, began right next door to the Martin home.[4] Separated from the construction site by one of the oldest graveyards in the city (where dissenting Protestants had been buried since 1681), Maria and her sisters were immersed in the grime and clamor generated by tradesmen as they put up new buildings out of stucco-covered brick.[5] Only the Sabbath provided a reprieve from the sights, sounds, and hazards of the workaday world but then the bustle of people heading to worship as the bells tolled in the neighborhood churches replaced the usual buzz of activity. In addition to living next door to the Congregationalist Church, the Martin family lived a few blocks north of St Michael's Episcopalian Church, a block west of both St. Philip's Episcopalian and the French Huguenot Church (also under repair after the fire of 1796), and less than a quarter mile south of St. Mary's Roman Catholic Church and Kahal Kadosh Beth Elohim, the Sephardic Orthodox synagogue located across the street from St. Mary's. The Martin family church, St. John's Lutheran, was equally close. It was just to the west on Clifford Street, and their proximity to it was not accidental. Maria Martin's world was defined by the faith of her ancestors, one of whom had been a pastor at St. John's Lutheran during the American Revolution. Her grandfather, John Nicholas Martin (1724–1795), a German émigré, solidified his reputation as a Patriot when the British "closed his church" because he refused to acknowledge their occupation from the pulpit.[6]

Located close to the church at the heart of their lives, enduring the dust and din created by carts and carriages—or by pedestrians and workmen—was merely another burden meted out by an all-knowing power. However, once inside, the Martin home was comfortable. Maria and her sisters were accustomed to the kind of home favored by both social elites and affluent tradesmen. The assessed value of their parents' two houses suggests that these side-by-side dwellings were three-storied "single houses" with the usual outbuildings.[7] Discretely out of sight, kitchens and laundries serving double duty as slave quarters typically flanked houses two rooms deep with a center hall that opened onto a private courtyard. Some two-thirds of these types of homes had shops or workplaces in the ground-floor rooms fronting the street, and at least one of the Martin houses had commercial space. Acquired from Rebecca Martin's first husband, John Duvall (who died c. 1782–1783), a stay maker who owned one of the first businesses on Meeting Street during the 1770s, this shop became a prosperous mantua-making business, presumably with a public entrance on the short end of the house where customers could enter.[8] Although Rebecca Martin worked in this shop for many years, whether she continued to run a mantua-making business out of her home or whether the commercial property was rented to tenants is unclear.

The Martin family might have used both properties, although they appear to have been more substantial than typical for private use among the artisanal class. In a city where many lived cheek by jowl in row houses, or built houses on lots fifty feet wide, the 80-foot frontage and slightly more than a quarter of an acre owned by Rebecca Martin suggests the presence of numerous outbuildings: storage sheds, barns, stables, perhaps even a carriage house.[9] While uncommon before the end of the eighteenth century, the Martin home probably had piazzas, or exterior porches attached to the long side of a house, when Maria was a youngster. Added strategically so as to catch ocean breezes, they offered respite during the stifling hot months of the year, and these attractive and practical structures were added to most elegant town houses in the early nineteenth century. Piazzas also allowed slaves to pass from room to room without intruding on their masters or mistresses, effectively permitting slave owners to pretend that the men and women who catered to their every need did not exist.[10] Given the number of enslaved men and women owned by the Martin family, this architectural feature would have been most convenient.

Maria and her sisters grew up with slaves preparing their meals, laundering their clothes, and caring for their basic needs.[11] Symbols of wealth and position, these men and women were, in turn, responsible for the material possessions of the household. Signs of status and prestige, the Martin family effects mirrored those of the elite in kind, if not in quality. There were, for example, no fewer than three dining tables, two tea tables, a sideboard, two and a half dozen mahogany chairs, mahogany beds and dressers, as well as office furniture that included a book case that, at the time, would have been a substantial piece of furniture with enclosed lower shelves and glassed-in upper shelves.[12] While considerably less refined than the furnishings found in homes where imported English furniture or locally made pieces by master craftsman Thomas Elfe (1719–1775) were common, those in the Martin home were nonetheless typical of affluent households. Mahogany rather than pine, curtains and linens, mirrors, fine china and silverware were the hallmarks of the upper class.

Maria and her sisters were accustomed to the accouterments of wealth. Tucked into four-poster beds at night, upon rising, the Martin girls ate meals prepared and served by slaves who also poured tea steeped in silver pots into fine china cups for guests seated at fancy little tables draped in white linen. If the Martin home did not quite approach the scale and luxury of the lavishly appointed mansions inhabited by wealthy planters a short walk away, it nonetheless signaled above-average affluence. Even Northerners known for criticizing Charleston domestic architecture as "unsightly," nondescript, and constructed of inferior materials would have detected differences between the house where Maria and her sisters lived and rental properties not far away.[13] Once inside, it was clear that the Martin girls lived in comfort, if not luxury.

Over all, their mother presided. Mistress of a large household, mother of four children and three times married, Rebecca Martin was described as a "lady of exemplary character, particularly remarkable for undeviating prudence and industry," as well as "amiable and affectionate."[14] In this and more, she was an inspiration. As a young woman, Rebecca was a mantua-maker, designing fashionable dresses for the wives and daughters of the rich and powerful, and even if she no longer worked in the shop she ran after the deaths of her first two husbands, her daughters could not but be impressed by her.

A force to be reckoned with even into old age, Rebecca was ambitious and creative as a young woman. Widowed not once, but twice, she managed a thriving business inherited from John Duvall. Apprenticed as a stay maker in 1774, she and Duvall married once her apprenticeship was finished and they went into the mantua-making business in 1781.[15] Although nothing is known of Rebecca's background before entering Duvall's employ—not even how she came to choose the occupation that would serve her so well—she probably came from a modestly affluent background because apprentices required a level of education beyond that found among waged employees. In the eighteenth century, apprenticeships tended to be "economically practical only for women of the upper middle class," who were capable of reading and bookkeeping, as well as being skilled in "decorative needlework, advanced clothing construction, and proper fitting techniques."[16]

But if Rebecca's educational record is obscure, the artistry, dexterity, and business acumen that made her a successful mantua-maker is not. When her first husband, John Duvall, died in the early 1780s, their open accounts equaled £1674.17.3, and when her second husband, Jacob Solzar, died in 1784, the amount owed them was £544.6.4.[17] This balance sheet was remarkably positive given that the shop had to adjust to shifting tastes and new ownership. In the early days, Rebecca would have been expected to custom-make Watteau gowns like those featured in publications such as the *Lady's Magazine*,[18] replicating them in all their metropolitan detail regardless of her views on tight fitting bodices, ruffled sleeves, and skirts with hoops "so wide that two women could not walk side by side down the walkways in front of the shops. . . . [or] walk through a doorway without turning to the side."[19] Then, to maintain profits as she did through the revolutionary years, Rebecca had to be adaptable. Because she catered to an affluent clientele rather than to women who purchased ready-made "English" clothes and accessories such as bonnets and aprons from local dry goods merchants, the boycott on imported goods may have affected Rebecca's business less than it did shopkeepers in her neighborhood. She had to adjust to shifting tastes, however, and in the postrevolutionary years, French fashions, especially the Polonaise gown, became popular. Made of silk or satin rather than the brocades or other heavy fabrics used for Watteau gowns, the Polonaise was easier to tailor because ruffled sleeves and hoops were abandoned for a more informal design.[20] Rebecca had to respond to customer demand or lose money. Her business would have languished had she not done so, and her accounts suggest otherwise.

Like most women of her generation, she remarried soon after being widowed. Her second marriage was less salutary than the first, but it did provide a valuable lesson. Not long after the nuptials, Rebecca's new husband, Jacob Solzar, placed the business she had built with John Duvall in his name. He appropriated property she deemed rightfully hers through honest labor, if not inheritance, and while perfectly legal under state law, when the opportunity presented itself, Rebecca took steps to avoid future forfeitures. In 1784, not long after Solzar died, she petitioned successfully to become administratrix of the estates of both deceased husbands.[21] Furthermore, as she contemplated a third marriage proposal from Maria's father, Jacob Martin (1763–1853), she had a "Marriage Settlement" drawn up.[22] Rebecca Murray Duvall Solzar had not spent fifteen years fitting clients and customizing hand-sewn, made-to-order dresses to hand over her property—including four slaves—to another husband.[23] Three days before solemnizing their vows before Reverend John C[hristopher] Farber, pastor of St. John's Lutheran Church, Jacob Martin signed a document stipulating he would not interfere with Rebecca's rights to use, sell, or dispose of her property once they were married.

Financially secure, Rebecca Solzar could have certainly provided for herself, but in a world where marriage was privileged over widowhood, and where "the ideal woman" was a pious one whose destiny as mother and wife was God's will, Rebecca chose marriage.[24] Why she chose Jacob Martin was another matter. As a woman of means, she was positioned to choose among many suitors, and yet she chose an impecunious son of an unordained Lutheran pastor. In a society in which church membership was an important identifier of place and position, with Anglicans or Episcopalians outranking all others, her decision to marry a Lutheran is curious, especially given that her marriage to John Duvall took place before Reverend Robert Cooper, a rector from St. Philip's Anglican Church, the official church of the colony of South Carolina.[25] While a shortage of clergy allegedly fostered a more ecumenical outlook among eighteenth-century Protestants than found among nineteenth-century denominations, Rebecca's decision nonetheless suggests movement down rather than up the social hierarchy. Even as Henry Melchior Muhlenberg (1711–1787), the "Patriarch of American Lutheranism," maintained "close relationships" with Anglicans, with revivalists such as George Whitefield, and with Quakers and Roman Catholics, there is no doubt that where one attended service was a factor in community affiliation and status.[26] More to the point, within his own church, John Nicholas Martin—Jacob's father—was not uniformly well regarded.

Categorized as a "vagabond preacher," a derisive appellation reserved for lay pastors who traveled about ministering to isolated congregations, Reverend John Nicholas Martin was "ordained" by pastors at the Lutheran settlement at Ebenezer, Georgia, and sent to Charleston in 1763, the year Maria's father was born.[27] When Muhlenberg visited Charleston in 1774, he tepidly supported Nicholas Martin's *in term* appointment as pastor of St. John's Lutheran. He doubted that his basic education from the German public school system prepared him for the pulpit of one of the largest and most affluent congregations in the region, and he was unimpressed that some in the congregation strongly supported Reverend Martin.[28] Unconvinced that Martin had the theological training necessary to fulfill his ministerial duties, Muhlenberg doubted that those who spoke the loudest in the pastor's favor were qualified to make such decisions. But, as the trouble "brewing" between the American colonies and the English undermined efforts to obtain a theologically educated replacement, Muhlenberg agreed that the "autodidact" could serve St. John's Lutheran until a more appropriate pastor could be found.[29] With such a reluctant endorsement, Martin's position was tenuous. Had it been otherwise, he would have been a member of the German Friendly Society, a philanthropic organization open to men of unimpeachable character, including the pastor of St. John's Lutheran, for whom an honorary membership was reserved.[30]

But if Rebecca was undeterred by their religious differences, the fact that Jacob did not seem to have a profession, or even an occupation, was another matter. Eventually becoming a clerk and bookkeeper at the Bank of South Carolina, when they married in 1789 Jacob Martin was listed as a merchant, although where he was employed in that capacity is unknown.[31] Indeed, a year later, when enumerators collected information for the First Census of the United States, Jacob's name does not appear. Rather, the Rebecca Martin household consisted of one free white man over the age of sixteen, two free white women, presumably employees in her mantua-making shop, and one slave.[32] It is possible that Jacob was a cabinetmaker, but he self-identified as a merchant and in doing so was being deliberately ambiguous about his line of work.[33]

Some of the wealthiest and most influential men in Charleston were merchants, but they were factors in the import-export trade. There were also many other "merchants" in Charleston, but they tended to be vendors selling goods and services to the public; they were far removed in power and prestige from the factors. Since Jacob Martin did not refer to himself as a factor, and since he was not listed in any business directories or census, whatever his occupation, it was closer to shopkeeper than factor. As a result, Jacob Martin's status would have been middling at best. As anything other than a factor, he would have been lumped in with the "vulgar" money-grubbing class; however, the extent to which the ambiguity surrounding his occupation caused concern is unknown. While living in a world dominated by the values of the "planting and professional classes—an aristocracy that took pride in its English antecedents, its public service, its standards of conduct and its guardianship of the social order," Rebecca Murray Duvall Solzar weighed her options and decided to take a chance on Jacob Martin.[34]

Certainly a well-situated widow could have found someone better fixed financially when choosing a third husband, but Rebecca clearly considered Jacob Martin an acceptable mate. Described by a nephew many years later as an honorable but poor man who brought "nothing" to the marriage "but that which is beyond all price, a good reputation and great industry,"[35] his suitability was, at least in part, due to the fact that he agreed to sign a marriage settlement. Jacob Martin's matrimonial options were limited. Descended from shoemakers and butchers who emigrated from the German Palatinate in the 1750s, Jacob stood to inherit lands acquired by his father, but it was a pitifully small patrimony that hardly compensated his many shortcomings.[36] Moreover, his father's estate was entrusted to his mother, Anna Katharina Schmidt Martin (1742–1800), until she died, and Jacob's inheritance from the less than three acres his father owned did not materialize until 1800.[37] In total, the farm located just beyond the Charleston city limits was worth £495, and Nicholas Martin divided it unequally among his seven children.[38] Jacob received a small piece of land 48-feet wide by 200-feet deep. Without position or property, Jacob could sign Rebecca's marriage settlement, he could look for another mate, or he could remain single. As Rebecca had a thriving business and assets that she was not prepared to lose through *femme covert*, they came to a mutually agreeable arrangement.

Jacob's impecuniousness made him powerless and consequently less threatening than better-situated men. Rebecca had already once lost her life's work through marriage, and she was not about to repeat the mistake made when marrying Jacob Solzar. If her third husband played a significant role in her mantua-making business, it was well hidden.[39] At the same time, Rebecca's assets grew after they married, and Jacob Martin has often been credited with their improved financial position. They added land and slaves, a commercial building and domestic dwellings, as well as personal possessions, household goods, bonds and cash to their belongings. Exactly how Jacob did so is unclear; why is less mysterious.[40] In transforming what was later referred to as "a decent competency" into something much more, Jacob Martin was following a well-established practice of Southern social climbers. Men who found themselves in a position to improve their status did so by purchasing land and slaves, preferably enough of each to approximate that owned by planters.[41] Additionally, at the same time as Jacob was adding to their holdings, he became a clerk at the Bank of South Carolina, a quasi-professional occupation that connoted a certain level of respectability, albeit far removed from that attained by lawyers, bankers, or factors. In any event, his efforts paid off as he earned the respect of both friends and family who described him as a "model" of "honor and integrity" within the "whole community."[42]

While such pronouncements were no doubt exaggerated, they were not entirely inaccurate. Although he had the misfortune to fall in love with another woman while married to Rebecca, he tried to keep his infidelity a secret and supported two households until he was found out and forced to decide between his so-called Philadelphia "Harlot" and his family. As a result, in 1813, he transferred ownership of considerable property to his wife and daughters before leaving Charleston for Philadelphia with Elizabeth Pennington. Admittedly, part of the settlement consisted of property protected by Rebecca's marriage settlement, but Jacob also deeded two dozen slaves, stocks, and real estate, specifically: two lots northwest of the city limits in Cannonsborough; a "large brick building on the head of Ropers late Geyers So. Wharf, commonly called the Custom House of Charleston"; a lot and house on Anson Street; and their home on Meeting Street to Rebecca. This, along with $7,000 for Rebecca and $15,000 for each of his four daughters, exceeded the properties protected in 1789.[43] Indeed, although Jacob's son-in-law, Martin Strobel

(1786–1838), castigated him for betraying his family and his good name by becoming entangled in polygamy, he admitted that the funds deposited to the account of his wife, Jacob's daughter Eliza, "placed him in very comfortable circumstances."[44] Yet unmarried, Eliza's younger sisters—Harriet, Jane, and Maria—could offer suitors equally comfortable circumstances.

Whether Jacob Martin was ever the "man of strict integrity, and rigid punctuality" described by Martin Strobel in a pamphlet castigating his adultery is difficult to determine. Hyperbole aside, his behavior seems typical. Far from unique in following the time-honored practice of marrying money and then adopting a "double standard," Jacob Martin was simply less successful than his peers when it came to extramarital liaisons.[45] Although Southern slave-owning households were rife with exploitative and nonconsensual sexual activity, Jacob made the mistake of relocating a white woman from Philadelphia to Charleston so as to have both a mistress and a wife in the same city. If it had not been for that fateful decision—and the fact that gossipy "tale-bearing old women" informed Rebecca of his transgression—then Jacob would have had a charmed life. Until exposed as a cad, "all nature smiled around him," but in 1813 Jacob was confronted with an uncomfortable decision: he could either leave his mistress, or leave town.[46] In what was interpreted as lack of character, he chose the latter.

In 1825, when rumors about Jacob's indiscretion reemerged, a pamphlet was penned to defend the family honor. News that Jacob had lawfully married his "paramour" had made its way to Charleston, and the claim was too much to bear. Affidavits from family, well-placed members of the community, and John Bachman, Rebecca's son-in-law and the pastor of St. John's Lutheran, were obtained so as to refute stories that simply could not be true. Reminding readers that the State of South Carolina did not permit divorce, witnesses also attested to the fact that Jacob and Rebecca were legally married and that contrary claims were false. Disputing rumors, often contradictory, that Jacob Martin had never been married, that he had been married but that he had divorced his first wife, that his wife and her sisters considered their father's Philadelphia "paramour" as their "dear mother," and that the "reputable people" of both Philadelphia and Charleston were among the couple's acquaintances, the pamphlet was published to set matters straight. Railing unrelentingly, Jacob was castigated for moral turpitude, although it was conceded that Jacob's depravity was not entirely his fault. When he first fell under Elizabeth Pennington's spell he was in a weakened physical condition that allowed a "prostitute female of Baltimore" to ply her "arts and vices."

Notwithstanding vulnerabilities beyond his control, Jacob was accused of causing both financial ruin and emotional trauma as "the acts and devices of the demon that seemed to guide him to his destruction" provoked indiscretions that left his wife and daughters destitute.[47] Well aware that Jacob provided adequately for his family and that Rebecca's property had been protected by a prenuptial agreement, Martin Strobel—the son-in-law who prepared the pamphlet—knew that his allegations were utterly disingenuous, but he nonetheless claimed that this "highly respectable and virtuous family" would have preferred to "have lived in poverty with him" and "grieve the demise of a honourable man" rather than lose him to scandal so serious that his fate was to "sink into the grave amidst the careless indifference of a Delilah and the pity and contempt of an insulted community."[48] At the same time, Strobel pointed out that when Jacob left Charleston his family chose to ignore his departure, assuming he would either come to his senses or suffer the consequences as the people of Philadelphia discovered he was living there under false pretenses. A contradictory message to be sure, but it does suggest that Rebecca carried on, head held high, in the community where she had lived for more than fifty years. Indeed, within a short time, Rebecca's name replaced Jacob's as a pew holder in the church where his father once preached.[49]

Only fourteen when her father made his fateful trip to Philadelphia, Maria Martin had spent her entire short life in her parent's home on Meeting Street or just north of the city where her grandparents owned a farm in Hampstead. Whether this farm was as extensive when Maria was a child as it was when John Nicholas Martin lived there in the 1780s is unknown, but even after his death it remained a working farm with at least ten slaves, including a currier and a gardener.[50] Destroyed by the British in 1779–1780, compensation claims itemizing damages suggest the "little farm" offered a comfortable retirement home consisting of two houses. The larger one was a well-lit, somewhat ornate, two-storied frame house (27 x 18 feet) with "15 windows, paneled shutters 12 lightsashes, 5 paneled doors, the whole of the upper part completely lined with boards from the floor upwards, with a ceiled piazza, one side and one end thereof, with floor and hand rail all compleat and well finished workmanship." The smaller one (20 x 14 feet) was a multifunctional dwelling with a detached, one-story kitchen (18 x 12 feet), a one-story stable (13 x 12 feet), a "necessary house," and a "fowl house." With several acres of land, it could have been the site described nostalgically by one of Maria's cousins as the "flower farm," so named for the reverend's love of flowering plants, or it could have been the place where "the pastoral sports of his children and their interesting little companions making the scene gay and lively" took place, but such romanticized recollections—simultaneously evasive and evocative—did not endear the man who had abandoned his wife and children to Maria.[51]

Maria Martin evinced little interest in the father who abandoned her, and when she visited Philadelphia in 1839 she made no effort to contact him. The passage of time had not healed past wounds, and Maria spent her days touring the sights. She went to the sculptural garden at Laurel Hill Cemetery, the art museum, the state legislature, the penitentiary, and the asylums built for the blind and the "Deaf and Dumb"—rather than seeking him out.[52] Similarly, others in her family showed little interest in Jacob. When Maria's niece, Catherine Lindauer Bachman, compiled letters and reminiscences for *John Bachman, the Pastor of St John's Lutheran*, she avoided genealogical information.

Admittedly, Catherine's stated goal was to memorialize her father's contributions to science and religion rather than recount the quotidian, but home and family dominated both the narrative and the contents of her biography. And her choices did not reflect an absence of material. Catherine chose carefully from her father's voluminous correspondence, avoiding information that might reflect poorly on family members, especially on the grandmother who was a role model and benefactor. She described Rebecca Martin as a "dear, aged saint," and she referred to her as a pious and dutiful Christian who was devoted to husband and family. She was, Catherine observed, so worthy of respect that her own father treated her grandmother with reverence and that his demeanor "was naturally adopted by the young members of his family."[53] Insofar as Rebecca Martin appeared in the pages of *The Pastor of St. John's Lutheran*, she was depicted as a woman to be emulated. She had raised her children to be God-fearing, responsible adults. She was an exemplary role model.

Rebecca Martin's marital history was not going to be placed on display as an embarrassing reminder of an episode better forgotten. Such revelations would, of course, have been in poor taste, and the obvious opprobrium attached to marital impropriety might have been reason enough to omit such information in the biography of a man whose reputation as a pastor and biblical scholar was indisputable. In particular, Bachman entered into a heated debate over the Lutheran view of marriage in 1853 that was not to be undermined by dredging up the past. He employed rational argument and righteous indignation to undercut Catholic charges that Luther sanctioned "concubinage, polygamy and adultery," and Catherine devoted a chapter to his efforts in the "Defence of Luther."[54] As he compared himself to the "Great Reformer," Bachman engaged in a lengthy dispute over *De Matrimonio,* arguing that Catholics were inherently biased against Luther, in part because they had not studied the fifteenth-century German texts appropriately: while Luther's language may have been common and vulgar, he described marriage as a "holy state," a "preservative against temptation to sin," and the only legitimate means to respond to God's command to "increase and multiply."[55] Catherine Bachman could hardly include information about her grandparents that would damage her father's reputation.

Possibly unaware of the scandal considered so heinous that Martin Strobel was prompted to defend Rebecca Martin's virtue a decade after the transgression occurred, it is more likely that information reflecting poorly on Rebecca and, by extension, the entire family, was suppressed. In any event, unwilling to divulge much beyond the fact that her mother, Harriet Martin, was descended from John Nicholas Martin, she referred to her grandmother—Rebecca Murray Duvall Solzar Martin—as Mrs. Jacob Martin. Nothing more was said about a woman who had a profound impact on her daughters and granddaughters. The life of Maria Martin's fascinating mother was protected from view, and the only reference to Jacob Martin was both perfunctory and enigmatic. His name was mentioned only to identify the woman who was "an honored inmate" in the Bachman home.[56] Otherwise, not one word was wasted on Maria Martin's father.

2

FAITH, THE LUTHERAN WAY

In 1845, just two years before Julia Bachman died of consumption at the age of twenty-two, Maria Martin wrote her niece a letter that revealed much about their world. Feeling compelled to explain why she had been so unrelenting, even unpleasant, in her efforts to make Julia compliant instead of willful, altruistic rather than selfish, Maria Martin wrote:

> You seem to take what I said about your teaching the children and making yourself useful as a reproach Dear Julia, and say that you hope to prove to me yet, "that you are not the worthless creature I think you." Perhaps the term worthless is too harsh a one and not exactly what you intended to say, and I should certainly not apply it to you. That I have sometimes been put out by your seeming want of energy and indifferent manner, I will candidly acknowledge, but there were many good traits in your character that, perhaps required circumstances to develope [*sic*] them and I think nothing will have a surer tendency to improve you than leaving home & having to exert your energies which perhaps were rather slumbering at home having nothing here to call them into action. I feared too that there might be some selfishness creeping in which is the principal ingredient in the character of almost every fashionable young lady of the present day, and it is one which I assure you is of all others the most to be avoided, if you would wish to gain the esteem of others. Why is Jane so general a favourite? Because she never thinks of herself but is always ready to renounce any trifling gratification if it will promote the happiness or pleasure of others. It is in the power of everyone to be pleasant, affable and obliging, and it does win the esteem, and insure so much gratification to the one who bestows and the other who receives it, that I am often surprised to see persons try so little to cultivate qualities that render them agreeable ~~to all~~ and gain for them the esteem of all. I have sometimes

> thought that you were quite too independent for a young person, and showed too great a disregard for the opinion and good advice of those who had more experience than yourself, and under the influence of such an impression may may [*sic*] have expressed myself, displeased or grieved at it, but if I had felt no interest in your welfare, I should never have reproved you, and for this reason you have drawn the conclusion that I dislike you and can never think well of any thing you do, but this is an error as no one would sooner give you credit than I would for the improvement of your mind or disposition, and I have no doubt that your own good sense will point out to you many little defects in your character, that you will be enabled daily to correct, and in doing so you will acquire that self command and discipline of mind that will render you not only happy yourself, but enable you to dispense happiness all around you.[1]

As the stresses and strains of motherhood left her sister Harriet unable to oversee the intellectual, moral, and emotional development of her children, Maria assumed responsibility for providing her nieces and nephews with "catechetical and moral instruction" expected in Lutheran homes. In a tradition going back to the Reformation, Maria accepted the role assigned first to the parent, and then to the school, as she taught "the fear of God and good behavior [*Gottesfurcht und gute Sitten*] and also [subjects] in the liberal arts, and honourable manners (*geistlichkeit, gute künste und ehrliche sitten*)" to the nine Bachman children.[2]

Such efforts reflected Maria's own upbringing. Although born a year after her grandfather died, she was raised in a home guided by his ideals. The "stern and authoritarian" pastor cast a long shadow, and if the home where Maria Martin lived was less rigid than the one in which her father was raised, it was nonetheless influenced by a man whom she had never met. Quick to react with "severity" and leaning to "despotic authority" both at home and at work, Reverend Martin was autocratic and dictatorial. According to one of Maria's cousins, these attributes were used to settle "serious family disputes, and [employed] on other occasions of a similar kind, when all other means of conciliation failed" among congregants. The Martin patriarch whose "fervid and intense disposition" surfaced regularly was not to be trifled with.[3] Nor, apparently, was his granddaughter Maria.

Like her grandfather, she made sacrifices for her flock, even though her responsibilities were more limited. Maria focused on the welfare of her sister's children rather than on the larger community of souls entrusted to a man of the cloth, but as Reverend Martin sacrificed creature comforts while roaming

"South Carolina in Deerskins" and living "out of doors in Gods fair Kingdom of wild things and flowers" so as to preach to impoverished backcountry men and women, Maria Martin accepted her duty as the spinster aunt to a large brood of nieces and nephews.[4] And, like her grandfather, she expected results. When John Nicholas Martin looked back on a twenty-year career, he was gratified to note: "My people run a neck and neck race with privation and have little to give to their preacher, but the gospel they receive with joy; I am met everywhere with hearty welcome and often with tears," and Maria Martin hoped for similar rewards.[5] Uncompromising in her efforts to instill Lutheran ideals, drastic measures were sometimes needed, especially with Julia. Comparing herself to Mentor in Homer's *Odyssey*, Maria explained this to her restive niece: "Remember that Telemachus [son of Odysseus and Penelope] would have been sacrificed to the enchantment of the Island of Calypso, if he had not had a kind Mentor [Odysseus's friend] at hand, who did not even hesitate to plunge him into the sea, and bear him to the land, rather than allow him to become enervated and helpless from the allurements of pleasure, and the moral may serve to show you that if my advice sometimes appears severe it is given with the same motive that influenced Mentor in his conduct towards his young friend charge—But you will say I am preaching you a sermon."[6] Her expectations were high, and not always easy to meet. Because Julia resisted her aunt's every admonition, the two were constantly at odds.

Maria Martin clearly considered Julia willful. In turn, Julia no doubt resented the extent to which her aunt controlled her life. From the time she was a youngster, her mother was little more than a shadowy presence, remembered affectionately as a "gentle sufferer" who played a small role in the day-to-day affairs of the household. Invalided by childbearing and chronic illness, Harriet Bachman also endured the emotional strain of losing five infants and two grown daughters (Maria Rebecca in 1840 and Mary Eliza in 1841) before she died of consumption in 1846. Her first loss occurred in 1821, when Cordelia died soon after birth, and before the decade ended she saw two infant sons—John (1822) and Henry (1824)—as well as twin daughters—Ellen and Clara (1828)—die. Often confined to her "chamber," Harriet was visited by her children in the room they described as a "quiet, peaceful spot, where we took our books to study a hard lesson, or to write our school composition." They reminisced about how: "Frequently, and not unwillingly, we shared with her, the dainties provided specially for the invalid." They recalled her perseverance with wonder, expressing gratitude for the "many daily lessons of fortitude" and for the example she provided in her "patience and unselfish devotion to God and duty."[7] Unavoidably playing a more passive role than Maria Martin when it came to ensuring her children knew what was expected of them, Harriet was clearly viewed as a perfect example of the pious mother esteemed in Lutheran doctrine. In their mother, the Bachman children saw living proof of lessons taught by Maria.

As Harriet endeavored to be the good wife, serving man and God, she foreshadowed her daughter's futures and provided a model for her sons, Samuel and William, for the day when they would choose wives of their own. Moreover, had they any doubts about women's roles, their father would have disabused them as deftly and decisively as he did parishioners who seemed confused over such matters. If less physical than Nicholas Martin in his ministrations, Bachman was equally unequivocal. When it came to the role of women, his views were clear. They were destined to be wives and mothers, and they were to "discharge their duties" by developing "industry, intelligence, refinement, and pure religion."[8] Ironically, as Harriet fulfilled her obligation to bear children, she was often unable to supervise her children's religious education or moral upbringing. Pregnant, recovering from pregnancy, or suffering from conditions for which there was no real treatment—tic douloureux (trigeminal neuralgia) and consumption—Harriet needed assistance. If her children were to serve God with the strength of character and self-effacing yet positive outlook needed to do good works—the hallmarks of pietism, a deeply personal approach to religious life that focused on faith and devotion to God rather than on outward displays of religiosity—they would need more guidance than she could provide.[9] Consequently, Maria Martin stepped in to help and, as a result, the Bachman children had both female role models esteemed by Martin Luther: the good wife who protected her husband from his baser instincts, and the companion who assisted him in his godly endeavors.

Although John Bachman sometimes questioned whether his children were becoming the God-fearing, self-sacrificing individuals he desired, he seldom criticized his sister-in-law for their failings. Indeed, he described Maria's efforts glowingly. Less than a year after the insouciant Julia was upbraided for doubting that her aunt's treatment was motivated by anything other than love and affection, Bachman could not praise Maria Martin highly enough. In a letter in which he confessed his dependency, he wrote one of Julia's older sisters, Jane, that he did "not know just now what we would do without your dear Aunt. She says she is ripping & shining—has given up her room for your sister Harriet—[and] is chief cook & bottle washer. I tell her if two years ago a clever young fellow had come to ask for her I would have given her up with some grumbling—now if a King came or even a Prince from Alabama I would set the dogs at his heels."[10] In large part, Bachman's admiration reflected need as well as accomplishment.

By 1846, Harriet was completely bedridden, and as she lay dying of the consumption that had afflicted her for years, Bachman was keenly aware of how Maria had stepped in when his wife was indisposed. She had, for example, accompanied him north on family business in 1827 when Harriet was pregnant, and she traveled to Cuba in 1841 when his daughter Eliza sought treatment for consumption. Both times Harriet was unable to even consider such a journey given her delicate health. When Harriet died in July, Bachman's grief and the gratitude he felt toward Maria for her care and compassion were intertwined. As he informed Jane of her mother's death, he told her that in their darkest days Maria had kept the family intact. She stepped in when needed and had, he wrote, "long been a slave to us all." Elaborating, he stated that she maintained "complete control of the children so that they have not given me a moments pain [adding] for a long time both Lynch & Catherine have excellent principles and the best of tempers."[11] Under Maria's guidance, three of his daughters—Jane, Lynch, and Catherine—had matured just as he wanted: Jane was a model of self-sacrifice; Lynch was "a treasure"; and Catherine "a most obedient & excellent child." When it came to Julia, however, Bachman's comments were more circumspect. He agreed with his sister-in-law. Her behavior was troubling. "She does her best," he wrote, "but is not so handy."[12] At twenty-two, she was well beyond the age when children knew enough to honor family expectations.

Lutherans were hardly unique in their view that once children began to develop their ability to reason they could become both willful and deceptive. Like others, they believed that if efforts to mold character were delayed beyond the age of six, attempts to do so were futile.[13] Despite such views, Maria Martin remained hopeful that Julia would become a model of Christian womanhood even as she left her adolescent years behind, and two years after chastising her niece for being apathetic and lazy, as well as selfish and headstrong, her prayers were answered. In 1847, Julia submitted completely to God's will as she passed from this life to the next. While seeking treatment at a retreat for consumptives in Red Sulphur Springs, Virginia, Julia had a deathbed transformation that was witnessed by her Aunt Maria, her sister Lynch, and her father. So miraculous was her redemption from subversive to submissive that a whole chapter of John Bachman's biography was devoted to the retelling of her ascent to God's kingdom.

In "Father and Daughter," Julia emerges as the embodiment of Christian womanhood. In death, her inner beauty and spirituality were described as surpassing her outer beauty, reputably considerable. Certainly those attempting to ensure she was a self-effacing and dutiful daughter viewed her physical attractiveness as a burden. With regard to her corporeal sufferings—allegedly over well before she drew her last breath—her father claimed he had "never witnessed in my long ministry so triumphant a death."[14] Writing those at home, he described her sad, yet glorious, departure to her final reward: "Her eyes were bright and her mind clear; her perceptions keen and her judgment strong; her words were submissive and her prayers fervent. Her whole soul so full of the love of God, and the mercy of her Saviour, that she seemed, almost to forget her great sufferings. The fear of death was entirely removed, and she triumphantly exclaimed, 'O! Death, where is thy sting? O! grave, where is thy victory? Thanks be unto God who giveth us the victory through Jesus Christ our Lord.'"[15]

Her childish ways forgotten and forgiven, Bachman returned to her final moments in a letter describing her fears, her despair, and her triumph as she accepted God's forgiveness and embraced her destiny. Breathless and weak, she asked her father to pray with her, as she was ready "for the joyful hour when her Saviour would call her to his blessed arms."[16] There, she believed she would be reunited with recently departed family members, and she welcomed her fate. Moved by the events, Bachman stated: "in death her face was like that of an angel, but her short religious life was brighter still. O, my children, will you not profit by this lesson!"[17] As someone who believed that good Christians anticipated a future when they would be reunited in heaven with those who had died before them, he was relieved that Julia had ensured that eventuality just before dying.

John Bachman was familiar with death. As a pastor who ministered last rites and dispatched deceased parishioners, and as a father who had buried seven of fourteen children, his commentary on Julia's "last days on earth" should be taken seriously. At the same time, it should not be accepted literally. Evangelical pastors were known to record such events "for the edification of others" who had not yet accepted the inevitability of death and the need for spiritual preparation.[18] Aware that passage from this world to the next would be determined by God, not man, when there was doubt over the views of the decedent "outward and visible proof" of true conversion was sometimes required, even among pietistic evangelicals who "emphasized an excessively inward and 'personal' relationship with God."[19] Known for his antipathy to emotionalism, and as someone who provided practical advice to bereaved parents, Bachman was uncharacteristically demonstrative when describing Julia's death: "Her perfect submission, and her exalted hopes, exceeded by far, anything I had ever witnessed. The parting scenes—the invoking of blessings—the beauty of her countenance—the brightness of her eye, and the thrilling tones of her voice were overpowering."[20] She evidently had, he opined, "deep thoughts on religious subjects" and "clear views" of God's "plan of salvation."[21]

At the same time, Bachman believed parents should not wallow in grief when others depended on them for moral and practical instruction; rather, they should focus on the living. They should stick to normal routines, maintaining ties "with those who are interested in your welfare, and in reading interesting works." He also advised keeping company "with a few choice, intelligent and pious friends, [and] above all, do not neglect self-examination, and intercourse with your Heavenly Father."[22] Easier to dispense than follow, the reverend usually practiced what he preached. Julia died on September 7, was interred on September 9, and her family began its journey home the next day. As they departed Red Sulphur Springs, Bachman remarked: "My duty to the departed has now been performed as far as I was able; and I will try to give my remaining strength and energies to those who are still left to me, and to the other manifold duties of my life."[23] Comforted by the knowledge that Julia attained everlasting life, her traveling companions returned home without delay. Similarly, when his eldest daughter, Maria Rebecca, died in 1840, he requested but "one day for the luxury of grief."[24]

While Julia's death is recounted as a testament to the power of man (her father) and God to quell the recalcitrant, that she accepted her fate—either in fact or as interpreted by those present—is hardly surprising. No matter how Julia resisted the teachings of her elders, she had lived her entire life, however brief, in a home defined by the precepts and practices passed from generation to generation. That she wanted to go to heaven "borne on the wings of my father's prayers" was as predictable as it was gratifying.[25] Moreover, such expectations were equally inescapable for her sisters, especially Catherine. Like Julia, she was singled out for special attention. Often the beneficiary of her aunt's advice, Catherine was reminded of her responsibilities from a young age.

Above all, Catherine was to think of others before thinking of herself. As Maria Martin enumerated her deficiencies in 1841, she pointed out that her duty was to please others, most especially the aunt issuing advice. She warned: "All that you study will be of little use to you unless you are obedient to your elders and kind and affectionate to your brothers and sisters. I hope to see you very neat in your person, with your hair well kept, and your shoes always tied. You were generally a good girl but latterly were a little too heedless, but as you have grown older, I hope you will also be more attentive to all these little matters that will please me. I do not wish to damp your spirits or check your innocent mirth, but to increase your happiness by making you so amiable, polite and well behaved, that everybody will admire and love you."[26] Only nine, Catherine was told to "make good use of your time" and to behave properly. And she did. Never marrying, Catherine lived her entire life serving family. In this she realized expectations made of her when just a girl: Maria Martin asked her to be her "constant companion and always be ready to assist and oblige me."[27] Like her aunt, Catherine was the dutiful daughter. There were many reasons why young women of the Civil War period did not find husbands, but counsel as well as circumstance determined her fate. Women of her generation were "ultimately and supremely" expected "to live for others."[28]

In the Bachman household, the values imparted by Maria Martin were formative, and they shaped the equally selfless, Jane, Catherine's sister. Plagued by eye trouble, Jane was periodically blinded by both affliction and the attempts of "occulists" to treat her, but she was nonetheless devoted to her family and did everything in her power to assist those around her. Despite being hampered by vision problems, Jane was her mother's constant companion, leaving her side only to assist others in greater need. In 1841, for example, she went to New York to care for her sister Eliza, who was dying of consumption. In 1864, Jane married William Elnathan Haskell (1805–1872), the widowed husband of her sister Harriet, and at the age of fifty-one, she assumed the role of mother to seven nieces and nephews between the ages of six and eighteen. In this, and more, she emulated her aunt: in 1848, Maria Martin married John Bachman two years after her sister Harriet died.

That Julia and Catherine required special effort to ensure conformity is more surprising than the self-sacrifice exhibited by Jane given that patriarchy and pietism were the norm in their home, and given that the rules and regulations dictating private and public life for Lutherans in America had been in place since 1787. That year, the Lutheran synod adopted a constitution outlining church governance, pastoral requirements, and congregational responsibilities that included instructions to the families of clergy. Article XI of *Unio Ecclesiastica* stipulated that a pastor was to bind "himself before God and the church, to administer his holy office, to adorn it with an unimpeachable walk and conversation" and to "admonish his household and children to walk in the fear of God."[29] Incorporated within the "Discipline" of the South Carolina Synod in 1803, these articles reminded anyone who might have forgotten, of the behavior expected of clerics and their families. Such prompting was, however, hardly necessary for the women and girls of the Bachman household. Pastors' wives had a long history of close scrutiny, and as descendants of Pastor John Nicholas Martin, they were accustomed to being held to a high standard.[30] Whether sitting at the dinner table, or in a pew reserved for female worshippers, they knew their place. Through tradition, through day-to-day practices, and through religious doctrine, they knew they were destined to be submissive wives and mothers, just as they knew that boys were expected to become authoritarian husbands and fathers. And Maria Martin played an important role in conveying these expectations.

Anything less than perfection was unacceptable. Maria Martin was unflinching in her commitment to the principles of modesty, humility, submissiveness, and piety, and in 1831 she copied a poem published in the *Mirror of Literature, Amusement and Instruction* (1823) that conveyed those sentiments. In elaborate cursive lettering, she reproduced a poetically paraphrased translation of *De cultu feminarum* by Tertullian (160–235) for the edification of her nieces. The excerpt was entitled "Receipt for a Lady's Dress," and Maria encircled the poem with decoratively painted flowers and leaves:

> Let Simplicity be your White,
> Chastity your Vermillion,
> Deck your Eye brows with Modesty,
> and your Lips with Reservedness;
> Let Instruction be your Ear-Rings,
> and a Ruby cross the front pin in your head,
> Submission to your Husband is your best Ornament;
> Let your garments be made with the silk of Probity,
> The fine Linen Sanctity,
> and the Purple Chastity.
> Let your breast pin be Virtue,
> encircled by the Pearls of Refinement.

Interestingly, Maria Martin omitted two especially repressive edicts even though she was not a progressive thinker on women's issues. Tertullian's admonition to women to: "Busy your hands with spinning; keep your feet at home; and you will 'please' better than (by arraying yourselves) in gold," rewritten in the *Mirror* as: "Employ your hands in housewifery, and keep your

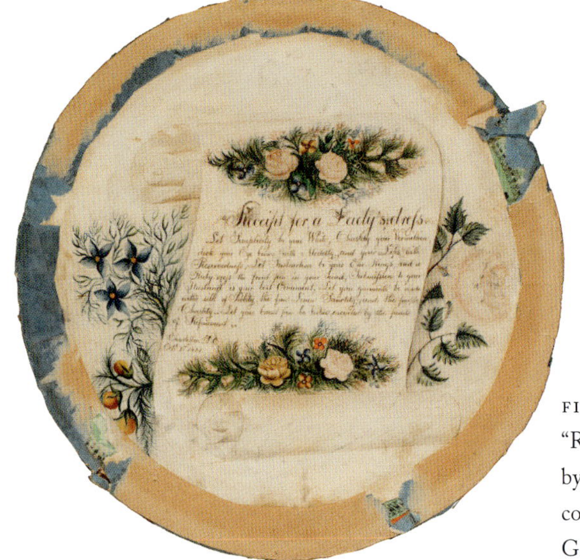

FIGURE 7. Floral Wreath: "Receipt for a Lady's Dress" by Maria Martin, 1831. Watercolor and ink. Courtesy of Jane Grimball Greely.

feet within your own doors" were left off her handiwork.[31] Although Lutherans accepted Tertullian's doctrine of the Trinity (Art. 1 Augsburg Confession), and theologians cited him as they rationalized their acceptance of confirmation, Maria Martin was not prepared to pass on his views of the carnality of women.[32] While accepting his pronouncements on women's destiny and duty, Maria Martin had no qualms about excising the offensive lines. Ever vigilant, she did not believe that the women in her family needed to be chastised for behavior they would not countenance, let alone commit. She knew this, as she had done her part in ensuring they were good Christians.

Such views were tested in 1853, however. Not everyone agreed that Lutherans were above reproach when it came to matters of the flesh, and John Bachman felt compelled to respond publicly to a charge that Martin Luther's tract on marriage, *De Matrimonio*, "sanctioned concubinage, polygamy, and adultery."[33] Despite prohibitions against sectarianism in the *Unio Ecclesiastica*, Bachman ignored church regulations in order to correct this shocking interpretation of the "Great Reformer's" work.[34] This was not the first time that the pastor of St. John's Lutheran had deviated from church policy—in 1841, he clashed with Catholic clergy when claims that Lutheranism was an attempt to restore Catholicism to its "original purity" gave offense—but in 1853 he published a five hundred–page tome entitled *A Defence of Luther* even as he averred antipathy to engaging in sectarian disputes.[35] Indeed, he went to extraordinary lengths as he extolled the virtues of Lutheranism and exposed the faults of Catholicism.

Initially Bachman had nothing to do with the squabble that elicited the weighty tome. Dr. John Bellinger (1804–1860), a Catholic alderman, initiated the dispute when he voiced concerns regarding an attack on his faith made in a public lecture by a former Trappist monk named Leahey who was visiting Charleston. Advertised as too salacious for "Ladies and Youths" who were "positively prohibited from coming to this lecture," Leahey's talk described the "unchristian treatment of females in the Confessional by Popish Priests," and Bellinger responded in kind.[36] His retort stating that Leahey's claims were nothing more than "Mean insinuation, founded upon a miserable perversion!" appeared in the *Catholic Miscellany*.[37] But he was also offended that local newspapers provided extensive coverage of the positive reception by local Protestants, and he leveled inflammatory accusations against Leahey's supporters. As the first Protestants, Lutherans received special treatment as Bellinger responded to Leahey's claims about the exploitation of women in the Catholic Church. Because he denigrated clerical marriage as a fate worse than death for women, it was unsurprising that Bachman rose to defend the founder of his church. In so doing, he offered his thoughts on women and marriage.

In a rebuttal that left that nothing to chance, Bachman attempted to show that Bellinger's charges against Luther were preposterous. Entirely confident of his position, he reprinted both sides of the debate, and letters published in the *Catholic Miscellany*, the *Richmond Watchman and Observer*, the *Southern Baptist*, and the *Charleston Evening News* were interleaved with his exegesis of Catholic doctrine. Drawing on his ability to read the "authentic" translations of Luther's early writings, he pointed out that Roman Catholics had misinterpreted Luther's texts, and he then went on the offensive with an exposition of instructions to seminarians based on the Moral Theology of Peter Dens (1690–1775). Published by the professors at Mechlin (*Theologia ad usum seminairi Mechliniensis olim sub nomine, P. Dens edita*), Bachman drew on this tract as he mounted a scathing attack on the papacy and the priesthood. Despite the fact that there were divisions within the Lutheran Church over "auricular confession"—that is, the practice responsible for the debate in the first instance—he did not hesitate to express his opinion on this matter. Moreover, because his fight with the Roman Catholics was separate and distinct from doctrinal debates inside the Lutheran Church, he did so with impunity.[38] Using his extensive knowledge of the Bible, Judaism, and Islam, as well as his expertise on the events of the Reformation, the Counter-Reformation, and the religious history of the United States, Bachman's volume combined learned matter with righteous indignation as he undertook to educate Catholics, especially Irish Catholics, of the error of their ways.

Although initiated by accusations about transgressions against women in the confessional, this debate revealed much about Bachman's views on marriage, family life, and the ideal wife. A man would be, he opined, fortunate if he were to marry a woman like Katharina von Bora (1499–1552). Described by her husband, Martin Luther, as "kind and submissive in all things," she was, Bachman elaborated, "meek and beautiful," a "virtuous, gentle and pious woman" who provided solace and service as she was able "to soften down the ruggedness of her husband's nature—to soothe him under cares and trials, and to be to him a companion in many an otherwise solitary hour."[39] He also praised Rosa Madiai, the devoted wife of Francesco Madiai, a recent Italian convert to Protestantism. She endured imprisonment rather than abandon her husband and their new found faith when persecuted by a "bigoted Romanist" in 1851, and Bachman was so impressed by Rosa Madiai that he reprinted a letter written by the woman he described as a "worthy . . . wife of a Christian hero" while awaiting sentencing for what he could only describe as the crime of reading the Scripture "in the privacy of their own humble dwelling."[40]

Sincere, if somewhat sensationalized, Bachman's *Defence of Luther* was instructive. Good Christian households would, he alleged, benefit by a literal interpretation of Reformation domesticity, and drawing on Luther's sermons and private correspondence, he outlined the ideal marriage. It should, he wrote, be "recognized as an ordinance of God, and is connected with purity, chastity and sanctity; that virginity is in no wise a purer state than that of marriage." Quoting Luther and the Bible, Bachman elaborated:

> The unbelieving wife is sanctified by the believing husband," and the contrary. 1 Cor [Corinthians]., 7 chap. He says, respecting the married: "God hath not called them to uncleanness, but to holiness." 1 Thess [Thessalonians]., 4th, 7th. He represents also the married woman's duty to be, "to continue in faith, charity, holiness, with sobriety." 1st Tim [Timothy]., 2 chap. 15. A Romish priest is poorly qualified to sit in judgment in regard to the purity of the matrimonial state. He can have no idea of the thousand nameless pleasures of sympathy, of companionship, of mutual encouragement in duty, of the softening down of the asperities of man's temperament by an association with a gentle, pure and virtuous wife, and of united prayers to the God and Father of their families. His grovelling ideas associate marriage with the gratification of sensual desires, and we object to him as an incompetent witness.[41]

Lengthy quotations on the duty to "increase and multiply" were also offered. Within marriage, men and women could undertake the "divine work" of procreation: "more necessary than eating and drinking, sleeping and waking. It is an implanted nature and disposition, even as the members which pertain to them. Therefore, as God has created man that they should be male and female, He has also ordered that they should multiply, and where men oppose this law, it leads them to fornication, adultery and secret sins."[42] In this, Bachman made a fortunate choice in Harriet Martin. She, like Katharina von Bora who gave her husband six children, accepted her special mothering role.

Harriet Martin Bachman delivered fourteen children between 1816 and 1832, burying seven before she died at the age of fifty-six. As a result, she was sometimes bored and anxious, and often pessimistic and fatalistic. She was worn out emotionally and physically by motherhood, and she was unable to muster even a scintilla of optimism as she counseled her visually impaired daughter, Jane, when she developed a growth in her "best Eye." Harriet simply reminded her daughter that her afflictions had a higher purpose and that she must choose stoic resignation. Harriet wrote: "you well know that I am never very sanguine in my expectations, but I trust and hope that all will eventually be for the best, and that any improvement [in your sight] will be a relief to you and us all; [adding] I have suffered so long & so severely, that from experience I have learned to be content and satisfied with my lot come what will, I view it all as coming from a kind providence intended for some wise purpose, and that it is our duty to submit, always hoping that some remedy will be sent us."[43] Harriet died two months later. In December 1848, not quite two years later, Maria Martin married John Bachman.

Elated with her decision, John Bachman wrote Audubon that Maria Martin had consented "to take the old man with all his infirmities of mind & eyes for better & for worse & thus lawfully become his nurse & his scribe Decm 28th."[44] In truth, she had long fulfilled these wifely duties. As early as 1827, Maria accompanied Bachman on a trip through the northern states. They visited family, toured battlefields, and saw the sights as Harriet awaited the birth of yet another child. When Bachman became ill, prolonging their stay, Maria nursed him through an ailment many feared fatal.[45]

Ever mindful of hearth and home, Bachman wrote Harriet reminding her of responsibilities for which she hardly needed prompting. Bachman feared that Harriet, confined with her tenth pregnancy, might neglect some of her duties, and he reminded her specifically to keep the slaves in check, to air out his library, to ensure the children went to school and did their homework, and to see that his ducks and geese were properly cared for and that the ripened peaches in the orchard were counted.[46] As he hinted that his traveling companion usually assumed such responsibilities, Harriet could hardly muster a half-hearted protest about being left behind while her sister was traveling with her husband. She needed Maria's assistance. Indeed, Harriet's reliance only increased as she spent more and more time in her private quarters. When Maria Martin married her widowed brother-in-law in 1848, she simply became the mistress of a household she had managed by proxy for more than twenty years.

3

PAINTING FROM NATURE

Maria Martin and John James Audubon

In 1829, just two years before Maria Martin met John James Audubon, Elizabeth Kent (1790–1861), the author of *Flora Domestica* (1823) pointed out that "girls are not only discouraged from the pursuit of natural history, but are very commonly forbidden it." Elaborating on the unfortunate consequences of such practices in "Considerations of Botany, as a Study for Young People," Kent noted that girls developed neither the skills needed nor an interest in science. Indeed, in the article published as part of a serialized column on "Papers Illustrative of the Linnaean System of Plants," she suggested that both poor preparation and prejudice impeded women's participation so that "young ladies are apt to be alarmed by the numerous terms of science; unacquainted with Latin, they shrink from this formidable difficulty, and either decide that, however sweet be the kernel, the shell is too hard for them to crack; or, if less diffident of their powers or sparing of their trouble, they are willing to surmount that obstacle, they are met by another, the dread of being branded with that fearful epithet—*blue*!"[1] Considered a suitable ladylike pursuit in the eighteenth century, it was less so by the time Maria Martin began painting botanicals for Audubon. Women were not generally encouraged to pursue botany by the 1830s and, in fact, anything other than the most superficial study of plants was closed to women. Botany, like other natural history avocations, was in the process of professionalization and was dominated by men.[2]

Given the prejudices described by Kent, and given that Lutheran doctrine rewarded women who accepted their destiny as wives and mothers, it would be surprising if Maria Martin had any curiosity about natural history as a young woman, and indeed there is little suggestion of either artistic ability or interest in science prior to 1831. Like most women of her generation, she was a skilled crafter, but artifacts such as a stylized wreath of nondescript flowers

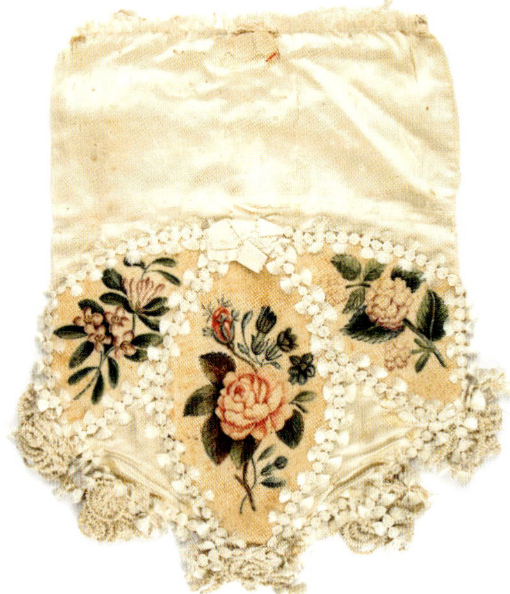

FIGURE 8. Reticule c.1820, Maria Martin. ChM HT 1505. Courtesy of the Charleston Museum.

encircling a poem intended to instill piety among her nieces, and a small purse decorated by lace and the same floral motif only hint at the artistry found in the botanicals and insects she added to Audubon's paintings. Painted just days before Audubon appeared on the doorstep of the home where she resided, Maria Martin's wreath consisted of garishly colored four-petalled flowers, feathery wisps of foliage, and insipid roses on poor quality paper. It demonstrated only the most elementary grasp of technique regarding form and color, and the details of plant anatomy she came to represent so authentically are absent. The roses are recognizable, although impressionistic, and the leaves are crudely rendered with exaggerated serration. Accompanied by matching buds, the flowers and foliage make an entirely contrived vignette. Bearing no resemblance to the fine work she later did for Audubon, the wreath nonetheless suggests familiarity with floral conventions. Poetry encircled by flowers was a common motif, even adopted by artists such as Pierre-Joseph Redouté.

That Audubon saw potential in Maria Martin is a testament to his powers of perception, but the progress she made is no less remarkable. Within months, she could paint birds, plants, and insects far superior to the stylized florals she was painting when they met, and while there were landscape painters and botanical artists, portrait painters and miniaturists, as well as artists employed by local theaters to paint scenes, if Maria studied with any of these "masters," she was still very much the amateur before Audubon.[3] The technical skill and aesthetic sensibility evidenced in botanicals such as trumpet creeper (*Campsis radicans*), loblolly bay (*Gordonia lasianthus*), and *Franklinia alatamaha* suggest she learned much from Audubon. As adept at identifying and cultivating talent as he was at charming complete strangers into opening their pocketbooks for his outrageous project, Audubon had the ability to recognize unvarnished talent and coax the best from those with it. At the same time, Maria Martin clearly had an aptitude for painting, and was able to capitalize on Audubon's expertise. As an artist whose images exhibited a "draftsmanly precision" that was "matched by a new mastery of color, sensitivity to modeling, and skillful execution of realistic detail . . . shaped by his singular combination of media: watercolor, pastel, and graphite enhanced with gouache, India ink, oil paint, gums, scraping, and metallic paint," he could guide protégés to do as he did.[4] As experts have noted, he was able to train students to use perspective, shading, and illusion so as to compose subjects in the archetypically neoclassical vignettes he admired, and within weeks Maria Martin painted a bamboo vine (*Smilax pseudochina*) that was added to Audubon's figure of the yellow-crowned night heron (*Nyctanassa violacea*, plate 336).

Over the next few months, she attempted even more difficult species as she made a monumental effort to move from the clumsy rendering of florals encircling her "Receipt for a Lady's Dress" to botanicals good enough for *Birds of America*. Exactly how many local plants, trees, and shrubs were painted over the winter of 1832 is unknown, but in the year following her first lesson with Audubon, several met his high standards. His fork-tailed flycatcher was perched on her *Gordonia lasianthus* in plate 168; his black-throated mango hovered beside her *Campsis radicans* in plate 184; and two birds named in honor of friends and colleagues, John Bachman and William Swainson, were accompanied by her botanicals. Bachman's sparrow was perched on a branch of the fever tree (*Pinckneya pubens*, plate 165) while Swainson's warbler was perched on a flame azalea (*Rhododendron calendulaceum*, plate 198). She also painted two butterflies—the Florida atala hairstreak (*Eumaeus atala*) and the common buckeye (*Junonia coenia*)—for that composition. An impressive list for a novice, it is inevitably incomplete because Maria Martin was not inclined to seek

FIGURE 9. (opposite) Trumpet creeper (*Campsis radicans*) by Maria Martin or, as she labeled it, "Bignonia," July 1832. Study for Havell edition, *Birds of America*, plate 184, black-throated mango (*Anthracothorax nigricollis*). Watercolor, graphite, and black ink; 53.7 x 35.1 cm (21⅛ x 13 13/16 in). 1863.17.184. Purchased by public subscription from Mrs. John J. Audubon. Collection of the New-York Historical Society. Digital image created by Oppenheimer Edition.

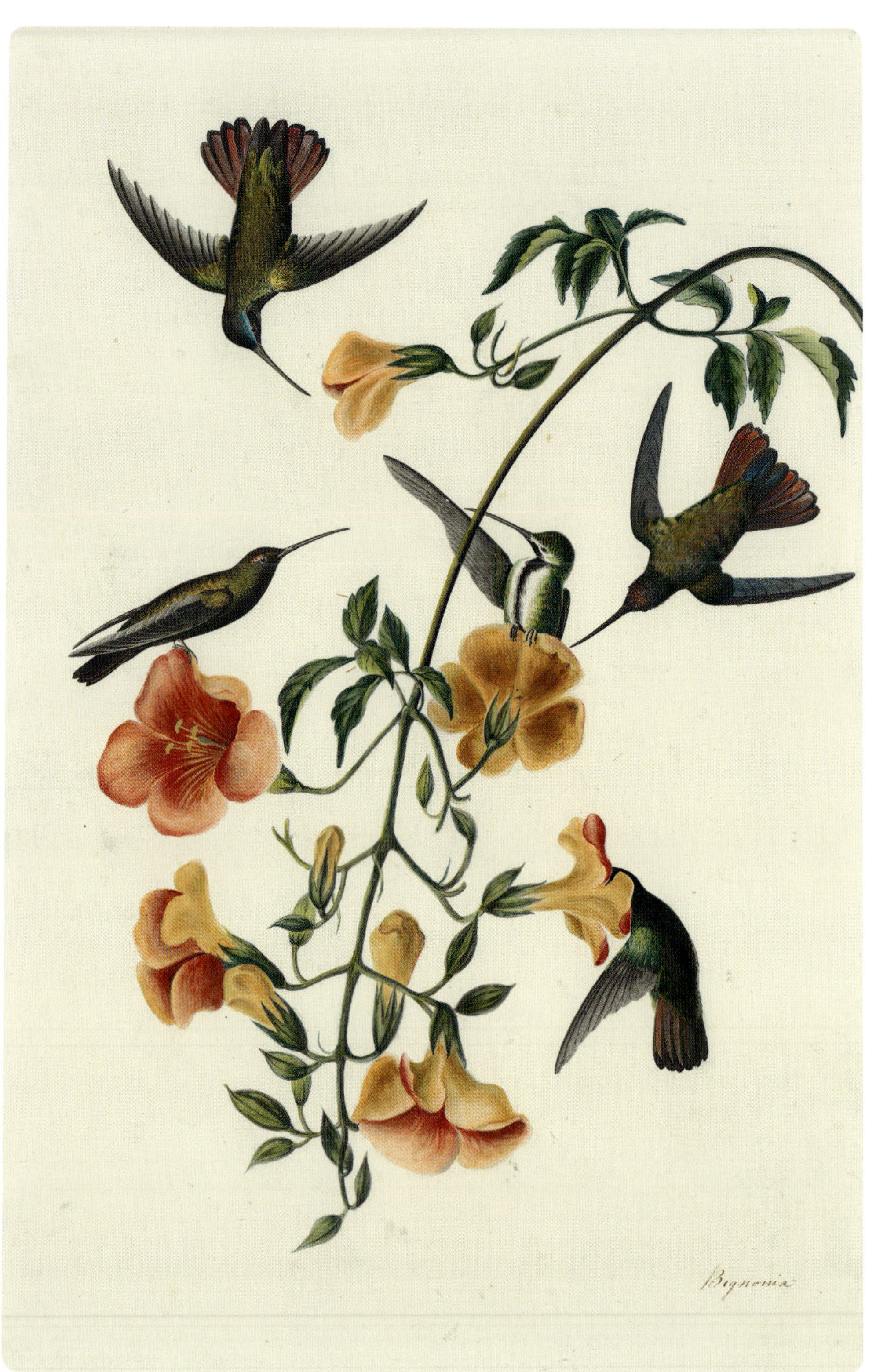
Bignonia

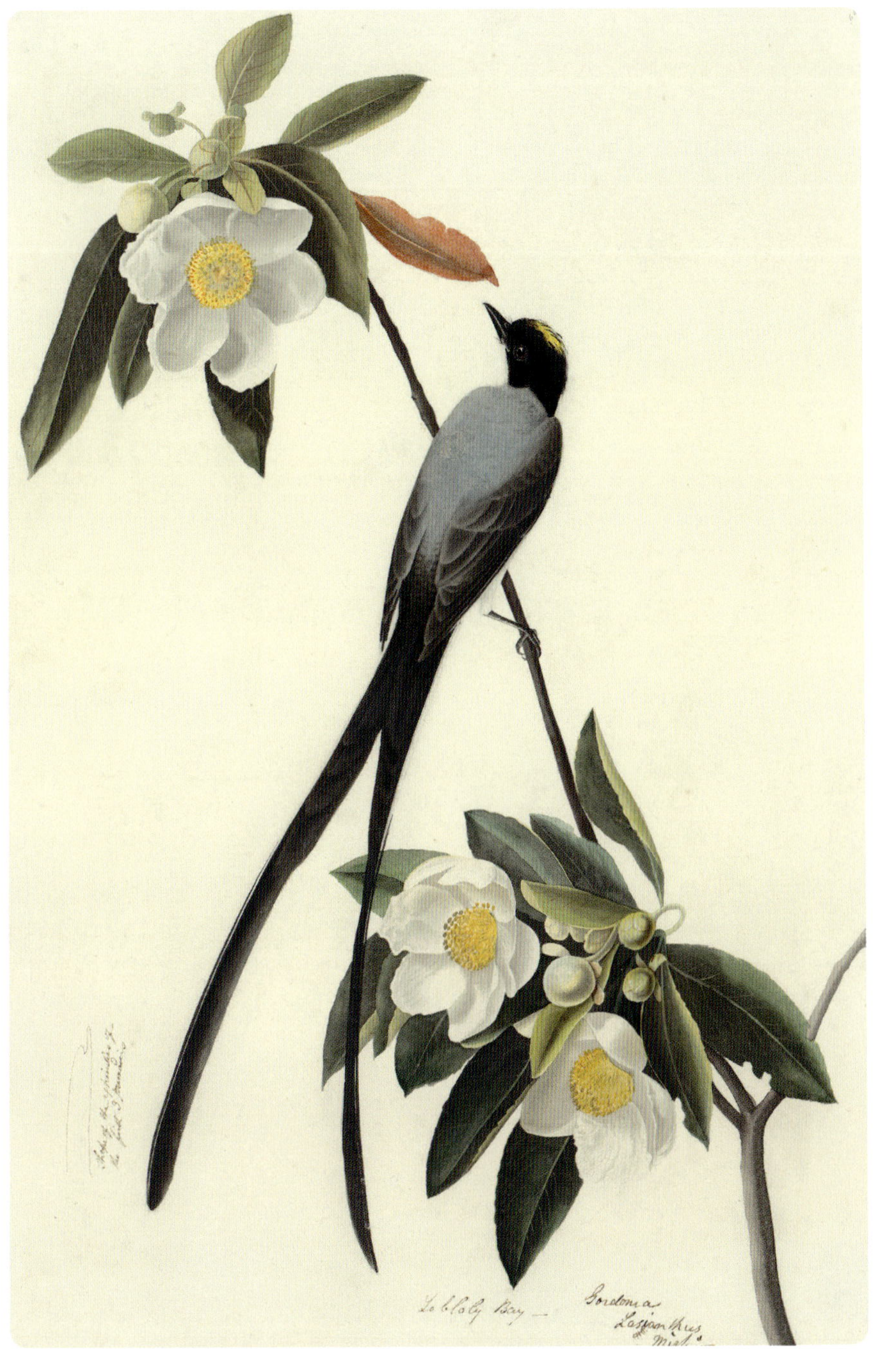

FIGURE 10. Loblolly bay (*Gordonia lasianthus*) by Maria Martin, June 1832. Study for Havell edition, *Birds of America*, plate 168, fork-tailed flycatcher (*Tyrannus savana*). Watercolor, graphite, black ink; 54.8 x 35.9 cm (21⁹⁄₁₆ x 14⅛ in). 1863.17.168. Purchased by public subscription from Mrs. John J. Audubon. Collection of the New-York Historical Society. Digital image created by Oppenheimer Edition.

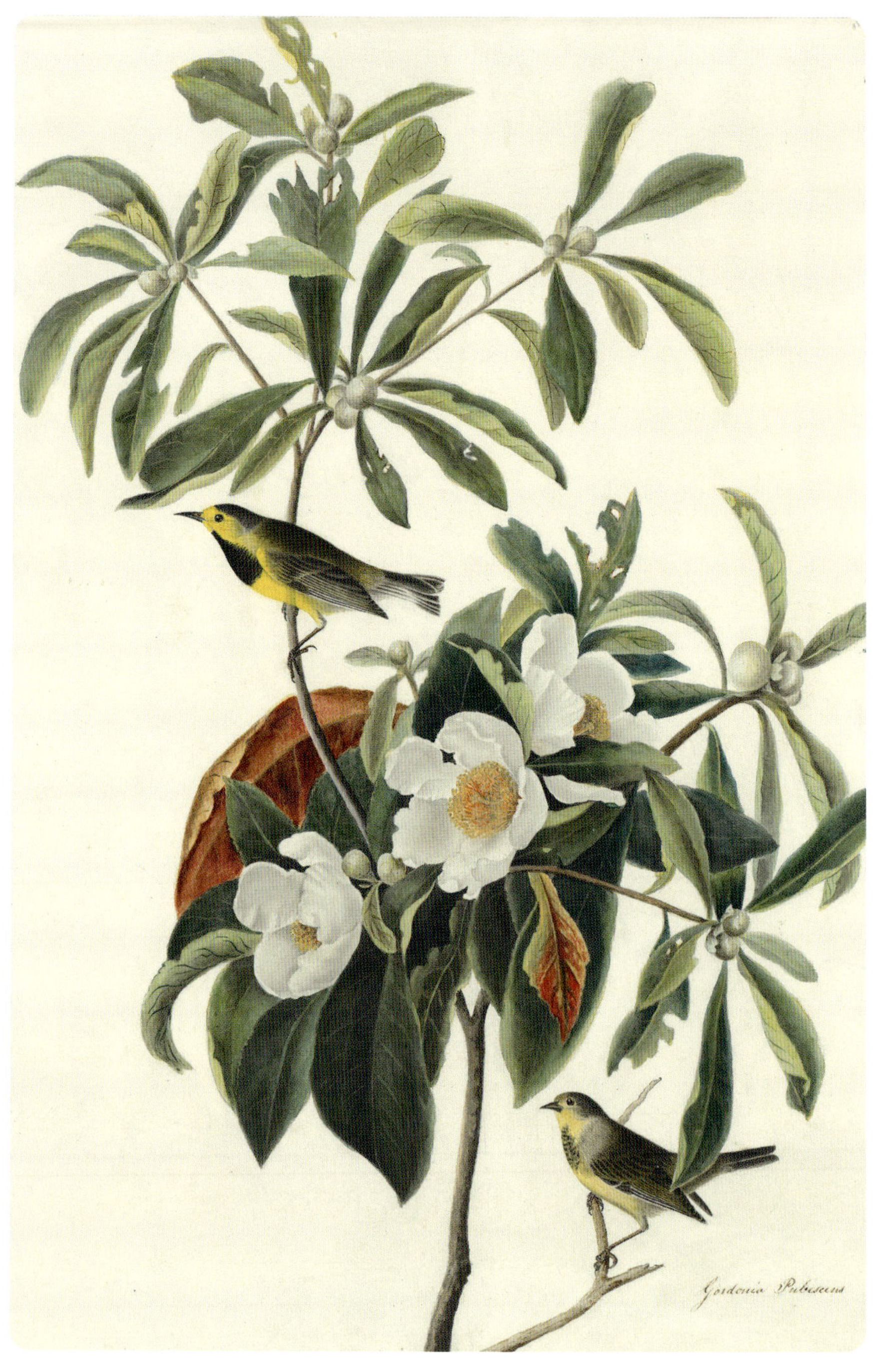

FIGURE 11. *Franklinia alatamaha* by Maria Martin, 1833. Study for Havell edition, *Birds of America*, plate 185, Bachman's warbler (*Vermivora bachmanii*). Watercolor, graphite, and black ink; 54.6 x 35.9 cm (21½ x 14⅛ in). 1863.17.185. Purchased by public subscription from Mrs. John J. Audubon. Collection of the New-York Historical Society. Digital image created by Oppenheimer Edition.

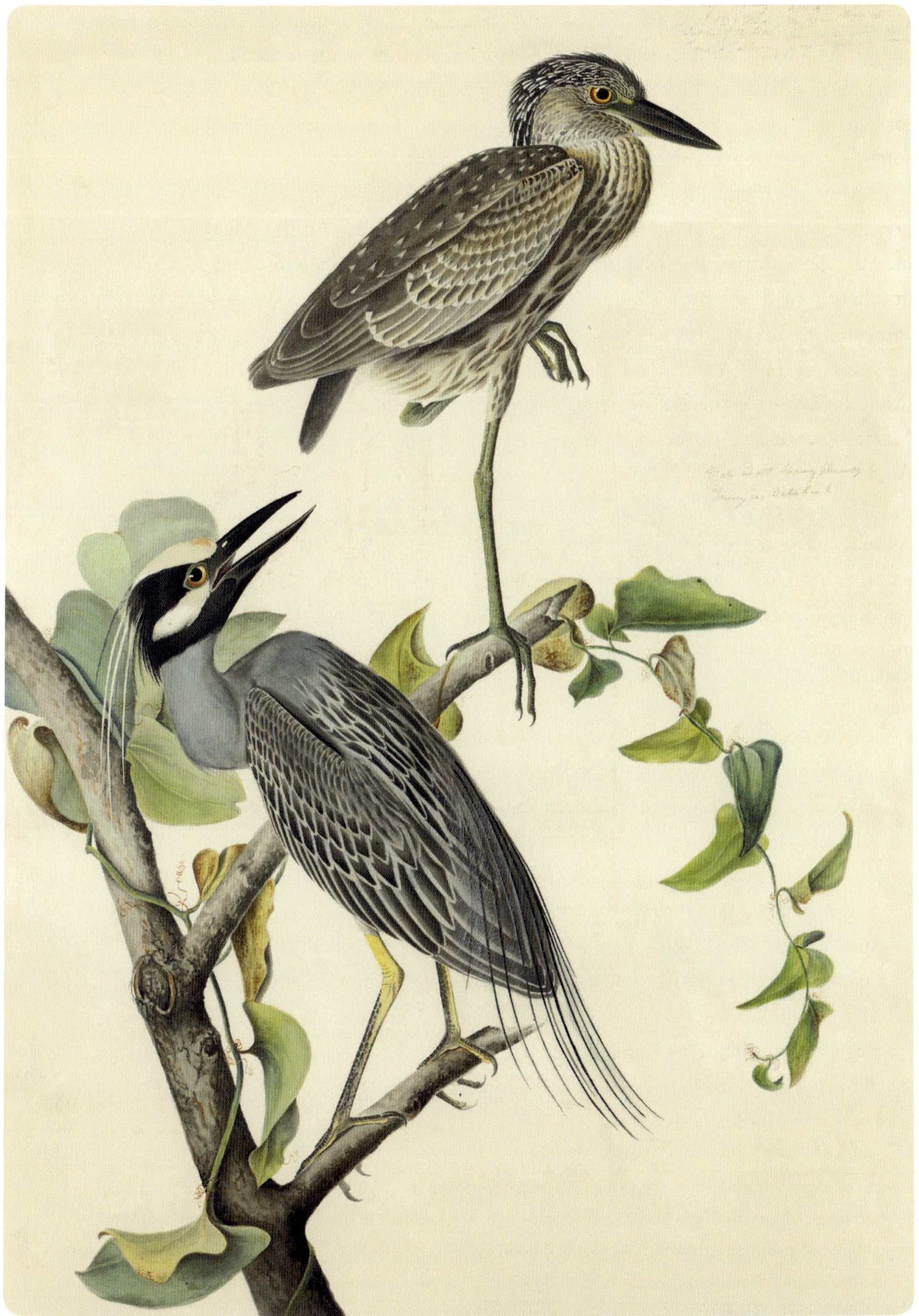

recognition for her work. Dutifully deferential, she never overstated her accomplishments or complained about the effort expended to meet Audubon's exacting standards. In July 1832, for example, she wrote Audubon that she was forwarding a painting of *Franklinia alatamaha*, drawn "from nature," as well as some "hibiscus" flowers she hoped would be acceptable.[5]

Always self-effacing, it was unsurprising that Maria Martin minimized her ability to paint plants and animals realistically and beautifully, but the men to whom she became indispensable were of the view that she took to natural history with alacrity. Audubon's praise was often exaggerated, especially compared to Bachman, for whom dignified reserve was the norm; however, the reverend could also be generous when it came to his sister-in-law's efforts. Prone to neither embellishment nor exaggeration, Bachman's assessment of Maria's painting could be flattering, particularly when corresponding with Audubon. Charmed by his new friend's knowledge of birds and by his enthusiasm for nature, Bachman took a childlike glee in everything associated with Audubon. He even claimed that their time together was "one of the happiest months of my life." Bachman was uncharacteristically effusive, and his gravitas disappeared as he explained his fondness to his new friend's wife. In a letter mailed immediately after Audubon left Charleston for Florida in November, Bachman wrote:

> Ornithology is, as a science, pursued by very few persons—and by no one in this city. How gratifying was it, then, to become acquainted with a man, who knew more about birds than any man now living—and who, at the same time, was communicative, intelligent, and amiable, to an extent seldom found associated in the same individual. He has convinced me that I was but a novice in the study; and besides reviving many lessons from him in Ornithology, he has taught me how much can be accomplished by a single individual, who will unite enthusiasm with industry. For the short month he remained with my family, we were inseparable. We were engaged in talking about Ornithology—in collecting birds—in seeing them prepared, and in laying plans for the accomplishment of that great work which he has undertaken.[6]

FIGURE 12. (opposite) Bamboo vine (*Smilax pseudochina*) by Maria Martin, Oct. 1831. Study for Havell edition, *Birds of America*, plate 336, yellow-crowned heron (yellow-crowned night heron/*Nyctanassa violacea*). Watercolor; 90.8 x 64.6 cm (35¾ x 25 7/16 in). 1863.17.336. Purchased by public subscription from Mrs. John J. Audubon. Collection of the New-York Historical Society. Digital image created by Oppenheimer Edition.

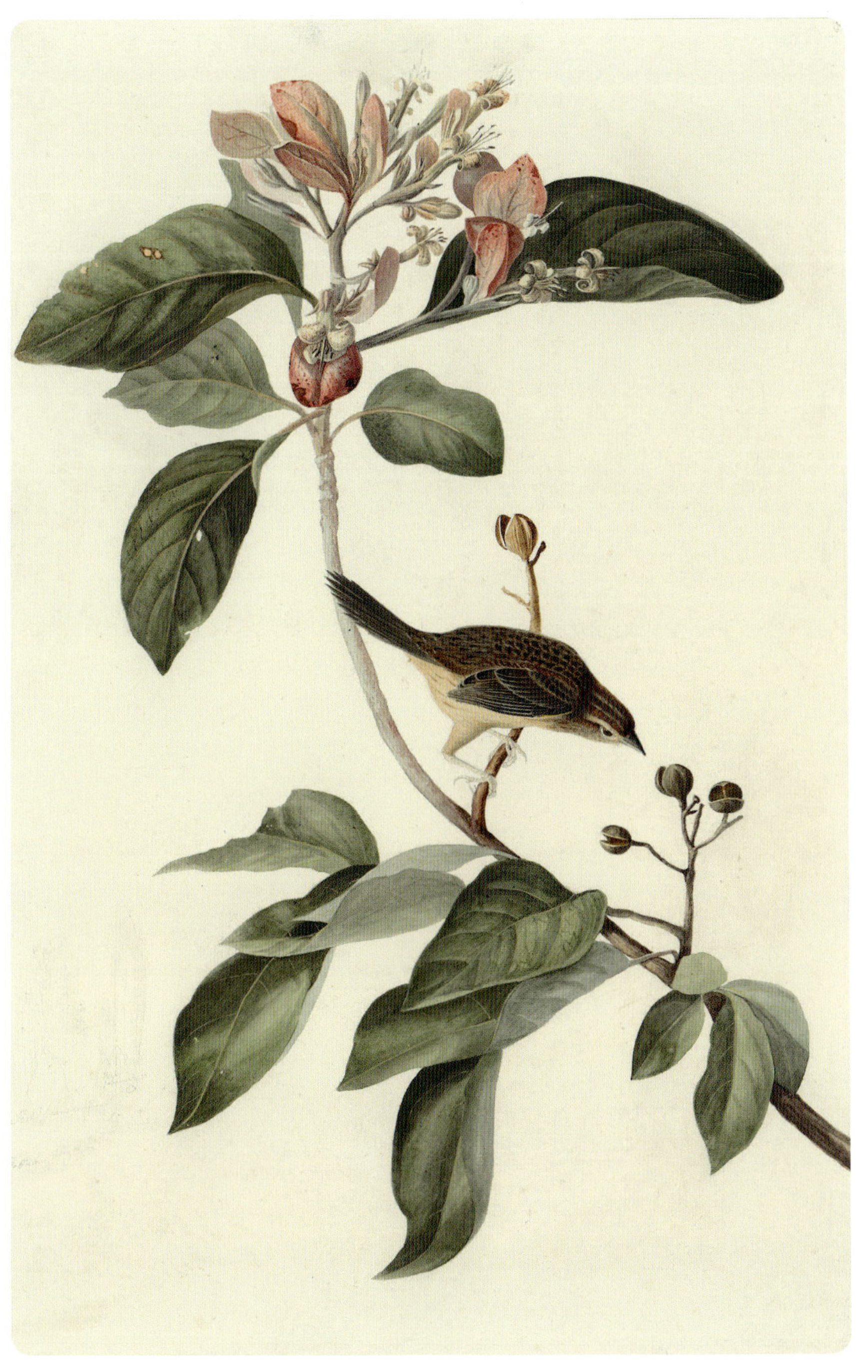

FIGURE 13. Fever tree (*Pinckneya pubens*) by Maria Martin, 1832. Study for Havell edition, *Birds of America*, plate 165, Bachman's sparrow (*Peucaea aestivalis*). Watercolor, graphite, black ink; 53.5 x 34.9 cm (21$\frac{1}{16}$ x 13$\frac{3}{4}$ in). 1863.17.165. Purchased by public subscription from Mrs. John J. Audubon. Collection of the New-York Historical Society. Digital image created by Oppenheimer Edition.

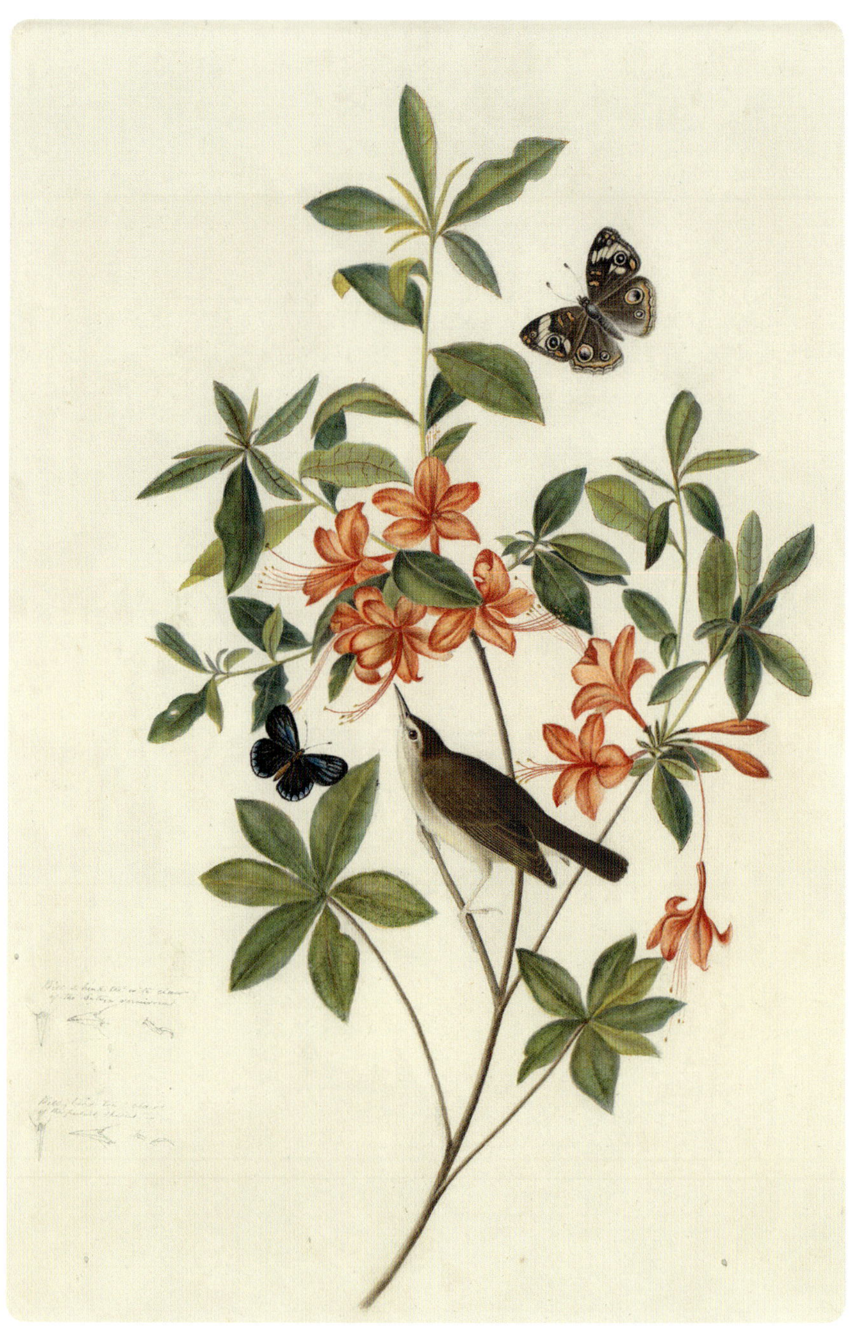

FIGURE 14. Flame azalea (*Rhododendron calendulaceum*) and two butterflies—Florida atala hairstreak (*Eumaeus atala*) and common buckeye (*Junonia coenia*)—by Maria Martin, Spring 1832. Study for Havell edition, *Birds of America*, plate 198, Swainson's warbler (*Limnothlypis swainsonii*). Watercolor and graphite; 53.8 x 36 cm (21³⁄₁₆ x 14³⁄₁₆ in). 1863.17.198. Purchased by public subscription from Mrs. John J. Audubon. Collection of the New-York Historical Society. Digital image created by Oppenheimer Edition.

He also assured Lucy that her husband was well received in his city, indeed "a general favorite," before ending his letter on a more personal note. Bachman wrote: "There seems quite a blank, in my house, since he has gone, for we looked on him as one of our family. He taught my sister, Maria, to draw birds: and she has now such a passion for it, that, whilst I am writing, she is drawing a Bittern, put up for her at daylight by Mr. Audubon."

While he overstated the salutatory effect of Audubon's visit on his youngest children and on the enslaved men and women of the household, Bachman understated the effect that Audubon's visit had on Maria Martin. If not quite as infatuated as her brother-in-law, Maria was nonetheless affected by Audubon, and in a letter written a month after his new friend's departure he had more to say about Maria Martin as he raved about their visit. He credited it with giving him "new life," and convincing him "to go carefully over my favorite study," but he also mentioned Audubon's effect on Maria specifically. He wrote she was "all enthusiasm, and I need not say to you that she is one of your warmest admirers, and were she not so closely allied to my family, I would say, that the admiration of such a person is very high encomium."[7]

No doubt accurately conveying Maria's views, Bachman had another reason for his comments. He hoped to impress Audubon sufficiently to entice him to return. The reverend longed to relive time spent with Audubon, and even as he prepared for one of the most important celebrations of the Christian calendar, he tried to lure him back by offering him Maria's paintings. Her birds were, he reported, becoming "better every day." Bachman's bait seemed to work. Audubon returned to Charleston in March, and remained there for six weeks.[8]

Longing for even more time with his new friend, Bachman used Maria's paintings yet again in July in an attempt to lure him back to Charleston. Whether he truly appreciated just how good her botanicals were is unclear; however, Bachman was as boastful as a cleric of his stature could be when he described the flowers she had painted in a letter to Audubon: "Maria has drawn for you the Franklinia, a very pretty Hibiscus, is preparing to do another of a white color and has also drawn a splendid Bignonia, the latter, which is very rare here, may be less so in the S. West and probably has already had the benefit of your pencil. She will not forget her instructor and I am sure will ever do you credit. She is making good progress both in ornithology and botany."[9] When this appeal did not produce the desired results, Bachman was not deterred. In October, he offered several more of Maria's "drawings," and suggested she could "draw" local water birds for the second volume of *Birds*.[10]

By November, it was clear that Audubon was not responding as hoped, and Bachman changed his strategy. Since efforts to use Maria Martin's paintings as bait had failed, he offered them unconditionally. He wrote Audubon promising to send "all the birds that I have a right to; the Humming Bird and the Sparrow, and the drawings and skins of the rest. Maria has figured for you the 'White Hibiscus,' and, also, a red one, both natives, and beautiful; a Euonymus in seed, in which our Sylvia is placed; the white Nondescript Rose; the Gordonica [*sic*], a Begonia [Bignonia?], &c."[11] Bachman's new approach was well founded. The aggressive tack he had adopted initially was unlikely to produce the intended results when Audubon's focus was elsewhere.

Audubon was looking north not south. Although he only ventured as far as Maine and New Brunswick in September through October before retiring to Boston, he spent his year painting birds, looking for subscribers, and planning an expedition to the avian breeding grounds in Labrador.[12] In fact, he stayed put until the end of May when he left for Labrador. He was in no position to accept Bachman's invitations, and he certainly was not encouraged to return south by his wife. Lucy was not impressed by his escapades in Florida or Charleston, and as the helpmeet who had followed him from place to place, often ending up stranded in unfamiliar surroundings where she took in students to support herself, her sons, and even her husband, she did not hesitate to express herself on important matters. And she did so when it came to the South.[13]

While in Charleston during the spring of 1832, Audubon received mail fairly regularly, and Lucy took the opportunity afforded by better communications to ask him to leave immediately. She implored him to "come home and put us all at ease," chiding him for becoming distracted with birds that did not fit into his project on the "*Birds of the United States*" and for "multiplying it into a universal history."[14] More to the point, she had a purely practical purpose for her request. While Audubon was incommunicado in the field, she was left to deal with complaints, and there were a number from their subscribers in Philadelphia. Similarly, when problems arose with the engraving process, they fell to her by default as he indulged his quest to depict every bird. Even though she tried to deal with the complaints by chastising Havell for shoddy work, she believed Audubon's presence was needed. It was clear to her that he had to go to London to supervise the engraving and printing of his paintings so that Havell would meet the standards required for "his success and reputation."[15] In her opinion, he had been roving long enough. His meanderings were, she believed, placing both his health and the entire venture at risk, and she was not about to let love and admiration trump common sense. She reminded him that "the South [has] never agreed with you," and she pleaded with him to "come away come away!"

Lucy Audubon was only half successful. Despite her best efforts to convince him that he alone could ensure promises made to subscribers were kept, Audubon did not go to London. He did, however, leave the South. After departing Florida on May 31, Audubon went to Savannah, where he stopped to meet potential subscribers before heading to Charleston. While there, he also oversaw the transfer of several "cartloads" of Floridian specimens shipped by boat. With fewer than three days to ensure his collections were safely stowed, Audubon had little time for his newest protégé, and Maria Martin would not see him again until October 1833, almost a year and a half later.[16]

In the meantime, she continued to paint botanicals and birds, and in March 1833, Bachman wrote Audubon regaling him with her progress. Among Maria's efforts were the promised water birds, specifically the "short-legged" sandpiper (pectoral sandpiper, *Calidris melanotos*, plate 294) and the "spotted" sandpiper (*Acitis macularius*, plate 310), and at least one passerine. Like before, her paintings were offered as an enticement, and Bachman was particularly pleased by a male Sylvia in "full plumage." He described her figure as "fairly drawn" and, more importantly, he believed the warbler was a new species. While hoping Audubon might consider Maria's figure good enough for publication, he hastily added that if her "drawing does not suit you, you may draw it over" so as to avoid causing offense.[17] Clearly presuming expertise he did not have, Bachman was nonetheless sure he had a bird not described or figured in Alexander Wilson's *American Ornithology*, and it would have been a shame if his invitation was sidelined by an offer that was supposed to be an inducement.

Maria's "Euonymus in seed, in which our Sylvia is placed" and some stuffed skins led Audubon to conclude that Bachman was right, but her efforts proved ineffective in eliciting Audubon's return.[18] The Sylvia was a new species, and Bachman's warbler (*Vermivora bachmanii*) appeared on a folio plate in fascicle thirty-seven. However, Maria's figure was not used. Although Bachman

FIGURE 15. (opposite) Strawberry shrub (*Euyonumus americanus*) and Bachman's warbler (*Vermivora bachmanii*) by Maria Martin, 1832. The botanical was later used in the Havell edition, *Birds of America*, plate 395, black-throated gray warbler (*Setophaga nigrescens*), hermit warbler (*Setophaga occidentalis*), Audubon's Warbler (yellow-rumped warbler/*Setophaga coronata auduboni*), winter 1836–1837. Watercolor, graphite, gouache, black ink and pastel; 51.6 x 35.9 cm (20$\frac{5}{16}$ x 14⅛ in). 1863.18.12. Purchased by public subscription from Mrs. John J. Audubon. Collection of the New-York Historical Society. Digital image created by Oppenheimer Edition.

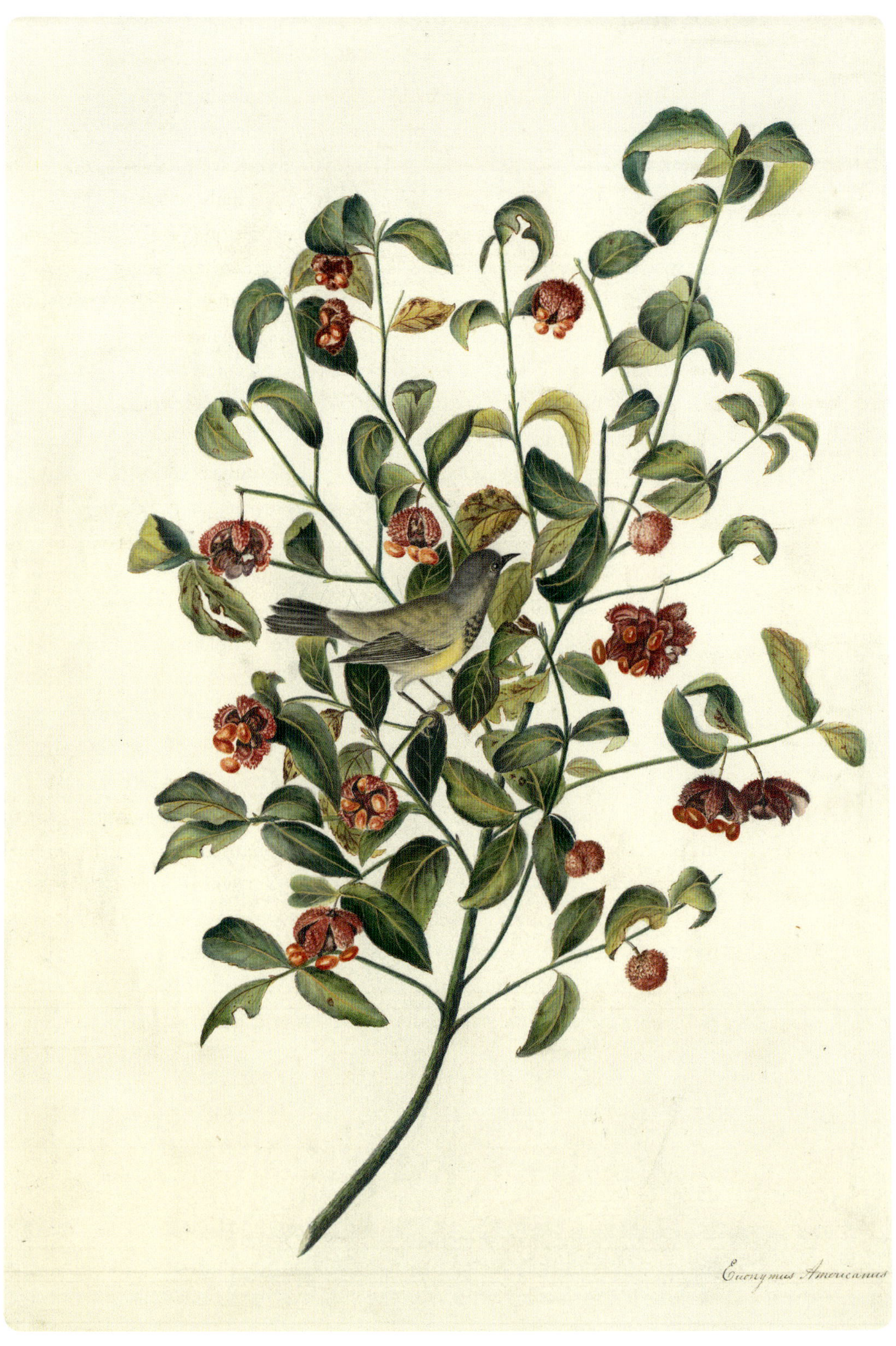
Euonymus Americanus

praised her painting, and Audubon expressed his "approbation of her efforts in drawing birds" more generally, it was just not good enough.[19] Rather, two warblers were placed on the branches of the rare Franklinia tree that she painted the previous year. Audubon needed her botanicals, not her birds. At the same time, if Bachman's ornithological inducement did not immediately prove successful, the effort was not entirely lost on his new friend. It was simply a question of timing, and seven months later Audubon returned to Charleston with his wife, Lucy, and son, John Woodhouse. They remained there from October 19, 1833, until March 14, 1834, and for four months Maria worked alongside the man who nurtured talents only hinted at when they first met two years earlier.

Maria Martin could do little better than learn nature painting from Audubon. No matter how absorbed he might have been by his monumental work, time under his tutelage was well spent. Additionally, after a three-year sojourn in Britain and France, his technical expertise was enriched by a deeper understanding of the world inhabited by serious artists. Between 1826 and 1829, he met members of both the English and Scottish Royal Academies, as well as at least one beneficiary of royal patronage in France, and he availed himself of every opportunity to examine works by the grand masters, by ornithological illustrators, and by those who painted the "game paintings" popular among the English gentry. He was especially inspired by the neoclassical masters he saw firsthand, and although Audubon's claim that he studied with Jacques-Louis David (1748–1825) has sometimes been dismissed as a fabrication intended to elevate his reputation, it is clear that he was influenced by the masters.[20] Whether in flight, fighting for survival, foraging for food, or at rest, his birds were as heroic as the human subjects portrayed by the neoclassicists, and this was the case well before he returned to Europe in the late 1820s. Even so, his immersion in the art world enlarged his knowledge of the academics of painting.

Armed with letters of introduction from Thomas Sully (1783–1872), a prominent Philadelphia portraitist, Audubon was received by important artists, perhaps most notably Thomas Lawrence (1769–1830), president of the Royal Academy (1820–30) and foremost proponent of neoclassicism in England.[21] His portraits "of royalty" in the Cotton Exchange Building in Liverpool were among the first important works encountered when Audubon disembarked there in July 1826, and he was initially impressed by Lawrence. Chuffed that an academician had praised his work, he even hoped Lawrence would teach him to use oils, but his admiration cooled when he heard that compliments to his face were countered in his absence. He reputedly described

Audubon's "drawing so-so, and the engraving and coloring bad," and whatever the accuracy of this rumor, Audubon began to question Lawrence's authority as a critic and his technique as an artist.[22] Admitting Lawrence "had a perfect idea of the rules of drawing any object whatever, as well as of the forms and composition, or management of the objects offered for the inspection of his keen eyes," he averred that watercolor applied in layers produced better depth, texture, and "transparency" than the thinly applied glaze the academician preferred. He also ridiculed Lawrence's practice of outlining his subjects in chalk and then glazing over "opaque" colors. By the time he finished his appraisal, Audubon questioned whether Lawrence knew anything at all about nature painting, expressing views that would have been foolhardy to air publicly.[23] "Sir Thomas," he confided in his journal, was "no ornithologist, and therefore could not well judge of the correctness of the detail of my drawings, which can be appreciated fully only by those who are acquainted with the science of which I myself am but a student." To the extent that Lawrence's shortcomings were overdrawn, they reflected Audubon's pique at his indifference: he neither promoted nor subscribed to *Birds of America*.

At the same time, even when dismissive, Audubon could not but benefit by studying European art. This was especially true when the paintings featured animals, even though he often claimed he found little to admire and did not hesitate to pass judgment on works many viewed positively. He was, for example, quite uncharitable to Frans Synders (1579–1657) and to the Dutch zoological painter Melchoir d'Hondekoeter (1636–1695). He was especially critical of the latter's animals, which he described as "destitute of life," and he observed that Synders's paintings had "great effect, fine coloring, and still finer finishing" but that the bear and dogs portrayed in them were "no Bear at all and the Dogs were so badly drawn, distorted, and mingled caricatures that I am fully persuaded that Snyders did not draw from specimens put up in real postures in my way."[24] Nor did he spare his contemporaries. The efforts of popular English animal painter Edwin Henry Landseer (1802–1873), for example, were described as stylized and inaccurate.[25] He also panned paintings owned by men who treated him as a friend and colleague. Scottish artists such as John Syme (1795–1861), Joseph Bartholomew Kidd (1808–1889), William Nicholson (1781–1844), and William Allan (1782–1850)—all members (and two presidents) of the Royal Scottish Academy—not only welcomed Audubon into their homes where he examined their personal art collections but also took him to galleries, museums, and the homes of their friends where he studied paintings by Rembrandt, Van Dyke, Claude Lorrain, Titian, and others.[26]

Such paintings impressed Audubon far more than those of watercolorist William Henry Hunt (1790–1864). One of the first artists he met after arriving in England, Audubon described the English-born watercolorist as the "best landscape painter" in Liverpool, but he did not find him particularly inspiring.[27] A founder of the English watercolor movement, Hunt had not yet shifted away from painting scenic vistas depicting country folk and countryside to the still life paintings that made him popular among Victorian art collectors and artists who endeavored to depict nature realistically.[28] With his early preference for somber tones and quaint subject matter, Hunt's efforts suffered by comparison to those of the grand masters, and it is unsurprising that Audubon saw more to emulate in them than in an artist in the early stages of a noteworthy career.

Interestingly, both Hunt and Audubon tried their hand at oil—Hunt more successfully, as he exhibited paintings at the Royal Academy in 1807 before abandoning it for watercolor. Audubon's exposure to the medium of the masters seemed to spur him on even as he was "disgusted" by his efforts. Not entirely unfamiliar with oil, he produced paintings in 1827 that were no better than the self-portrait he painted in 1822–1823. Although he was "perfectly confident that the delineations are correct to perfection and the habits of the individuals quite at my disposal, through a long course of experience," he knew his paintings in oil were inferior.[29] He knew they were bad because only his "friends" purchased them. This was quite a blow because oil paintings promised to be a lucrative source of income. In America, he sold watercolors and portraits drawn in charcoal to underwrite living expenses as he traveled about painting birds and selling subscriptions, but in the British Isles oils were more desirable and his efforts were just not good enough.[30] Indeed, the economic potential of oil paintings was so great that in 1831 Joseph Kidd was engaged to reproduce the first volume of folio plates in oil. Aside from the fact that Audubon's multimedia approach to ornithological figures was superior to oil, a "misunderstanding" over the terms of their agreement undermined the project and the plan to reproduce the plates in volume one of *Birds of America* was not completed.[31]

Although in the vanguard of a movement that became increasingly popular during the nineteenth century, Audubon could easily be denigrated as an amateur. At the time, many considered watercolor inferior to oil.[32] Additionally, his lack of formal training was apparent as academically trained artists befriended him. Even his old friend Thomas Sully was well versed in neoclassicism. In fact, Sully recommended that aspiring artists consult the *Seven*

Discourses on Art (1769–1776) by Joshua Reynolds (1723–1792).[33] Directed toward those with the discipline and talent to become artists of the highest caliber, the deceptively simple *Discourses* were delivered to the students of the Royal Academy when Reynolds was the president. Sully considered Reynolds required reading, and whether Sully convinced the "American woodsman" to read the *Discourses*, in Audubon's only essay describing his views on nature painting he agreed with much of the academician's advice.[34]

From a practical perspective, Reynolds's admonition that artists were duty bound to emulate the masters, first copying images placed next to their easel and then drawing "by memory" so as to improve both technique and composition, could not but have resonated with the self-taught American. When Reynolds outlined how "the most eminent masters" balanced creativity and realism by adhering to fundamental principles and techniques, his description of how the artistic geniuses of the Renaissance created their greatest works bore a strong resemblance to Audubon's method. According to Reynolds, when "they conceived a subject, they first made a variety of sketches; then a finished drawing of the whole; after that a more correct drawing of every separate part, heads, hands, feet, and pieces of drapery; they then painted the picture, and after all re-touched it from the life." Artists were to draw and redraw similar "forms" of the same subject in order to avoid interpreting unique characteristics as common, or as Reynolds put it, "mistak[ing] deformity for beauty."[35]

In fact, Audubon adhered to such dicta more faithfully than the acclaimed academician himself. Experts have described Reynolds's portraits of the rich and famous as stylized and formulaic, whereas Audubon sketched and resketched his birds. He drew them as he observed them in the field, and then he retired to a painting room or makeshift camp studio to finish the figures using specimens mounted "as in life" on boards. He sought perfection through repetition, and he encouraged his protégés to do likewise. Audubon wrote little on how to paint "from nature," but whether depicting birds or backgrounds they were to be drawn as realistically as possible, and in 1828 he published an essay on his approach.

Swearing that his "style of painting" was unique, Audubon's "Account of the Method of Drawing Birds employed by J. J. Audubon, Esq." (*Edinburgh Journal of Science*, 1828) has an uncanny, if spare, resemblance to Reynolds's classic statement on "the great style." In particular, Audubon appealed to the masters, and he reiterated the view that the fundamental objective of art was a search for truth in "grace and beauty." As Reynolds reminded his audience that learning from the masters was a means to an end, and that art had a grander purpose than mere beauty, Audubon strove "to distinguish the true from the false" in nature.[36] Aesthetics aside, Reynolds stated that art was to reveal "a nobleness of conception, which goes beyond anything in the mere exhibition, even of perfect form, [and] there is an art of animating and dignifying the figures with intellectual grandeur, of impressing the appearance of philosophic wisdom or heroic virtue."

Less eloquently, Audubon made similar claims. He saw himself as offering more than beautiful images. He approached his avian subjects as more conventional portraitists did their human subjects, and he compared his work to that of the very masters lionized in the *Discourses*. Audubon wrote that just as the great Renaissance painter Raphael (1483–1520) would have fallen short had he "not fed his pencil with all belonging to a mind perfectly imbued with a knowledge of real forms, muscles, bones, movements, and lastly, that spiritual expression of feelings that paintings like his exhibit so beautifully," his avian "portraits" would have failed as both art and science had he not painted living birds in their natural environment.[37] Then, appealing reverentially to Rembrandt (1606–1669), Audubon claimed that avian character was more fully and accurately revealed through art than text. "Why," he asked, "should the reader be tormented with descriptions? Where is the amateur of paintings who could bear the reading of a description of the structure, muscles, and expression of the face of such a man as Rembrandt, after gazing at the portrait of that eminent artist by himself?"[38] As biography paled next to Rembrandt's visage, those who focused on naming and describing birds could never, in Audubon's opinion, match his efforts to reveal their true nature through art.

In 1831, Maria Martin benefited from Audubon's technical skills and his accumulated knowledge, both practical and academic. She learned to paint by emulating him. However, she was also able to expand her knowledge of the ideas informing his work. She had access to two impressive libraries established in Charleston in the early nineteenth century. In addition to hundreds of volumes in the German Friendly Society library, there were more than twelve thousand monographs, travelogues, journals, and pamphlets in the Charleston Library Society.[39] Because the Charleston Library Society was a circulating library, and because John Bachman had been a member since 1822, Maria Martin could acquaint herself with topics discussed only by men and generally in public. In the privacy of her own home, she had access to the neoclassical ideals espoused by the artistic community and common currency among educated people.[40] She could consult Reynolds's *Discourses*, as well as scientific serials such as Curtis's *Botanical Magazine* and the *Transactions of the Linnaean*

Society. Standard works such as *System of Vegetables* (translated by Dr. Murray, 1783) and *Families of Plants* (translated by Erasmus Darwin, 1787) by Carl Linnaeus could be borrowed from the Society library holdings, as well as botanical works such as William Curtis's *Lectures on Botany* (1803–1815), William Withering's *Systematic Arrangement of British Plants* (1801), D. C. Willdenow's *Principles of Botany and Vegetable Physiology* (1805), Edward Smith's *Introduction to Physiological and Systematical Botany* (1809), and Benjamin Waterhouse's *Botanist* lectures (1811). Books on indigenous species were less common, but there was valuable information in Stephen Elliott's *Sketch of Botany of South Carolina and Georgia* (2 vols. 1821–1824), Thomas Walter's *Flora Caroliniana* (1788), Benjamin Smith Barton's *Elements of Botany* (1803; 1804 ed.), John Drayton's *Carolinian Florist* (1798), John Shecut's *Flora Caroliniensis* (1806), and in books by André (1746–1802) and François Michaux (1770–1855): *Histoire de Chênes de l'Amerique Septentrionale*, 1801; *Flora Boreali-Americana*, n.d.; *Histoire des Arbres Forestiers de l'Amerique . . .* ,1810–1813; and *North American Sylva*, 1817.

Equally important were the society's illustrated books. As Maria Martin perfected her botanicals, she could copy images by the preeminent botanical artist, Pierre-Joseph Redouté (1759–1840).[41] *Les Liliacées* (486 plates in eight volumes, 1802–1815) and *Les Roses* (169 plates in three volumes, 1817–1824) were, for example, both in society holdings, and the paintings in these volumes elicited uncommonly strong praise from Audubon. Of all the collections he visited when he went to Paris in 1828, none matched what he saw in Redouté's studio. He wrote glowingly: "His flowers are grouped with peculiar taste, well drawn and precise in the outlines, and colored with a pure brilliancy that depicts nature incomparably better than I ever saw it before. Old Redouté dislikes all that is not *nature alone*; he cannot bear either the drawings of stuffed birds or of quadrupeds, and evinced a strong desire to see a work wherein nature was delineated in an animated manner."[42] So impressed was he with Redouté that he referred to him as "the flower-painter *par excellence*" and called him "le Raphaël des Fleurs." Less flamboyantly, Maria Martin referred to Redouté as the "French florist."[43] She was, however, clearly influenced by Audubon's Parisian adventures.

Working side by side, stories about "le Raphaël des Fleurs" were inevitable. In Paris to obtain subscribers in 1828, Audubon met the man whom he viewed as the best botanical painter of the day. In his opinion, Redouté's botanicals held their own when compared to the zoological and botanical velins (c. 1630s) by des peintres du Cabinet du Roi at the Jardin du Roi/Jardin des Plantes.[44] Equally significant though was the affirmation offered by Redouté's approach to painting. Audubon visited his studio a number of times, spending hours studying hundreds of drawings, and after more than three hours with them one day his admiration was irrepressible. When he opened his journal that night, he recorded his thoughts, writing, "never have I seen drawings more beautifully wrought up, and so true to nature."[45]

Redouté was equally impressed with Audubon. Although he later subscribed to *Birds*, in 1828 he could not "afford" his new friend's paintings. A trade was thus worked out between the two artists, and Audubon left Redouté's studio with "nine numbers of 'Belles fleurs,'" and a promise that *Les Roses* would follow.[46] Within the month, the promised volumes arrived. With forty-five plates from *Choix des Plus Belles Fleurs* (1827), a work containing images that could be used by students learning how to draw botanical specimens, Audubon had at his disposal incomparable teaching aids.[47] Then, in early 1834, Redouté sent Audubon another batch of plates from his newly published florals—some "4 cahiers of flowers," and he promised to forward more as soon as he received them from the engraver.[48]

Between Audubon's plates and volumes owned by the Charleston Library Society, Maria Martin had access to an impressive array of botanical paintings. Redouté's roses, peonies, irises, gladiolas, camellias, hibiscus, passion flower, amaryllis, woody plants with fruit, and more were all beautiful images for aspiring artists to emulate and Maria not only studied his botanicals but also copied them. How many she copied is unknown, but one is extant. Her copy of his Cherokee rose (*Rosa laevigata*) serves as a backdrop for Audubon's figure of a Townsend's bunting (*Emberiza townsendii*), and while beautiful, it does not appear in *Birds of America.*

Given that in the space of a year Maria Martin's botanicals were so good that Audubon declared he was "extremely desirous to Introduce them in my 2d Volume,"[49] she applied herself diligently whether copying Redouté, Audubon himself, or others such as George Lehman. A Swiss-born landscape painter, Lehman was hired to paint backgrounds, and while the record is all but silent on how he passed the time in Charleston as he awaited their departure to the wintering grounds in Florida, Lehman most certainly showed Maria how to

FIGURE 16. (opposite) Cherokee rose (*Rosa laevigata*) by Maria Martin, n.d. This is a copy of a botanical by Pierre-Joseph Redouté in *Les Roses* (1817–1824). Maria Martin probably painted the unidentified butterfly accompanying Townsend's bunting (dickcissel/*Spiza americana*) as well. Watercolor, graphite and black ink; 51.1 x 35.4 cm (20⅛ x 13 15/16 in). 1863.18.13. Purchased by public subscription from Mrs. John J. Audubon. Collection of the New-York Historical Society. Digital image created by Oppenheimer Edition.

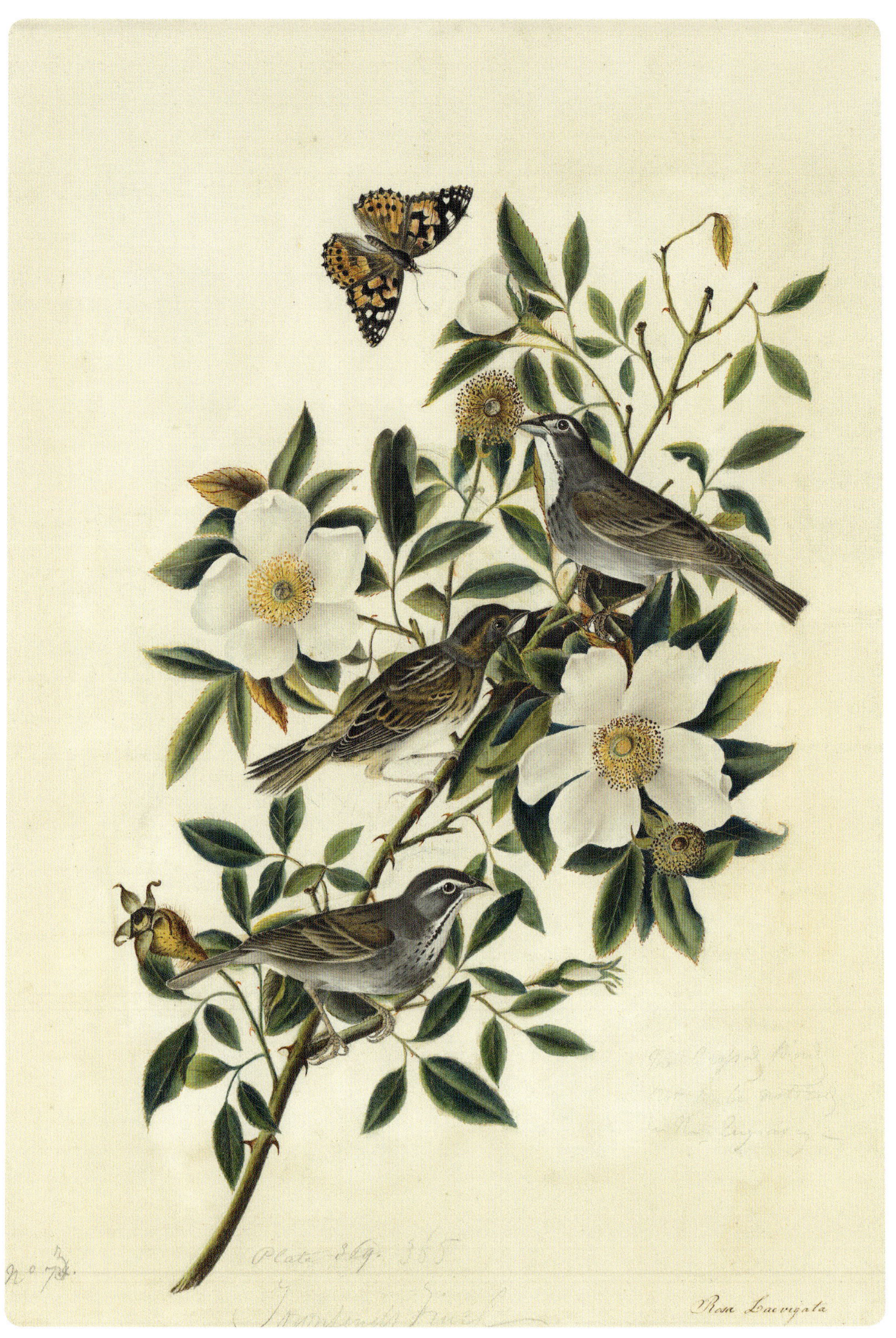
Rosa Laevigata

mix and apply pigment to paper. When Audubon was out courting potential subscribers, off looking for birds, or hobnobbing with natural history devotees, Lehman stayed behind, presumably painting backgrounds for water birds. As a result, Maria could turn to him for advice as she learned to paint by copying and, unsurprisingly, she painted his backgrounds. As she copied Audubon's tricolored heron (plate 217) and white egret (plate 242), Maria copied the skies and water, marshes and plants, and even the buildings added by Lehman. But she also copied a "wild" orange (*Citrus trifoliata*) that Lehman painted while in Charleston.[50] Although not typically noted for his botanicals, he was a paid employee who produced what was needed, when it was needed, and Lehman painted at least a dozen plants and trees for *Birds of America*.[51]

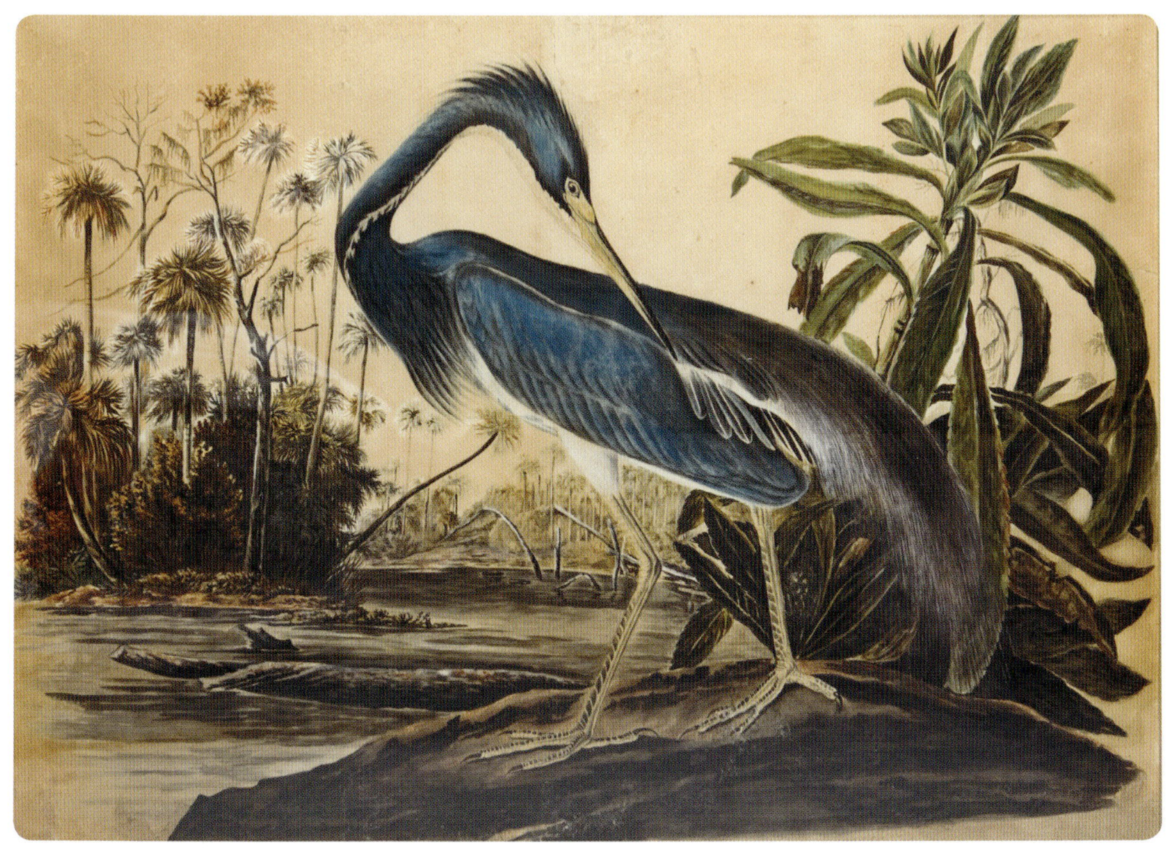

FIGURE 17. Maria Martin's copy of Audubon's tricolored heron (*Egretta tricolor*) and George Lehman's background for *Birds of America*, plate 217, 1832. Watercolor, graphite, pastel, gouache, and black ink. 76.67 x 53.35 cm (29 x 21 in). Courtesy of the Charleston Museum.

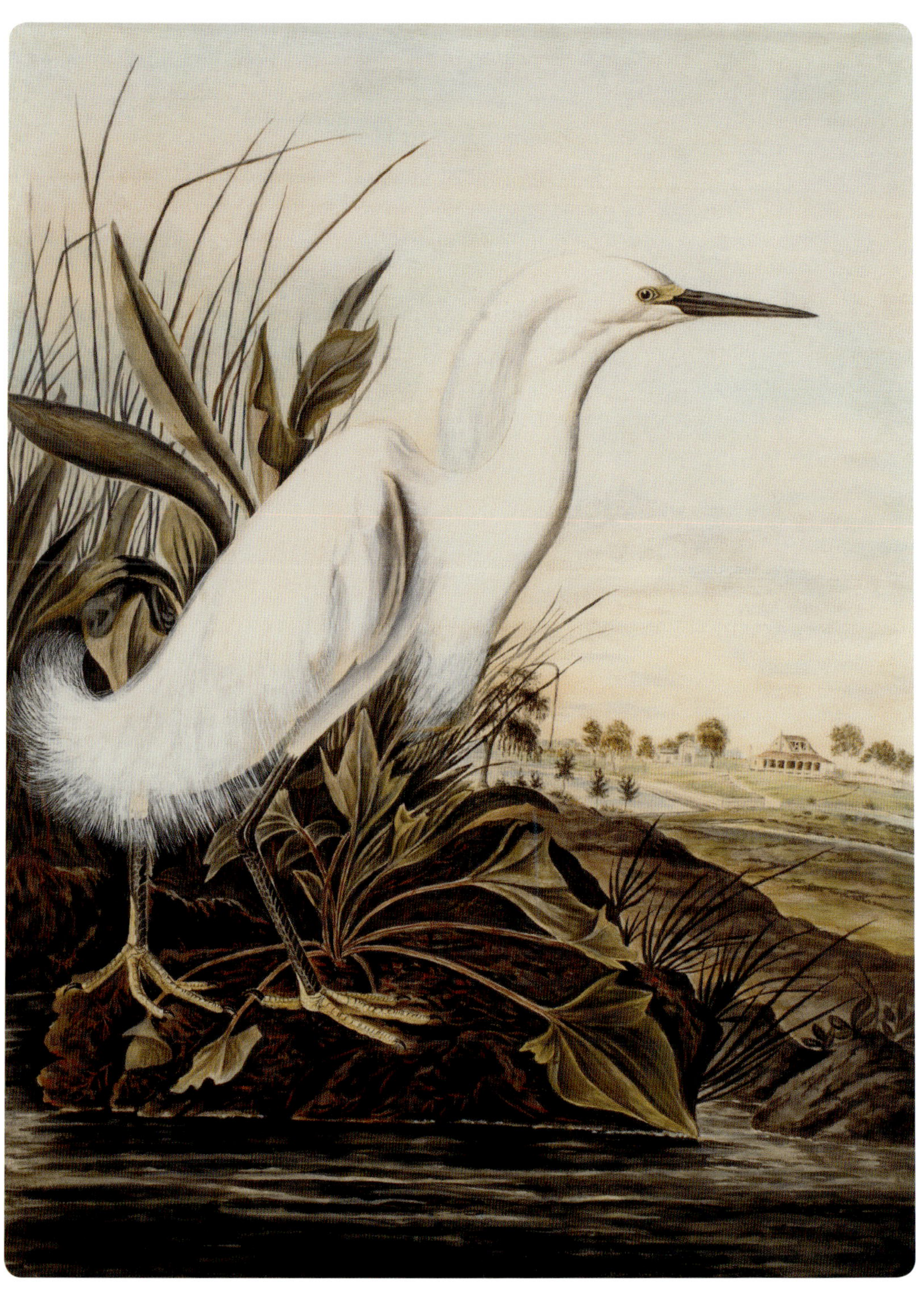

FIGURE 18. Maria Martin's copy of Audubon's snowy egret (*Egretta thula*) and George Lehman's background for *Birds of America*, plate 242, 1832. Watercolor, graphite, gouache, and black ink. Courtesy of Jane Grimball Greely.

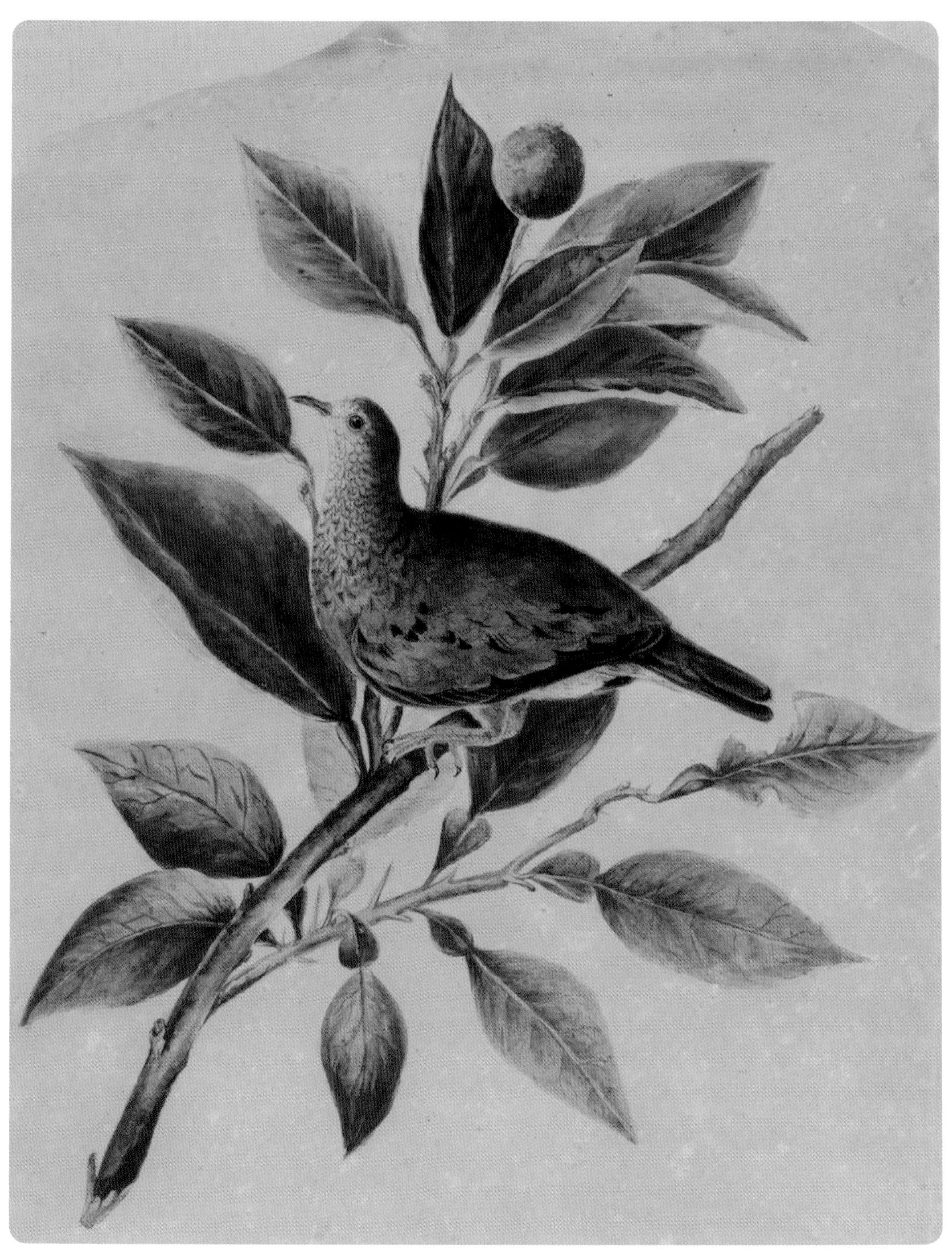

FIGURE 19. Martin Martin's version of Audubon's ground dove (*Columbina passerina*) and George Lehman's wild orange (*Citrus trifoliata*) for *Birds of America*, plate 182, 1832. Watercolor, graphite, and black ink. Original. Courtesy of Jane Grimball Greely.

Painting alongside Lehman offered yet another opportunity to hone her skills, and as Maria Martin copied his wild orange and Audubon's dove, she moved beyond replication to interpretation: she painted a simplified version of Audubon's ground doves roosting in Lehman's botanical. Because Audubon chose assistants whose work melded with his so seamlessly that their contributions were indistinguishable from his, Lehman's advice surely reinforced instructions already given. Similarly, after Audubon left Charleston, she put into practice what had been conveyed in person. Before leaving for Florida, he promised to send a copy of the first volume of *Birds of America*, and as she anxiously awaited the opportunity to improve her skills by copying, Maria Martin painted "from nature."[52] In the spring of 1832, for example, she produced a trumpet creeper (*Campsis radicans*) that was far different from the *Bignonia capreolata* painted by Audubon to accompany the yellow warbler (*Setophaga petechia*) for plate 65 and distributed as part of fascicle fifteen.[53] While her trumpet creeper was less striking and more simply composed than the one painted by Audubon, it was good enough for *Birds of America* and five black-throated mango hummingbirds hover around her figure. Indeed, the fact that her trumpet creeper was less showy than it might have been was essential to its inclusion.

Of the many differences between their botanicals, the orientation of the flowers and the color palette are notable. While Audubon's figure has forward-facing flowers, all but one of those on Maria's plant is viewed from the back. Interestingly, the one forward-facing flower has more intricately reproduced stamens and pistil than found in Audubon's bignonia, but there is a minimalist approach to her plant that complements the birds perfectly. Depicted as rather drab little creatures, the hummingbirds face forward, poised to extract nectar from backward-facing flowers. Despite their small size, the viewer is drawn to them even though their plumage lacks its characteristic iridescence. They are the focus of the vignette because Maria Martin's botanical is colored conservatively. Although a member of *Bignoniaceae*, a family with many dramatically colored species, Maria's *Campsis radicans* is a less vibrant species than most, and Audubon's diminutive birds are shown to advantage.

More to the point, Maria Martin managed to ensure that Audubon's birds were not eclipsed by her botanicals. Whether she was instructed to choose unobtrusive rather than showy botanicals, she tended to paint dusky toned rather than vibrantly colored species. She also tended to choose plants with minimal contrast. The spider flower (*Cleome hassleriana*) she painted to accompany the ruff-necked (rufous) hummingbird (*Selasphorus rufus*, plate 379) has, for example, pale pink and grey petals rather than the vivid pinks and violets common

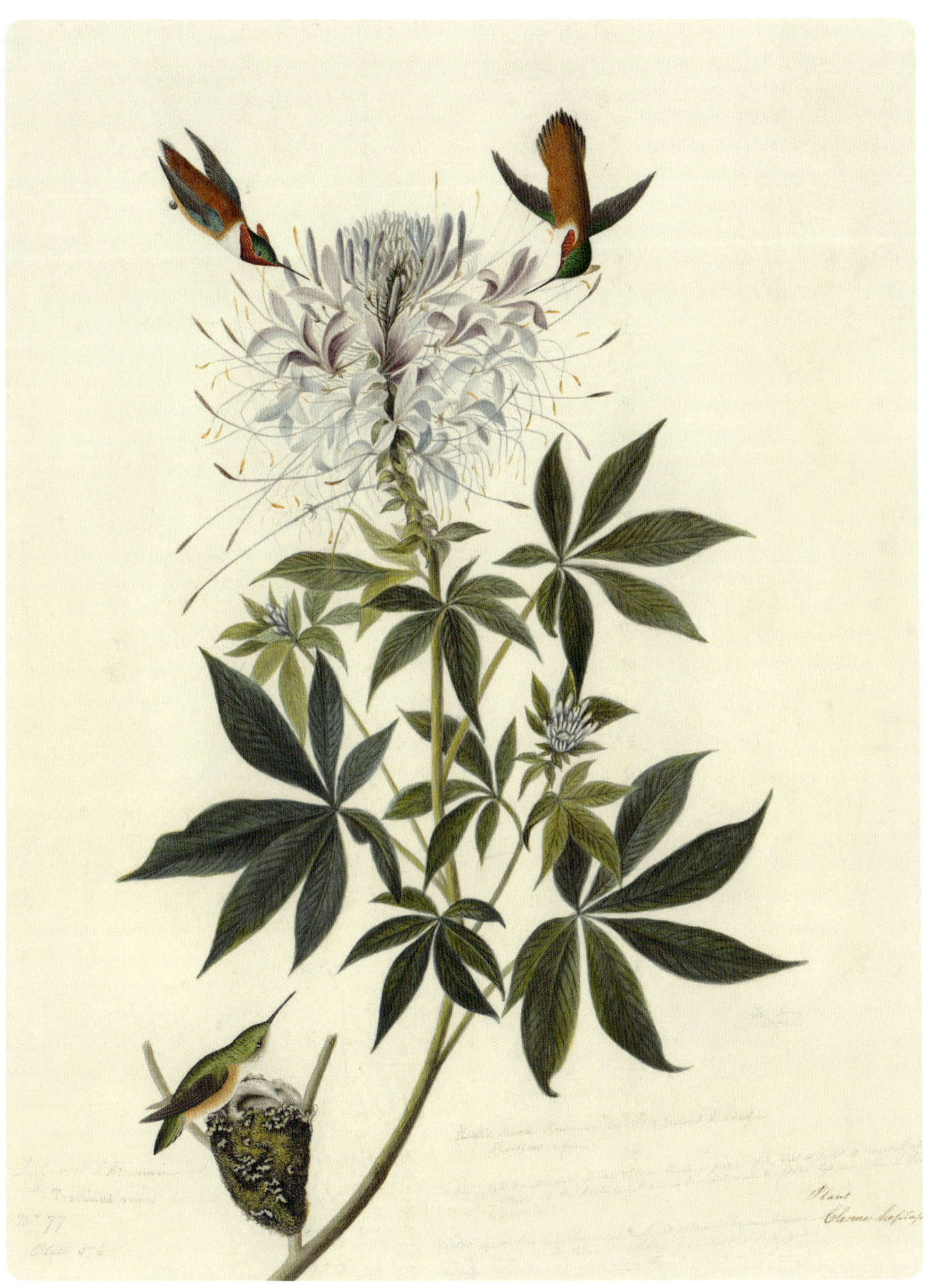

FIGURE 20. Spider flower (*Cleome hassleriana*) by Maria Martin, winter 1836–1837. Study for Havell edition, *Birds of America*, plate 379, ruff-necked (rufous) hummingbird (*Selasphorus rufus*). Watercolor, graphite, black ink, and gouache; 53.7 x 40.5 cm (21⅛ x 15 15/16 in). 1863.17.379. Purchased by public subscription from Mrs. John J. Audubon. Collection of the New-York Historical Society. Digital image created by Oppenheimer Edition.

to the species.[54] Likewise, the foliage is dark and drab. Her botanical could not have been duller. As a result, the two tiny birds hovering over her *Cleome* stand out. No matter how beautiful, most of her botanicals—especially those painted in response to requests from Audubon—recede into the background so that his birds seem to naturally stand out and capture the attention of viewers.

Maria Martin's color palette was almost always muted. The flowering botanicals she painted tended to have petals or bracts in whites and pastels, and those with more vivid coloring were typically mixed with grey to produce more subdued hues that did not compete for attention with Audubon's figures. There were, of course, exceptions but even when her botanicals were more conspicuous, they were complementary. One of the best examples of how even the most striking botanical could be used to foreground a bird is found on the painting used to create plate 168. Easily one of her most exquisite botanicals, the loblolly bay (*Gordonia lasianthus*) could have overshadowed the fork-tailed flycatcher (*Tyrannus savana*) it accompanies, but it does not. Placed on the diagonal and stretching from one corner of the sheet to the other, the yellow-centered, white-flowered branch could have dominated the painting; instead, it serves to accentuate the yellow-tufted, long-tailed, black and blue bird by counterbalancing it. Smaller than Maria's *Gordonia*, the flycatcher is deftly perched so as to dissect the page at right angles to the botanical in a manner that emphasizes its unusually elongated form and dark silhouette.

Whether Maria Martin would have offered Audubon such an eye-catching painting unsolicited is uncertain; however, she had no difficulty producing one when asked. Similarly, in 1836–1837 when he needed a botanical to accompany some of the most colorful birds of North America, she painted a Carolina allspice (*Calycanthus floridus*). With dark brownish-red flowers, the allspice was one of the most colorful shrubs she painted for Audubon, but that was irrelevant when compared to the markings of the birds perched in it. Townsend's warbler (*Setophaga townsendi*) has bright yellow and black striping on its breast and head, and two of the bluebirds have vivid blue plumage. The females of the Arctic [mountain] bluebird (*Sialia currucoides*) and the western bluebird (*Sialia mexicana*) have subdued coloring but that of the males is intense. Maria's allspice was painted out of season and was no match for Audubon's figures. Her botanical had just three of the densely colored blossoms and very few leaves on a species characterized by dense ovate foliage and numerous laterally placed flowers. Interestingly, her stark portrayal was altered before being engraved and printed. The addition of two flowers for a total of five produced a more symmetrical vignette, while the removal of a number of leaves emphasized that symmetry.[55]

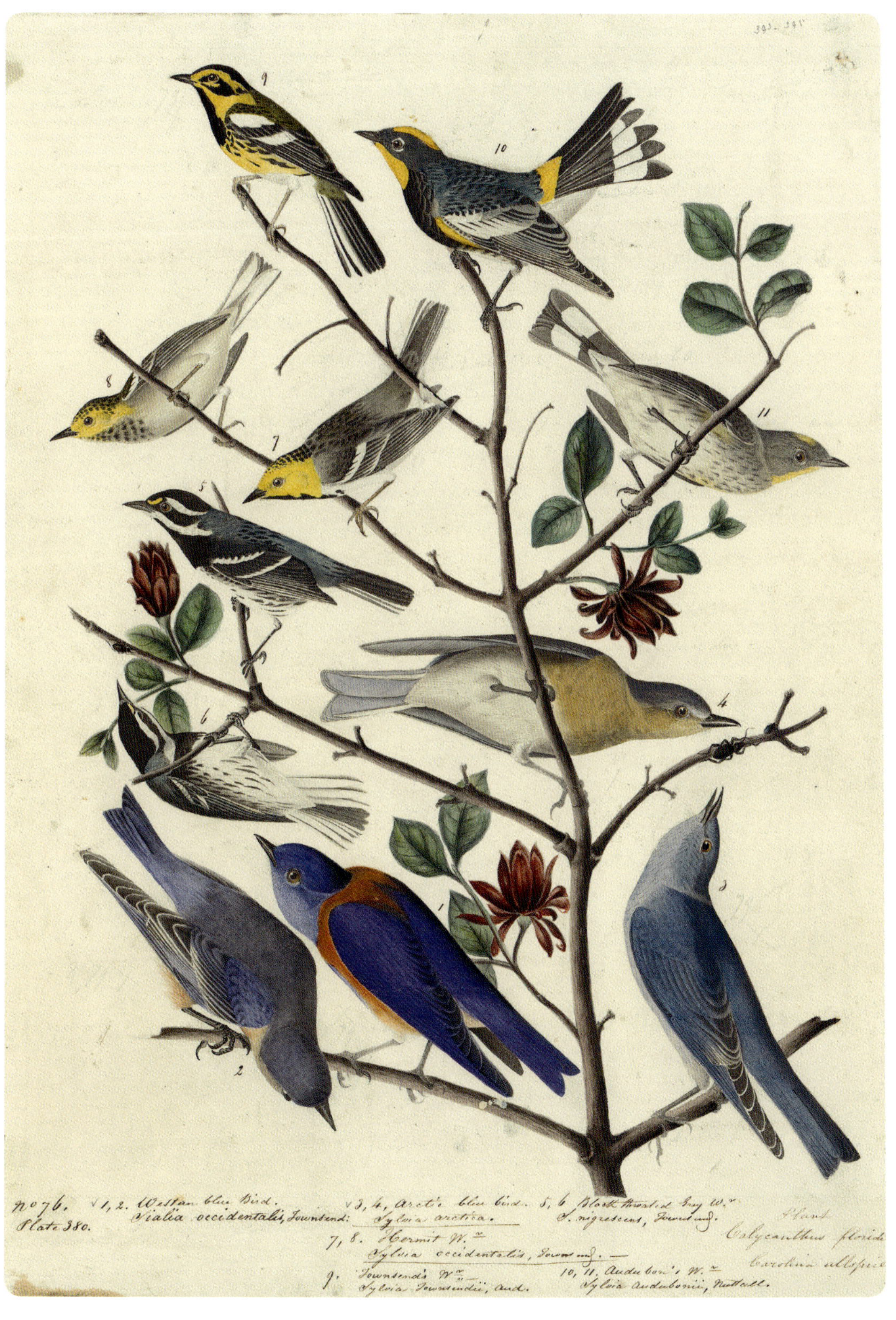
No 76.
Plate 380.
1, 2. Western blue Bird.
Sialia occidentalis, Townsend.
3, 4, Arctic blue bird.
Sylvia arctica.
5, 6 Black throated Grey W.r
S. nigrescens, Townsend.
7, 8. Hermit W.r
Sylvia occidentalis, Townsend.
9. Townsend's W.r
Sylvia Townsendii, Aud.
10, 11, Audubon's W.r
Sylvia auduboni, Nuttall.
Plant
Calycanthus
Carolina

As Maria Martin assisted Audubon prepare the last studies for engraving, earlier efforts were sometimes revisited. The American strawberry bush (*Euonymus americanus*) painted in the autumn of 1832 was, for example, resuscitated and replicated as a background for three western species (yellow-rumped warbler/*Setophaga coronata*; hermit warbler/*S. occidentalis*; black-throated gray warbler/*S. nigrescens*) depicted in plate 395. Unusually full, Maria's euonymus attests to her artistry and technical skill, particularly in the half-elephant folio format used for the three small paintings found in the fascicles or "numbers" presold to subscribers. When bound, the pages making up *Birds* were all the same size, however each fascicle consisted of one large (approx. 100 x 67 cm) painting, one medium (approx. 61 x 49 cm) painting, and three small (approximately 52 x 36 cm) paintings; as Audubon contemplated the contents of these "numbers," he had to consider many factors, including what birds to offer in each grouping and how to use his artist-assistants to best effect. Landscape artist George Lehman, for example, added backgrounds in all three sizes: he provided backgrounds for eight large folios, nine medium, and several small. Of the more than twenty botanicals added by Maria Martin, only one graced a full-size folio and the bamboo vine (*Smilax pseudochina*) accompanying the yellow-crowned night heron (*Nyctanassa violacea*, plate 336) was her least accomplished effort. She clearly excelled in a smaller format, and because Audubon insisted on accuracy as well as artistry, her contributions appeared where they were as close to perfect as possible.

Audubon was obsessed with verisimilitude. It not only dictated choices about the birds in the foreground but also determined the plants and scenery in the background, and he believed contextualization was essential. It was, he pointed out, misguided to ignore habitat and habits, and misrepresenting scale was equally problematic. Whether perched on a branch, feeding upon the nectar of flowers, guarding chicks or eggs nestled in a hollow, or any number of other scenes found in nature, the environment had to be portrayed accurately. He wrote, "The woods that I continually trod contained not only birds of richest feathering, but each tree, each shrub, each flower, attracted equally my curiosity and attention, and my anxiety to have all those in my portfolios

FIGURE 21. (opposite) Carolina allspice (*Calycanthus floridus*) by Maria Martin, winter 1836–1837. Study for Havell edition, *Birds of America*, plate 393, Arctic (mountain) bluebird (*Sialia currucoides*), Townsend's warbler (*Setophaga townsendi*), western bluebird (*Sialia mexicana*). Watercolor, graphite, and black ink; 50.8 x 36.2 cm (20 x 14¼ in). 1863.17.393. Purchased by public subscription from Mrs. John J. Audubon. Collection of the New-York Historical Society. Digital image created by Oppenheimer Edition.

introduced the thought of joining as much as possible *nature as it existed*. [adding] I can assure you that all these were copied with the same exactness with which all the birds are represented, [so] you will no doubt view them with as much pleasure."[56] Like the insignia of office that portraitists included in their paintings of great men and women, the forests, skies, and waters inhabited by Audubon's birds were fundamental to his "ornithological delineations or portraitures."[57] He disparaged artists who depicted only the "*necessary characteristics*" of birds—no matter how accomplished or accurate—as he believed that backgrounds had to be rendered no less carefully than the birds in the foreground. In 1828, for example, he described botanicals examined in Britain as "washy, slack, imperfect messes" that were inferior to the backgrounds he demanded of himself and of those who assisted him.[58]

Nothing less than perfection was required, and Maria Martin responded admirably. Under Audubon's tutelage, she was transformed from a "dauber," whose decorative efforts made no pretense of representing reality, to an artist able to render flowers and buds, stems and leaves, butterflies and beetles that were as beautiful as they were accurate. She learned the fundamentals and more within a few months. Exactly how this transformation occurred is unclear though. Any account Maria Martin might have created no longer exists, and Audubon wrote little on the matter even though he had an aptitude for seeing talent and teaching to it. Indeed, without the recollections of an assistant who described how Audubon used a "position board" to replicate avian behavior, descriptions of how he painted "from nature" would be entirely speculative.[59] Likewise, knowledge of his tools and supplies would be slim had a list compiled in 1836 detailing items he considered absolutely essential for scientific illustration not been forwarded by Charles Pickering (1805–1878), a naturalist from Philadelphia, to the Secretary of the Navy.[60] As a member of the United States Exploring Expedition, Pickering was in a position to appreciate Audubon's preference for expensive and imported supplies. And while locally available gamboge, gum arabic, corks, India rubber, and India ink were satisfactory, Audubon viewed American-made paper as substandard—not even good enough for plates copied from his originals—and he was equally discriminating when it came to pigments, pencils, and brushes. He preferred pastels, black chalk, watercolor brushes, and port-crayons from Paris, but recommended London suppliers for graphite and watercolor pigments. He specified Brookman and Langdon for leaded pencils (treble B to treble H), and advised purchasing pigment cakes from Giovanni Arzoni, the "celebrated" manufacturer of ultramarine. Well known as a premium supplier of pigments, Arzoni and his entire family died—most probably, local physicians speculated, from work-related poisoning—in 1841, but until then Maria Martin worked with Arzoni pigments, Parisian brushes, and English paper.[61]

Thus supplied, she made the best of opportunities offered while working alongside Audubon in the studio set up on the north side of the ground floor of the Bachman home. Like Audubon, she would have applied both natural and manufactured pigments such as red lead, white lead, Prussian blue, indigo, red lake, and chrome yellow after outlining figures in pencil.[62] Honing her skills as she sketched intricately drawn insects and delicately outlined plants, Maria Martin learned to apply pigments mixed with water gradually so as to convey texture and produce intense colors like those on the flowers of the Carolina allspice, the strawberry shrub, and the flame azalea. Dark or vibrantly colored flowers were only achieved through constant mixing and layering of colors from the painter's palette, especially as Audubon drew on a small number of pigments to produce a wide range of tones and hues.[63] Less complicated perhaps, but equally important, was the foliage. Following standard practice, it was painted last, and on some of her botanicals it was among the most challenging to depict realistically. She replicated, for example, the shiny stiff elliptic leaves of the loblolly bay, the distinctively veined and slightly hairy leaves of the western dogwood, the fine serrations of the strawberry shrub, the inwardly curled heart-shaped (cordate) leaves of *Smilax pseudochina*, and more, with felicity and finesse. As Maria did not normally use gouache, she had to either lift color or leave blank areas so fine details such as veins could be added later. Interestingly, her rendition of the sweetgum tree (*Liquidambar styraciflua*) painted during the winter of 1836–1837 was superior to the one painted by Joseph Mason, one of Audubon's most accomplished assistants. Similarly, in volume one, Audubon's figure of the willow flycatcher (plate 45) sits atop a branch depicting the unusual cork-like scales characteristic of the species, but the accompanying leaves are flat and lifeless. Maria Martin's image, on the other hand, has both depth and complexity. Although the distinctive scales are absent, her botanical includes the anatomical feature used by botanists to identify and classify species, and the fruits are rendered artistically: burr balls dangle from branches used as perches for four different species (Clark's nutcracker/*Nucifraga columbiana*; scrub jay/*Aphelocoma californica*; Stellar's jay/*Cyanocitta stelleri*; and yellow-billed magpie/*Pica nuttalli*). In other instances, she painted relatively uncomplicated branches and tree trunks, but the level of verisimilitude she achieved was remarkable; the detail in the bark and epiphytes such as moss matched that of the plumage and other identifying characteristics

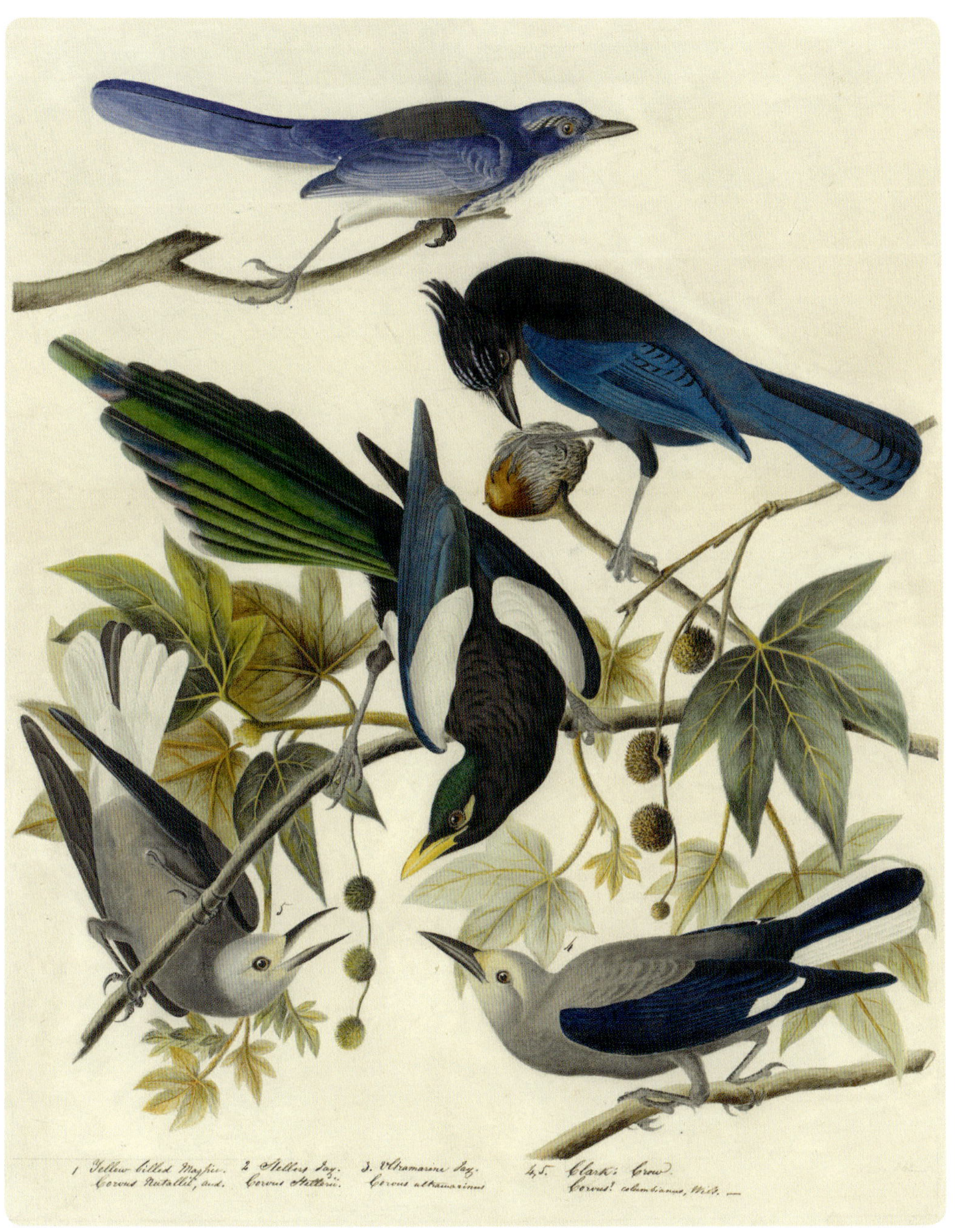

FIGURE 22. Sweetgum tree (*Liquidambar styraciflua*) by Maria Martin, winter 1836–1837. Study for Havell edition, *Birds of America*, plate 362, Clark's crow (Clark's nutcracker/*Nucifraga columbiana*), ultramarine jay (scrub jay/*Aphelocoma californica*), Stellar's jay (*Cyanocitta stelleri*), yellow-billed magpie (*Pica nuttalli*). Watercolor, graphite, and black ink; 64.9 x 55.6 cm (25⁹⁄₁₆ x 21⅞ in). 1863.17.362. Purchased by public subscription from Mrs. John J. Audubon. Collection of the New-York Historical Society. Digital image created by Oppenheimer Edition.

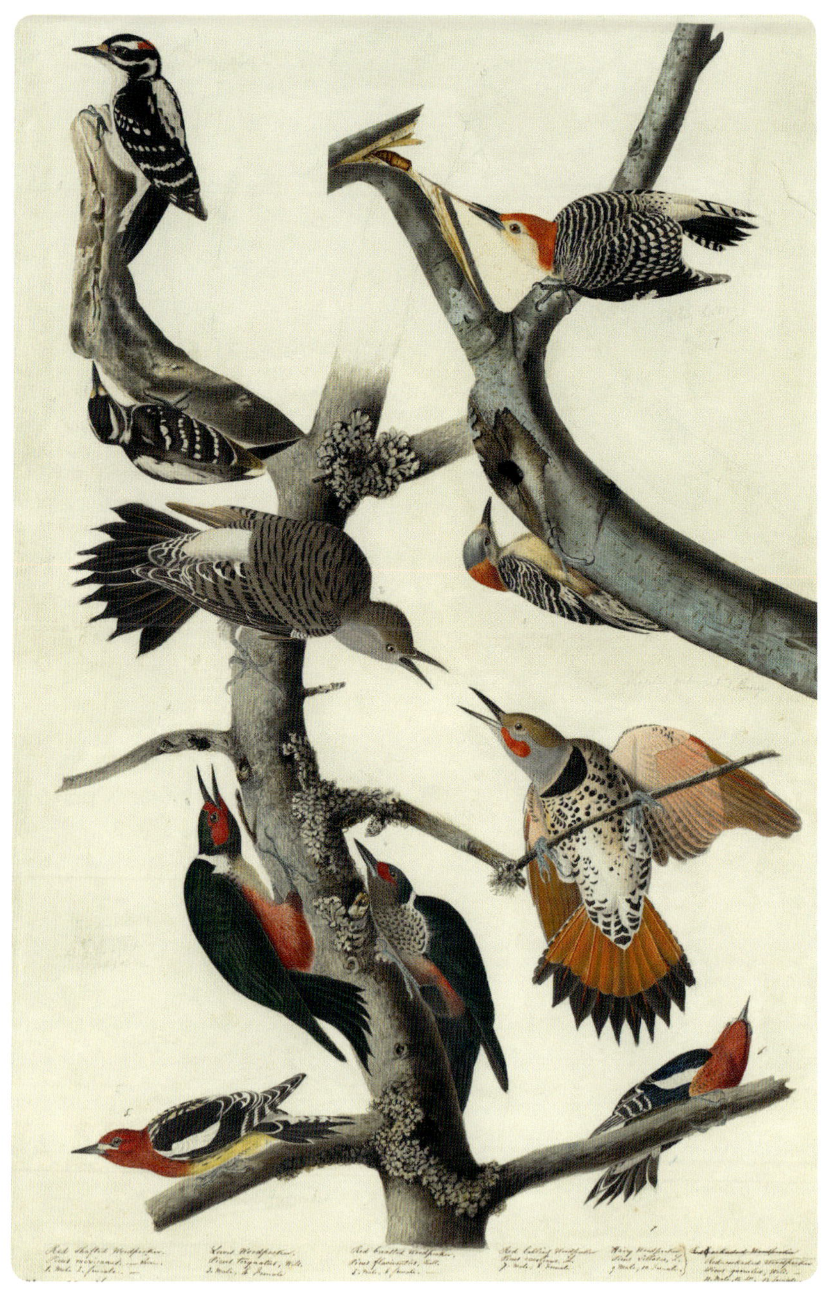

FIGURE 23. Dead tree limb by Maria Martin, winter 1836–1837. Study for Havell edition, *Birds of America*, plate 416, hairy woodpecker (*Leuconotopicus villosus*), Lewis's woodpecker (*Melanerpes lewis*), red-shafted woodpecker (northern flicker/*Colaptes auratus*), red-bellied woodpecker (*Melanerpes carolinus*), red-breasted woodpecker (red-shafted or red-breasted sapsucker/*Sphyrapicus ruber*). Watercolor, graphite, and black ink; 94.5 x 61.8 cm (37 3/16 x 24 5/16 in). 1863.17.416. Purchased by public subscription from Mrs. John J. Audubon. Collection of the New-York Historical Society. Digital image created by Oppenheimer Edition.

minutely portrayed by Audubon. Such detail is only accomplished through close examination and study of plant morphology, and Maria Martin employed her scientific knowledge, no less than her artistic gifts, so as to ensure that her botanicals would be as realistic as Audubon's beautiful birds.[64]

While Maria Martin's figures of botanicals and insects were so beautifully rendered they were saved among family memorabilia, they also reflect her practical nature. Fanciful notions that she could paint anything had no appeal to a woman schooled in pietistic principles. Fortunately, she was spared having to paint botanicals larger or smaller than they were "in nature" because Audubon chose to paint his birds "life size" and in their natural environment. Flowers and seeds, leaves and stems, as well as branches and bark were thus reproduced exactly as they appeared before her. With the issue of scale resolved, Maria Martin could focus on artistry and accuracy. Without diminishing her accomplishments, it is obvious that she chose simple botanicals deliberately. Able to step into a garden filled with several varieties of roses, irises, lilies, "jessamines," and myrtles, as well as honeysuckle, verbena, alyssum, mignonette, petunias, pinks, camellias, milkweed, cigarette vines, quince trees and more, she preferred naturalized or indigenous species that were less complex than the ornamentals a few steps from the painting room.[65] Similarly, the Lamarque double roses, the white and yellow Banksia double roses, and the red camellias growing in the garden were not among the botanical paintings offered Audubon. If she did attempt to paint these varieties, her sketches have disappeared. Only the beautifully simple Cherokee rose (*Rosa laevigata*), long naturalized in the south and familiar to both gardeners and devotees of Redoutés's *Les Roses*, is extant.[66] At the same time, although three of her most exquisite botanicals—*Gordonia lasianthus*, *Gordonia pubescens* (or *Franklinia alatamaha*), and *Cornus nuttallii*—have relatively simple structures, their flowers or bracts required considerable skill to create. They were white, and she did not use either gouache or the white pigment available at the time.

Talented but untrained, Maria Martin mastered the practicalities of painting "from nature" because Audubon nurtured ability not fully developed, roused interest in nature lying dormant—if there at all—and provided instruction to guide her. In turn, he became accustomed to her assistance. If not quite indispensable, her attention to detail and eagerness to please were welcome attributes, and once her botanicals were good enough for *Birds,* Audubon ceased to employ artist-assistants. He also began to view her artistic talents and botanical knowledge as at his disposal. He assumed she would paint for him no matter where his work took him, and before leaving for Britain in

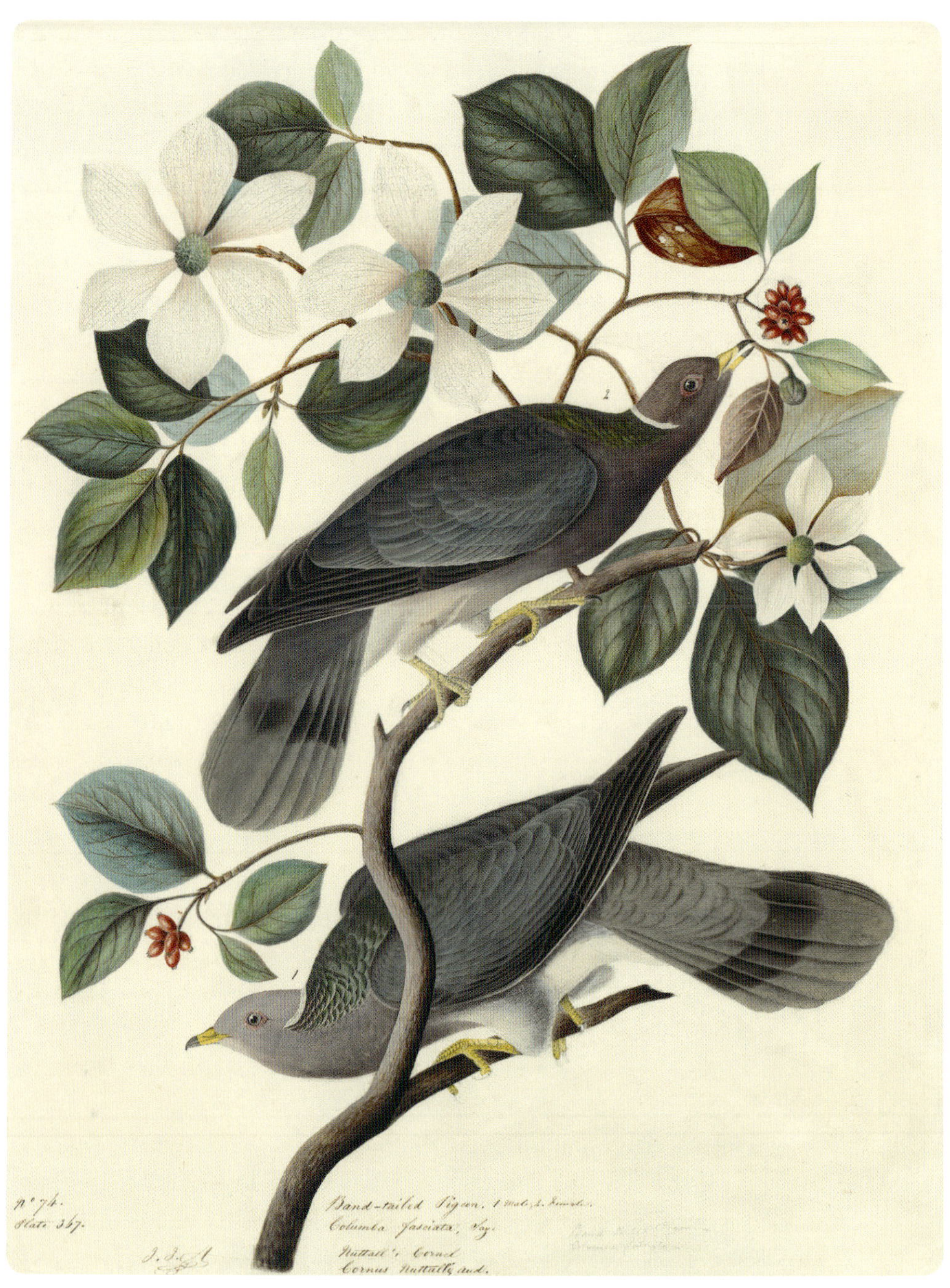

FIGURE 24. Western or mountain dogwood (*Cornus nuttallii*) by Maria Martin, winter 1836–1837. Study for Havell edition, *Birds of America*, plate 367, band-tailed pigeon (*Patagioenas fasciata*). Watercolor and graphite; 67.8 x 52.4 cm (26 11/16 x 20 5/8 in). 1863.17.367. Purchased by public subscription from Mrs. John J. Audubon. Collection of the New-York Historical Society. Digital image created by Oppenheimer Edition.

1834, he sent her brushes and encouraged her to "wear [them] out by the 1st of November" when he hoped to be back painting alongside her.[67]

That plan never materialized. Under pressure from subscribers who wanted orders filled and sets completed, Audubon endeavored to oblige them. Instead of returning to America, he stayed in Britain until August 1836 to supervise the preparation of plates for the third volume of *Birds*, to paint figures for the last volume, and to complete the accompanying text for the *Ornithological Biography*.[68] He also sent requests for assistance with increasing frequency and urgency: he needed information on habitat, habits, and the anatomical structure of birds, and he needed backgrounds for the paintings he was desperately trying to complete. And he was not shy about asking for either. Nor was he diplomatic.

By December 1835 Audubon was overwhelmed. He careened between commendation and disparagement when dealing with his Charleston friends, and he wrote a particularly incendiary letter as the month drew to a close. He chided Maria Martin for inactivity and accused Bachman of being "extremely Lazy! Frightful—horrible—Disgraceful." He admonished the reverend to "stir up for the sake of yourself and that of an Old Friend—climb up trees! Seek the 'rara avis' and then all will be right!" He berated Maria for being "somewhat slack in ornithological Delights or stil worst [*sic*] on Botanical ones," and as he did so he opined condescendingly that as "one of the *Slenderer Sex*" she could be pardoned for frailties for which men had no excuse.[69]

Truthfully his aspersions were groundless. In fact, he had largely ignored her for the previous eighteen months while he was preoccupied with painting water birds and seascapes. However, as he anticipated the end of his project, his priorities changed. He wanted to make good on his promise that *Birds of America* would be comprehensive and complete, and Maria's botanicals were highly desirable as he raced to finish plates promised subscribers.[70] Leaving aside water birds and returning to Columbiformes, Passeriformes, Piciformes, Cathartiformes, Falconiformes, and Strigiformes, he assumed his Southern friends would be spurred to action when they heard that the first set of plates for the last volume was being engraved and that "the enormous work will be finished and compleat in *22 Months*"—if the paintings he was rushing to complete reached Havell in a timely manner. He certainly felt no need to atone for ill-considered comments made only a month earlier, and without a hint of an apology, Audubon wrote Bachman asking for "finished" paintings from Maria as well as for preserved specimens and anatomical information.[71]

With many partially finished paintings awaiting backgrounds, there was cause for concern. Even though sons John Woodhouse and Victor Gifford worked alongside him, neither could reasonably be expected to do more: John Woodhouse worked on figures while Victor Gifford assisted with landscapes and attended to the technical and financial details so crucial to producing *Birds*. Indeed, from 1832, Victor spent long periods overseeing affairs in England, and his younger brother rarely left their father's side after the Labrador expedition of 1834.[72] Quickly mastering taxidermy, by early 1833 John Woodhouse was also a fine artist. So impressive was his progress that John James wrote Lucy in May that John Woodhouse "certainly surpasses all I had anticipated and I hope to see him *complete* many a fine drawing for our *family work*."[73] By December, Audubon's wish was fulfilled: John Woodhouse was able to work on his father's figures so that his brush strokes blended invisibly. He was, Lucy Audubon reported to Victor, the "drawer of [the] fine parts that your Father does not see so well."[74] Close to fifty, Audubon was suffering from presbyopia, an affliction that could only worsen. His dependency on his sons could only increase, and Maria Rebecca, one of John Woodhouse's daughters, described their working relationship as symbiotic. She claimed they worked together "in the utmost unison, [the sons] with perfect freedom from all jealousy," so that they "merge[d] their genius so wholly in his, that their identity as artist was lost."[75] What was not noted by Audubon's granddaughter was that botanicals and ephemera were, of necessity, also left to others, and it was Audubon's good fortune that Maria Martin was as capable and as self-effacing as his sons. In addition to having an aptitude for botanicals, she was willing to paint other elements of avian habitat. She was not reticent when it came to drawing nests or nonavian species promised in the Prospectus, and she tried her hand at the "Insects, Reptiles, or Fishes, that form the food of the birds" added to Audubon's vignettes.[76] Equally important, she did not hold a grudge.

Even though Maria had heard nothing from Audubon since being castigated, she would not withhold her services unless she had family obligations, and on the very day that Audubon wrote requesting "finished" paintings, John Bachman penned a letter describing her efforts in that regard. Calling her a "good girl," he informed Audubon that Maria "has sent you a few drawings of shells [that is] evidence of what she will send you in a few weeks." Further attesting to her charitable nature, Bachman referred to her as "my right hand still—[she] paints for me bugs, butterflies & even toads & snakes if I should wish them—makes caps for the girls & breeches for the boys & works for every body but herself."[77] Signaling that Audubon's outburst had been forgiven, Bachman's letter permitted a return to the amicability that normally characterized their relationship.

Although it is unclear that Audubon was troubled by his gaucherie, any misgivings he might have had about the rough handling of his collaborators were set aside, and by early March his correspondence was much friendlier as he inquired about Maria's drawings and the much-needed specimens. Fearing they were lost at sea, he suggested that future packages be addressed to him at the customhouse and sent via merchant marine.[78] A month later, still minding his manners, he sent detailed instructions. Through Bachman, he asked Maria to "draw plants, and branches of Trees for Me to the Number of 15 or 20 Drawings for small plates—Anything not published in my *Two first* volumes would prove a valuable acquisition, and [if] She would send them 5 or 6 at a time . . . our Son Victor would know how to use them by placing them to Birds which I have drawn without plants."[79] It was mid-June and, as only half of the last one hundred paintings were engraved, Audubon was under enormous pressure. Confident that Maria was familiar with the birds and plants in the first two volumes and that she was sufficiently knowledgeable about avian habitat, he trusted her to pick the appropriate botanicals for the paintings he was trying to complete before returning to America.

By October, Maria was more favorably disposed toward the churlish Audubon. He was planning to return to Charleston, and he had sent her a small gift, a book by Arthur Parsey (1791–1857) on *The Art of Miniature Painting on Ivory*.[80] In turn, she apologized for "having done so little for you in the painting line" and promised to make up for her deficiencies once he was in residence. She would then, she wrote, be at his "disposal." She offered to be his "amanuensis, painter or anything else that will be an assistance to you; not forgetting the darning of socks which you know was my employment on a former occasion, during the absence of your good wife."[81]

A woman of her word, Maria Martin could hardly have guessed just how busy she would be when John James and John Woodhouse arrived a month later. In addition to finished figures awaiting backgrounds, there was a number of entirely new specimens collected in the far west by John Kirk Townsend (1809–1851) to paint. Audubon was loath to declare *Birds* complete without these birds, and with Maria Martin and John Woodhouse at his side, he hoped to paint the Townsend specimens between mid-November and mid-February.[82] Less thrilling perhaps, but nonetheless important, were the plants collected by Townsend's traveling companion, Thomas Nuttall (1786–1859). While the Audubon men painted western ornithological specimens, Maria Martin drew western plants collected by this accomplished botanist, although exactly how many is unknown because her contributions in 1836–1837 do not bear her distinctive handwriting in the lower corner of the paintings.

In the rush to completion, Audubon offered only vaguely worded acknowledgments of Maria's efforts. He noted, for example, that she painted some of the Nuttall specimens, specifically the western dogwood (*Cornus nuttallii*, Aud., plate 367), the California sycamore (*Platanus racemosa*, Nutt., plate 362), and a western spider plant (*Cleome integrifolia*, Torrey and Gray syn. *Cleome hassleriana*, plate 379), and identified a few particularly beautiful botanicals such as the Carolina allspice (*Calycanthus floridus*, plate 393), the strawberry tree (*Euonymus americanus*, plate 395), the pink azalea (*Rhododendron periclymenoides*, plate 398), and the Virginia saltmarsh mallow (*Kosteletzkya virginica*, plate 425) as her drawings, but he only casually mentioned that she painted the trees and branches appearing in three other plates (399, 414 and 416) and said nothing definite about work added discretely elsewhere.[83] He summed up her efforts briefly when he wrote that he had been "assisted in the finishing of the plants, branches of trees, and flowers, which accompany these figures, by my friend's sister-in-law Miss M. Martin."[84] In other words, she painted more than the ten botanicals specifically attributed to her.

While it is true that Audubon painted exquisitely beautiful botanicals, in the rush to include the Townsend-Nuttall specimens it is unlikely that he painted the wild bergamot (*Monarda fistulosa*) accompanying five figures of various Passeriformes depicted in plate 394, the river hawthorn (*Crataegus rivularis*, Nutt.) accompanying a hermit thrush, a Townsend's solitaire and a grey jay in plate 419, or the common snowberry (*Symphoricarpos albus*)—that is reminiscent of the mistletoe (*Phoradendron serotinum*) she painted to accompany Audubon's varied thrush (*Ixoreus naevius*) and mountain mocking bird (sage thrasher/*Oreoscoptes montanus*) for plate 369—in plate 375 containing the common redpoll (*Acanthis flammea*). Although these could have been painted by Audubon or by his sons—whose contributions were also typically under acknowledged—it is not probable.[85] John Woodhouse was fully occupied in assisting his father complete the seventy figures they painted while in Charleston, and neither he nor Victor painted botanicals. Fully employed with their normal responsibilities, it is more likely that Maria Martin painted them.

Whether it was the press of time or the fact that *Birds* had become so thoroughly collaborative that specific acknowledgement seemed pointless, Audubon tended to pick and choose when assigning credit. He acknowledged,

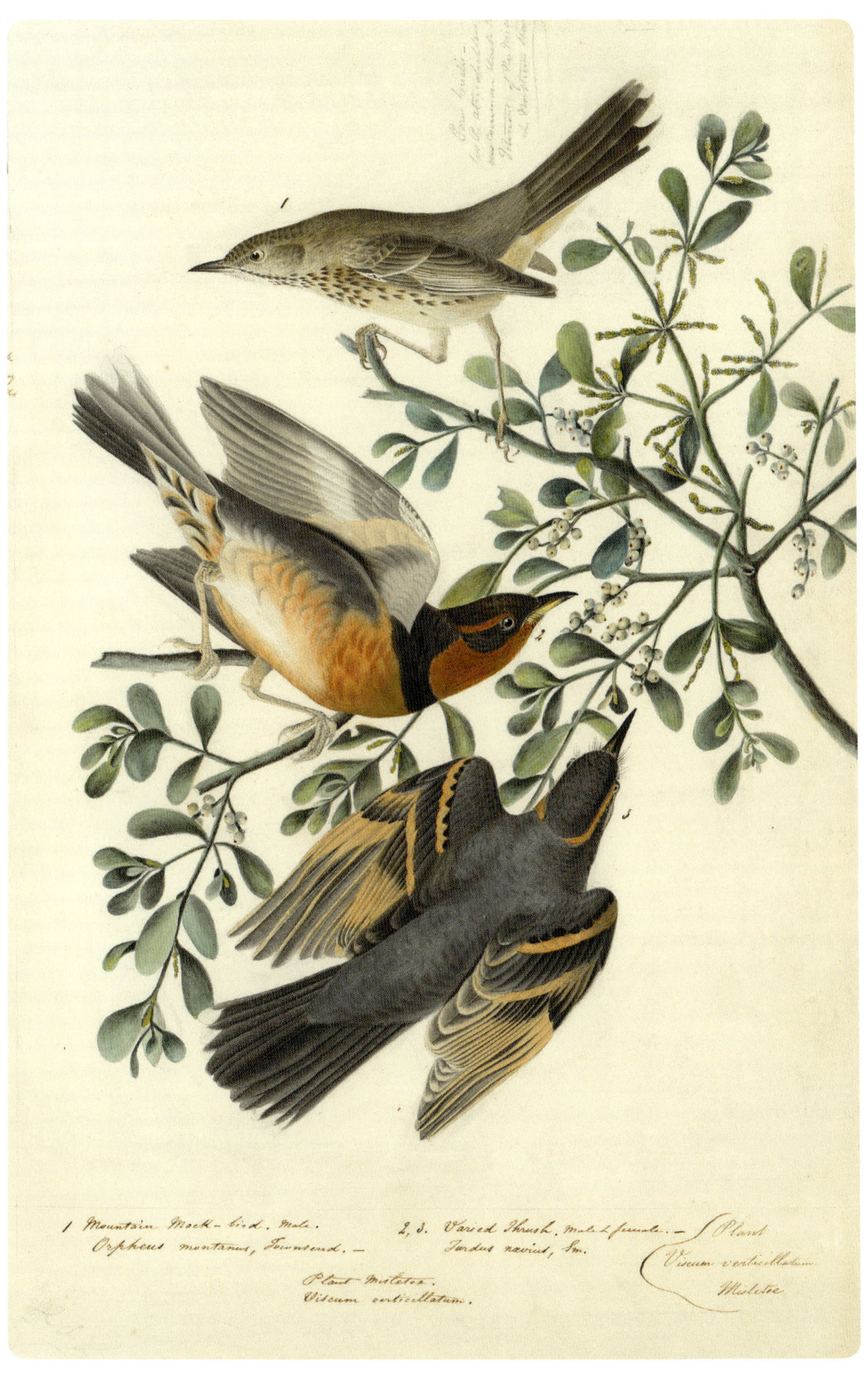
1 Mountain Mock-bird. Male.
Orpheus montanus, Townsend. –
2, 3. Varied Thrush. Male & female. –
Turdus naevius,
Plant Mistletoe.
Viscum verticillatum.
Plant
Viscum verticillatum
Mistletoe

for example, that Maria Martin painted the nest of the chestnut crowned titmouse (*Psaltriparus minimus*) used in plate 353, but ignored entomological contributions such as the white peacock butterfly (*Anartia jatrophae*) found in plate 355. Perhaps it could not have been otherwise: Was it wise to acknowledge the extent to which he depended on others? Should he have drawn attention to the fact that John Woodhouse had to fill in details he could not see, or that he relied on Maria Martin to reproduce the intricate (and equally invisible) parts of plants accompanying the birds painted with his son's help? Could he have acknowledged fully those who collaborated so willingly, especially in those last hectic months?

While his genius is evident in every painting, emanating from every figure and every background, by 1833 Audubon needed help and he knew it. As the year drew to a close, he even began to recognize that if his original timetable seemed reasonable when conceived, it was increasingly less so. At the outset, he believed he should offer twenty-five plates a year because, as Audubon reasoned, to do more "would make it too [financially] heavy to my Subscribers and indeed would require many more persons employed than I could find at present," but by November 1833 (if not sooner) he began to doubt the wisdom of this plan.[86] He needed to accelerate his production schedule if *Birds* was to fulfill promises made in the prospectus, and he thus proposed publishing "8 or 10 Numbers per annum," or twice as many plates as previously thought advisable.[87] As predicted, many more people were needed to meet this ambitious goal even though there were already dozens of colorists and engravers, as well as his son Victor and collaborators such as William McGillivray working on *Birds* in Britain.[88] From 1833, John Woodhouse became more involved as both taxidermist and artist; Lucy Audubon assumed greater responsibility in arrangements and continued to work as a teacher to support her family; John Bachman became more involved in collecting specimens and information; and, Maria Martin did her part by painting botanicals and insects in the studio on the ground floor of her home in Charleston.

It was Audubon's good fortune that in Maria Martin he found an assistant who valued service to others. She found it next to impossible to do less

FIGURE 25. (opposite) Mistletoe (*Phoradendron serotinum*) by Maria Martin, winter 1836–1837. Study for Havell edition, *Birds of America*, plate 369, varied thrush (*Ixoreus naevius*) and mountain mocking bird (sage thrasher/*Oreoscoptes montanus*). Watercolor, graphite, and black ink; 54.3 x 35.2 cm (21⅜ x 13⅞ in). 1863.17.369. Purchased by public subscription from Mrs. John J. Audubon. Collection of the New-York Historical Society. Digital image created by Oppenheimer Edition.

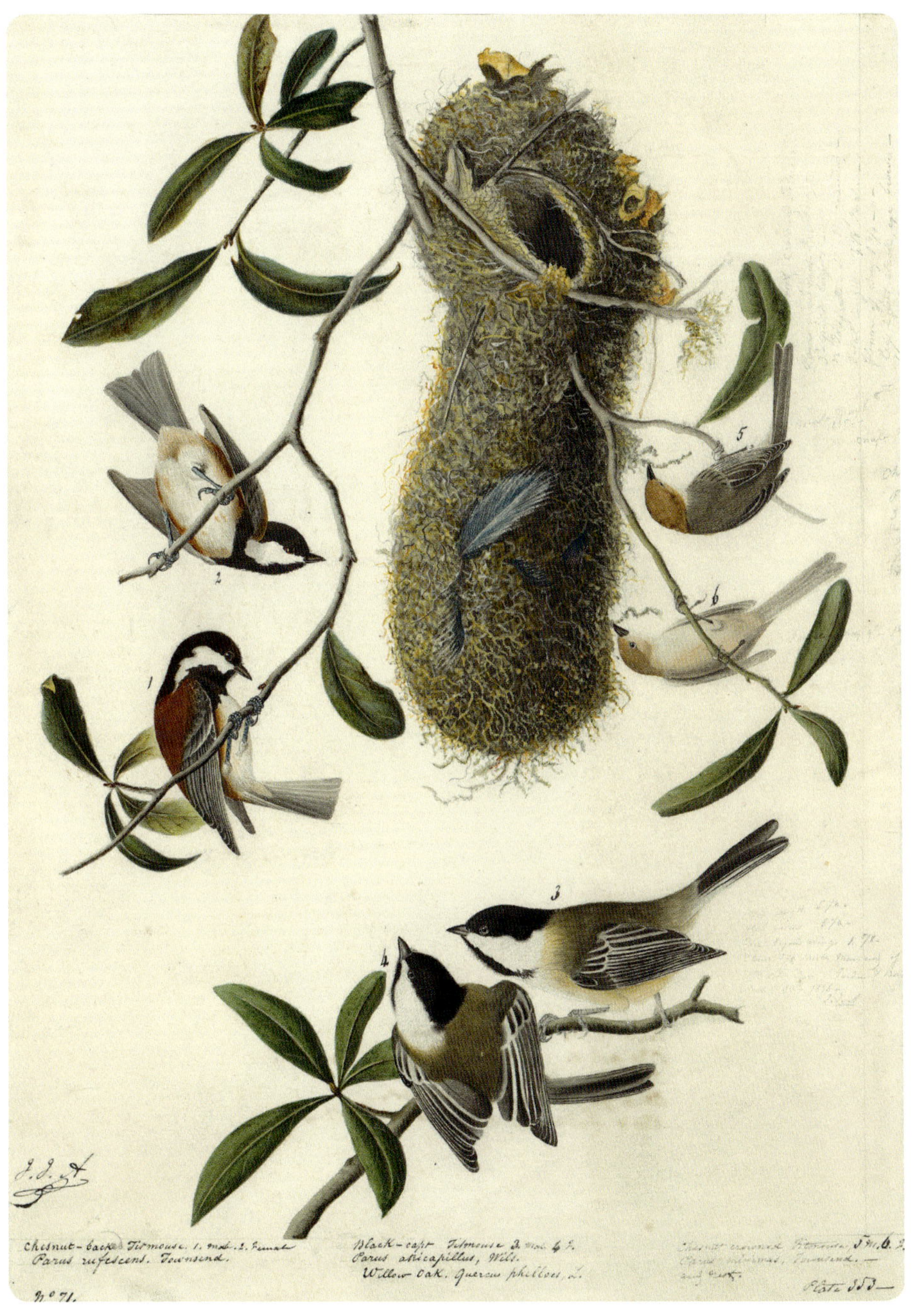

FIGURE 26. Willow oak (*Quercus phellos*) and bird nest by Maria Martin, 1836. Study for Havell edition, *Birds of America*, plate 353, chestnut crowned titmouse (bushtit/*Psaltriparus minimus*), black-capt titmouse (black-capped chickadee/*Poecile atricapillus*), chestnut-backed chickadee (*Poecile rufescens*). Watercolor, graphite, gouache, and black ink; 48.4 x 34.6 cm (19 1/16 x 13 5/8 in). 1863.17.353. Purchased by public subscription from Mrs. John J. Audubon. Collection of the New-York Historical Society. Digital image created by Oppenheimer Edition.

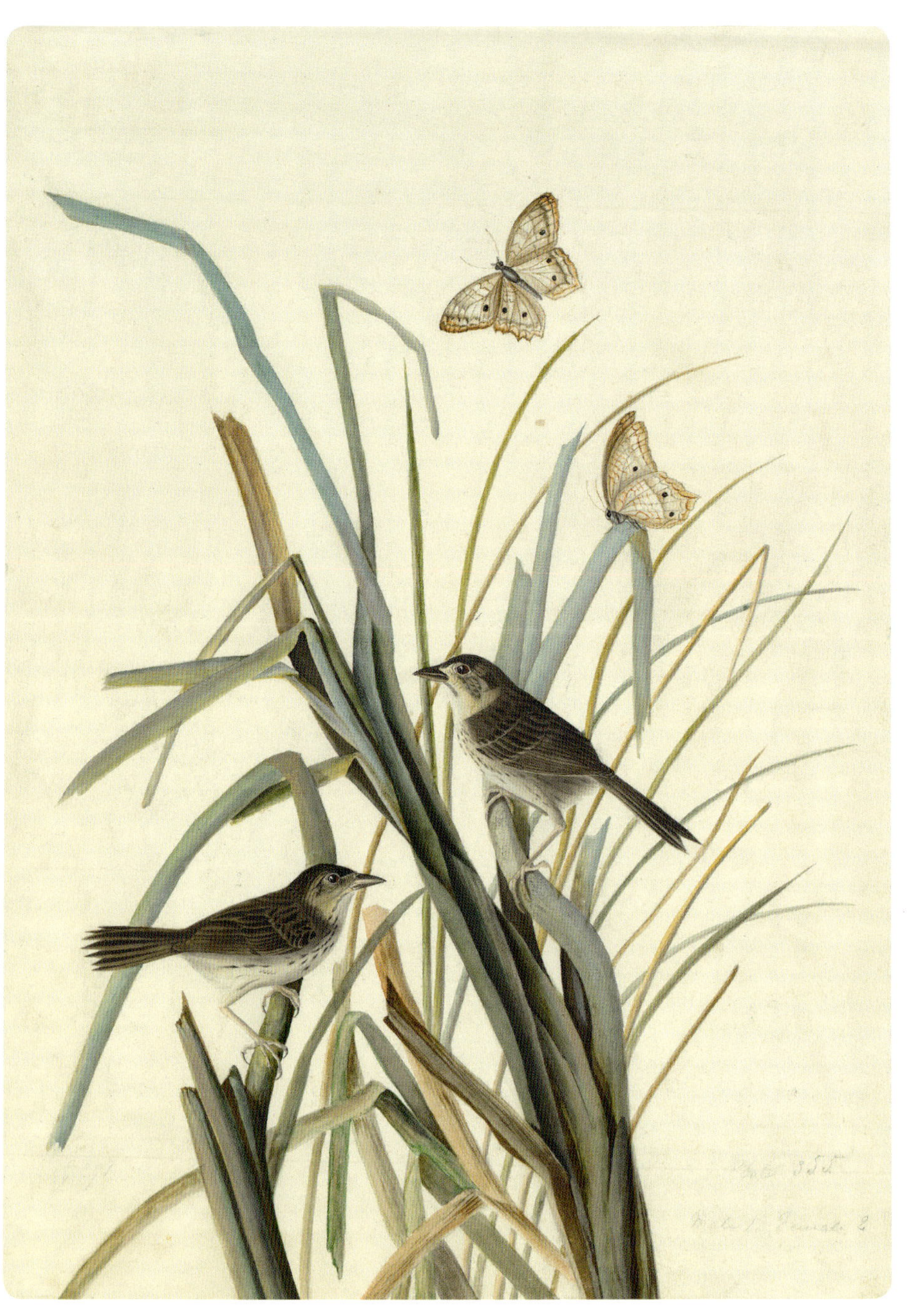

FIGURE 27. Reeds and white peacock butterflies (*Anartia jatrophae*) by Maria Martin, Dec. 1833. Study for Havell edition, *Birds of America*, plate 355, McGillivray's Finch (seaside sparrow/*Ammodramus maritimus*). Watercolor and graphite; 50.6 x 36 cm (19 15/16 x 14 3/16 in). 1863.17.355. Purchased by public subscription from Mrs. John J. Audubon. Collection of the New-York Historical Society. Digital image created by Oppenheimer Edition.

than requested, and as revealed in a letter requesting Bachman to collect and preserve birds in the one month of the year when church duties could not be set aside, he knew it. In November 1834, Audubon suggested that if responsibilities associated with the annual synod meeting meant the reverend was unable to fill his requests "punctually," he should "tell our Dear Sweetheart to attend to it—[adding] I know her well—nay better than you do yourself and I am thereby assured that she will do all for my sake in her power."[89] Although Audubon had not called on Maria's assistance for the six months previous, he did not doubt she was at his disposal and, for the most part, he was correct. When, for example, it became clear that drawings of insects could be of use, Maria Martin turned her attention to entomology.

With few models to emulate in what was still a nascent science in the United States, Maria Martin nonetheless adopted the approach that had worked when learning to paint botanicals: she copied the work of other artists. Her aesthetic and subject matter suggest she may have consulted John Abbot's *Natural History of the Rarer Lepidopterous Insects of Georgia* (two volumes, 1797), but most of her inspiration came from Thomas Say's *American Entomology* (3 volumes, 1824–1828).[90] She copied the butterflies and moths, wasps and flies, midges and weevils, locusts and beetles by Charles-Alexandre Lesueur (1778–1846), W. W. Wood, H. B. Bridport, and Titian Peale (1799–1885), the artists who illustrated Say's volumes.

Typically taking her lead from Audubon, she had to use her own judgment when it came to entomology. He was not at his best when painting insects, and he was unlikely to recommend Say's work as her inspiration. Whether he approved of figures drawn by Lesueur, Wood, or Bridport is unknown, but he was not impressed by Titian Peale, and his opinion of Say was little better.[91] When the first volume of *American Entomology* was published, Audubon ridiculed it by comparing it to *Wanderings in South America* (1825), an often-embellished and fanciful book by Charles Waterton (1782–1865), an amateur naturalist in England. He mocked Waterton for having mentioned insects fewer than six times in a book purportedly on natural history, and especially for his claim to have seen but one "bug" between New York and Quebec. Audubon believed his knowledge of the insect world vastly superior to

FIGURE 28. (opposite) Large orange sulphur butterfly (*Phoebis agarithe*) by Maria Martin, c. 1832–1833. This figure was possibly inspired by the American brimstone butterfly (*Papilio eubule*) depicted by John Abbot in *The Natural History of the Lepidopterous Insects of Georgia* (1797), 1:9. Watercolor; 24 x 17.8 cm (9.5 x 7 in). 1918.14.15. Courtesy of the Charleston Museum.

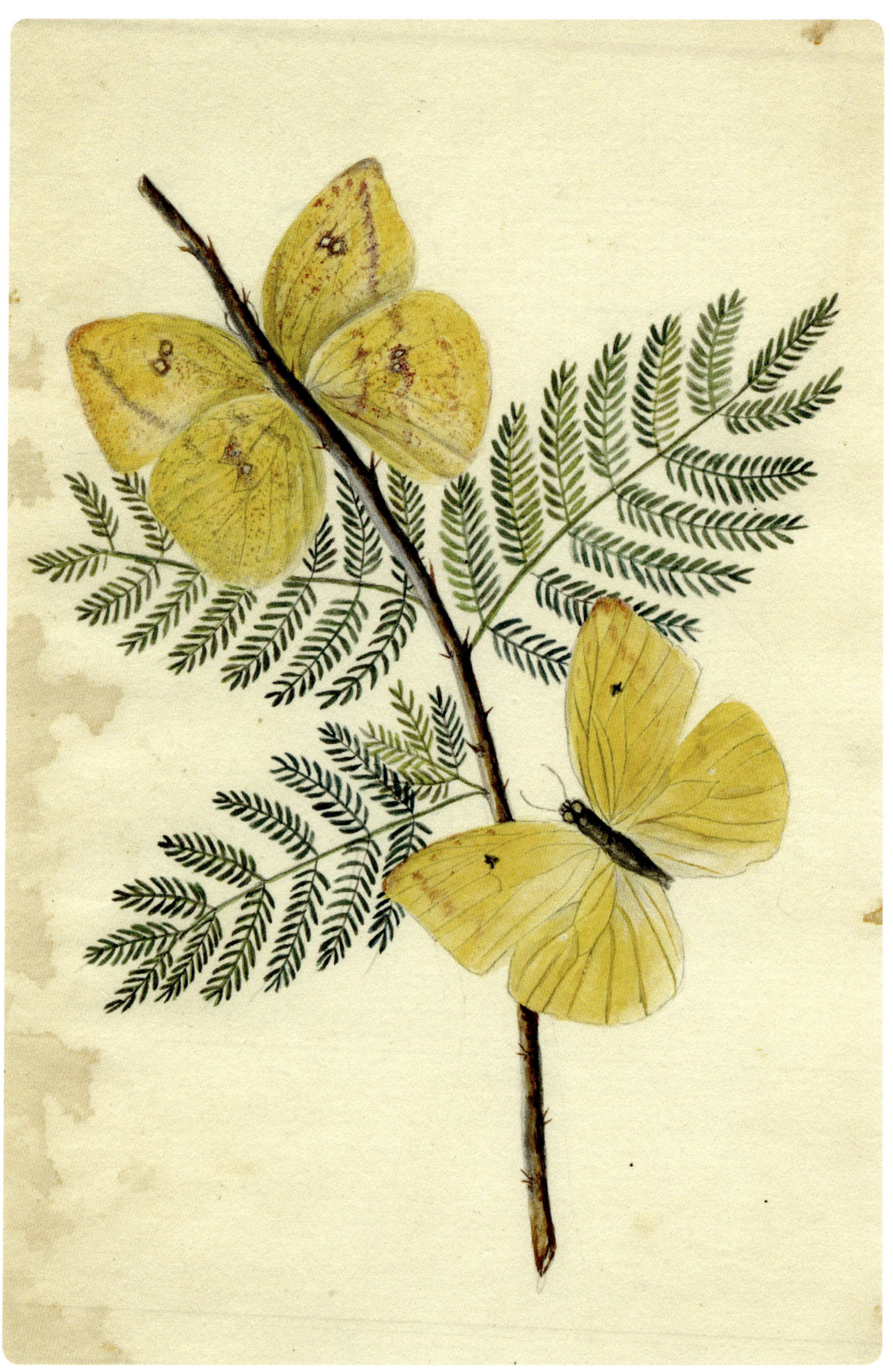

both, and he wondered how such allegedly learned men could know so little about insects, writing contemptuously: "American bugs!!! Waterton only saw one—I have seen millions. . . . And Thomas Say [1787–1834] has described the same species over and over again, probably hundreds of times."[92] Admittedly *American Entomology* was preliminary and partial, but Audubon would have had difficulty recommending a better "American" source. In 1833, it was the best monograph on the main orders—the Diptera, Lepidoptera, Hymenoptera, and Coleoptera—as well as on the Orthoptera and Neuroptera.

Maria Martin's knowledge of entomological illustration benefited greatly by studying the images in Say's volumes, and she filled two sketchbooks with "ugly worms & pretty butterflies." Some were identical replicas of illustrations in *American Entomology*; others, like the Florida atala or coontie hairstreak (*Eumaeus atala*; Poey, 1832), were rare; and yet others were still unidentified species. Cherished family possessions, her sketchbooks were prized for their artistry more than for the scientific information they contained, and while some might have viewed her sketchbooks as deficient because she did not always provide names for the figures she painted, such criticism ignores that her ability to provide names for the species she painted was limited. Even though many of them had been identified and classified by Linnaeus or by his student Johan Christian Fabricus (1745–1808), these men focused on describing and classifying new species. They provided little assistance to novice entomologists who needed illustrations in order to identify specimens. As a result, access to Linnaeus's *Ordines et genera insectorum; or, Systematic arrangement of insects collated with the different systems of Geoffrey, Schaeffer and Scopoli* (translated by Thomas Pattinson Yeats [d. 1783], 1773) and to *Entomologia* (1789) did not aid her. In fact, many of her figures were painted from specimens. Using her keen powers of observation rather than familiarity with the scientific literature, she portrayed insects so accurately that they can be identified from her images. Species such as the faithful beauty or Uncle Sam moth (*Composia fidelissima*; Herrick-Schäffer, 1866), the Florida purplewing (*Eunica tatila tatila*; Herrick-Schäffer, 1855), and the snout butterfly (*Libytheana fulvescens*, Lathy, 1904) had not yet appeared in the scientific literature but Maria Martin painted them beautifully and accurately.

FIGURE 29. (opposite) Monarch butterfly (*Danaus plexippus*) by Maria Martin, c. 1832–1833. This is a copy of a figure by Titian Peale in Thomas Say, *American Entomology* (1824), plate. 54. Watercolor; 24 x 17.8 cm (9.5 x 7 in). 1918.14.2. Courtesy of the Charleston Museum.

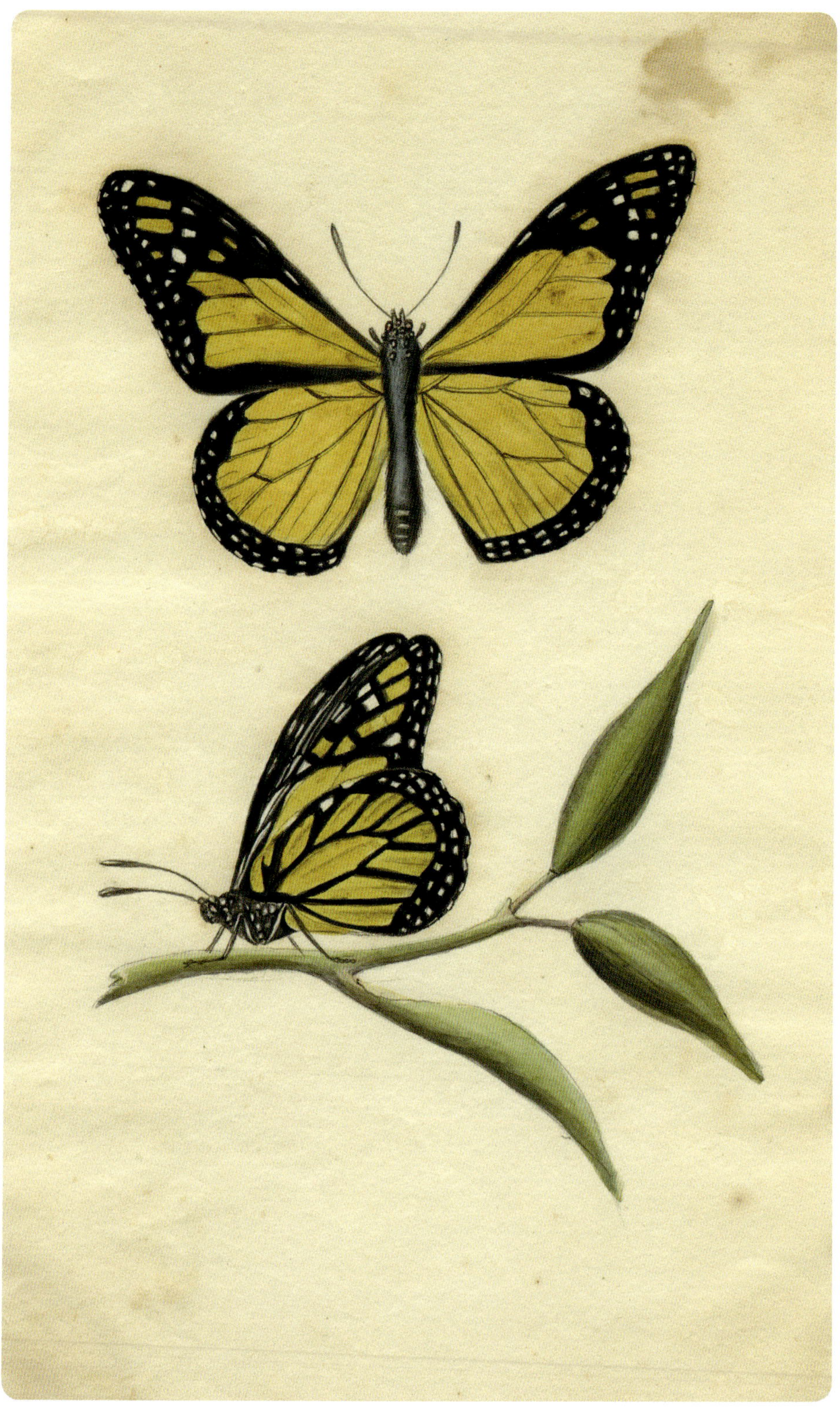

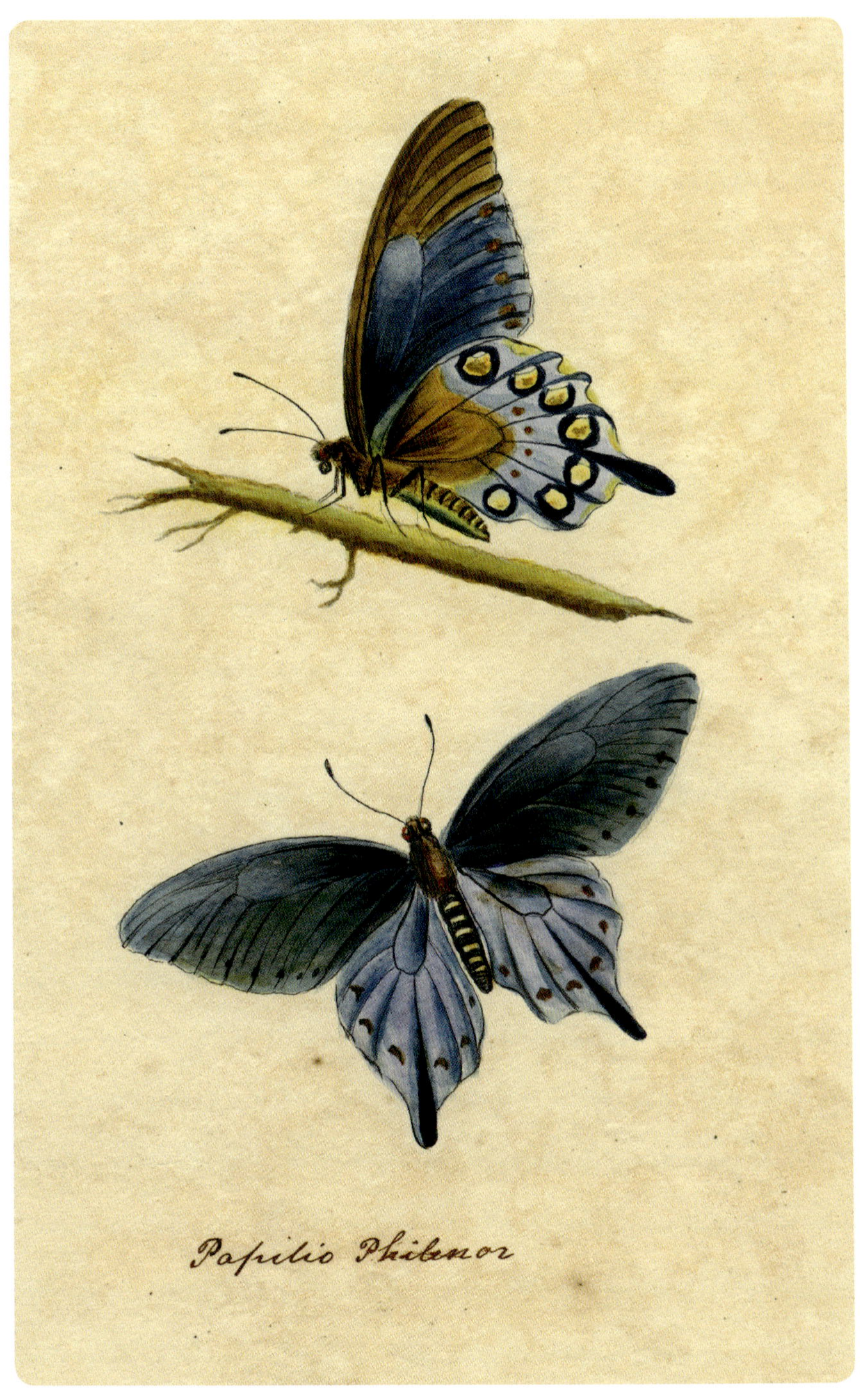

FIGURE 30. Pipevine swallowtail (*Battus philenor*) by Maria Martin, c. 1832–33. This is a copy of an unattributed figure (*Papilio philenor*) in Say, *American Entomology* (1817; 1824), plate 1. Watercolor; 24 x 17.8 cm (9.5 x 7 in). 1918.14.29. Courtesy of the Charleston Museum.

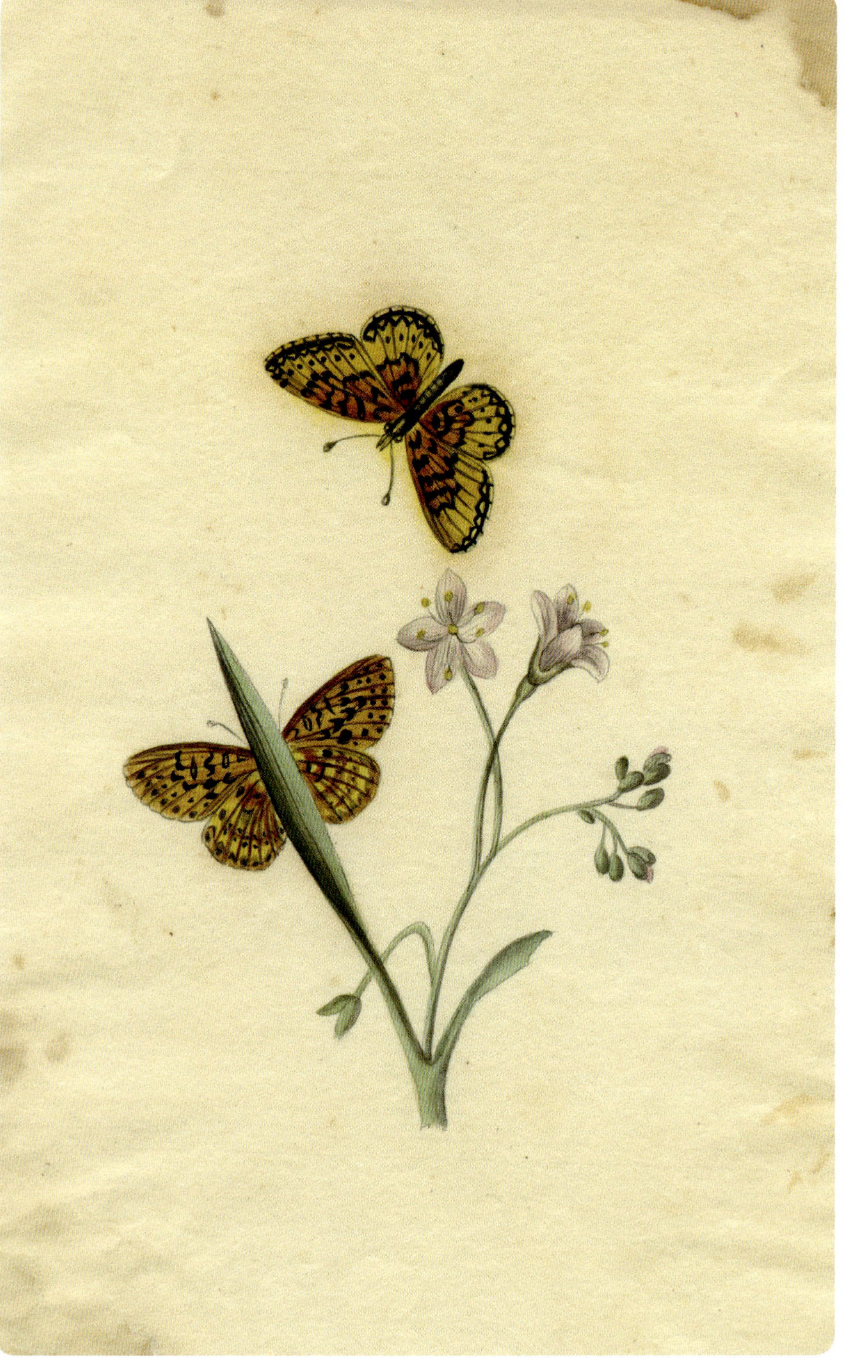

FIGURE 31. Small pearl bordered fritillary (*Boloria selene*) by Maria Martin, c. 1832–1833. This is a copy of a figure (*Melitaea myrina*) by Titian Peale in Say, *American Entomology* (1824 and 1828), plate. 46. Watercolor; 24 x 17.8 cm (9.5 x 7 in). 1918.14.7. Courtesy of the Charleston Museum.

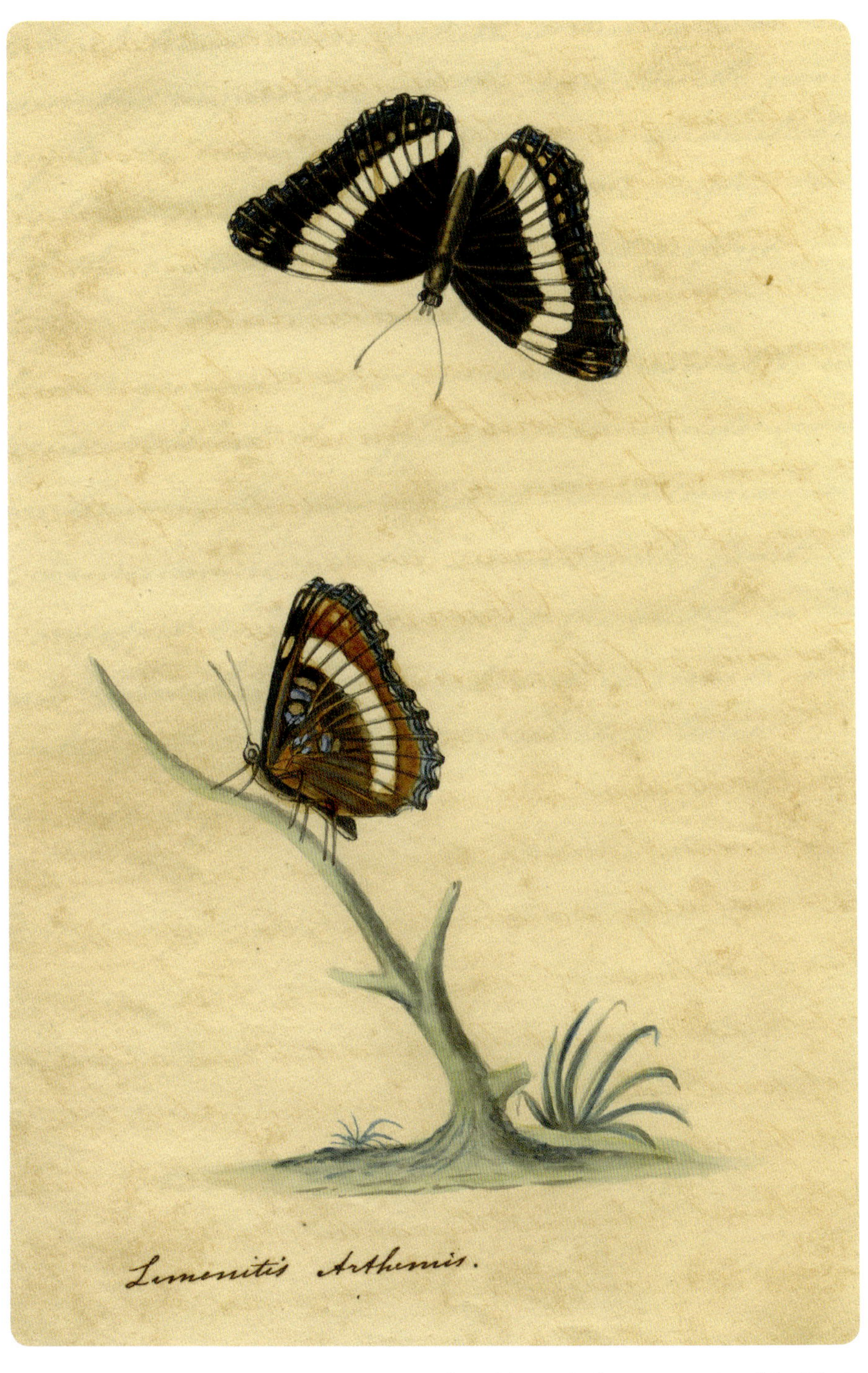

FIGURE 32. Red-spotted purple or white admiral butterfly (*Limenitis arthemis*) by Maria Martin, c. 1832–1833. This is a copy of a figure by W. W. Wood, in Say, *American Entomology* (1825), plate 23. Watercolor; 24 x 17.8 cm (9.5 x 7 in). 1918.14.29. Courtesy of the Charleston Museum.

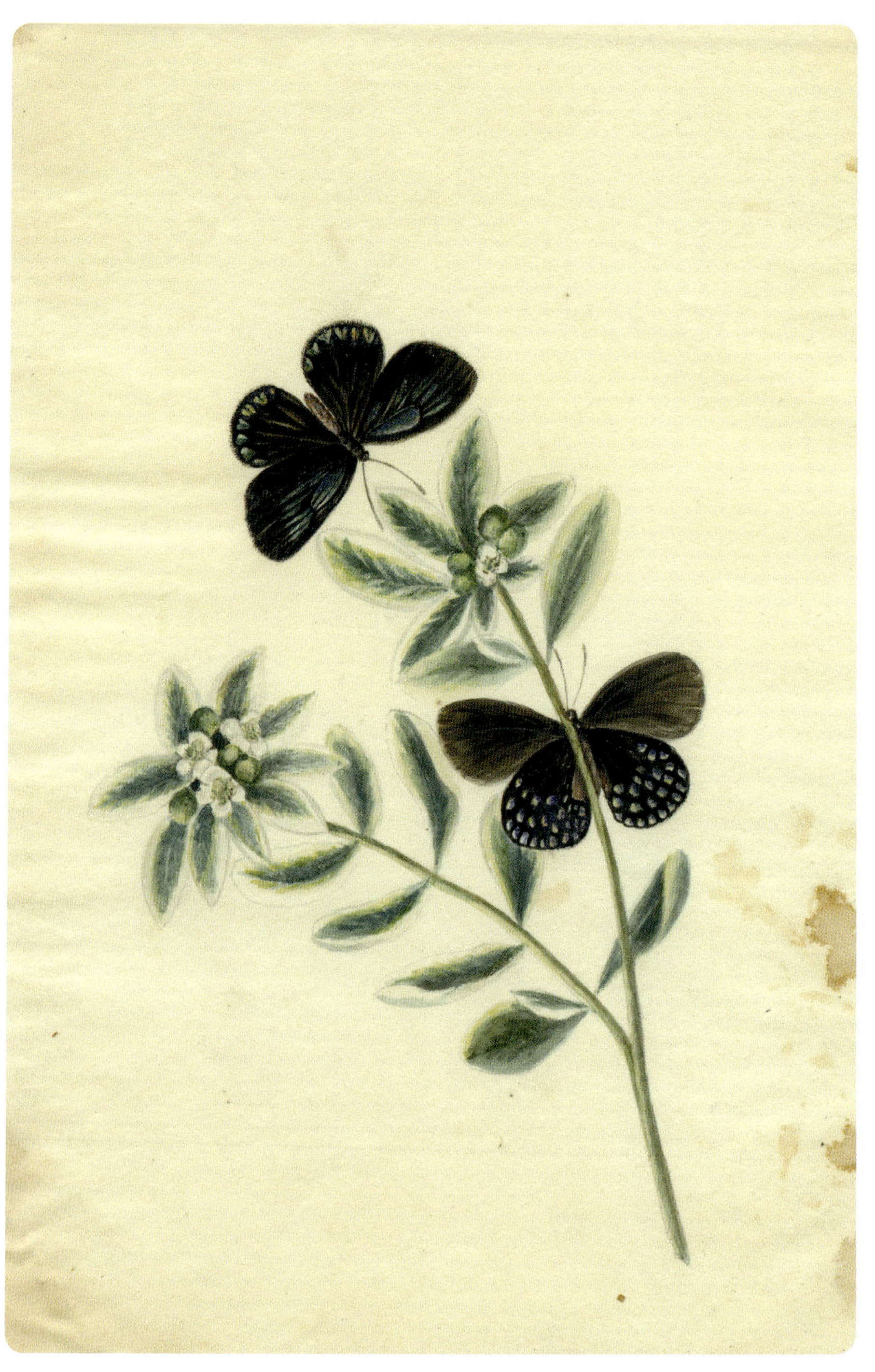

FIGURE 33. Melissa Arctic butterfly (*Oeneis melissa*) by Maria Martin, c. 1832–1833. This is a copy of a figure by Titian Peale in Say, *American Entomology* (1828), plate 50 (*Hippcarchia semidea*). Watercolor; 24 x 17.8 cm (9.5 x 7 in). 1918.14.24. Courtesy of the Charleston Museum.

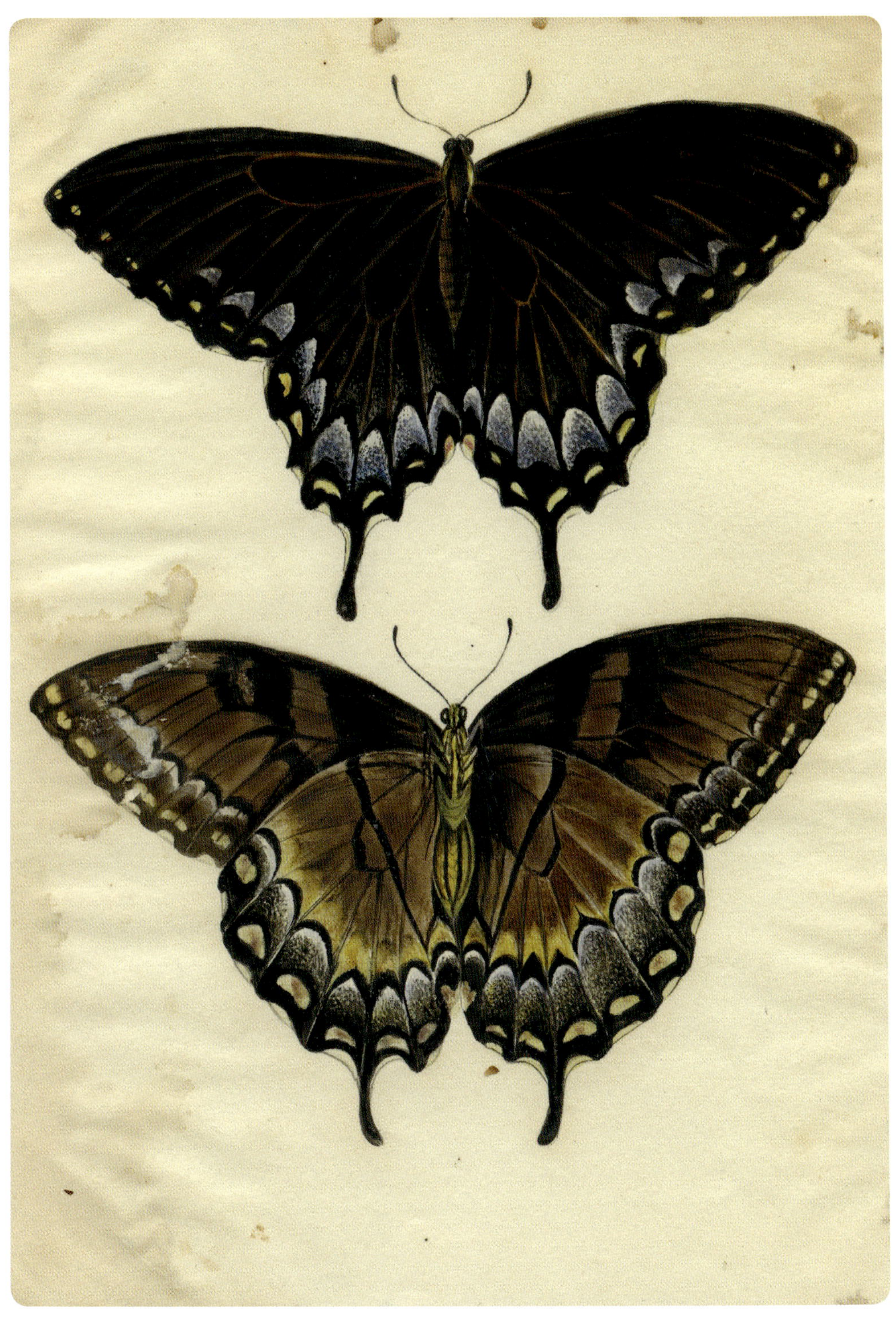

FIGURE 34. Spicebush swallowtail (*Papilio Troilus troilus*) by Maria Martin, c. 1832–1833. Watercolor; 24 x 17.8 cm (9.5 x 7 in). 1918.14.6. Courtesy of the Charleston Museum.

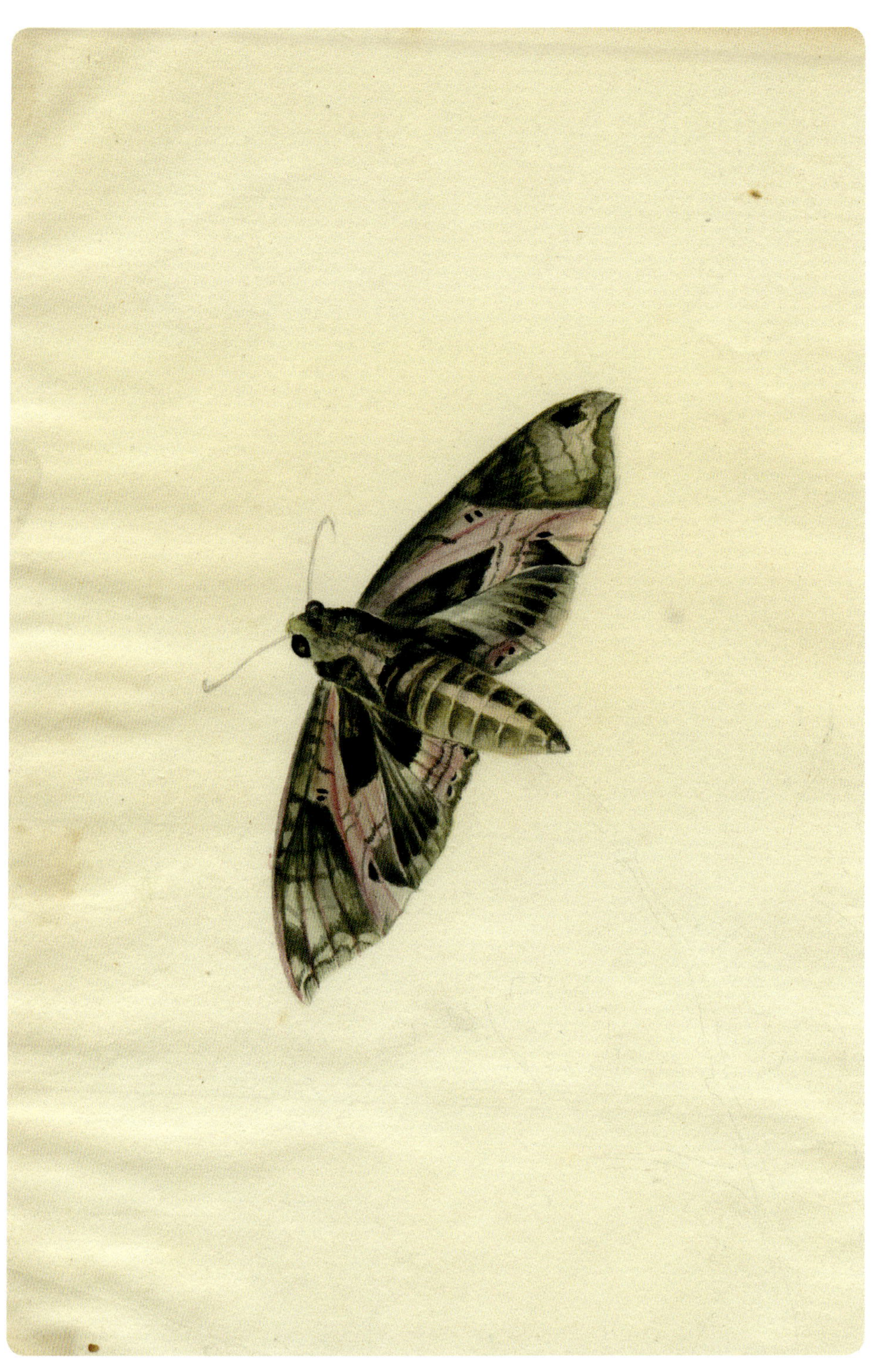

FIGURE 35. Pandorus sphinx moth (*Eumorpha pandorus*) by Maria Martin, c. 1832–1833. Watercolor; 24 x 17.8 cm (9.5 x 7 in). 1918.14.14. Courtesy of the Charleston Museum.

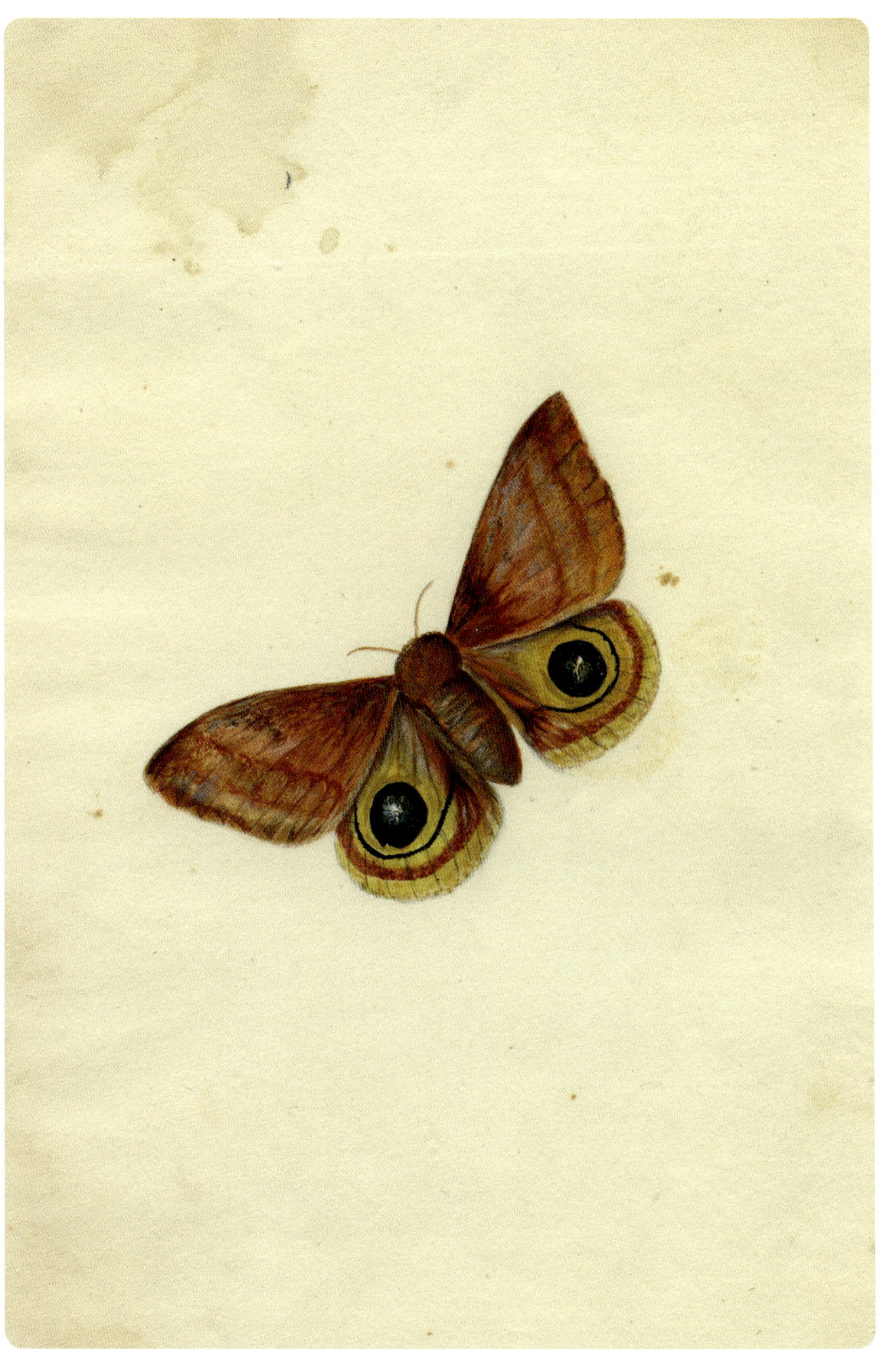

FIGURE 36. Io moth (wild silk moth/*Automeris io*) by Maria Martin, c. 1832–1833. Watercolor; 24 x 17.8 cm (9.5 x 7 in). 1918.14.19. Courtesy of the Charleston Museum.

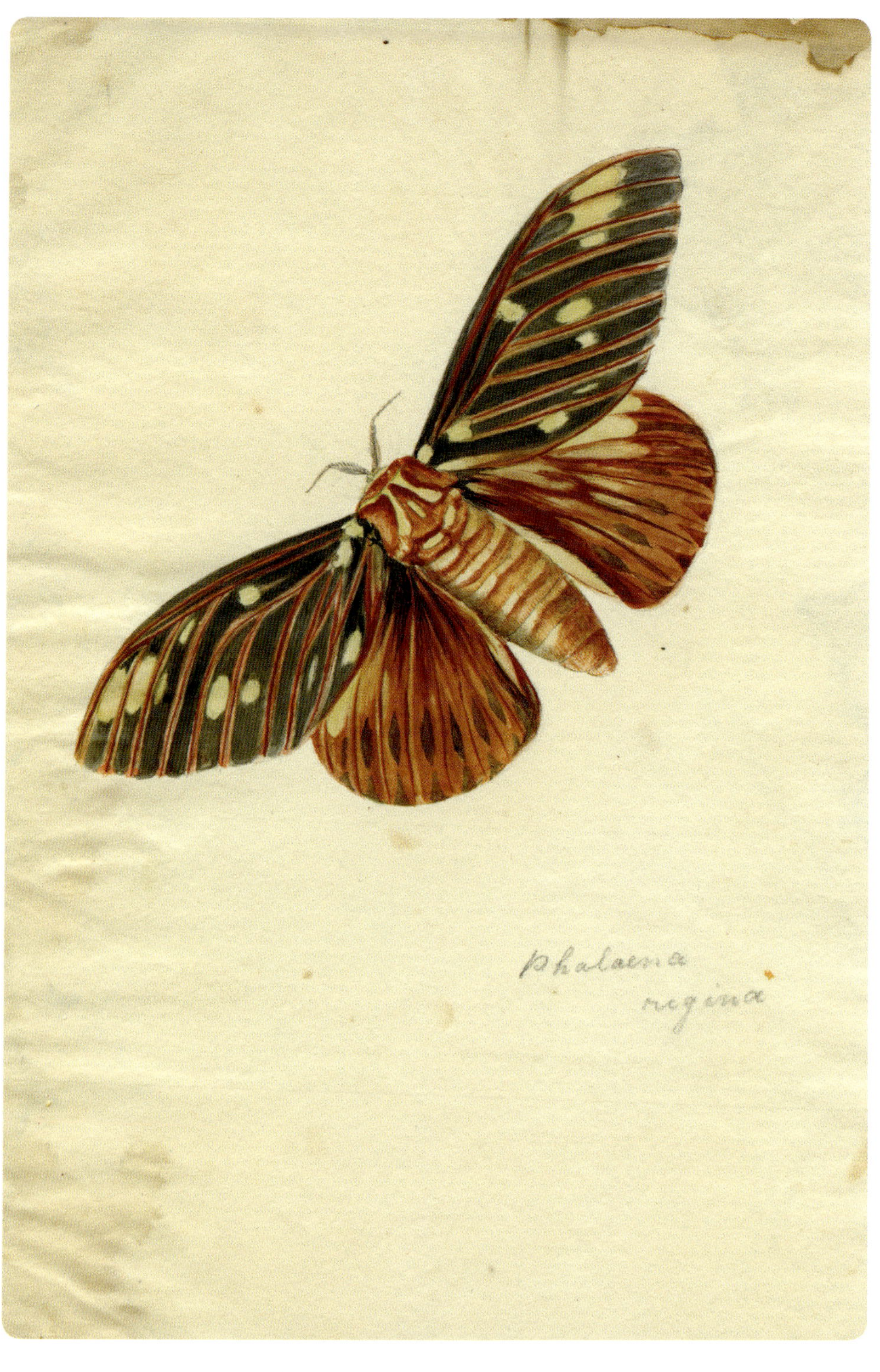

FIGURE 37. Royal walnut moth (*Citheronia regalis*) by Maria Martin, c. 1832–1833. Watercolor; 24 x 17.8 cm (9.5 x 7 in). 1918.14.21. Courtesy of the Charleston Museum.

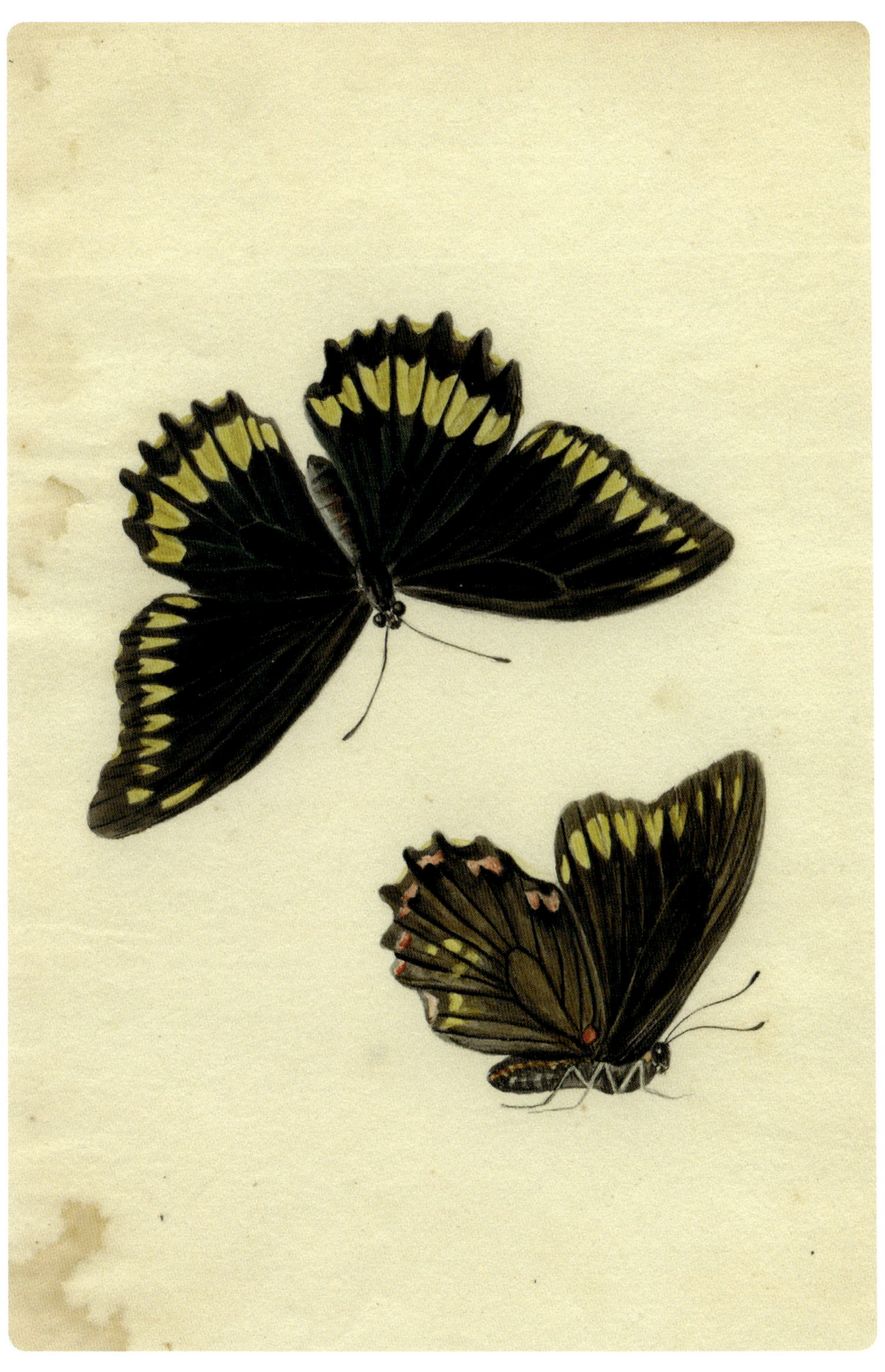

FIGURE 38. Gold rimmed swallowtail (*Battus polydamas*) by Maria Martin, c. 1832–1833. Watercolor; 24 x 17.8 cm (9.5 x 7 in). 1918.14.22. Courtesy of the Charleston Museum.

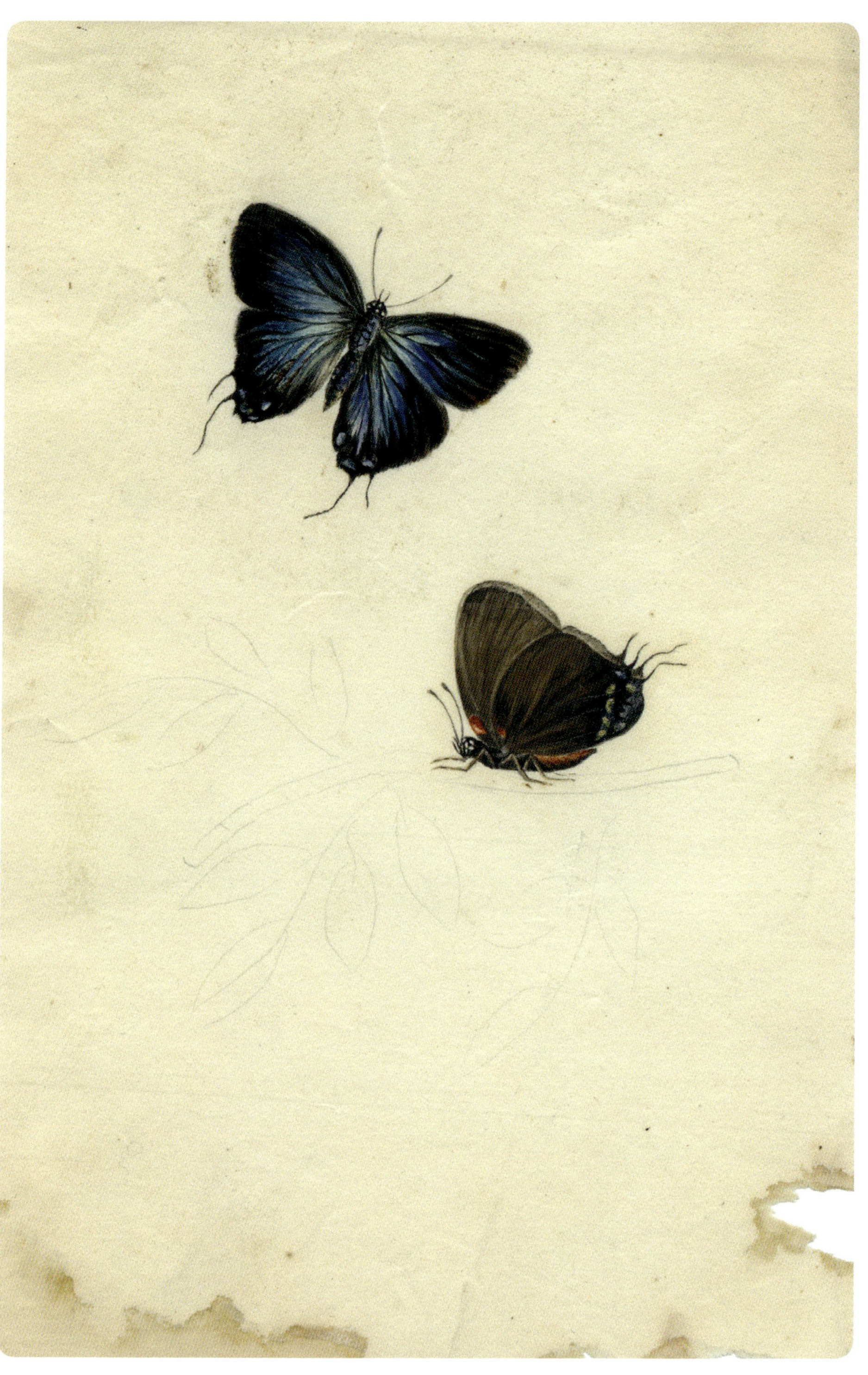

FIGURE 39. Great blue hairstreak (*Atlides h. halesus*) by Maria Martin, c. 1832–1833. Watercolor; 24 x 17.8 cm (9.5 x 7 in). 1918.14.5. Courtesy of the Charleston Museum.

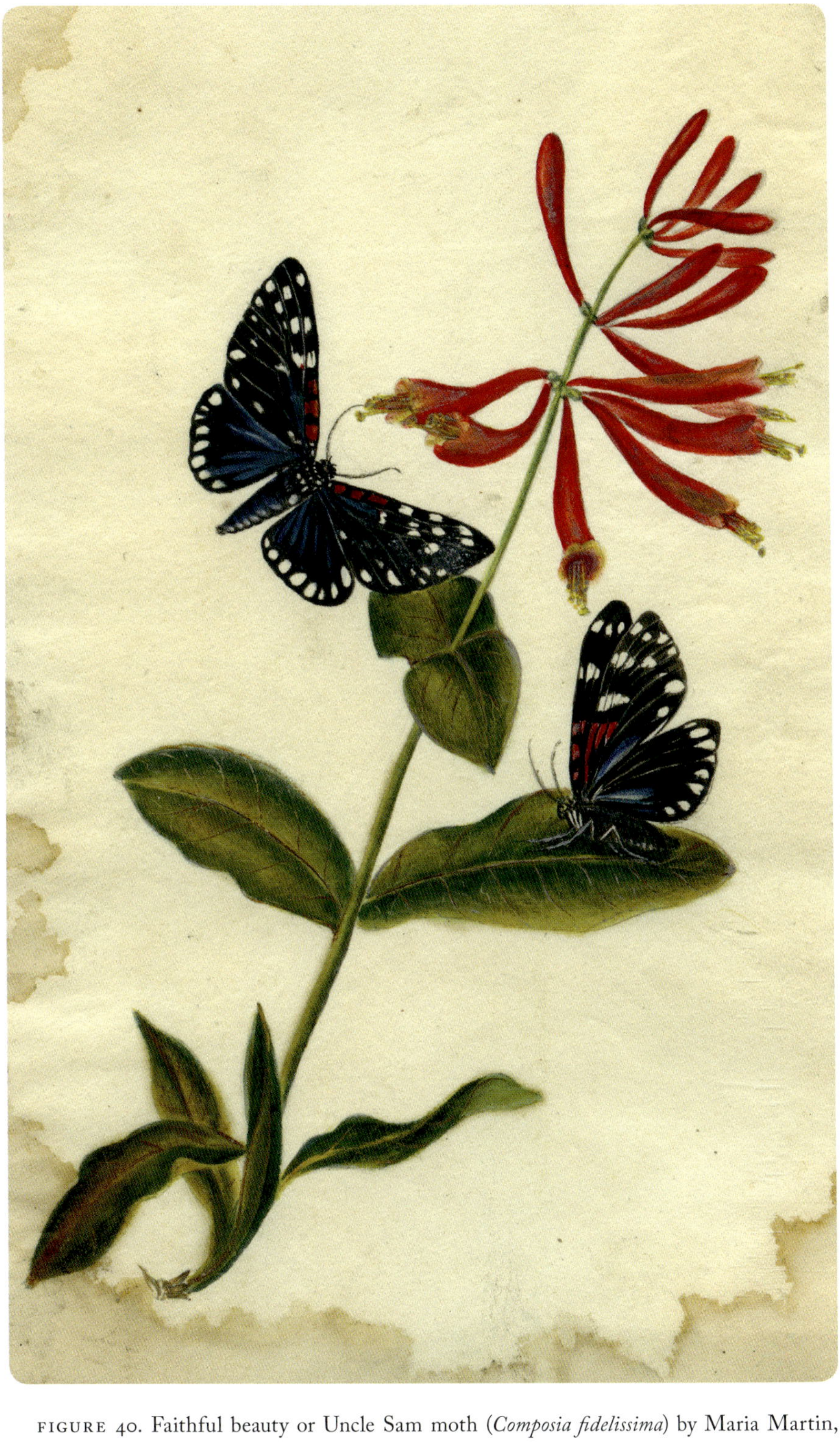

FIGURE 40. Faithful beauty or Uncle Sam moth (*Composia fidelissima*) by Maria Martin, c.1832–33. Watercolor; 24 x 17.8 cm (9.5 x 7 in). 1918.14.1. Courtesy of the Charleston Museum.

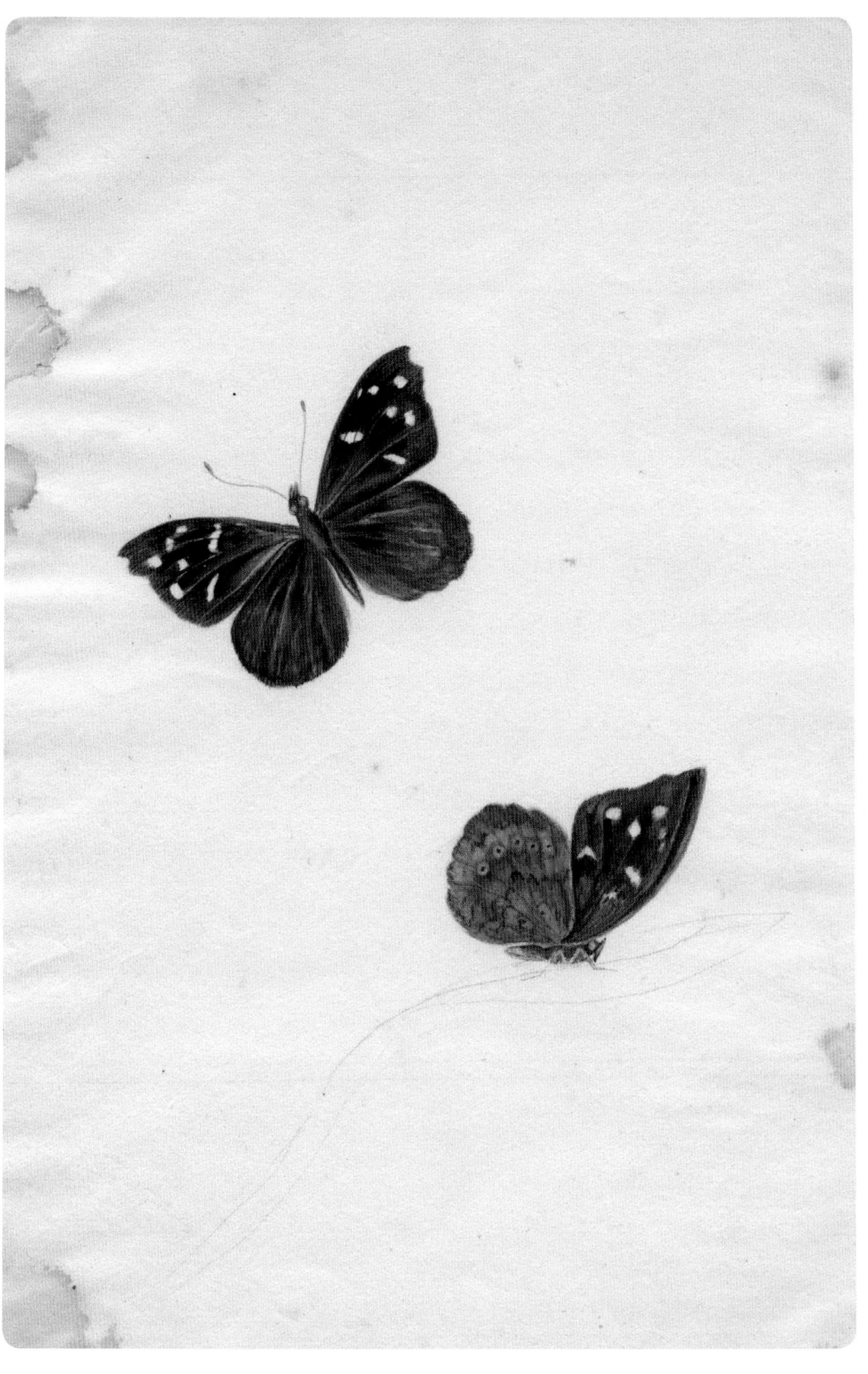

FIGURE 41. Florida purplewing (*Eunica t. tatila*) by Maria Martin, c. 1832–1833. Watercolor; 24 x 17.8 cm (9.5 x 7 in). 1918.14.23. Courtesy of the Charleston Museum.

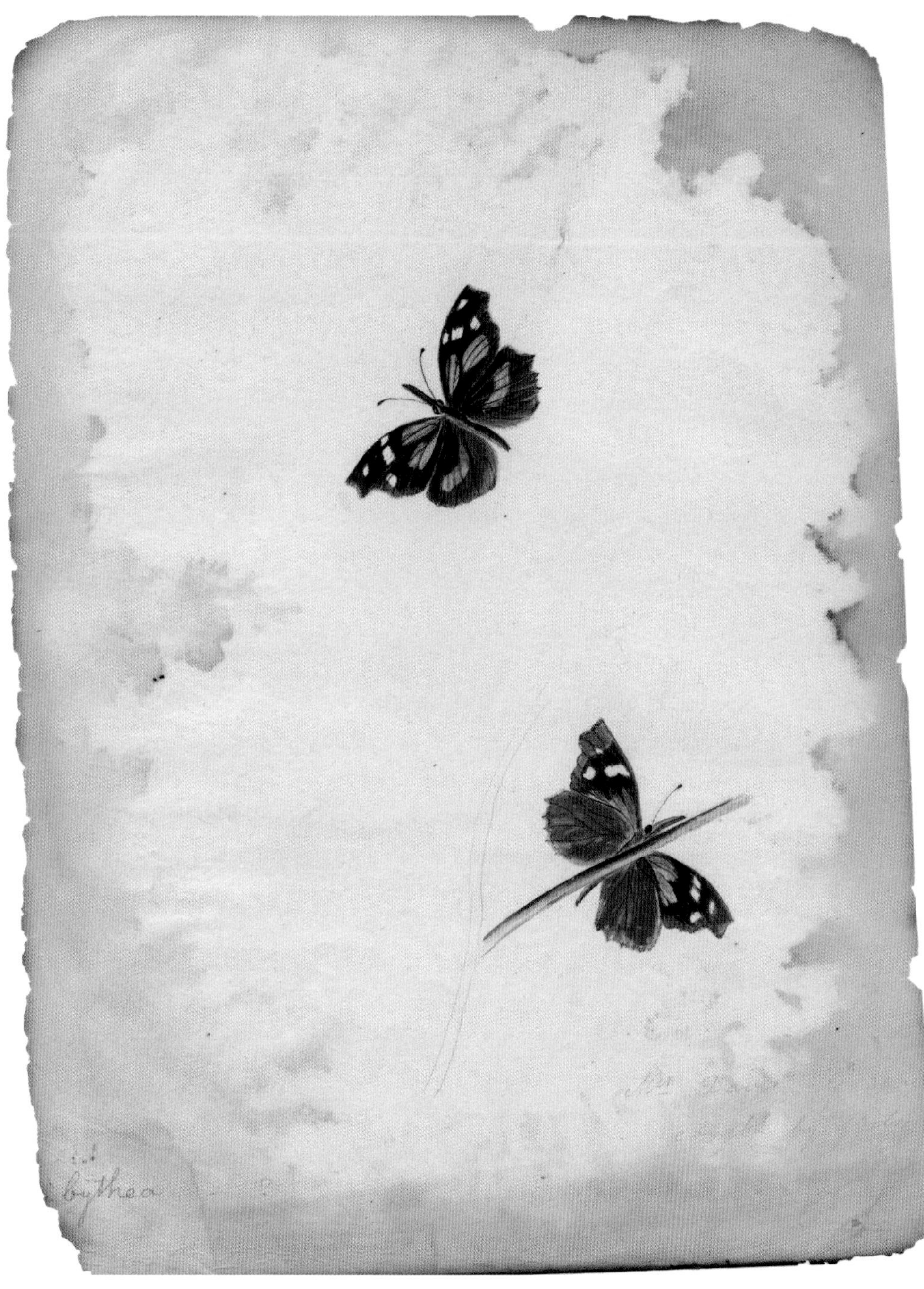

FIGURE 42. Snout Butterfly (*Libytheana fulvescens*, Lathy, 1904) by Maria Martin, c. 1832–1833. Watercolor; 24 x 17.8 cm (9.5 x 7 in). 1918.14.20. Labelled *Libythea bachmani* on the sheet; a notation indicates it was discovered nearby, in the garden of family friend Mrs. Davis. Courtesy of the Charleston Museum.

So accomplished did she become at entomological illustration that Audubon referred to Maria Martin's insects as "perhaps, the best I've seen" as early as 1833. He also added her figures to a number of his paintings: her common buckeye (*Junonia coenia*) and the coontie hairstreak (*Eumaeus atala*) joined her flame azalea in the painting of Swainson's warbler (*Limnothlypis swainsonii*, plate 198), her white peacock butterfly (*Anartia jatrophae*) hovered near the reeds she painted for Audubon's figure of the seaside sparrow (*Ammodramus maritimus*, plate 355), and a scarab beetle (*Dynastes tityus*) was added to Audubon's study of the white-tailed kite (*Elanus leucurus*).[93] Had she the time to paint insects while assisting Audubon with the Townsend-Nuttall specimens in 1836–1837, she could have painted more of these little creatures, and it is quite likely that she added the beetles placed on the Carolina allspice (*Calycanthus floridus*) on plate 393 and the beetles and larva found on the dead tree limb on plate 416; however, the western birds were painted hurriedly, and only a few of the insects collected by Thomas Nuttall found their way onto the paintings.[94] Audubon added, for example, a pair of sheepmoths (*Hemileuca nuttalli*; F. H. H. Strecker, 1875) to his painting of Say's phoebe (*Sayornis saya*), western kingbird (*Tyrannus verticalis*), and scissor-tailed flycatcher (*Tyrannus forficatus*) for plate 359, and a zephyr anglewing butterfly (*Polygonia gracilis*; W. H. Edwards, 1870) appeared alongside the black-headed grosbeak (*Pheucticus melanocephalus*), the evening grosbeak (*Coccothraustes vespertinus*) and pine grosbeak (*Pinicola enucleator*) perched in the branches Maria Martin added for folio plate 373.[95] Although uncredited for this figure, Maria Martin's deft touch suggests she painted it. This finely detailed image is far superior to the clumsily rendered moths painted by the visually impaired Audubon.

Despite being good at painting insects, Maria Martin was not fond of doing so. She was especially averse to painting butterflies.[96] Observing them flit around the garden as she sketched them "from nature" was one thing; pinning them to a board so as to complete the painting another. According to Edward Donovan (1768–1837), author of the preeminent work on entomological specimen preparation, anyone working with insects had to know how to capture and "manage" living specimens, how to preserve insects, and even how to kill them so they remained useful for scientific study.[97] Procedures both cruel and humane were laid out in his book, and neither was for the faint of heart. For example, while some entomologists were able to eviscerate and skin caterpillars without first anesthetizing them, Donovan suggested dropping them into boiling water before submerging them in spirits. When it came to butterflies and moths, advice intended to minimize cruelty was almost useless, especially

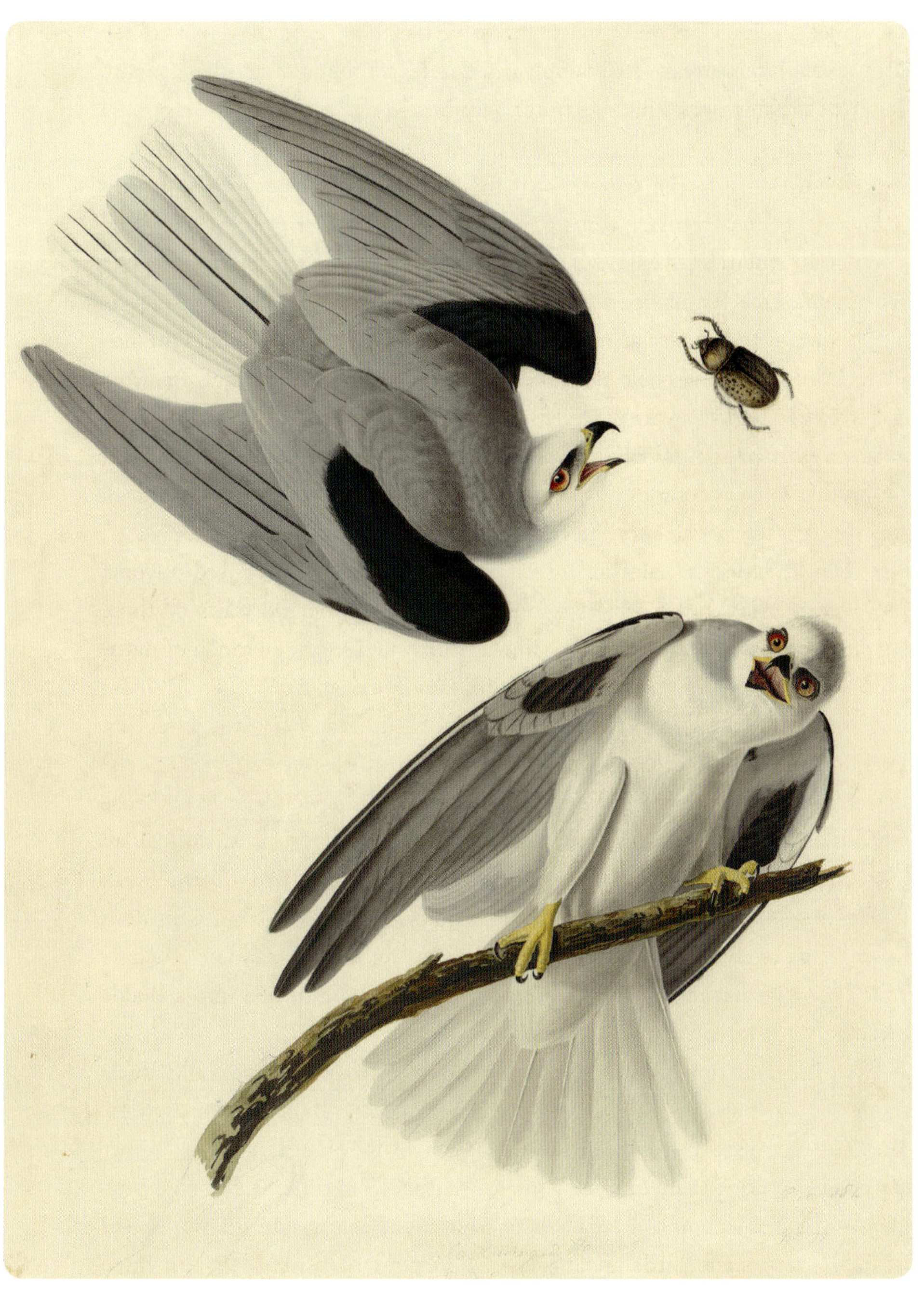

FIGURE 43. A female beetle (*Dynastes tityus*) by Maria Martin, 1834. Drawn on Audubon's study of the black winged hawk (white-tailed or black-shouldered kite/*Elanus leucurus* or *Elanus axillaris*), it was removed before engraving plate 352 for *Birds of America*. Watercolor, graphite, black ink, and gouache; 72.9 x 54 cm (28 11/16 x 21¼ in). 1863.17.352. Purchased by public subscription from Mrs. John J. Audubon. Collection of the New-York Historical Society. Digital image created by Oppenheimer Edition.

for larger species. Donovan admitted they were seldom euthanized by sticking pins through the thorax. They simply did not die from impaling. He therefore suggested dipping the impaling pins in nitric acid and placing a drop of acid in the pinhole.

Available from the Charleston Library Society, Donovan's *Instructions for Collecting and Preserving Various Subjects of Natural History* (1805) provided detailed instructions to aspiring entomologists, and while Maria's familiarity with Donovan is less obvious than her knowledge of Say's *Entomology,* she was well aware of the cruelty associated with the study of insects. As an entomological illustrator, she could not avoid it; and, as a close student of *American Entomology,* she was aware of contemporary debates.[98] Modeled on Donovan's *British Insects* (1805), *American Entomology* contained comments on preserving procedures in Say's description of the eastern tiger swallowtail (*Papilio glaucus*), and this was one of the butterflies Maria Martin copied in her sketchbook.

Her distaste for painting insects could hardly have surprised anyone; however, Maria Martin worked tirelessly, perfecting her portraits of these small creatures. In the process, she unwittingly indulged in a branch of natural history that was becoming both popular and profitable. Much to the dismay of her mentor, this burgeoning branch of natural history was rendering his efforts to sell ornithological specimens to collectors overseas difficult. Although Audubon shipped innumerable entomological specimens in response to requests from individuals such as John Children (1777–1852) at the British Museum, by 1835 he viewed the growing fascination with "*Bugs*" with shock and horror.[99] While "*mounted*" bird specimens were being sold for a pittance in England, a beetle sold for fifty pounds sterling (or $250.00), and he was provoked to write Bachman that: "I almost wish I could be turned into a Beetle myself!"[100]

At the same time, Audubon had long enjoyed the company of individuals interested in "bugs." The Liverpool merchant and entomological aficionado, André Melly (1802–1851), for example, was one of the first naturalists he met after disembarking there in 1826.[101] Invited frequently to dine, Audubon examined Melly's collection of exotic Asian insects, and he gave him a watercolor depicting two water birds and three Lepidoptera. In turn, Melly provided Audubon with letters of introduction. Setting aside his animosity toward those paying outrageous prices for bugs, he contacted Melly thinking he could facilitate Bachman's entomological interests by arranging a shipment of insects from his old acquaintance. Apparently lost in transit, the collection was never received by Bachman; nonetheless, Audubon urged him to strike up a conversation with a man whose expertise was indisputable. Melly had "a collection of 13,000 species of Insects *named* and *described*," and Bachman could not but benefit from his knowledge. All might not be lost with the specimens.

Bachman began the suggested conversation a year later, in 1836, but it was not with Melly. He had alluded to his views on entomology in 1833 when he gave a talk to the horticultural society of Charleston, but as Audubon was packing to leave England, Bachman was writing a paper "On the Habits of Insects."[102] Published before the end of the year in the *Southern Literary Journal*, his essay was republished many times as "The Morals of Entomology." Aimed at an educated readership that might not be acquainted with entomology but would nonetheless be impressed by his familiarity with Linnaeus and Fabricus, Bachman's article was a combination of fairly objective observations and moralistic musings. With a nod to serious scientists, Bachman provided a few general descriptions of insect behavior before concluding rather improbably that the humanlike qualities he detected in these tiny creatures could only cause entomologists to be "at a loss to discern where instinct ends, and where reason begins."[103] Then, in an about-face, he devoted much of the remainder of his essay to demonstrating that insects lacked a vital human characteristic: the ability to feel pain. With a level of conviction that blinded him to the flaws in his argument, he abruptly transitioned to the heart of the matter. Entomologists were often accused of treating insects cruelly, and this was a charge he disputed.

Hardly unique in attempting to dispel this criticism, Bachman provided a lengthy disputation based on the assumption that if insects did not feel pain then entomologists could not be guilty of cruelty. Even though "acid, alcohol and steam" were used to euthanize specimens, he argued that an absence of struggle suggested insects died without pain. He could not contemplate any other possibility, and given that experts like Linnaeus held similar views, there was scant reason for him to do so. As he pointed out, the great classifier "denied the existence of a brain in insects," and this was support enough. And, in case there were lingering doubts about the significance of the anatomical deficiencies of insects, Bachman explained: "from their formation, they cannot be as susceptible of pain as beings, whose internal organization approaches nearer to that of man. And the more we examine their habits, the more sensible we are made of this truth." He concluded with a flourish, stating what he believed was obvious: "Now if insects were as susceptible of pain as man, think you that they would exhibit such insensibility to pain?"[104]

Unlike Thomas Say, who brusquely dismissed accusations of cruelty as unfounded, Bachman felt compelled to disabuse his accusers. He was wounded by the accusations, and he turned his attention to the main critics of entomology: women. Once refocused, he set aside what he considered objective evidence supporting his view that insects did not suffer as a result of entomological studies and he lectured those who might not be convinced by empirical evidence and logic—that is women, for being hypocrites. Women, he alleged, bore more guilt for suffering in the insect world through housekeeping than the entomologist did while fulfilling his sacred duty to uncover "God's revealed word." Forgetting he had just mustered evidence to show that insects felt no pain, he seemed to accept the views of his detractors when suggesting that the "fair" sex would embrace science if "collecting and preserving, admiring and studying those works of God, in which we behold his glory reflected" were substituted for criticism. He wrote passionately on behalf of his newest avocation, belittling those with contrary views: "Away with this affectation of sensibility; this generation will not pass away before the subject will be better understood, and woman, the fairest of God's works, will, instead of condemning, assist us in his study; and, as from the occupation we sometimes form an estimation of the character, let me ask, when and where have you ever found the student of nature a cruel man?" Unable to resist extolling the "innocent pursuits" of the naturalist, what began as a defense against the charge of cruelty concluded by pointing out that those who pursued "the cause of science" made everyone "better fitted for that higher state of intelligence, and that perfection of happiness, to which immortal minds are privileged to aspire." If his moralizing was insufficient to convince critics that the study of insects was a sacred quest, Bachman hoped that the moralizing of others might work, and he appealed to the literary leanings of his readers as he quoted one of the most popular poets of the period, James Thomson (1700–1748). With three lines from "Spring," his dour invocation of God's laws was enlivened by the romanticized allusions for which the Scottish poet was known. Bachman concluded his polemic with the hope that he had "said enough to convince you, that the science which has beguiled many a lonely hour of the naturalist is neither devoid of interest nor utility."[105]

As the reverend turned philosophical, extolling the "wonder and astonishment" of this godly pursuit, Maria Martin worked away painting specimens pinned to boards. If she was offended by the fact that Bachman published his views on the hypocrisy of the "fair sex," she left no indication. Their relationship was close, and she might have had a quiet word with him, but it would have been out of character to voice contrary views publicly. Moreover, Bachman was not likely to entertain them with an open mind. Remembered fondly by a colleague at the College of Charleston, the reverend was nonetheless described as "dictatorial" and unable to "brook opposition" when contradicted on matters of importance to him.[106] As Frederick Adolphus Porcher (1824–1888) reflected on the man who was "loved by his associates," he was perplexed by how someone so "apparent[ly] genial" could also be so intolerant and ruthless, but he concluded that the pastor's disposition was likely an occupational hazard. And perhaps, in part, it was.

Like Maria's grandfather, John Nicholas Martin, John Bachman stood at the head of a community defined by patriarchy and pietism, but these were views that Maria Martin accepted wholeheartedly. That she devoted her time, her talent, and her moral authority to the glory of God through art and science, despite criticism from men she admired, is therefore entirely understandable. Even so, given Maria's contributions, Bachman's characterization of women as obstacles to men's efforts to "read the book of Nature" was particularly uncharitable. Indeed, his comments exemplify the concerns of Elizabeth Kent and other "bluestockings" over the treatment of women with scientific aspirations: even when women made valuable contributions, men treated them as outsiders. At the same time, it is doubtful that Maria Martin agreed with those women who desired a life in science. She gave no evidence of wanting public recognition, and she could easily have considered Bachman's thoughtless comments as intended for those women who believed themselves the intellectual equal of men. Indeed, neither Bachman's criticisms nor Audubon's churlishness diminished her enthusiasm for natural history. If anything, it grew as science and family became more closely intertwined.

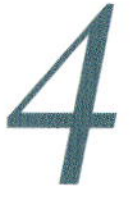

Living Together / Working Together

Collaboration and Kinship

As John James Audubon made his way to rooms prepared for him in 1831, no one could have anticipated how an impromptu invitation would affect an intensely devout and overwhelmingly female household: it united two families as well as two men. During that first encounter, John Bachman seemed blissfully unaware of anything other than their mutual interest in natural history, and Maria Martin left no hint of the important roles she would come to play in *Birds of America* and in fostering a lifelong relationship with the peripatetic artist-naturalist and his family. Nonetheless, two years later when John James, his wife, Lucy, and their son, John Woodhouse, appeared on the doorstep of the Bachman household, the bond established earlier was deepened, and the ties that were to unite them with the Bachman family for more than thirty years were firmly established. For four months, Audubon and his family lived in a world where kinship, religious observances, and ecclesiastical affairs were paramount, but as natural history came to assume an increasingly important role in the home on Rutledge Avenue, an intensely devout and overwhelmingly female household was transformed.[1] As these two very different families lived together and worked together—collecting, preparing, drawing, and describing plants and animals—both underwent profound change.

Among the least significant of these changes was perhaps the most noticeable: normally reserved, Bachman's enthusiasm for natural history and his new friend was boundless, and he sometimes behaved quite out of character. An invitation extended in September 1833, for example, began grandly: "Hail! My old Friend, all hail! Health, success and happiness, attend you—the wind, the waves, the heavens and fortune, have all smiled on you. Welcome, thrice welcome, to the homes and hearts of your friends!" And his gushing continued: "You must pay me a visit this autumn; you must just pay me a visit. Bring, if you can, the wife and son; you shall all be welcome—doubly so."[2] Restrained even with his wife and family, Bachman addressed his new friend fulsomely.

Bachman's effusiveness was at odds with his well-known aversion to emotionalism, but if Maria had qualms about his extravagant language, she was discreet enough to keep them to herself.[3] Additionally, the reverend regained his composure quickly, and when he wrote Audubon a week later he was less expansive. It occurred to him that Lucy Audubon might be unprepared for boarding in a home where there were few entertainments, especially for women and girls, and his remarks were cautionary rather than cajoling as he reiterated his invitation and informed Audubon that Maria Martin was in charge of arrangements. Indeed, at that very moment, she was readying a recently renovated space next to the dining room for their use.[4] Repurposed to accommodate the reverend's elderly mother when she relocated from New York to Charleston, this main floor gathering room was an unusual location for private quarters, but it would serve nicely as a bedchamber for John James and Lucy in the cloistral-like environment of the Bachman home.

If anyone missed the inference that daily routines were sufficiently dull so that even the most personal of spaces could coexist with more public ones, Bachman provided a more pointed reminder that John James could pass on to his wife. Although reasonably sure there was no need to note the differences between staying in his household and living off the land, the reverend was less sanguine about whether Lucy Audubon really understood how little her future home would resemble those occupied in metropolitan centers such as London and Liverpool—even Boston—and he instructed Audubon to prepare her: "Tell Mrs. A we are as plain as a pikestaff—few servants and some of these lazy—Clergymen ought not to be frolicsome so we do not see much company at dinner parties. But such as we have we will give unto you—and we will do it most cheerfully—we make no compliments and there is little fudge about us—no grog—no snuff—what an improvement in us both—we have reformed all these bad habits, except that of now then telling a long yarn and as for myself this will like second nature sometimes force itself out in spite of myself."[5] Mailed just a week after the grandiose invitation, this communication foreshadowed a retraction made within the month. The impending visit coincided with one of the busiest times on the church calendar, and as Bachman prepared to attend synod, a fellow clergyman and his wife occupied his guest room.

As Maria Martin supervised those who readied the room for John James and Lucy, Bachman turned his attention to the many duties under his charge as president of the South Carolina Synod. The meeting that convened every November was in Lexington, a village located a few miles west of Columbia, and Bachman had to write the opening address as well as draft position papers on constitutional change and union with the General Synod. Perhaps most importantly, however, was the impending debate on the establishment of a theological seminary.[6] Bachman had been promoting the creation of a Southern seminary for at least five years, and this meeting was potentially the penultimate step in realizing his dream. To that end, he invited the reverend Dr. and Mrs. Ernest Hazelius to board with him so they could prepare arguments supporting the seminary to present to synod.

Clearly Bachman did not contemplate problems when he suggested that this highly respected theological scholar stay in his home. Invitations to Audubon had been rebuffed many times and, in any event, he had convinced Hazelius (1777–1853) to leave the Gettysburg seminary in Pennsylvania for a professorship at a seminary that had not yet been approved.[7] It was imperative that members of the synod meet Hazelius and confirm his appointment at the institution they were about to create. Bachman had a dilemma. Two of his dearest friends and colleagues were to arrive almost simultaneously—both accompanied by their wives—and so he apologized for what was surely an unintended gaffe, and asked Audubon to postpone his visit. "Here I sigh," he wrote, "for although I am truly anxious to see you yet it so happens that I shall be almost compelled to turn you out should you come too early."[8]

Although excited by the prospect of seeing Audubon, Bachman could not rescind his invitation to Hazelius, nor would he have wanted to do so. Religious matters were paramount. He discussed doctrine as happily as he did natural history, and less than a month after telling Audubon he was "Welcome, thrice welcome," Bachman rephrased his invitation less magnanimously. He described his situation clearly: "If you come earlier you will till the 12th find me full and after that absent, the latter is the least inconvenience. You know my friend how I am situated—I have not much room—nor many servants—my heart I think is better than my means—as a man of sense and as a friend you will see precisely how I stand and will act as you may under all circumstances believe best."[9] Lodgings had quite simply been offered to more guests than could reasonably be accommodated.

By the time Bachman's letter was posted, it was too late for rescheduling. John James and Lucy were already in Richmond, and as the letter traveled toward them, they were on route to Charleston.[10] They therefore arrived to find the house filled to capacity. In addition to the usual occupants—the reverend and Harriet Bachman, their nine children, elderly mothers, and Maria Martin—they found Reverend and Mrs. Hazelius, as well as John Woodhouse. Lucy described the household as consisting of 17 "white" people, as well as "a good many *droppers in*"[11] Her description was not quite accurate as the many enslaved men, women, and children were mentioned only in the most general terms. She wrote Victor: "We are in as amiable a family as can be, but I should not choose (not that I know New England) to live in a slave state on many accounts, but certainly this family have as little the habits arising from slaves as any I ever knew."[12] At the same time, she was happy to find herself living with a hospitable family, and she set aside any discomfort she might have felt over the fact that domestic labor was performed by slaves rather than by servants.

Realistically, Lucy Audubon had little choice but to go along with whatever domestic arrangements her benefactors preferred. Her family had survived upon subscriptions and what she could earn as a teacher for at least a decade, and their finances were as precarious as ever in 1833. At least, however, the indignity and disappointment experienced a few years earlier when inquiries about "boarding" *en famille* were rebuffed unceremoniously by ornithologist William Swainson (1789–1855) would not be repeated in Charleston. Swainson informed Audubon that such arrangements were only resorted to "as a matter of necessity or profession" in England, and in his particular case long-term guests would "be attended with so many changes in our every-day domestic arrangements, that it becomes impossible" to contemplate.[13]

Swainson was right: generosity required effort, and if hosting out-of-town guests was uncommon in his circle, it was less so in the residence that was reputedly "always open to strangers and newcomers." While Swainson was cool to the idea of hosting, John Bachman was happy to have guests stay for as long as they wished. Other occupants were apparently equally amenable, and his grandchildren recalled houseguests with fondness.[14] One granddaughter did, however, note that there were sometimes more people in residence than could reasonably be accommodated in the fifteen rooms normally occupied by family, but comments about the inconvenience and extra work associated with long-term visitors were noticeably absent among those living in a home where domestic labor was performed by enslaved men and women. Because Maria Martin typically assumed responsibility for ensuring that the domestic workforce provided for the care and comfort of guests, she was unlikely to complain. Like the other women of her generation, she believed this was one of the many burdens she was born to bear.

The youngest of four girls, Maria Martin was destined to serve, and she was the dutiful daughter, stand-in mistress, and surrogate mother before becoming a wife in 1848. Her fate was sealed by birth order and shaped by events: she became her mother's companion when her parents separated in 1813; and, a few years later, she became her brother-in-law's assistant and a care-giver to her sister and to the nieces and nephews who appeared almost annually between 1816 and 1832. While some families relied on grandmothers in similar circumstances, such was not the case in Maria's family. Although Rebecca Martin was venerated as an example of Lutheran womanhood, her days as an active participant in raising children were long behind her by the time Harriet required assistance with her brood.[15] She and John Bachman's mother were "honored inmates" in the home where Maria Martin lived, and their care also fell to Maria. She cared for them as chronic illness left Harriet unable to perform many of the duties expected of the good wife.

Over time, John Bachman depended increasingly upon Maria Martin. He lamented Harriet's indispositions, sympathizing with her suffering and hoping that divine intervention or a medical miracle might improve her condition, but he came to rely on Maria long before she assisted with his scientific endeavors.[16] In 1827, for example, when Harriet was unable to leave her infant twins and five other children to accompany her husband on a trip to his ancestral village, Maria went instead to serve as his amanuensis. She also assumed the role of nurse on this trip, which was undertaken to settle some family business. But Bachman became ill while they were in New York, and for nearly a month Maria nursed him as he hovered between life and death. It was thus hardly surprising that the woman who was both caregiver and assistant was described as "more than a right hand" by her sister's husband. Moreover, her role as artist-assistant benefited not only *Birds of America* but also her brother-in-law's aspirations as a man of science.

In 1831, Bachman had little more than hospitality and some well-placed introductions to potential subscribers to offer Audubon, but once it became clear that Maria Martin had a gift for botanical painting he had something much more compelling to give his new friend. Bachman's expertise and contacts were admittedly important, but as Audubon's strove to complete his monumental work, he came to rely on the assistance of others—including Maria—and Bachman appropriated her efforts as if they were his to commandeer. Once it became clear to him that Maria Martin had superior artistic abilities Bachman encouraged her to pursue her new avocation, thus strengthening his ties to Audubon and moving him ever closer to being a real scientist rather than a dilettante. It was therefore entirely natural that Maria assumed a pivotal role, as the home where she lived became a "home away from home" for Audubon and his family.

The fact that Bachman was occupied with church business when Audubon arrived also increased the likelihood that Maria would spend time with her mentor. In 1831, Audubon was away from the painting room a good deal as he and Bachman went hunting upcountry or fraternized with men interested in the arts and science, but as Bachman prepared for synod, he was only able to find a few moments in the evening for natural history. Moreover, by the time he was free to talk about birds, Audubon was too exhausted to do so. He had been in the painting room all day with John Woodhouse and Maria Martin, and his regimen of painting from dawn to dusk left him "weakened & fatigued." In fact, the imminent completion of volume two and one hundred new "drawings" for volume three did not assuage his fears, and after a month of concentrated activity he was concerned he might not live to complete his project.[17] He even confessed as much to his engraver. He wrote Havell that "the machine me thinks is wearing out" and, by early December, his worries seemed real.[18] He was bedridden with hemorrhoids, an affliction commonly associated with aging, and he was laid low for ten days.[19] John James did not visit the studio until December 7.

In the meantime, John Woodhouse and Maria Martin were painting without him and doing quite well. Upon inspection, John James was "delighted" with his son's "*industry* and his work," and he was impressed by Maria's "superior talents."[20] In particular, there were three passerines that caught his attention. Although then focusing primarily on water birds, both figures and backgrounds for the seaside sparrow (*Ammodramus maritimus*, misidentified as MacGillivray's Finch), a sedge wren (*Cistothorus platensis*, misidentified as Nuttall's Short-billed Marsh Wren), and Swainson's warbler (*Limnothlypis swainsonii*) impressed him. He believed them to be new species, and he named the warbler in honor of William Swainson, the wren in honor of Thomas Nuttall, and the sparrow in honor of William MacGillivray (1796–1852).[21] Two weeks later, Audubon repeated his good impression of his son's figures. He wrote Victor that: "John has drawn a few Birds as good as any I ever made," adding that "ere a few months I hope to give this department of my duty altogether to him—"[22]

But as John James saw signs that the apprentice was on the road to becoming a master, it was the "ephemera" painted by Maria Martin that dominated this vignette. Her flame azalea (*Rhododendron calendulaceum*) spreads across two-thirds of the sheet, and the Florida atala hairstreak (*Eumaeus atala*) and common buckeye (*Junonia coenia*) that hover over the shrub compete with the warbler for attention. Although the folio painting is among the smallest published in *Birds* (53.7 x 35.1 cm), in a world where finding new species trumped describing or painting well-known ones, an aesthetically pleasing vignette both dramatized and normalized new discoveries, and Maria Martin's plant and insects achieved that objective admirably. That Audubon did not acknowledge Maria's skills as an entomological artist as quickly or as robustly as he did his son's efforts in ornithological illustration is unsurprising: she never sought commendation for her services. This oversight was, however, soon corrected. In his next letter to Victor, John James referred to her insects as "perhaps, the best I've seen."[23]

With John James recuperated and John Bachman home from Lexington, progress improved. Two months into their stay, Lucy Audubon described their routine as one in which "we write, read, work and walk by turns," and she was pleased to report that her son was "learning the scientific terms and descriptions of the Birds by heart under Mr B's tuition, who says he makes quick progress."[24] Even though painting was confined to daylight hours, her comments clearly reflect the many hours devoted to natural history. Taxidermy, for example, could be performed under artificial light, and because painting was limited to no more than ten hours per day—between 8:00 A.M. and 4:00 P.M.—in winter John Woodhouse was often employed skinning and staging birds until well after midnight.[25] Likewise, descriptions for the second volume of *Ornithological Biography* could be composed in the evening, and many were devoted to writing biographies credited by Audubon as a group effort.

Nonetheless, work on *Birds* proceeded more slowly than desirable at least in part because Maria's talents were not fully deployed. The botanicals that had proven so useful in the past were not needed for the water birds being painted, and while Bachman had a high opinion of her birds, Maria Martin was but a talented imitator. The copies she made of Audubon's tricolored heron and the snowy egret in spring 1832, for example, were truly beautiful but they were not to his standards. Nor were those that followed. Six months later, when Bachman proposed that Maria could paint ducks not readily available near Boston where Audubon was residing, he did not respond positively.[26]

Maria's paintings of the "short-legged" sandpiper (pectoral sandpiper, *Calidris melanotos*, plate 294), the "spotted" sandpiper (*Actitis macularius*, plate 310), and a simplified version of his green-winged teal (*Anas carolinensis*) were just not good enough. Her talents lay elsewhere. When her botanicals and insects were not needed, her potential was not fully realized.

Additionally, in mid-December when Audubon was well enough to paint, and Bachman could be more attentive to natural history, another matter emerged to distract them. Work slowed as time and energy were devoted to addressing criticisms of Audubon's work by Charles Waterton, whose history

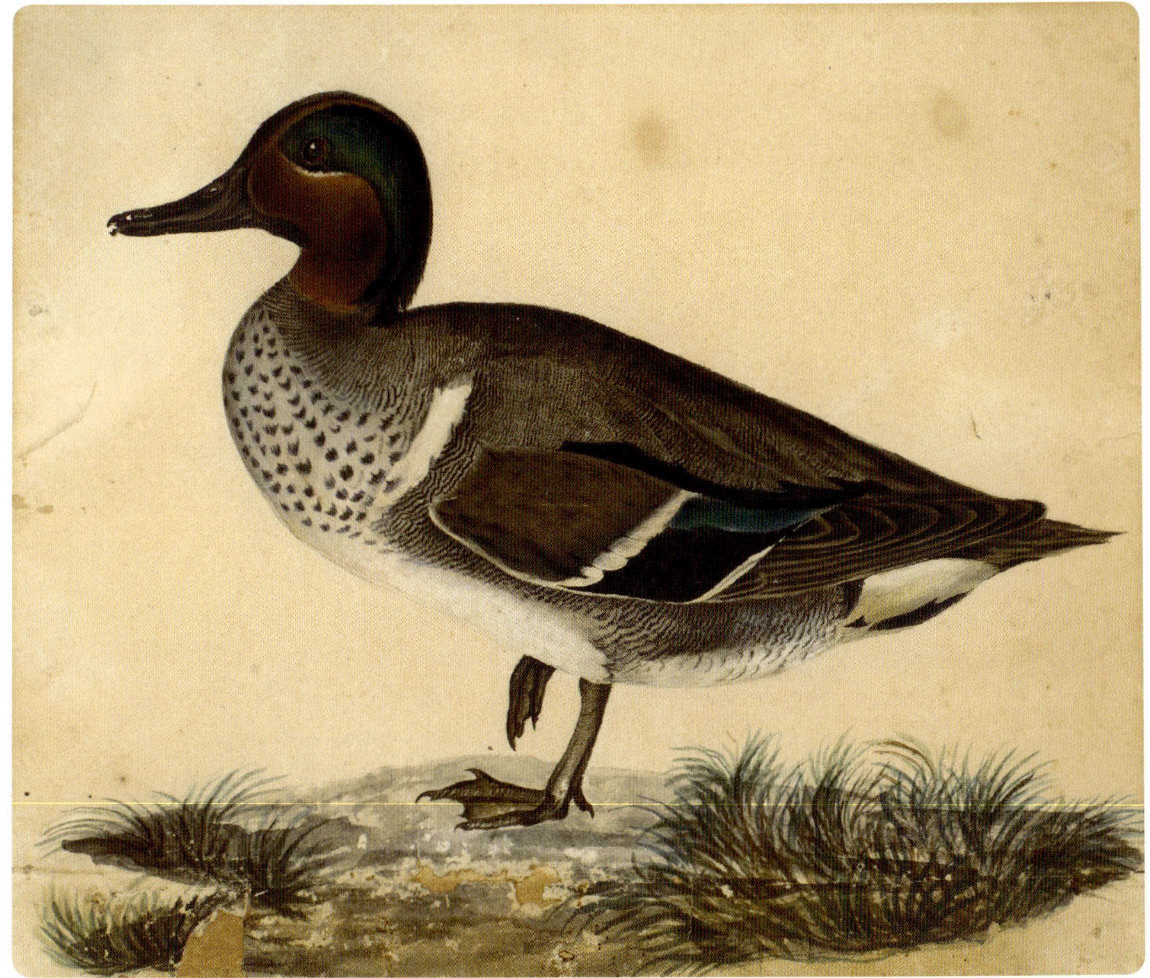

FIGURE 44. Green winged teal (*Anas carolinensis*) by Maria Martin. Courtesy Haskell Grimball Carr.

of attacking those with whom he disagreed was well established.[27] In this case, the criticisms were a reprisal of an attack launched two years earlier. In a paper that appeared within months of the publication of volume one of the *Ornithological Biography*, he claimed that Audubon had either erred egregiously or that he deliberately misled those unfamiliar with avian behavior when he claimed that vultures were anosmic (*Edinburgh New Philosophical Journal*, 1826), and he returned to that topic in early 1833. Indeed, his attacks were even more acrimonious than two years earlier as he reviewed the *Ornithological Biography* and accused Audubon of plagiarism. In addition to stating that someone else had written the bird biographies, he taunted Audubon by describing his "drawings" as mere "work[s] of art."[28]

Ever spiteful, Waterton took aim at two *bêtes noires*—Audubon and James Rennie (1787–1867), naturalist and editor of the second edition of George Montagu's (1753–1815) *Ornithological Dictionary* (1802)—as he reviewed the *Ornithological Biography*.[29] Like Audubon, Rennie had been the subject of Waterton's wrath when his edition of Montagu's *Dictionary* appeared in 1831. When Waterton returned to Rennie in 1833, he did so, at least in part, because his book *Wanderings in South America, the North-West of the United States and the Antilles* (1825) was ignored while classical studies by Francois Levaillant (1753–1824), René Antoine Ferchault de Réaumur (1683–1757), John Ray (1627–1705), Gilbert White (1720–1793), Alexander Wilson, and others of similar stature—including Audubon—were recommended in Rennie's edition.[30] *Wanderings* was Waterton's major scientific contribution, and such treatment was insulting. Waterton thus skewered both men as he attempted to redeem himself by showing that it was wrong to view the "American woodsman" as "an ornithological luminary of the first magnitude."[31]

A month later, he was at it again. This time, Waterton ridiculed Audubon for stating that eagles had uropygial glands.[32] Four months after that, he revisited the debate on vultures, and before the year was out, he expanded his philippic. In essays that were far from courteous, he countered Audubon's views on hummingbirds, partridges, and rattlesnakes. Nonetheless, his greatest concern was Audubon's work on vultures. He took issue with it because, he noted, if it "were allowed to stand, my statement in the *Wanderings* must necessarily fall to the ground."[33]

Given the polemical nature of Waterton's essays and given that his publisher, *Loudon's Magazine of Natural History and Journal of Zoology, Botany, Mineralogy, Geology, and Meteorology*, welcomed reader commentary, it was not surprising that several letters supporting Audubon were published. But if anyone thought such testimonials would settle the matter, they were quickly disabused. Waterton pursued both Audubon and anyone who supported him aggressively, and he was especially acerbic after being chided by Victor Gifford for waiting until his father left England to pan the *Ornithological Biography*. In fact, Victor's comments could have been harsher as Waterton actually published his review fully two years after the book appeared, but even his modest scolding triggered a quick response. Waterton fired off a demeaning rebuff in which he informed Victor that he was a poor substitute for his father.[34] He wrote: "If Mr. Audubon, junior, feels alarmed for his father's reputation as a naturalist, at the menacing attitude I have assumed in defence of my own book (bless the bantling!), I would recommend to him either to refute my arguments, or send over an express to his father to come back from America without loss of time, and mount guard over his own *Biography of Birds*; which shall feel the weight of my arm in earnest, if the son returns me sarcastic thanks a second time."[35]

Three months later, Victor responded in kind, and the reaction was immediate. When he accused Waterton of writing "an amusing book; but whether of facts, or of fables," the retort was vicious.[36] In November, Waterton penned one of the lengthiest verbal drubbings of the entire episode, even dredging up the fact that Audubon had been rejected for membership in the Philadelphia Academy of Natural Sciences in 1824. But more specifically, he accused both father and son of hoodwinking an unsuspecting British public with tales simply too fantastic to be true. His contempt was palpable as he pointed out that if such "astonishing" observations had merit, they would surely have been published in America, as Audubon's countrymen would no doubt want "the honour" of claiming him as their own.[37]

Rejoinders dripping in sarcasm appeared regularly, and Waterton only treated Perceval Hunter (1812–1878), an as-yet unknown natural history enthusiast who early on weighed in on the dispute, more diplomatically.[38] Waterton's response was, however, unsurprising given that Hunter believed Rennie was mistaken in omitting *Wanderings* from his bibliography—a point that did not escape Waterton's notice. By the autumn of 1833, Waterton had abandoned any pretense of objectivity. He went well beyond the norms of scientific discourse when he accused Audubon of loving the limelight, pandering to acolytes, and misrepresenting himself as a man of science, and it was feared the assault was far from over. Although John James drew some satisfaction at having stayed out of the squabble, in December a plan was developed to counter the heckling.[39] Thus it was that when those in the Bachman household should have been working on *Birds*, they embarked on a protracted set of experiments on avian olfaction.

Conducted in the gardens just steps away from the painting room where Maria worked, the experiments were intended to provide empirical evidence to refute Waterton's rhetoric. Additionally, whereas Waterton tended to seek support for his ideas in popular opinion, their findings would be placed before the scientific community. In a letter posted not long after Victor had been on the receiving end of Waterton's insults, Lucy Audubon reported there was a plan in the works to put an end to the harassment published in *Loudon's Magazine*. Lucy wrote that they planned to obtain validation from experts and avoid debating with a man reputedly considered "crazy–or nearly so" by many British scientists.[40] She elaborated: "Mr B is going to write a paper, not a reply, but a series of facts concerning your Fathers work and the authenticity of it," and consequently make short work of "that self-sufficient puppy Mr Waterton." A week later, John James added his comments, writing Victor they would prove that "Turkey Buzards are first gregarious as well as the Carrion Crows—that they eat fresh meat in preference of Putrid stuff—that they eat birds newly killed, either plucked or not, *even of their own Species*—that they suck Bird's eggs and devour their callow young—that they come to their food by their sense of Sight and not by that of smell—and lastly that they cannot Discover by any sense of smell, the most putrid of matters, even when this putrid Substance is within a few feet from them & *out of their bright eyes*! —"[41]

John Bachman was a crucial partner in this venture. Without doubt, loyalty was a deciding factor in his decision to participate in a rather elaborate plan intended to defuse Waterton's increasingly vicious attacks, but the English naturalist's antipathy to Lutheranism and his low opinion of American scientists surely contributed as well.[42] That Waterton's views were often contradictory was irrelevant. He chastised Audubon for avoiding scrutiny from his own countrymen while expressing contempt for American scientists other than ornithologist George Ord (1781–1866), and such insults could not go unchallenged. As a result, it was decided that the only prudent course of action was to disseminate the results of their buzzard experiment widely. Not only would this tactic enhance their own reputations, but it would also forestall the inevitable accusation that they contrived to guarantee positive reviews by only sharing results with sympathetic Southerners and gullible Britons (meaning Robert Jameson [1774–1854], MacGillivray and Swainson).

It did not take long to move from planning to action. Bachman's manuscript was published in early 1834 as a scientific article in *Loudon's Magazine*, and their results were presented to the Boston Society of Natural History and to the Academy of Natural Sciences in Philadelphia before spring. Because *Birds of America* might be deleteriously affected if Waterton could influence the views of those who were devotees rather than men of science, copies of the paper were also mailed to Audubon's subscribers and to "others whom it may concern."[43] Whether these recipients were impressed by evidence showing that the "imperfectly developed" olfactory organs of vultures were not used when searching for food is unclear. Likewise, whether they noticed Bachman's cautionary remarks is equally uncertain. Less sure of their findings than Audubon, Bachman admitted that vultures had a sense of smell but he added that neither acuity nor function could be verified conclusively through their olfactory experiments. This admission made no impression on Waterton. He was determined to discredit their work and, armed with a copy of their manuscript, he drafted a response that appeared in the same volume as their paper. In it, he reiterated his view that Audubon was a poser, and he ridiculed the "American philosophers" who witnessed the experiments as deficient in both scientific reasoning and common sense.[44]

Although this was the last word from Waterton until 1835, countering his accusations consumed much time and energy. Rather than painting specimens and writing "biographies," Audubon and Bachman were often found experimenting on avian olfaction. If Maria Martin was painting regularly, her confrères were most certainly not, and whatever she or others in the household were doing, it was impossible to ignore the experiments taking place in the garden. The proceedings were malodorous and gruesome, and no amount of self-discipline could overcome the temptation to check out the commotion created by hundreds of vultures attacking a painting of a disemboweled sheep as they tried to make a meal of an illusory morsel. Similarly, who could resist sneaking a peek at a macabre experiment in which vultures were blinded deliberately so as to test the veracity of a folk tale claiming their down had restorative powers? No less compelling were the captive birds. A number were captured using rattraps located next to bait laid out in the yard; others were survivors of the "cruel" blinding experiment. And if having caged blinded birds and committees of sighted ones hovering and landing in the back garden were insufficiently distracting, the accompanying odor was more than most people would bear willingly. No doubt accustomed to disgusting smells, especially when Audubon was in residence and decaying birds were deposited by the dozens in the back garden, familiarity provided small comfort as a noxious fetor hung heavily and attracted dogs and other pests.[45]

Although the weather was cool, putrefaction, bloat, and decomposition were delayed, not arrested. The fact that "trials" were suspended on Sunday and Christmas day did little to reduce the stench, and by the second week even Bachman conceded that the "dainty mess" was "offensive."[46] In large measure the degree to which the bait generated its stench was determined by the apparatus used: a special frame was constructed so as to ensure the pile consisting of discarded birds from the painting room, others killed by dogs, and offal from local "slaughter-pens" was not discovered by scavengers prematurely. Every effort was made to encourage maximum decomposition, and the miasma generated by "the effluvia" from the maggoty liquefied tissues protected by this specially built apparatus drew swarms of vultures, attracted vermin, and repulsed hyposomics.

Despite the unpleasantness of this makeshift laboratory, these experiments offered an opportunity to incorporate an actual example of scientists at work into lessons on natural history. Even though some of the Bachman children had already studied natural history, it would be difficult to overemphasize the pedagogical value of the grisly activities taking place just beyond their classroom. Moreover, had Audubon known it was possible to do experiments on rattlesnakes in South Carolina, he would have extended their knowledge of herpetology as well. Waterton had ridiculed his description of a rattlesnake swallowing a squirrel tail first, and he longed to defend his reputation against yet another attack by his most vehement critic. "Were rattlesnakes as abundant near Charleston as Buzards," he stated, "that Business would soon be equally set at rest—for this however Time is needed and the time will come."[47] And so it was for lessons in herpetology. Moreover, if the Bachman children were to have such lessons they would get them from Maria Martin.

Maria painted specimens for John Edwards Holbrooks's (1796–1871) *North American Herpetology* (1838–1842), and she learned about snakes in much the same way she learned about plants. A practical person, Maria applied lessons learned when copying Audubon's birds or Redouté's flowers to painting snakes and, by first replicating models, she went on to produce images of snakes with felicity and finesse. At the same time, the woman who surpassed Audubon when it came to Lepidoptera was less gifted when it came to other creatures, most obviously birds, but also snakes. Fortunately, *Birds* contained three herpetological species she could copy: the infamous tree-climbing rattlesnake attacking the nest of a mockingbird (plate 21), an eastern coral snake (Audubon's Harlequin snake/*Elaps fulvius*; *Micrurus fulvius*) being shooed away by chuck-will's widow birds (plate 52), and a black snake (*Coluber constrictor*) looking to make a meal in the nest of a ferruginous thrush (plate 116). Her figures are not exact replicas of those in *Birds* but by copying Audubon and by painting from specimens, she was able to produce beautifully rendered figures such as the *Coluber constrictor* (1842, 3: plate 11, p. 55). It is also likely that she painted the eastern coral snake (1838, 2: plate 18, p. 87). Given that *Birds* provided a model and that the artist who provided this image is unnamed in a work characterized by scrupulous attention to the crediting of artists, there is a very good chance that the woman accustomed to anonymity drew this small poisonous creature.[48] Of Holbrook's artists, Maria Martin was the least likely to complain when a volume went to press without acknowledgment. Indeed, she seemed to prefer anonymity, and there is one case where it was preferable to the notation received: Maria Martin's painting of the scarlet kingsnake (*Coluber elapsoides/Lampropeltis elapsoides*, Holbrook, 1838) has bad coloring, lacks physiognomic detail, and is ill-defined.

The quality of the scarlet king snake also suggests that Maria painted from specimens on occasion. Holbrook preferred that his artists paint from living specimens, and perhaps her poor rendering is because there was no model for this snake. In any event, it stands out as substandard in a work intended to convey taxonomic information visually as well as through text. As a result, her figure only appeared in the first edition of *Herpetology* (1838, 2:123). Maria's scarlet king snake was deleted in subsequent editions: it simply was not good enough for inclusion in a reference work attempting to systematize Classes, Orders, and Families. Unfortunately, as Holbrook strove to ensure high-quality, accurate images, he replaced Maria's poorly executed illustration with two that were beautifully rendered but incorrectly classified. Clearly superior, the redrawn figures in the 1842 edition of *Herpetology* were mislabeled as an Asian species (*Calamaria elapsoidea*) and an African/European/west Asian species (*Coronella doliata*).[49] To Maria Martin's credit, the black snake and the unattributed bead snake were reproduced in the second edition.

Exactly how many species she attempted to figure is unknown, but Bachman boasted that she was willing to paint virtually anything asked of her—"even snakes"—and as someone accustomed to painting specimens and images over and over again as she perfected them, she assuredly painted more than the two figures credited to her in *Herpetology*.[50] But when it came to ophiology, Maria Martin stood alone. John Bachman was pleased to offer her services to his friends, and he was more than willing to assist Audubon conduct experiments on avian olfaction, but he was not eager to venture into the field of ophiological behavior.

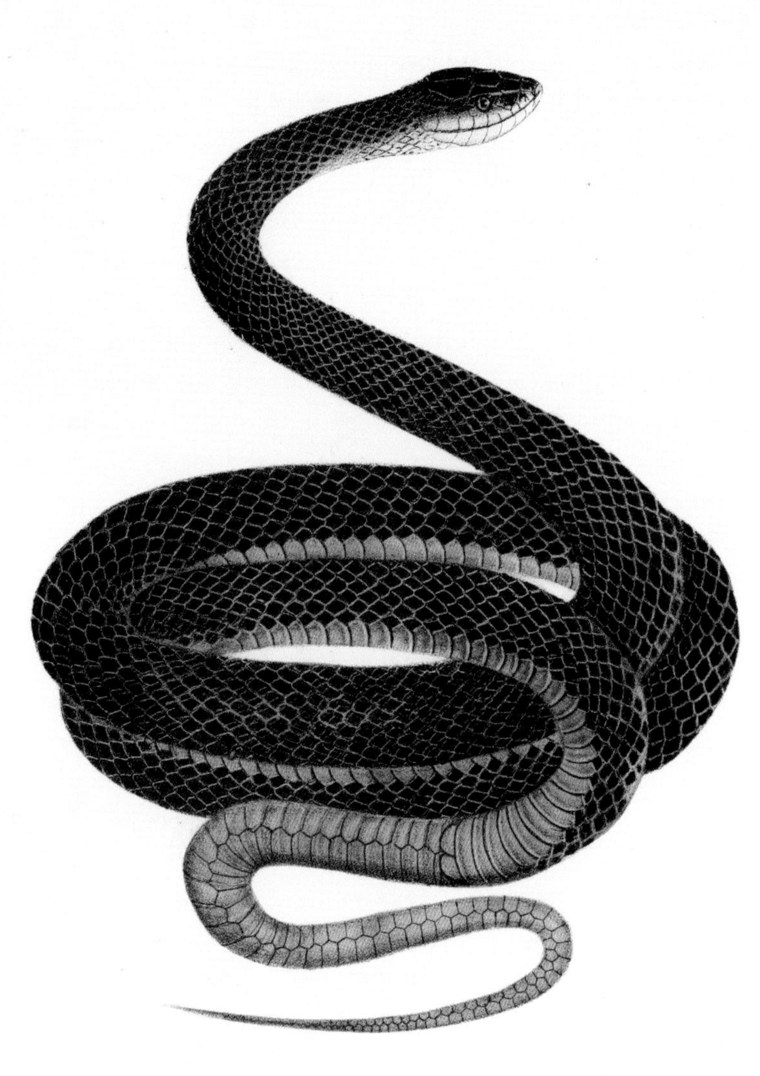

FIGURE 45. Black snake (*Coluber constrictor*) by Maria Martin for *North American Herpetology* (1842), 3: plate 11, p.55. Courtesy of the Smithsonian Libraries, Washington, DC.

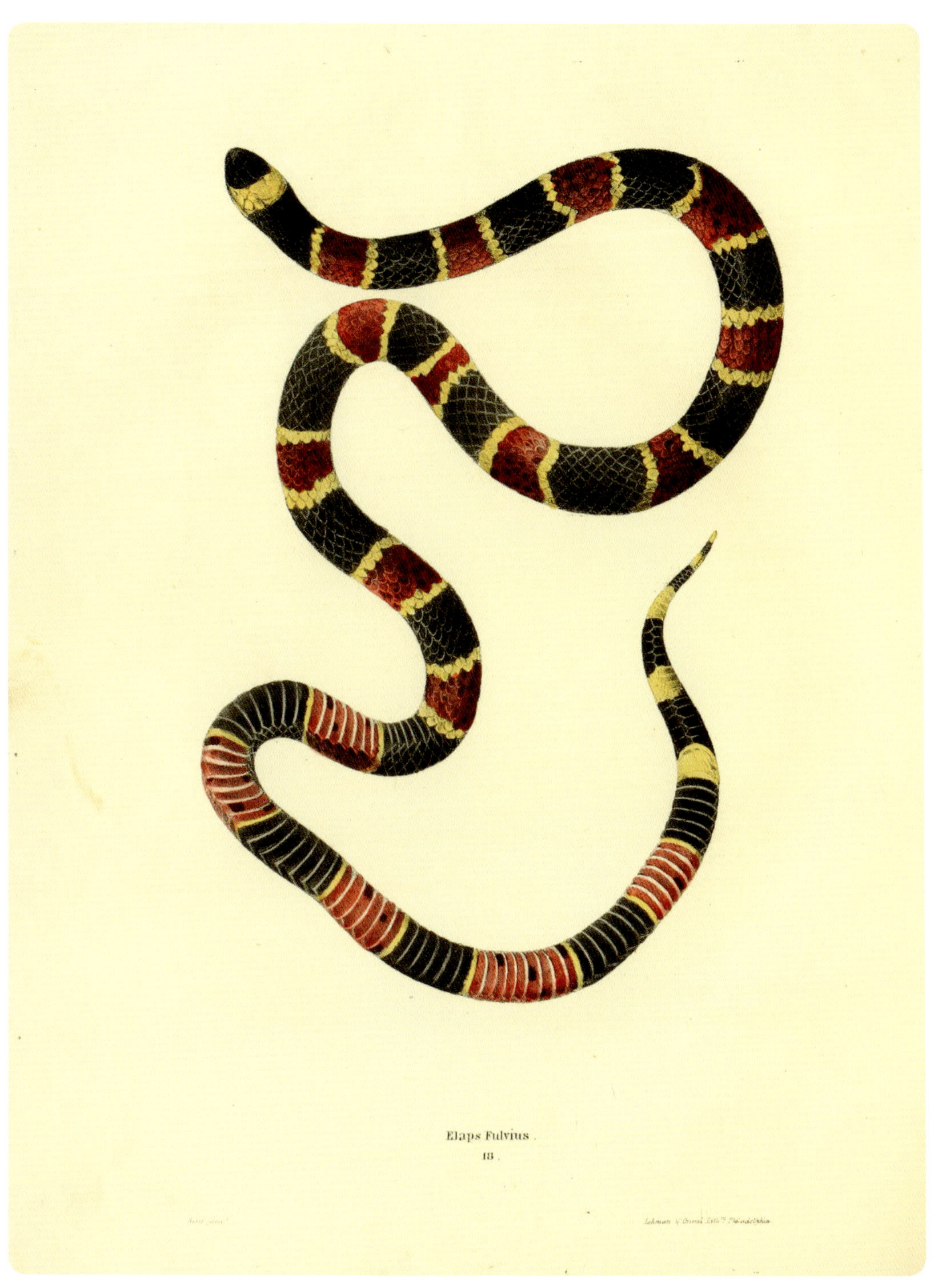

FIGURE 46. Eastern coral snake (*Elaps fulvius/Micrurus fulvius*) in John Edwards Holbrook, *North American Herpetology* (1838), 2: plate 18, 87. Courtesy of the Smithsonian Libraries, Washington, DC.

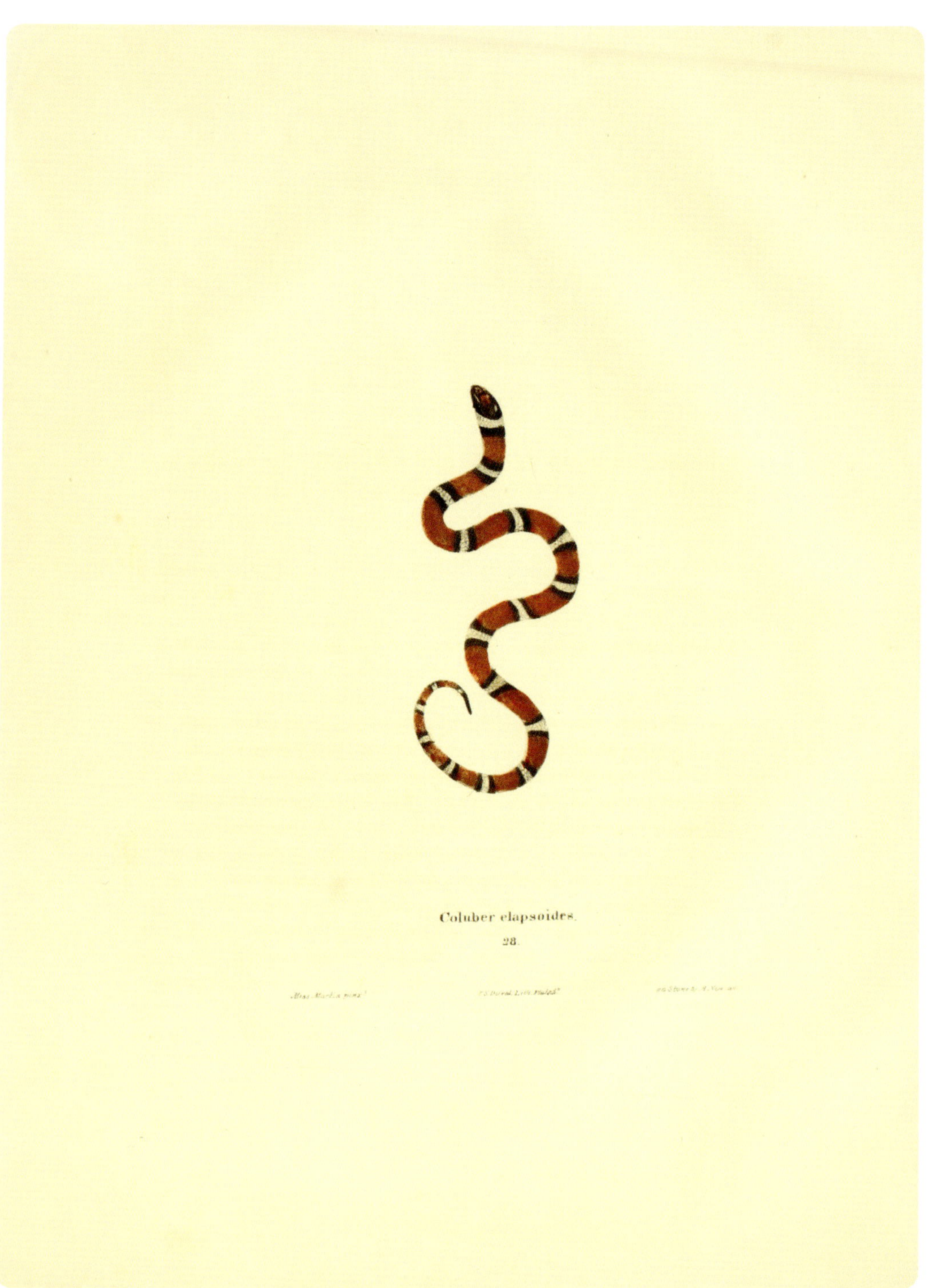

FIGURE 47. Scarlet king snake (*Coluber elapsoides/Lampropeltis elapsoides*) by Maria Martin for *North American Herpetology* (1838), 2: plate 28, p. 122. Courtesy of the Smithsonian Libraries, Washington, DC.

As Audubon threatened to counter Waterton's accusations that his descriptions of a rattlesnake climbing a tree and eating its prey tail first were figments of his fertile mind, Bachman was not entirely sure he agreed with his friend's account. In fact, he shared Waterton's concerns and offered conflicting comments on the rattlesnake issue in the preamble to the buzzard paper in *Loudon's*. Rather than avoiding the issue, Bachman went out of his way to state that he could not discuss a topic when he had not read the article responsible for the disagreement. But he did not stop there. He then speculated that Audubon may have "ascribed to the rattlesnake some of the habits of the common black snake (*Coluber constrictor*, Lin.)."[51]

That Bachman made these comments was surely disquieting to Audubon. At the same time, however, he did not divulge information that would have undermined his friend: there were rattlesnakes in South Carolina, and whether Bachman had seen the timber rattler (*Crotalus h. horridus*), the eastern diamondback (*Crotalus adamanteus*), or the Carolina pigmy (*Sistrurus m. millarius*) on his many hunting expeditions, a learned man would have been aware of the fact that *Vipera caudisona Americana* and *V.c.a. Minor* were described by Mark Catesby (1683–1749) in *The Natural History of Carolina, Florida and the Bahama Islands* (*1731–1743*).[52] But no matter how qualified the comments, it was enough that Bachman thought Audubon mistaken, and in the very volume containing the results of their buzzard experiment, Waterton referred to Audubon's claim that rattlesnakes climbed trees and swallowed squirrels "tail foremost" as reason to doubt all of the "narratives which may come from Mr. Audubon's zoological pen."[53]

While Waterton's badgering was a constant irritant, Maria Martin's efforts to replicate Audubon's figures could only be welcome. But if chuffed by her attempts to master his techniques and aesthetic, Audubon's conceit was misplaced. His apprentice was focused on the task at hand and on teaching her new skills to her nieces. Moreover, while John James facilitated Maria's transformation from an undistinguished to an extraordinary painter, it was Lucy Audubon who showed her how to pass on acquired expertise to the next generation.[54] A private tutor and teacher for more than a decade, the well-educated "Madame" Audubon had both subject matter and pedagogical experience at her disposal, and finding herself among friends who believed that girls required "moral and mental training" as well as "the essentials of a solid English education" required few compromises in content or conduct.[55] And in Maria Martin she had an assistant accustomed to tutoring children. Long responsible for ensuring her nieces and nephews completed both academic and catechetical lessons, Maria simply took on new responsibilities as she and Lucy worked with children for whom academics were as much a matter of common sense as a matter of principle.

With scholastic experiences closer to those who attended private academies (Southern or Northern) than to the girls in neighboring homes, Maria's nieces were encouraged to take their studies seriously. Although discouraged from developing the independence of mind associated with "Blue Stockings," they were aware of their father's censure of Southern education and of the importance of developing the intellect bestowed by God. But if he criticized Southern planters and professionals for allowing their daughters to be superficial and "frolicksome" instead of ensuring that they developed both moral and mental discipline, his views on the education of girls were nonetheless shaped by patriarchy and pietism.[56] Husbands needed an educated helpmeet who understood both the divine and the mundane of God's creation, and his daughters studied botany, history, chemistry, natural philosophy, and drawing preparatory to their roles in marriage. Any questions about the importance of their destiny as God-fearing wives and mothers or about the role of scientific education in it, the aviary in the garden and specimens mounted under glass in the parlor were constant reminders of how and why they should study God's creatures.[57]

The Bachman children were also beneficiaries of a tradition going back to the Reformation. In fact, education was so important within the Lutheran community that the German Friendly Society provided schooling for children of less affluent families, and leading men—for example, Maria Martin's father and John Bachman—served on a committee that underwrote the costs of tuition for children in families unable to pay. Normally classes at the school were coeducational, but Maria's three eldest nieces—Maria Rebecca, Mary Eliza, and Jane Lee—were among twenty-two pupils who participated in a short-lived experiment with gender-segregated classes. Between 1829 and 1833, they attended an all-female branch of the school, which had a "thoroughly equipped . . . department of natural sciences,"[58] and they followed a regimen that included arithmetic, geography, and history, as well as "natural and experimental philosophy," the classics, French, German, and Latin. Clearly, by the time Lucy Audubon arrived, they were well prepared to delve into more complex studies in natural history.

Already involved in her niece's academic and religious education, Maria Martin could not but be an important participant in their scientific studies; however, like other "ladies of Charleston" with an interest in "the Floral department," Maria's knowledge of natural history was practical and her reference point biblical. Entirely familiar with Bachman's reverential description of gardens as repositories of "the great truths of religion as contained in the word of God" and with his view of gardens as sources of sustenance for those who made "them subservient to the best interests of mankind," during the 1830s she also came to see them as places where scientists collected specimens and conducted experiments.[59] Never doubting that they were "the first habitation of man," Maria acquired botanical knowledge through close observation. And so did her nieces. However, after studying with Lucy Audubon, they were all better acquainted with the finer points of descriptive botany.[60]

As they gained proficiency, specimens collected, pressed, and identified by the "ladies" of the household were included in Bachman's first botanical publication. A modest effort entitled "Catalogue of Phaenogamous Plants and ferns native or naturalized found growing in the vicinity of Charleston, (S.C.)," native plants as well as "exotics which may now be said to be fairly naturalized around Charleston" were listed alphabetically rather than classified according to Linnaean criteria. But however elementary, the "Catalogue" nonetheless benefited from expertise developed by the women and girls of the Bachman family, and Maria Martin's role is obvious.[61] Several species enumerated in the Catalogue were painted for *Birds of America*, and while Bachman may have been familiar with them, Maria knew them through careful study. After all, the botanicals she painted for *Birds* were identified at the bottom of the folios in her hand; Bachman's distinctive penmanship is not to be found on the sheets containing her figures.

While few had her artistry and knowledge, Maria Martin nonetheless exemplifies how talent could be nurtured through instruction. A model student, Maria also endeavored to pass on what she had learned to her nieces and nephews. Perhaps children accustomed to seeing adults devote hours to mastering the scientific names and taxonomic information of artfully displayed botanicals and dead animals arranged in lifelike positions would be drawn to natural history, but transforming interest into action took effort, and Maria Martin was crucial to making science an important part of their lives. In fact, even those familiar with the trials and tribulations of doing natural history could mistake opportunity for aptitude or interest.

John James Audubon, for example, believed that the Bachman children would take to drawing and natural history with alacrity as an antidote to ennui. While it is true that the women and girls of the Bachman family lived quiet uneventful lives—quite unlike the adventuresome one his wife led while on the Kentucky frontier or traveling about America and the British Isles—but Audubon was nonetheless a little self-satisfied and uninformed when it came to the reality of daily routines in his friend's home. He assumed the Bachman children lacked purposeful and stimulating occupation, and he had no sooner left their company than he wrote encouraging them to continue their lessons: "I am delighted that you all are interesting yourselves in botany & Drawing, nothing starts the blues so effectually than constant employment."[62] Thinking he saw evidence of the ill-effects of boredom among the youngsters, he advised natural history as a tonic to stimulate those whose time and talent could be put to good use. Admittedly, the Bachman children escaped the daily round of chores expected of their less affluent peers, but they were not idle.

Maria Martin's nieces were accustomed to academics and religious studies, and the no-nonsense attitude of their elders meant that adding science and drawing to their daily regimen had less impact than might be anticipated by an outsider. Not only had the three oldest girls been introduced to natural history in the short-lived experiment in same-sex education at the German Friendly Society School, but they were also accomplished in many other areas.[63] Familiar with seventeenth-century pietistic poets such as Isaac Watts (1674–1748), as well as with eighteenth-century sentimental and "Churchyard" poets such as James Thomson (1700–1748), Nathaniel Cotton (1707–1788), Oliver Goldsmith (1728–1774), Thomas Campbell (1777–1844), William Cowper (1731–1800), and Edward Young (1683–1765), they also read nineteenth-century poets from both sides of the Atlantic. Less serious than the Augustans and preromantics, American poets such as James Nack (1809–1879), Hugh Peters (1807–1831), William Cullen Bryant (1794–1878), Theophilus Fisk (n.d.), and Caroline Howard Gilman (1794–1888), as well as British poets such as Maria Jane Jewsbury (Fletcher) (1800–1833), George Gordon, Lord Byron (1788–1832), and Sir Walter Scott (1771–1832) were also well known to them.[64]

The Bachman girls were eminently capable of tackling specialized material, but it helped that Maria Martin and Lucy Audubon introduced them to botany and ornithology. The latter was kindly and patient, even solicitous of those who tried to please her through hard work. At the same time, "Madame" Audubon also garnered a healthy respect from her students. Even those who tended to be "mischievous or playful at inopportune times" were apparently well behaved in her classes, and she impressed students by her "tireless passing from one child to another, seeing that each was properly at work, helping, explaining, encouraging."[65] Even her best scholars were mindful that her agreeable nature depended upon their effort. In this, she was not so different from Maria Martin.

With a stern demeanor that elicited both respect and affection, Maria was well positioned to learn from Lucy's impressive pedagogical skills. Known to set aside a lesson plan in order to take advantage of youthful curiosity when an interesting bird was sighted outdoors, Lucy Audubon exemplified emerging trends that emphasized study through hands-on experience rather than by sitting in a classroom.[66] Experts were questioning the wisdom of trying to interest children in science through book learning, and such an approach could not but have resonated with Maria Martin, a woman who tramped through woods to observe water birds in their natural surroundings, collected plants, and painted botanicals, birds, and insects from nature.[67] Whether familiar with the "common sense" approach advocated by "an experienced teacher" in *Essays on School Keeping* (1831), Lucy and Maria certainly taught ornithology and botany as if they agreed wholeheartedly. When it came to natural history, expert Allison Wrifford (c. 1780–1844) argued: "the demonstrative and practical method of instruction is the only suitable one for any of the branches of natural science. A mere recitation of text books, without experiments and demonstrations is nearly useless, as it furnishes a parcel of words without the corresponding ideas—a smattering of science without those habits of observation and reflection which are indispensable to any practical acquaintance with scientific objects."[68] What book could teach form and function, or habits and habitat, better than nature itself? There were pedagogical benefits to active participation and observation; and whether aware of contemporary theoretical discussions, activities in the Bachman household offered many opportunities to move beyond the classroom.[69]

Lucy Audubon employed hands-on instruction because it made sense to do so, and this approach was not completely unfamiliar to the Bachman youngsters. Although accustomed to the lecture and memorization approach found in most schools, they lived in a home that became a living laboratory during their formative years, and they could learn about the natural world as easily in the garden as they could in the parlor.[70] And yet they lived in a home where books were valued, some especially so out of affection for Audubon, and they could leaf through *Birds of America* and the *Ornithological Biographies* when studying natural history. What else they read is less clear. John Bachman certainly had access to books in the collections of the German Friendly Society and the Charleston Library Society, but it is unlikely that classical treatises, taxonomic and classificatory manuals, or the highly detailed monographs found there were of much use.[71] Whether it was Pliny (*Natural History*) or Linnaeus (*Entomologia* and others), Buffon (*Natural History of Birds*) or Miller (*Gardener's Dictionary*), Michaux (*Histoire de Chênes de l'amérique*) or Smith (*Introduction to Physiological and Systematic Botany*), the children neither could have nor should have attempted these books. As experts knew, many students learned little more than elocution as they learned to read; if books containing complicated subject matter were to be of any use, they had to be thoroughly and completely simplified.[72]

Truthfully, the Bachman girls favored magazines that focused on religious and moral questions. They read *The Casket, The American Farmer*; *The Monthly Traveler*, and the *Southern Literary Messenger*, and although *Parley's Magazine for Children and Youth* contained fascinating articles on plants and animals as well as the usual fare, it is unclear whether they had copies at their disposal.[73] What is certain, however, is that they had access to information found in *Parley's* on naturalists such as Buffon, John Latham (1740–1837), Francis Willoughby (1635–1672), Thomas Bewick (1753–1828), Georges Cuvier (1769–1832), Alexander Wilson, and even John James Audubon. They learned about these men and their work through Lucy Audubon, who had a wealth of practical knowledge gleaned from a lifetime of assisting her naturalist husband, and then through Maria Martin. Even better, they woke every morning in a home that was a living laboratory. There were preserved and stuffed specimens on the ground floor; there were collections of mounted insects, pressed plants, and other curiosities in the parlors; and there were gardens filled with ornamental and useful plants as well as domesticated and wild animals in varying states of confinement.

It would, of course, be foolish to dismiss the importance of books entirely. Their father was a learned man who counted among his friends important scientists such as Audubon and Stephen Elliott (1771–1830), the first president of the Literary and Philosophical Society. Through Audubon's generosity, he owned copies of volume one of *Birds* and the *Ornithological Biography*, and in 1834, shortly after the departure of the Audubon family, Bachman purchased Elliott's *Sketch of the Botany of South Carolina and Georgia* (1821).[74] With fifteen hundred pages in two volumes, it had extensive summary remarks in lay terminology detailing where a plant was found, when, and by whom, and it provided easily understood information on morphology, geographical distribution, and plant propagation.[75] Equally important was the fact that Latin and English names were used in conformity with the principle of priority and binomial nomenclature. In all, Elliott exemplified the scientific principles and practices that increasingly preoccupied Bachman, and his *Sketch* also held great potential as a reference for budding botanists. At the same time, Elliott's work had limitations. The line drawings appended to it provided little inspiration to Maria Martin.

While Elliott's descriptions were useful, she preferred to learn about plants in the field rather than in the study. Actual specimens were endlessly intriguing, and Maria expressed this sentiment poetically in a "Keepsake Album" belonging to her niece Eliza:

> A plant, a leaf, a blossom, but contains
> A folio volume.—We may read, and read,
> And read again; and still find something new;
> Something to please and something to instruct,
> Even in the humble weed.[76]

Beyond observation, botanical expertise was acquired through drawing, a self-evident fact to a published illustrator like Maria. But leaving nothing to chance, Audubon sent a reminder that the students left in her care should "not neglect Drawing."[77] If he did not mention Maria Martin specifically in the letter posted not long after he left Charleston, her role was nonetheless clear. Her expertise would guide them as they undertook to "outline flowers or Plants of any sort correctly" so as to not forget what they had learned before he could "forward them good models" to copy. This was good advice. The models did not arrive for another five months.

Perhaps Audubon did not look hard enough for the promised models. He admitted to spending but a half-day in April searching for them; however, he claimed that his efforts were "in vain" because "New York with a population of 250,000 souls, possesses only 2 Drawing Masters—those instruct 3 *months* and starve for Nine of the year."[78] The search resumed when he got to London, and Audubon sent a "book of Instruction in the Art of Painting" to his Charleston protégés in August.[79] Intended for beginners, George Brookshaw's *Groups of Flowers, Drawn and Accurately Coloured after Nature, with Full Directions for the Young Artist, containing six plates and accompanying instructions* (1817) provided directions to transform even the most inexperienced amateur into a credible painter.[80]

A decorative furniture maker and botanical illustrator who also published under the pseudonym John G. Brown, Brookshaw (c. 1751–1823) produced highly simplified painting manuals. Apparently it was possible to become a botanical artist by tracing the "patterns" provided and by following a few elementary directions; unfortunately, Brookshaw's instructions were less helpful than intended. How, for example, did advising a novice to vary "tints" or to apply darker colors over lighter ones facilitate efforts to master shading? Equally unhelpful were his instructions that fine details could be drawn in with a pencil or India ink and that "softening" could be achieved by adding intermediary "tints" between primary "tints." Elaboration was missing when it came to technique and erudition absent when he tried to include theoretical material. Brookshaw's references to Joshua Reynolds, or that "great master of elegance," for example, advanced neither practical skill nor academic knowledge. Snippets from the *Discourses* would have been lost on the uninitiated and superfluous to those who cared not that the academician "strongly recommends historical painters to study and paint from groups of Flowers, as objects the best calculated for a free and graceful manner of composing."

Shortcomings aside, Maria Martin had the practical knowledge needed to use Brookshaw's manual to best advantage, and she guided her nieces as they learned the basics. Although none became accomplished illustrators, they painted for their own edification, and Maria Rebecca painted flowers while living in England and Eliza's keepsake album was filled with drawings by herself and others.[81] They also developed an aptitude for botany that pleased their father. After four months of study with Lucy Audubon and their aunt Maria, John Bachman declared his children were far superior to the "fashionable Boys & Girls" who were unable to "tell a thistle from a cauliflower."[82]

Modestly put, Bachman's compliment was nevertheless unusual. If he was encouraging in person, he left little to posterity in that vein. A dedicated correspondent who wrote much about natural history, he wrote little about his children's accomplishments, and when he did mention them it was not out of fatherly pride. For example, when he relayed the part played by his children in creating "his" herbarium some thirty years after the plants were picked and pressed, he did so incidentally. Indeed, he only mentioned their role when responding to accusations that he had mistreated Northern soldiers during the Civil War. Because the charge was leveled by a pastor from Philadelphia, his defense was vigorous and went well beyond the matter in dispute as he recounted depredations of Union soldiers that included the wanton destruction of his books. Emphasizing the tragedy of his loss, Bachman remarked that among the most prized of his possessions burned in the City of Columbia was a collection of preserved plant specimens described as "the labor of myself and the ladies of my house for many years."[83] Normally, however, little was said about work done by others in the Bachman household.

For the most part, Bachman's correspondents needed no reminding of who performed the mundane tasks of "doing" science or of what those tasks were, and so when his silence was broken there was usually a good reason. In 1835, for example, he relayed an anecdote about his eldest daughter, Maria Rebecca, to highlight her virtues as she neared marriageable age. He reported that Ria, as they called her, was collecting birds' heads "as industriously employed as if she was to have a share in the profits."[84] Cast in an amusing light, her efforts reflect considerable hands-on experience and familiarity with at least some of the ornithological literature. Although the contents of her father's library cannot be determined conclusively, by the end of 1834 Ria had access to at least two of the volumes of the *Ornithological Biography*. She also had access to Elliott's *Botany*, Thomas Bewick's monographs on birds (two volumes, 1797–1804), and William Yarrell's (1784–1856) work on swans (*Linnaean Society Transactions*, v. 16. 1830).[85] In other words, she had the means to develop her intellect, and she did. But as delighted as any parent might be when a child is both intelligent and hard working, Bachman's comment suggests something else. His daughter had been raised to be a good wife and helpmeet and that was worth mentioning. Indeed, two years later, as Bachman contemplated Ria's betrothal to John Woodhouse Audubon, he was pleased to report she was "prudent and industrious" as well as possessed of an "education and habits" that "will, I think render her an assistant, as well as a blessing to you."[86] If John Woodhouse was not quite what the pastor of the most affluent congregation in the state desired in a son-in-law, Ria would not fall short as a wife and mother, and her aunt Maria played an important role in ensuring she met the high standards expected of women in her family.

Although a spinster, Maria Martin could conceive of no other fate than marriage for her nieces, and their husbands would not suffer because her nieces had been poorly prepared. First and foremost, they were to be submissive to the men they married, and it was thus entirely predictable that Bachman denounced the "fashionable, lazy young lady, who spends her nights at balls, and her days in lolling on the sofa with a novel, leaving her poor mother to toil, economize–and to speculate for her" while Maria agreed in silence.[87] Normally circumspect, Maria seldom asserted herself, although she could not quite resist when observing a mismatched married couple. On this one very unusual occasion, she spoke her mind as she predicted an unhappy future for a woman

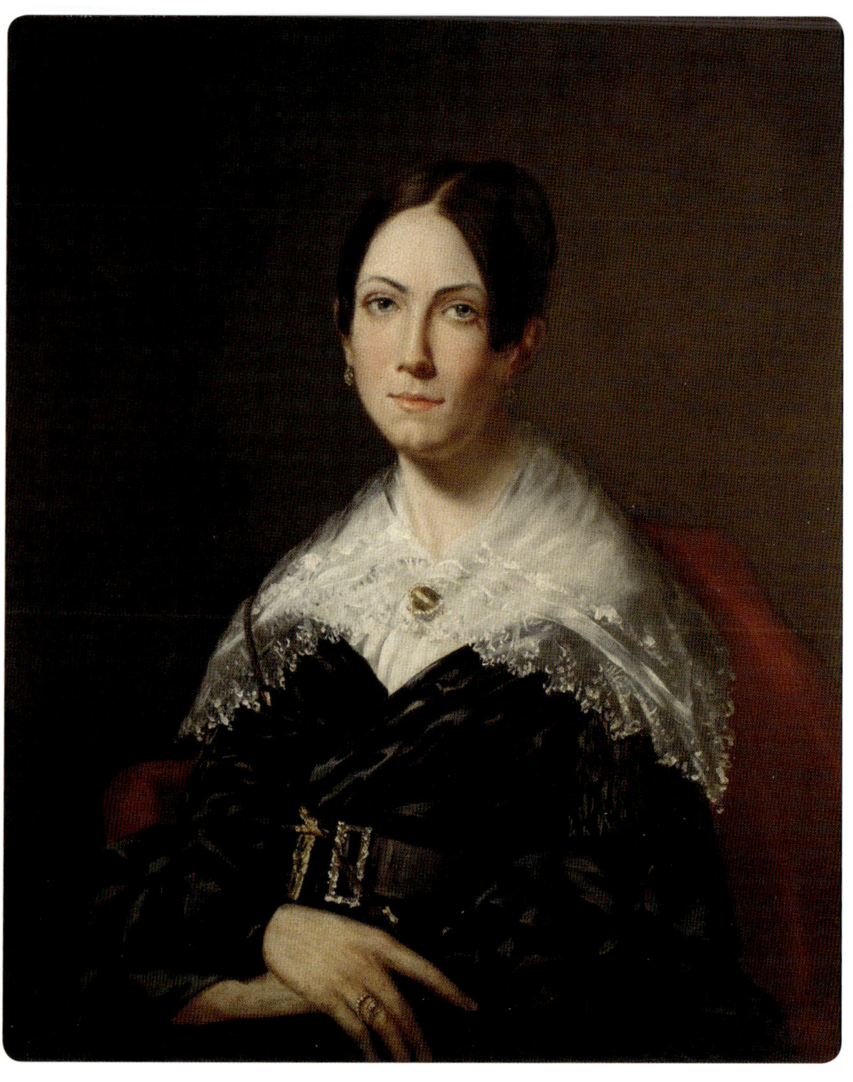

FIGURE 48. Maria Rebecca Bachman Audubon (1816–1840) by John Woodhouse Audubon, 1838. Courtesy of Ann Carr.

unprepared for "the realities of life" as "the wife of a visionary author."[88] In her world, it was simple: women existed to make men's lives easier. They were to suffer in silence and defer to husbands in public. It was crucial that such training began early so that the next generation of wives and mothers acquired the necessary attributes for their divinely dictated responsibilities, and Maria Martin was often in charge of that training. Although she stepped into this role in her sister's stead, she was unfazed that she was there by proxy. She did not shrink from pointing out lapses in her nieces' behavior or from reminding them that they must be cheerful and polite, thoughtful of others, and "acquire the habit of doing all things well."[89] Indeed, with Maria Martin in charge, Bachman could be confident that his daughters would be well prepared for their roles as wives and helpmeets to the next generation of Lutheran leaders and scholars.

Bachman's confidence was no small compliment. Moreover, as Maria's efforts proved successful, the reverend's enthusiasm for female education grew. In 1857, for example, as Bachman enumerated the many reasons to support a preparatory school for young men, he spoke of the salutatory effect such a college would have on young women. In a speech that might have alarmed more conservative clerics and congregants assembled to celebrate the laying of the cornerstone at Newberry College, Bachman actually promoted education, although not egalitarianism, as he pointed out the merits of such an institution: "Where men are well educated, their wives, sisters, and daughters will not consent to remain far in the rear. Woman is the companion and the equal of man, and it will soon be perceived, that although she is not destined to occupy the posts designed for the more rugged sex, yet that in all that is valuable in education—in all that can inform the mind, regulate the affections and adorn her character as a Christian woman, she is fully capable of qualifying herself for her high destination."[90] In many ways, these words simply articulated long-held views. Twenty years earlier, as he described attributes possessed by his eldest daughter, his perspective on the importance of a well-educated helpmeet was both well formed and well founded. That he was so inclined was in no small way due to Maria Martin.

When the matter of whom Maria Rebecca might marry arose, Maria Martin undoubtedly had an opinion, but no trace of her view remains. Certainly, the possibility that their children might marry presented itself as the two families lived together and worked together—especially as Maria Rebecca and John Woodhouse became sufficiently enamored of one another that upon his departure they began to correspond almost daily; however, despite Bachman's genuine affection for Audubon and his family, the reverend was not immediately convinced that nineteen-year-old John Woodhouse was a good match for his fourteen-year-old daughter.[91] Admittedly, Ria's scientific knowledge and artistic skills prepared her to assist a husband whose avocation (or even vocation) would have benefited from such abilities, but John Woodhouse was just too young to be assessed on his virtues as a husband. He was bright enough, successfully memorizing scientific names and descriptions of birds, but just two years earlier his own mother thought him insufficiently motivated and his "reflective powers" underdeveloped.[92] Such considerations aside, there were more important concerns: as a pastor's daughter, it was assumed that Ria would marry a pious Christian, preferably a Lutheran—and John Woodhouse was neither.[93]

Indeed, the son may have been just a little too much like the father. Despite a healthy fear of God, John James's views of organized religion were problematic. When he exclaimed in 1833 that Bachman was "the *only parson on Earth* for me!", he was hardly endorsing Lutheranism.[94] Rather, his turn of phrase was intended to emphasize the esteem he had for a man who would have to work mightily to overcome his disdain for religion. He considered clerics to be charlatans and, whether highly organized or loosely configured, Audubon found fault even in his experiences as a young man boarding with Quakers. He described his life then as being "little livelier than a prison."[95] Even though John Woodhouse had spent most of his formative years with a woman who lived her life "as if I was to be called to the other world [at] any moment" and who reminded her sons to "preserve" their morals so she would "never have to blush for you or shed a tear of reproach," Audubon's irreligious views affected him deeply.[96] And he knew it. Upon meeting his future father-in-law in 1833, John Woodhouse confessed that his "religious education has [*sic*] been much neglected," and he promised to "improve" and "always go to Church on Sunday provided my Father has no hurry work for me to do."[97]

Trying to please, John Woodhouse was too guileless to respond other than honestly to prodding, and his frank admissions about religion could hardly have endeared him to the cassocked pastor whose daughter could have found any number of better-qualified suitors closer to home. Nonetheless, by the time John Woodhouse left Charleston five months later, he was referring to "my Maria." And he was doing so with his mother's consent: Lucy Audubon approved of the match almost immediately. John Bachman, however, was more cautious. He did not concede to the match until almost four years later when he spoke on behalf of himself and Harriet as he gave their "full consent and blessing." All John Woodhouse had to do was prove "himself a man in intelligence and in the practice of those virtues which will render him a blessing to society and an ornament to his name and family with the means of a moderate support."[98]

It was hardly surprising that financial considerations were a concern, and well before Bachman agreed to the betrothal, discussions occurred about how a man who earned his keep by assisting his father as a taxidermist and painter might provide for a wife and family. For his part, John Woodhouse was willing to do whatever necessary to secure the financial means and respectability needed to convince Ria's family that he was a suitable husband. As he and his parents prepared to depart Charleston, a plan was hatched to transform him into suitable husband material. Unsurprisingly, it drew upon the only life he had ever known.

Ignoring the fact that his mother had labored as a teacher to sustain the family when subscriptions to *Birds* barely funded fieldwork and supplies, John Woodhouse surmised that a similar project might provide the "moderate support" expected of him, and he proposed a book on mammals. John Bachman was studying mammals, and as he collected specimens and information on rabbits, hares, and shrews it became apparent that there was an opportunity for a nature artist in this field.[99] Desperate to please Bachman, John Woodhouse wrote Victor proposing they publish a book on quadrupeds: "I am to learn Landscape painting or Engraving which ever your judgment should approve and if neither of those are to your liking you must find something more profitable for *both*. I have had *a castle* going up for some time but I am afraid to venture to far as I have not the foundation *certain*.—but the plan is to publish with you the 'Quadrupeds of America' but I am not able to come to any conclusion for want of your advice, and that will be had when we meet."[100] It was hypothetically possible that such an endeavor just might prove lucrative.

John James and Lucy were equally determined to make the match, and they outlined their son's prospects the following year. They reminded Ria's family that John Woodhouse was part of a "Working Family," and that he and his brother were not only gainfully employed, but also that any leisure time they might have was well spent. According to John James, his sons kept company with "Learned & Aimiable" [*sic*] individuals," and he assured Bachman that their collective efforts would "leave my Sons in a good way, having the hope that when all is settled each will have a very fair amount to go on with."[101] He also periodically offered further evidence of John Woodhouse's character and initiative. By the end of 1835, for example, John James reported his son was becoming a highly sought after portraitist who could "Maintain *Two* very decently in Edinburgh through his art."[102]

Partly pretense, partly true, Audubon's optimism failed him as he faced 1836. If he made extravagant claims that John Woodhouse had a bright future as a portrait painter at the beginning of December, he ended the month by imploring John Bachman and Maria Martin to work harder "*for the sake of our Dear Children* whom I Know are truly busy themselves!"[103] He was almost frantic with worry that his son's matrimonial plans would collapse and there was little he could do about that as he labored mightily to complete the *Ornithological Biography*, paint figures for the last volume of the elephant folio, and supervise the engraving and coloring of plates. Much of 1835 was spent in England working on *Birds*, and any hopes John Woodhouse entertained for a speedy reunion with *his* Maria were fading as their stay was extended indefinitely. There had been a fire in New York that destroyed Audubon's guns, and because he wanted English gunsmiths to replace the lost firearms, the entire family was detained several months.[104] In an attempt to make the best of a bad situation, John James and Lucy sent their sons to Europe to see the sights while they awaited their departure.[105] They also tried to impress Bachman by claiming that the trip would be of "Immense benefit" to them. While not normally impressed by the idle rich who sent their sons on a "Grand Tour," Bachman would have been favorably disposed to their peregrinations: they spent the better part of four months in Italy examining classical art, many works depicting "scriptural subjects," and they also searched out exotic animals in captivity and visited natural history "cabinets."

In some ways, Bachman's consent was a matter of time. John Woodhouse had made every effort to prove his worthiness, and Lutheran doctrine recommended parental approval but advised against undue interference in choosing spouses.[106] When John Woodhouse returned from London, Bachman agreed to the formal courtship. In October, he informed John James that he was amenable to "let[ting] the young folks court & post away" with the proviso that they must continue "their drawing & improving each other, especially in French."[107] A month later, John Woodhouse was in Charleston. While there he became better acquainted with Ria, and he and his father painted specimens collected in the far west by Thomas Nuttall and John Kirk Townsend. Together with and Maria Martin, they completed the last fifty plates of *Birds of America* between November and mid-February. When John Woodhouse departed Charleston after four months of hard work on *Birds,* he was much more confident of Bachman's view of him as a prospective son-in-law, confiding to Victor that he was "much higher in favour with Mr Bachman now than when I left this just 11½ months and two years since."[108]

Bachman's confidence in John Woodhouse was also bolstered because the plan to replicate the success of *Birds* with a book on mammals was beginning to take shape. The reverend's interest in mammals was producing results as papers on rodents and lagomorphs were drafted, and both John James and John Woodhouse were attentive to his burgeoning vocation. When they left Charleston for lands along the Gulf of Mexico, they added mammalian species to the list of birds sought in these territories—a gesture that could only improve John Woodhouse's standing as a prospective son-in-law.[109] Also important was the new dynamic that emerged during this expedition. As squirrels, rabbits, hares, and even a wild cat were collected and forwarded to Bachman, the nature of the working relationship between the men changed. Until 1837, John Bachman supplied John James with specimens and information; with the western expedition, John James and John Woodhouse became collectors and, over time, this role reversal became increasingly pronounced. Initially, Bachman focused on squirrels, and his goal was modest: he wanted to obtain every American species of Sciuridae. But as his interests expanded to include other quadrupeds, he needed more and more specimens, and no matter how important father and son were to painting species for the *Viviparous Quadrupeds of North America*, as the project grew into a multivolume work, Bachman was clearly in control. As usual, Maria Martin played an important, if subordinate, role.

When father and son reappeared on her doorstep in November 1836, Maria was ready to resume her former role, advising Audubon in advance that she would be "quite at your disposal."[110] She promised to paint, do secretarial work, or anything else that might be asked of her. And she was as good as her word. She was his amanuensis, forwarding information to Lucy in London. She also painted botanicals and helped to some extent with collecting and preserving—or skinning and stuffing—birds.[111] In many significant ways, her efforts made the visit in 1836–1837 one of the most productive periods devoted to *Birds*—even as she was being pulled in other directions. Her interest in botanicals was as strong as ever, but she added bromeliads such as *Tillandsia* and tropical (or neotropical) plants such as *Bauhinia*, *Heliconia*, *Alpinia*, the candelabra tree (*Senna didymobotrya*) and poinciana shrub, as well as orchids and passion flowers to the native species painted for Audubon.[112] More importantly, however, she was also assisting John Bachman at this time. Although her brother-in-law sometimes joked that he could not induce her to abandon "beautiful flowers" for "shrews & rats," the fact is that when he needed assistance as he dissected and described mammalian specimens, he turned to Maria Martin.[113]

Less pleasant than working at her easel, particularly *en plein air*, Maria had worked next door to the taxidermy room for years and was better acclimated than most. Nonetheless, working side by side on mammalian specimens required a strong constitution. It was bad enough that the odoriferous haze of the workroom clung to clothing and repelled those who got too close, it was far worse to be in close proximity to the decaying carcasses.[114] In any event, Maria responded as expected. No matter how she felt about rodents and insectivores,

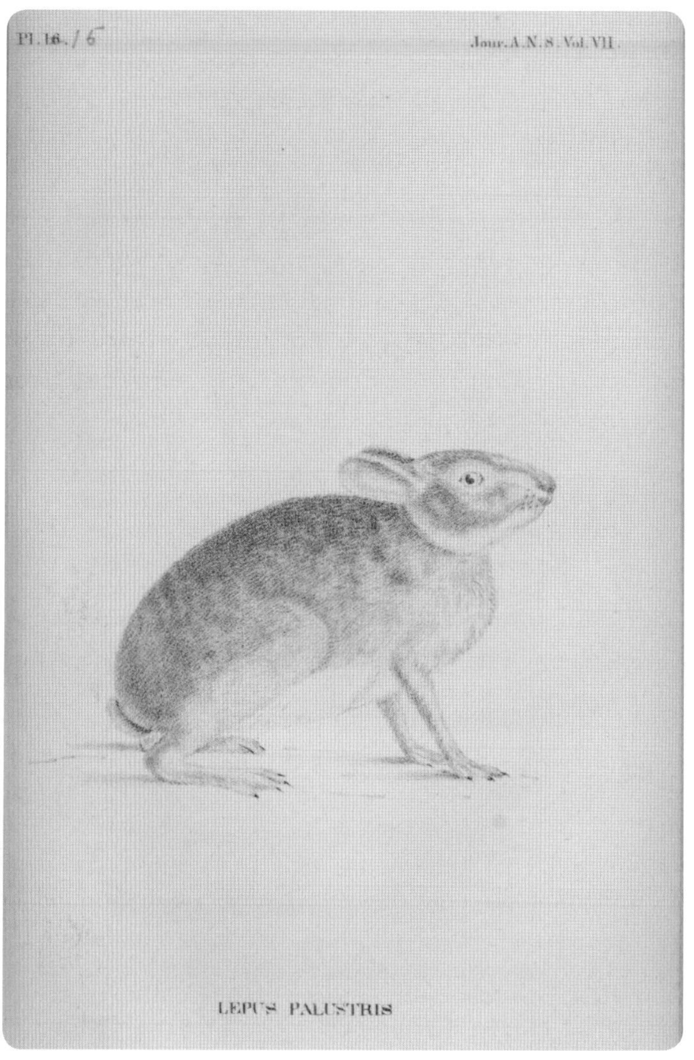

FIGURE 49. Maria Martin sketched two plates for John Bachman, "Description of a New Species of Hare Found in South Carolina," *Journal of the Academy of Natural Sciences of Philadelphia* 7, pt. 2 (1837): 194–199, plates 15 and 16. Depicted here is a specimen in its entirety, plate 15. The species was incorrectly identified as *Lepus palustris* and has since been classified as *Sylvilagus*. Courtesy of the Gerstein Science Information Centre, University of Toronto Libraries. (Public Domain)

Maria Martin sketched them for Bachman. Freely admitting his ineptitude as an artist, the sketches of the ears and hind feet of two rabbits (incorrectly identified as hares and named *Lepus Palustris* and *Lepus Americanus* [*sic*]), as well as four species of shrew published in the *Journal of the Academy of Sciences of Philadelphia* in early 1836, bear a strong resemblance to a muskrat foot Maria

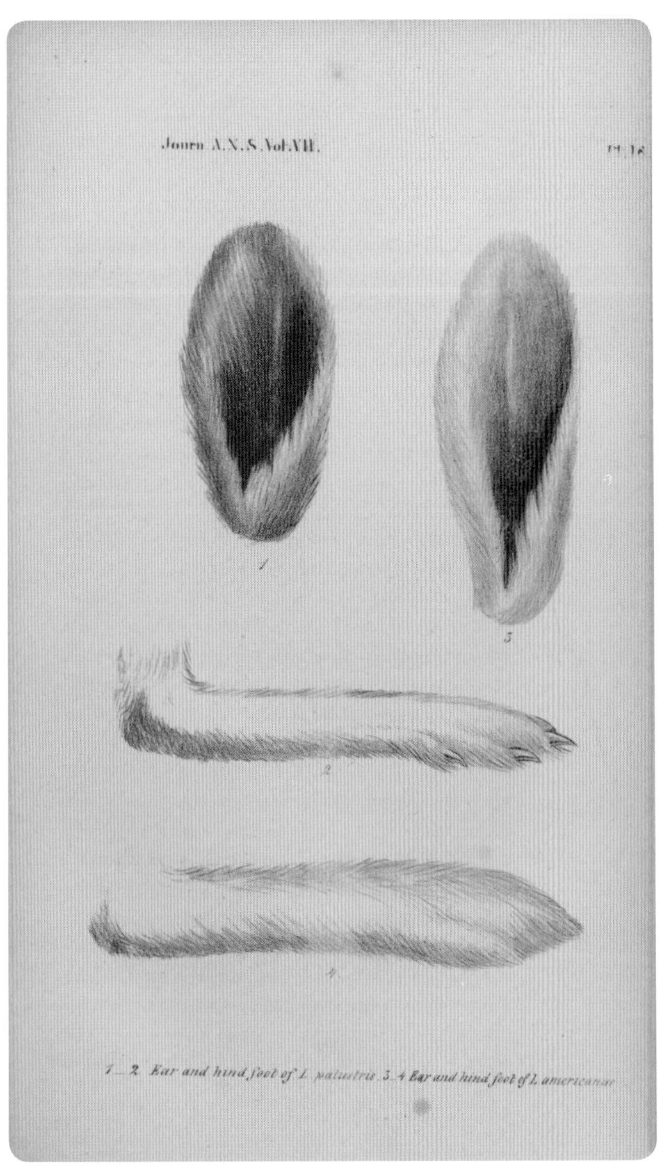

FIGURE 50. The second plate drawn by Maria Martin for "Description of a New Species of Hare Found in South Carolina," *Journal of the Academy of Natural Sciences of Philadelphia* 7, pt. 2 (1837): 194–99. Plate 16 depicts the feet and ears, significant anatomical parts in the identification process. Courtesy of the Gerstein Science Information Centre, University of Toronto Libraries. (Public Domain)

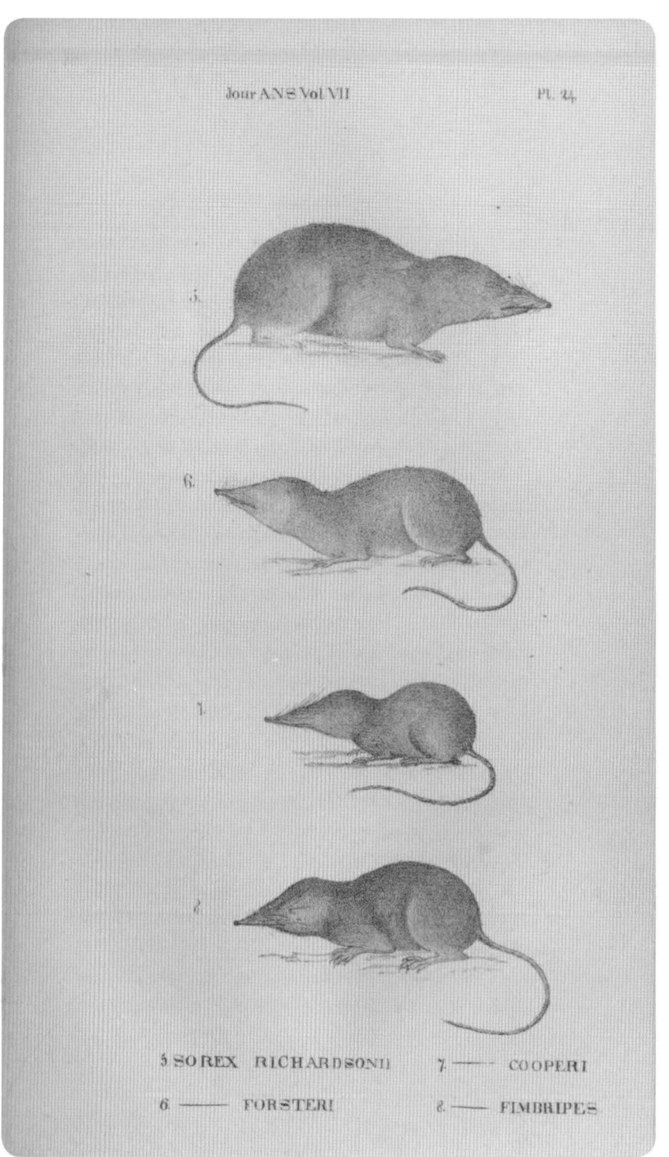

FIGURE 51. Maria Martin sketched four shrews for Bachman, "Some Remarks on the Genus Sorex [Shrews], with a Monograph of the North American Species," *Journal of the Academy of Natural Sciences of Philadelphia* 7, pt. 2 (1837): 362–402, plate 23. Bachman stated he had found four species and Maria Martin thus illustrated from specimens: *Sorex carolinensis, S. longirostris, S.cinereous*, and *S.Dekayi*. Of these, only the southern short-tailed shrew (*Blarina carolinensis* and *Blarina c. carolinensis*) and the southeastern shrew (*Sorex* [*Otisorex*] *longirostris* and *S.* [*Otisorex*] *l. longirostris*) were new species. Courtesy of the Gerstein Science Information Centre, University of Toronto Libraries. (Public Domain)

Martin sketched as they tried to determine whether a local specimen was the "common" muskrat or a new species.[115] Bachman might have asked John James or John Woodhouse to prepare the illustrations but they were far away when the articles went to press and, in any event, his sister-in-law was quite capable. That she was not acknowledged formally would hardly have mattered. Maria Martin had a history of working anonymously.

Before the year was out, John Woodhouse and Maria Rebecca were married; the appearance of the last volume of the elephant folio (and companion biographies) was imminent; and planning had begun on an octavo edition of *Birds*. The proposed project on quadrupeds was on hold, although John Bachman had published some articles on small mammals, and he was about to enter a new phase in his life as a scientist. With Maria Martin at his side, everything seemed to be coming together nicely. However, as work shifted from *Birds* to the book on quadrupeds, there was one impediment after another, and the woman who had been so helpful when working on *Birds* was often of little assistance. Rather, Maria was overwhelmingly preoccupied with caring for family members, several of whom died after lengthy illnesses. While prevented periodically from assisting Audubon during the 1830s because she was "nursing the sick"[116]—that is, taking care of her nieces and nephews when they came down with the usual childhood maladies or tending to her sister's chronic afflictions—during the 1840s Maria Martin was almost entirely focused on her family. It was not that she did not take her work for Bachman and Audubon seriously; she simply had obligations that were more important.

5

FAMILY AND SCIENCE

Beyond Botanicals

In the summer of 1839, Maria Martin went to New York City. It had been more than a decade since she had strayed so far from home, and only an extraordinary event like the birth of a great-niece could tempt her to do so again. That spring, Ria had given birth to her second daughter, Harriet (1839–1933), and if Maria wanted to meet the new babe, there was only one way to do so as Ria's confinement was prolonged by complications. At the time, there was no inkling that her difficulties were caused by consumption, but her delayed recovery meant that she was housebound, and so Maria Martin went to her. Even more remarkable: Harriet Bachman went, too.

Between 1815 and 1831, Harriet Bachman was confined at least thirteen times, and after that she was frequently indisposed by illness. She rarely left home, and when she did, she never ventured far from Charleston. She boarded periodically with friends and family whose homes were located inland and thus had climates considered conducive to her health, but she did not travel for anything less consequential. In 1839, however, Harriet joined Maria in traveling to meet her two granddaughters: the infant named in her honor and little Lucy (1838–1909)—or LuLu—who was born the previous year while John Woodhouse and Ria were in London working on *Birds*. No doubt envious that her husband had the good fortune to meet LuLu while on a physician-prescribed European tour intended to restore his health, she and her sister went to New York accompanied by a nephew, Maynard Strobel (1812–1868).

While there they visited friends as well as family, did some sightseeing, and even went shopping along Broadway. Their rooms were not far from the bustling thoroughfare, and although Maria found the "noise and turmoil" enough to drive her "crazy," she ventured out from time to time. Her interests tended to the more educational though and she was complimentary about the academy at West Point.[1] The same could be said about choices made elsewhere—for example, Philadelphia. The trio stopped there on the way home, and Maria was particularly impressed by the penitentiary, by the schools for hearing and visually impaired students, and by the state house. But the place that made the most lasting impression was Laurel Hill Cemetery.

Newly established five miles north of Philadelphia along the east side of the Schuylkill River, Laurel Hill mimicked a style pioneered recently in France.[2] Most graveyards were macabre reminders of the horrors of death, but the French model recommended arcadian vistas and sculptural gardens intended to comfort the bereaved, and Maria Martin praised the architects of Laurel Hill for producing the desired "romantic" effect. She wrote at length to her niece Eliza about the solace derived from such surroundings:

> On entering the gate the first object presented is a group of Statuary by [James] Thom. (in coarse stone similar to Tam O Shanter) of Old Mortality, his Poney [*sic*] & Walter Scott listening to him. It is a striking group, and seems to be appropriate as the first object that introduces you to many a storied urn, and animated bust. Numerous and beautiful are the monuments which adorn these peaceful shades, and the dead seem to repose here on beds of Roses, and the rural quiet that reigns around, the natural garlands and beautiful verdure that mingle with the chaste columns and sculptured marble, renders it a scene of varied beauty, and the landscape that meets your view at every opening of the foliage, seems to bring the last sad abode of man to our contemplation with less terror and dread, than when we view the narrow mound in some desolate Church yard covered by rank and noisome weeds.[3]

A survivor of the illnesses to which five of her siblings had succumbed in infancy or early childhood, Eliza Bachman was all too familiar with the fleeting nature of life, and her aunt's description could not but have resonated with her.

The reassurances offered by Laurel Hill would be sorely needed over the next decade. Six more members of Maria's family, including Eliza, died after months of agony. The threat of mortal illness was ever present and traditional therapeutics—blistering, bleeding, purging, and puking—did little to ameliorate physical afflictions or the "desponding" attitudes accompanying unbearable pain and suffering.[4] While the Bachman household reported no deaths from accidental injury, from poisoning due to contaminated food or drink, from complications arising from minor injuries, or from diseases such

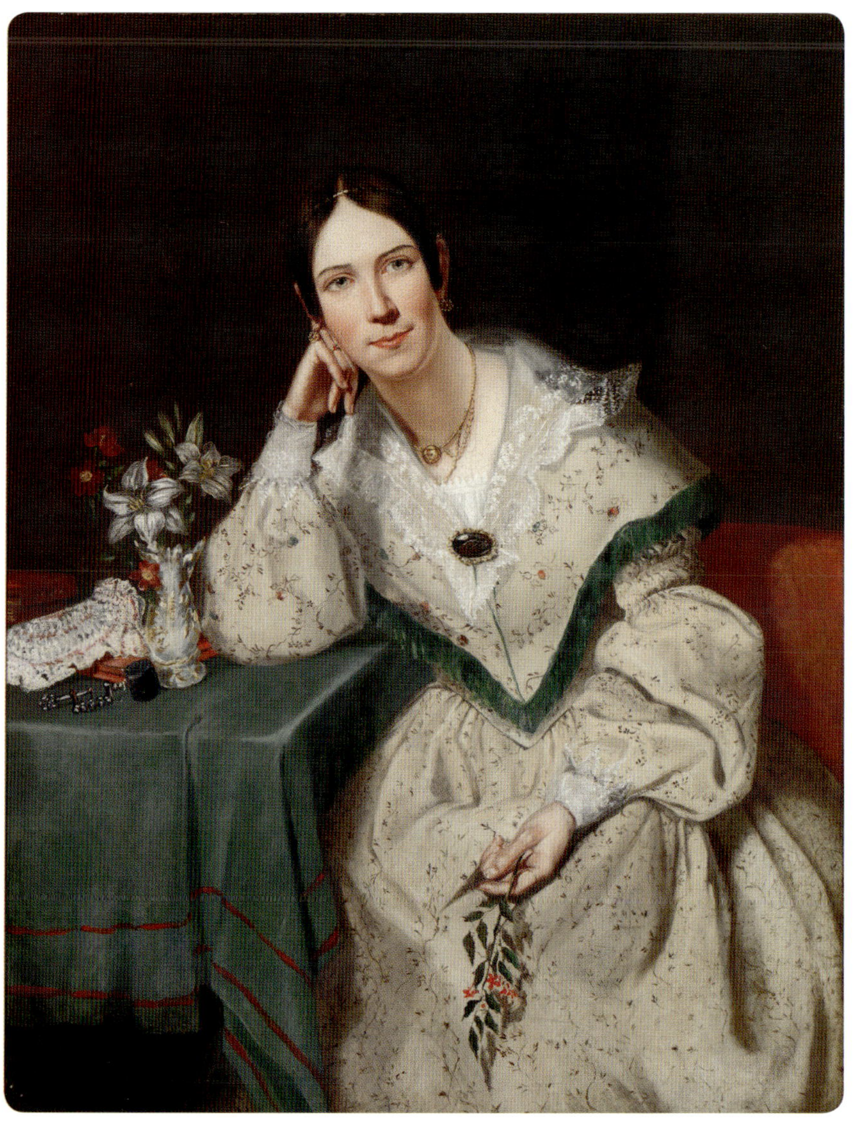

FIGURE 52. Eliza Bachman Audubon (1818–41) unsigned and undated oil attributed to Victor Gifford Audubon, 1840 (Anne Coffin Hanson). 105.4 x 83.2 cm (32.75 x 41.5 in). Courtesy of Blaine Garson.

as malaria and yellow fever, there were plenty of reasons to be concerned about mortality, and it was one of the most frequently invalided, Harriet Bachman, who put into words what others kept to themselves. She described yellow fever with dread, referring to it in 1827 as one of the great "evils" borne by Southerners, and she was sufficiently frightened to propose leaving her childhood home so she and her family could go "to some healthy spot and settle."[5] In this case, however, her concerns were largely unfounded. Most local families were largely untouched by the disease that devastated recent arrivals who disembarked from ships infested with the mosquitos carrying the virus that caused yellow fever.

There was, however, more than enough misery to go around. Fevers, digestive complaints, colds, influenzas, and childhood diseases (measles, diphtheria, scarlet fever, and whooping cough) passed through with sufficient regularity to justify Harriet Bachman's fatalistic outlook, and after decades of chronic illness and the anguish of burying seven children, it was unsurprising that Harriet faced death as if it were long overdue. Just weeks before she died of consumption in 1846, she felt compelled to pass on to her daughter Jane what she had learned from a lifetime of hardship, writing: "you well know that I am never very sanguine in my expectations, but I trust and hope that all will eventually be for the best . . . I have suffered so long & so severely, that from experience I have learned to be content and satisfied with my lot come what will, I view it all as coming from a kind providence intended for some wise purpose, and that it is our duty to submit, always hoping that some remedy will be sent us."[6] Like everyone else in the Bachman family, Harriet believed in an omniscient power whose wisdom exceeded that of mere mortals, but her fatalistic outlook also reflected a lifetime of suffering.

When Ria began to exhibit signs of consumption, her condition was taken in stride. Described matter-of-factly by John Bachman as the "disease from which our family has suffered so much," Ria's symptoms were taken as a sign that Divine Providence was testing her. Deeply religious, the family met such trials with pious resignation. But if the fate of God's creatures rested ultimately with the Creator, it was nevertheless important to aid and comfort the afflicted. In the Bachman home, neither effort nor expense was spared in providing care and, as Ria's condition worsened, it was decided to take her to Virginia Springs. Pulmonary problems were reputedly ameliorated by the mineral waters found there and, in July 1835, John Bachman and Maria Martin took Ria to the Springs.[7]

The first of many fruitless excursions in search of a cure, the trip was a reminder of the reality of life for the maiden aunt who had devoted many months to painting plants and insects in the four years since meeting Audubon: when Maria Martin's family needed her, everything else was set aside. That this was the case was not necessarily obvious, and Audubon, in particular, only discovered just how important his assistant's family obligations were in the summer of 1836. He needed her to paint botanicals as he rushed to complete *Birds*, but she was unable to oblige because she was nursing the sick.

Audubon thought her behavior inconsiderate, and he could not be faulted for thinking so. Until then, she had done everything asked of her and more. Further, not long after his request was rebuffed, she was working alongside him in the painting room on the ground floor of the Bachman home. By November, the sickly season had passed, and Maria returned to painting because she could. It was quite simply Audubon's good fortune that when he drew upon her assistance in 1831, 1832, 1833, and 1834, her family was in good health. It was thus easy to overlook the fact that Maria Martin had commitments that could not be ignored and that painting was set aside when she was needed elsewhere. Indeed, as John Bachman pointed out, she and Harriet could only leave home in 1839 because everyone in his household had been "unusually healthy all summer."[8] At the same time, it would be inaccurate to describe Maria Martin as completely carefree. She had been her mother's companion and assistant for more than twenty-five years, and had Rebecca Martin been obviously ill Maria would not have left her side; however, she was frail, and Maria worried that she might suffer some debilitating setback. In fact, her trip north was marred by what she called "gloomy reflections" on her mother's condition, and she was no doubt relieved to find her little worse than when she left.[9]

Maria Martin did not leave her mother again. Over the winter, Rebecca Martin's health declined, and by the end of April she was "in such a helpless condition" that Maria's days were "almost entirely taken up in attendance on her."[10] However, Maria's assistance was also in demand elsewhere, and she juggled Rebecca's needs with others, particularly those of her niece Eliza, who was showing signs of consumption. To make matters worse, Eliza contracted dengue fever in the autumn. Her father claimed that the "breakbone fever" did not undermine her overall health, but she was sufficiently indisposed that plans to marry Victor Audubon were affected.

Eliza was disappointed. She begged and pleaded with her father, assuring him that she was completely well, until he performed the marriage ceremony on December 4.[11] Hardly less disappointed by the delay, John James and Lucy were anxious to have Victor married and back in New York to assist with the family business. More to the point: John James and Lucy had been promoting the match for at least six years. In 1834, Audubon even drew Maria Martin into the plan as he wrote her in hopes that she could influence Eliza's parents on the matter. He described Victor's accomplishments saying he painted "pretty well," could "scrape God bless the King on the Violin," was studying piano, and had some fluency in "French, German, Spanish and English."[12] He made the best case he could for his son's ability to provide for a wife and family. As John Bachman had pointed out when John Woodhouse first indicated his desire to marry Ria, financial considerations were at least as important as academic and artistic achievement, but the best that could be said for Victor was that he was frugal: he could live on a thousand dollars per year. Nonetheless, with characteristic bravado, John James summed up boastfully claiming that: "If he is not a man fit for any fair maid my name is not John J.A!"

By 1839, Victor had apparently demonstrated himself a worthy suitor, and in anticipation of returning to America, Lucy Audubon outlined how they could reunite with the Bachman family so as to be together for the impending wedding and resume their work in natural history. Although the plans changed between June and December as John James and Lucy decided to resettle in New York City, a letter posted in Edinburgh laid out their aspirations for Victor's future:

> My plan as Papa agrees, of all going to Charleston for the Winter to be confined, to be married[,] to draw and write about quadrupeds and consider where the permanent abode should be is a good one provided you find a roof to shelter us, however we have it in the hands of you all on that side [of] the Sea and we shall be content on looking over the items you will see what seems the Birds of America required and I am sure without that (tho' we lived by it) you would find our expenditure quite moderate, for the number of us and the comfort we have had.[13]

There was much riding on this marriage. It not only represented an important step in the development of the family business but also brought an end to what had been a longstanding worry that Victor would fall short in his duty to the family.

Of the two boys, Victor Gifford was considered the clever one. He was expected to shoulder greater responsibility for *Birds*, and he often did as he supervised the printing and distribution from London. His personal life caused concern though.[14] As early as 1831, Victor was cautioned to avoid "embarrassing [*sic*] engagements." He clearly did not heed this advice, and his indifference did not go unnoticed. In 1836, he was on the verge of marrying songstress Adelaide Kemble (1815–1879), whose talents were well known to London opera fans in the 1840s, and Lucy was concerned. Nor did it help that her older sister, Fanny Kemble (1809–1893), was a well-known actress. Lucy made sure that Victor knew how she felt about his infatuation, writing him that Miss Kemble's "peculiar education and circumstances" would be contrary to the "feelings, inclinations, and habits" valued by his family.[15] Confident that her remonstrations would elicit the intended result and that Victor would "not forget what is due to his parents," Lucy was overoptimistic. It was not long before Victor entertained similar aspirations for Blanche Sully, a sister of his father's friend Thomas Sully. In 1839, however, John James and Lucy were rewarded for their diligence. Victor was betrothed to Eliza Bachman, and she, like her sister Ria, had many virtues. She was, they were happy to report, "so amiably inclined that I trust my dear child will reap all he deserves from the union. [adding] These changes make me feel my children have arrived at maturity and we are passing away from the checquered [*sic*] Scene."[16]

In the end, the nuptials were only slightly delayed. Still feeble, Eliza managed to convince her father that she was well enough to marry and move to New York City, and by mid-December the newlyweds were with John James and Lucy in their rented home in lower Manhattan.[17] Eliza was confident she would be fine. After all, her father had told her of how he had been "cured" of a "hemorrhage of the lungs" as a young man, and physicians were of the view that consumption could be cured repeatedly.[18] She had every reason to hope that her improvement was permanent; however, she never really shook off the "cold" that delayed her marriage. Moreover, her optimism could not but have been dampened when she arrived in New York and saw her sister. Ria was desperately ill. She rarely left her chamber, and she could not even care for her children.

When Ria left Charleston in 1837, she was in good health. Admittedly, there had been a bout with consumption that sent her to Virginia Springs but it was believed she had bested the dreaded disease. However, after two years in the British Isles and Northern states—both considered consumptive climates—she was very ill. While Ria's debility, specifically her difficulty walking, was noticeable more than a year earlier, it had been attributed to childbirth. When Eliza arrived in New York, it was clear that Ria's frailty was caused by something else, and she said so. She wrote Mary Davis, a longtime family friend, describing Ria's decline:

> By this time you will be aware of the indisposition of dear Ria and this I'm sure will be a sufficient excuse for me. Mamma's [LBA] time has been so fully occupied in taking care of the little ones and in preparing delicacies to tempt the appetite of the invalid that my time has been fully taken up in keeping dear Ria's company and trying to raise her spirits. The poor girl has suffered severely from a sore mouth and a general weakness, which rendered us all for a few days quite anxious about her but she has had such kind attendance and so skilful a Physician that she is now in

> a fair way of recovering, this morning we took a ride through the city together, which seemed to refresh her very much and this evening she was downstairs, eating her bread and milk on the sofa. The weather I hope will soon moderate and we will then be able to take some delightful walks together.[19]

Eliza had come face-to-face with the ravages of consumption, and Ria's condition did not improve. Rather, it deteriorated in the new year. She developed "a bad cold after she had been a week, about the house," and was then "seized with an intermittent and could not regain her strength sufficiently to nurse the Babe."

This turn for the worse prompted those around her to suggest a change of scenery. Any plans Eliza might have had about rekindling sisterly bonds were dashed as Ria, John Woodhouse, and their eldest daughter, Lucy, left for Charleston, where it was hoped Ria would rally in "the land of early days and young associates."[20] Such benign efforts were futile. The warmth of the Southern sun and the comforts of her childhood home effected little improvement and her physicians advocated heroic measures.[21] Countless rounds of blistering seemed to harm more than help, and the same could be said for the laudanum, calomel, anodynes, mercury, and herbals prescribed by her doctors. Nothing seemed to work. By mid-April, her physicians conceded defeat and recommended a "change of air."[22]

It was hoped that a visit to Aiken, a defunct railroad hub just southeast of Columbia, would help. The dry, balmy climate there was reputedly beneficial for consumptives, and such rumors were enough to convince John Woodhouse that he should do everything in his power to relocate Ria to a place where her constant coughing and bodily wasting might be forestalled. Ever the optimist, John Woodhouse reported that Aiken had produced the promised effect, but John Bachman was skeptical. He decided to go to Aiken and witness the alleged improvement for himself. Ria had left home just two weeks earlier but what he saw shocked him. He quickly returned to Charleston to fetch one of her physicians and arrange to have her carried home "on a bed."[23]

When the group arrived in Charleston, John James was there. He, too, was shocked by Ria's condition, and he could not hide his concern. He wrote Victor that she was so "feeble and so emaciated that it gives me pain to look at [her] face."[24] And Ria was not the only invalid in the house: the grandmother for whom Ria had been named was also bedridden. Moreover, his normally stoic assistant was overwhelmed by her responsibilities. As Rebecca Martin became increasingly infirm, she required constant attention but Maria Martin also had to assist, where and when she could, with her desperately ill niece.

This was hardly the first time there had been more than one invalid in the Bachman home, but in 1840 Maria labored under unusual conditions: her slaves were, she reported, unable to perform their normal tasks let alone nurse the sick. Even while Ria was in Aiken, Maria found herself overextended, writing Eliza, "Your mother Jane and myself have scarcely a moment at our disposal." She editorialized as she elaborated: "When I tell you that Venus has never done the most trifling thing since you have been away, and that Thomas is obliged to supply her place in the kitchen, and that Nancy is in a particular way which you know always makes her lie by for three or four months at least, and she is now in chamber and of no use, you will be able to form some idea of the inconvenience we are suffering, and although Mrs Audubon complains of having to change her servants we cannot but think that you are much better off as we are burdened with sick ones, and have a parcel of noisy little blacks about the premises to annoy us."[25] In other words, neither Bachman nor Audubon could expect Maria's assistance. She was otherwise occupied. So too was Bachman's gardener and right-hand man in the taxidermy room. Thomas had to prepare food for invalids while the cook was indisposed. Whether his expertise in the kitchen matched that in the garden, Thomas was charged with preparing easily digestible soups, bland puddings and custards, as well as gruel made out of corn, oats, or rice, and broiled or roasted meat and fowl. The entire household was in disarray, and Maria Martin was unhappy.

Admittedly, the extent to which she or the other women of the family provided the physical labor needed to care for patients and the "sick rooms" they occupied is unclear. Their nursing duties may have amounted to little more than being hypervigilant but, according to medical expert James Ewell (1773–1832), even this was a significant matter in the restoration of health. So important was nursing to patient care and recovery that Ewell provided guidelines for home nursing in the 1827 edition of his self-help manual, *Medical Companion, or Family Physician*. The highly popular American publication provided information on common diseases and their remedies, including a detailed list of useful pharmaceuticals—especially medicinal plants—but by 1827 when the seventh edition was published, Ewell laid out the important role of nurses who could follow physician's orders and who "possess[ed] *honesty, sobriety*, and *fidelity*."[26] As he pointed out that nurses must be especially attentive to cleanliness, he was not suggesting that such roles were to be assumed by slaves; however, in the Bachman household it would have been more common for slaves to open windows so as to air out sickrooms or to provide fresh bedding when patients had "diseases of a putrid nature" than it would have been for the woman who supervised their work to do so. No doubt Maria assumed responsibility for administering medicines ordered by physicians and for ensuring that sick rooms promoted rather than hindered recovery, but the extent to which she performed the personal care—bathing, oral hygiene, and other tasks of an intimate nature—outlined is unclear.

Aside from the question as to whether Maria Martin and her sister could manage to keep two sickrooms in good order without assistance, it was almost impossible to abide by Ewell's dictum that caregivers must always appear optimistic and cheerful. By early June, Ria's condition was far worse, and despite Thomas's best efforts, she was not eating. Tempted only by wild fowl, the few morsels she managed to swallow did nothing to improve her health, largely because her bowels were deranged by medication and likely affected by the tubercle bacilli.[27] Moreover, Maria Martin was entirely occupied with the practicalities of caring for the sick. She wrote Eliza that she was housebound except "to go for an hour or two to King Street occasionally when your mother or I are in want of supplies. I have not been to Church once since Maria's [Ria's] arrival here, and do not expect to visit or go about while mamma lives."[28] Luckily, John Woodhouse was completely devoted, caring for Ria as she suffered the ravages of pulmonary and intestinal inflammation. As his father-in-law stated, he was "not only one of the most attentive of husbands but the best of nurses I have ever known."[29]

Ever hopeful, John Woodhouse believed his wife was improving, but John Bachman despaired and, in early May, he wrote Victor that the doctors "leave us nothing to hope for but the interposition of providence on her behalf."[30] A month later, the news was no better, and the "ladies" of the house were "depressed & almost worn out" from caring for two seriously ill women.[31] Well aware that their efforts on behalf of Ria and Rebecca Martin were palliative, Maria Martin and Harriet Bachman were experiencing considerable emotional strain on another front as well: John James was being difficult.[32]

Audubon arrived in April, and it did not take long for him to become "miserable." The collaborators on whom he had come to depend focused on the welfare of their loved ones rather than on natural history, and because he had offended Bachman twice in the previous months, their relationship was strained. His first transgression was to release a prospectus for their project on quadrupeds without first consulting Bachman; his second *faux pas* was to be presumptuous toward Maria Martin.[33] Assuming she was at his disposal,

Audubon speculated they could produce the first set of engravings in a few months if she applied herself. It did not take long for Bachman to set him straight.

He pointed out that collaborators discussed matters before acting. Moreover, when they first contemplated the project, they had agreed to act cautiously because there was much at stake: their book on quadrupeds was supposed to provide an income for their married children. By 1839, however, the project was equally important to Bachman. He was developing a reputation as a mammologist, and he had come to see *Quadrupeds* as a "partnership" between equals. Any missteps would affect him no less than it would his children, and, in one of his first letters of 1840, he cautioned Audubon to avoid further blunders. He believed the project unachievable without his full participation, and he told John James that he was "willing to have my name stand with yours, if that will help the sale of the book" but he was not about to risk his funds or his reputation. He continued: "The expenses and the profits shall be yours or the boys [and he added] I am anxious to do something for the benefit for Victor and John, in addition to the treasures I have given them—and this is all I can do."[34] Either unfazed or deliberately ignoring Bachman's carefully crafted scolding, Audubon's reply focused on the octavo edition of *Birds*. Instead of responding to his friend's concerns, he crowed about how many subscriptions he had sold and he directed Bachman to tell Maria Martin to paint botanicals "such as I have not yet published" for the small edition.[35]

Maria Martin did not respond as she had in the past. Certainly able to paint the beautiful but uncomplicated botanicals being added to the octavo plates, she was far too occupied for even the sparse backgrounds or highly simplified foliage and flowers wanted by Audubon. And if he thought that being in residence would elicit the desired cooperation, he discovered differently when he arrived on her doorstep. Audubon hoped to replicate the experiences of 1833–1834 and 1836–1837, but this time things were different. He had hoped that the trio that had collaborated so well on the elephant folios would reunite, but neither John Woodhouse nor Maria Martin were able to help him. He was sorely disappointed with his reception, and he wrote Victor that he wished he "had not come South this Year."[36] His hosts were of like mind.

The timing of Audubon's visit made it appear as though his daughter-in-law's health was his foremost concern, but he really viewed the trip as a chance to work on his latest project, and he saw no reason why his assistants could not paint even as they cared for Ria. When John Woodhouse and Maria Martin did not join him in the studio, he behaved badly. He drove his "sweetheart" to tears, and he embarrassed his old friend. Bachman blamed Audubon's misadventures on "intemperance," and he wrote at length about the situation to Victor:

> Shortly after your Father's arrival I discovered that he used liquor too freely. In the afternoons especially he was almost unfit for conversation. He became garrulous—dictatorial & profane. He stated as facts things which I knew were not such & which he seemed not even to recollect on the foll'ing day. The ladies in my family all remarked it, & begged me on those occasions to let him have his own way. I bore with it for many weeks. I have a perfect abhorrence of intemperance & when I perceived he had taken too much I had only one resort, to go into my front room & lock the door. Thus time passed away—in the midst of other heavy trials & afflictions. But things grew worse. There were scarcely three days during the last month of his stay in which he was not the worse for liquor in the afternoon & on several occasions before dinner. . . . I saw one whom I esteemed beyond almost any other living man ruining his health & his intellect, setting a bad example to my children & rendering me perfectly miserable.[37]

Only in Charleston for a month and a half, Audubon's stay was trying. Well known for his antipathy to alcohol, Bachman was hosting an inebriate whose behavior was all the more problematic when he had two desperately ill women under his roof.

Caught in the middle, John Woodhouse became increasingly despondent as his family pressed him to work on the octavo edition and to return north with his wife.[38] His mother was convinced that Ria would obtain better care in New York, and when John Woodhouse was unmoved by her arguments, others chimed in. Victor, for example, wrote that if he knew how his behavior affected the welfare of his infant daughter and their mother, he would return home immediately. He reported that Lucy Audubon's health was not as robust as usual, and that even though she had a baby nurse, caring for Harriet was taxing. But John Woodhouse barely heard their arguments. Focused on his wife's situation, he could not consider their requests seriously, and he simply ignored their overtures.

His intractability only made his family more determined. By June a new tactic appeared: the trip north would be feasible, they argued, if Maria Martin accompanied them. This was not the first time such an invitation had been extended but, like in the past, Maria declined. As someone who left Charleston only reluctantly, Maria Martin responded no differently than in 1837, when she had been urged to go to London and work on the last volume of *Birds*.[39] Truthfully, Ria was too delicate to travel, and the pleading from New York made little difference. By this time, however, Maria Martin had her own reasons for staying close to home. She had to deal with pressing legal matters associated with her mother's estate.

For the most part, Rebecca Martin's Last Will and Testament was as expected. She bequeathed her property to her three living daughters: Harriet Bachman, Eliza Strobel (1790–1851), and Maria Martin; and to the granddaughters left motherless when Rebecca's daughter, Jane Lee (1793–1825), died. However, she went further and disinherited her son-in-law and four grandsons. Such a provision was unusual but not out of character for a businesswoman who had personal experience with what could happen when the law did not protect a woman's property. Rebecca Martin had once lost control over property she believed was rightfully hers, and she was not about to let a similar fate befall her granddaughters, even if it meant she had to direct her executors to distribute property in a manner contrary to common practice and risk having her will contested.

While such a possibility did not deter Rebecca from settling her affairs as she wished, John Bachman worried that litigators might meddle with the family inheritance, and he believed Maria Martin's presence necessary to ensure her mother's stocks, cash, and slaves were disbursed as stipulated.[40] The extent to which intervention was required is unclear, but Maria simply could not go north while the matter was being settled, and John Bachman wrote Victor Audubon to forestall further harassment. By the end of August, approximately a month after the will was probated, the matter was settled and Victor congratulated Maria Martin on being "well off in money matters" in a letter reminding her that her presence was long overdue in New York.[41] In fact, by this time, Maria was resigned to going north. The departure date was, however, far from settled.

Ria's condition declined precipitously throughout August, and the steady stream of letters urging them to go north failed to elicit the desired response. Nor did changing tack help. Victor and Lucy moved away from arguments that Ria would receive better care in New York, to those based on the potentially tragic consequences of staying put, to no avail.[42] Lucy Audubon accused John Woodhouse of jeopardizing his health as well as that of little Lucy by exposure to consumption or yellow fever, but her fear mongering did not garner the hoped for result. Even when told that he was putting Eliza's health at risk because the "cold" she could not shake was aggravated by excessive worry, he would not budge. His wife was just too delicate to travel. Ever resourceful, Lucy Audubon proposed using a palanquin so her daughter-in-law could lie down on the journey north.[43] But nothing worked: not bribery, not bullying, not even plaintive entreaties disguised as helpful tips.

The fact that Dr. Eli Geddings (1799–1878), who recently returned from Maryland to assume the chair of "pathological anatomy and medical jurisprudence" at the Medical College, and Dr. Elias Horlbeck (1804–1881), president of the Medical Society of South Carolina, were in charge of Ria's care did little to stem the steady stream of advice sent south.[44] Even though Ria was under the care of two distinguished and academically trained physicians who checked on her frequently, communications from New York reinforced the suspicion that Northerners believed Southern medical care was inferior to that available elsewhere and did nothing to convince John Woodhouse to return north. At the same time, Victor's view that her physicians were overmedicating with mercury was legitimate. She was losing teeth, and even her doctors attributed her sore mouth to their ministrations.[45]

The Audubon family made countless suggestions and, while mercury was not removed entirely from the recommended course of treatment, their suggestions tended to be more benign than the tonics prescribed by Geddings and Horlbeck. Lucy, for example, suggested that Ria take "the smallest quantity of the excellent blue pills" she used when feeling poorly. Better known as the Edinburgh puke and purge pills, they were commercially manufactured tablets that contained minute amounts of mercury mixed with rose "confection" and liquorice root, but they were not going to improve Ria's health any more than the heavy metals administered by her physicians.[46] Nor were the less harmful but equally useless tonics and botanicals recommended from afar going to help. At one point, Lucy proposed wearing a girdle of cinchona or Peruvian bark (*Cinchona officinalis*), commonly used to treat deranged bowels, while Victor mentioned a "remedy" that also allegedly calmed overactive bowels: the benne leaf (*Sesame folium*).[47] Even the devout Eliza, whose inclination was to depend on Divine dispensation and offer religious platitudes, made suggestions.

She relayed a story that was nothing less than miraculous and recommended a course of treatment followed by a woman whose symptoms seemed uncannily similar to those experienced by Ria. The woman was, Eliza wrote, cured by a course of "teped [*sic*] salt water baths." The doctor's conclusion that this woman's symptoms signaled "neulagea" [*sic*] rather than a life-threatening illness was also comforting, and both diagnosis and prescription were embraced enthusiastically.[48] Unlike Ria's physicians who seemed to favor calomel and fasting (when she was unable to digest her food), the Northern homeopath prescribed a trip to the Virginia Springs. Ignorant of Ria's actual condition, Eliza was optimistic she had discovered a cure. She was pleased to forward such good news, and it was surely no coincidence that when faced with the same disease eighteen months later, she opted for homeopathic medicine.

By the beginning of September, John Woodhouse was losing hope, and being under quarantine exacerbated his pessimism. The dire predictions from New York seemed to be coming true as he was prevented from traveling inland, or even into town, for fear he would catch a fever. Alternatively exhausted and depressed, he was also under pressure to contribute to family finances. Victor wrote him that his wife's medical bill would "probably absorb the amount due by Dr Geddings to Papa for the large work," and while that would settle some of their account, John Woodhouse needed to do his part by painting and by being frugal. However, John Woodhouse had no "spirit for work," and he only managed to outline a few animals before Ria died on September 15.[49] Not long after, he, little Lucy, and Maria Martin left for New York.

What greeted them there was disheartening. Eliza was despondent and sickly, and Victor was planning a trip to Cuba. This was a destination frequented by consumptives, but the idea of a woman traveling such a distance in search of treatment for pulmonary problems was unconventional.[50] Admittedly, Eliza's sister had traveled in search of relief, but she ventured no farther than Red Sulphur Springs in West Virginia. Because those mineral waters had not helped, Victor hoped a more exotic location would be beneficial.

There was, however, an obstacle: Victor had to convince two sets of parents that such a trip was a good idea. He had seen the effect of disagreements between parents and children when Ria was dying, and he wanted to avoid repeating that experience, but Victor needed financial assistance as well as approval in principle and so he began preparing his case by discussing the idea with Richard Harlan (1796–1843). A physician and naturalist from Philadelphia who had supported Audubon against his American critics in the 1820s, and again during the 1830s against Charles Waterton, he was considered a close family friend and his thoughts would bear weight.[51] If Harlan thought the idea sensible, it was likely that John James would be favorably disposed, and Victor spoke with him as Maria Martin, also an integral part of his scheme, departed Charleston.

By mid-September some of his plan had fallen into place. Victor was pleased to tell his father that Harlan believed the Cuban trip "wd benefit her greatly," and if Victor overstated his endorsement, he did not misrepresent him entirely.[52] Harlan had, after all, advised Lucy Audubon to return to "the free air from the broad rivers and lofty hills of our own free land" as an antidote to the "pent up atmosphere of London" in 1838.[53] Moreover, John James could be convinced of the utility of the trip if it offered opportunities to collect and draw botanicals, birds, and mammals, and such an argument might convince John Bachman as well. Certainly, he had to come up with something because Harlan's endorsement of the plan was worse than useless with his father-in-law: in 1834, Bachman shared specimens and information with Harlan but his contributions were not acknowledged.[54] Additionally, even though Bachman admitted the benefits of a sea voyage, he had grave misgivings about the journey, especially the costs and the dangers associated with traveling through miasmic lands along the Gulf of Mexico and into Catholic territory.[55]

If Victor hoped to convince Eliza's father, he had to show that they were taking every precaution. To this end, Maria Martin's presence as a traveling companion was essential. Admittedly, it was uncommon for women in the Bachman family to travel, but Maria traveled under exigent circumstances, and Eliza's case was dire. Plus, her natural history skills meant that she would be more than a chaperone. She could paint plants and collect specimens, and such opportunities were clearly taken into account as the two families weighed the benefits of the proposed journey. The trio had barely set foot on the island when correspondence containing accusations of inattentiveness to natural history arrived.

The criticism was, in fact, accurate; however, Victor was focused on his wife's condition rather than on the family business, and over the next few months his interest in natural history diminished as Eliza's condition deteriorated. From the outset, his goal was simple—to cure Eliza—and not long after leaving New York in early October, he thought he found a way to achieve it: aboard ship he met a man whose respiratory illness had been "cured" by homeopathy. Victor was impressed. This man's story was a welcome alternative to the experiences of consumptives who doctored with regular practitioners. He knew that their reliance on mercury, blistering, and purging had done nothing for Ria, and Victor wrote his brother asking him to seek out the man responsible for the recovery of his new acquaintance: Dr. Federal Vanderburgh (1788–1868).[56]

A well-known practitioner from New York, Vanderburgh was a regular physician who adopted homeopathic therapies after meeting Hans Burch Gram (1786–1840), a German émigré trained by Samuel Hahnemann (1755–1843), the founder of homeopathy. Hahnemann's principle of "like produces like" formed the basis of Vanderburgh's treatments, and whether John Woodhouse had as much faith as Victor in the idea that very weak concentrations of botanicals or other "natural" substances that produced consumptive symptoms in a healthy person would cure his sister-in-law, he did as he was asked. After all, regular medicine had only increased his wife's suffering. There was, of course, one other problem. Eliza was in Cuba, and Vanderburgh was in New York.

Like most physicians, Vanderburgh did not believe in diagnosing from afar. Nonetheless, he offered a very general opinion on Eliza's condition: he speculated that her "system generally is out of order and *not the Lungs*."[57] Although her symptoms were indisputably those of a consumptive, Vanderburgh was not entirely misguided as organs other than those of the pulmonary system are often affected by the tubercle bacilli. However, the herbals and "natural" minerals he prescribed were no more going to cure her than the "poisons" offered by regular physicians, especially considering his goal was to increase her "vital heat" while reducing chest pain and the production of sputum.

Eliza began treatment in early January, but her symptoms were unchanged even though instructions accompanying the first shipment of medicines were followed faithfully. After a month of treatment, her temperature still fluctuated wildly; her pulse was high; her breathing was shallow and fast; and the pains in her torso were undiminished. Moreover, she developed a new and worrisome problem: she had become "troubled with bad dreams" and only slept fitfully.[58] Vanderburgh's reluctance to doctor from afar was clearly well founded, and Victor concurred. Convinced Eliza would do better if she consulted the homeopath in person, he was determined to take her to Vanderburgh as soon as they left Cuba.

By the end of February, Lucy Audubon believed Victor should concede defeat. Despite having spent two months in the salubrious climate of Mantanzas, specifically in the town of Limonar, which was described as a "perfect Lacedaemon" and "a favoured retreat for invalids from the United States" by Dr. John George F. Wurdemann (1810–1849), a fellow consumptive from Charleston who was also there in 1841, Lucy viewed Victor's "experiment of Cuba for our dear girls health" a failure.[59] She believed they should leave immediately, and Vanderburgh agreed. The homeopath was of the opinion that warm weather was more "debilitating" than cold weather, and he pointed out that he could not effect any change in Eliza's condition unless he saw her in person.[60] Exactly what the good doctor might have suggested beyond the Lycopodium, Bryonia, and calcarea [calcium carbonate] he had already prescribed is unclear; however, the homeopathic *materia medica* was at least no worse than the elixir of vitriol—a mixture of sulphuric acid, alcohol, water, aromatic herbs, and fruit essences—that Eliza was taking to combat night sweats.[61]

Even John James thought Victor should come home. His reasoning differed from that offered by Lucy and Vanderburgh, though. He had hoped the trip would produce some interesting finds in natural history, but he was sadly mistaken. Victor obtained subscriptions for the octavo edition while in New Orleans, but he seldom painted.[62] In any event, his exertions were never enough, and John James reminded him of that when he advised Victor to return home where he could be of use in overseeing the publication of the new edition of *Birds*. He knew full well that Victor had done little in the way of painting or collecting, concluding his letter sarcastically: "We will be delighted to see your Pictures."[63]

Victor was also under pressure from John Bachman. Although he did not berate him directly, he wrote Maria Martin bemoaning lost opportunities. He was working on the genus Sciurus but had been compelled to use species found locally and in California (as well as a few specimens examined in London at the Zoological Society), and although he thought Victor would be able to add to his collection while traveling through Louisiana, he was disappointed by his son-in-law's inattentiveness. Soon after they left Charleston, he wrote Maria only half in jest: "I wish you could skin squirrels—& I would commission you to get the skins in N. Orleans—of a small brownish black squirrel—a larger black—& a reddish brown one found in the N. Orleans Market. If Victor was good for anything beyond accounts & painting he might have spunk enough to attend to this."[64] Once in Cuba, the prodding continued. While Victor saw their primary purpose as Eliza's health, everyone else believed they should be doing something in natural history. They had no sooner set foot in Havana when a letter reminding Victor and Maria that they were to paint and collect specimens arrived, and John James insisted they start without delay because work would be next to impossible once the weather became hot.[65] He also pointed out Victor's financial obligations: he was supposed to obtain subscribers for the octavo edition and paint landscapes that could be sold to offset expenses.

Victor understood well enough the need to sell paintings to finance the trip, but he was not entirely sure why his father wanted him to collect specimens. He had not been in Cuba two weeks when he learned that its natural history was already in press with "a work on the birds of Cuba now publishing at Paris," presumably *Ornithologie* (1839) by Alcide Dessalines d'Orbigny (1802–1857)—part of *Histoire Physiques, Politique et Naturelles de L'Ile de Cuba*, 1840, by Ramón de la Sagra (1798–1871). More importantly, he was unimpressed by the birds he saw, and he found little else of interest. "There was," Victor wrote, "only one quadruped found originally on the Island, it is something like a rat . . . [and] There are said to be no venomous snakes on the Island, and only scorpions & large spiders which bite so as to cause much inflammation."[66] He had also seen the collections made by Dr. Wurdemann and did not consider the results worth the effort. The twenty skins he had were uninteresting, and his father's concern about the Cuban climate was correct—but John James underestimated the situation. It was already too hot and humid for preserving specimens. Even so, exactly one month after being contacted by his father, Victor received a stern rebuke from John Woodhouse.

Worried that little had been done and that the time of their departure was fast approaching, he demanded to know: "What have you been doing for two months in Cuba without putting 'brush to canvas'"[67] John Woodhouse should have understood Victor's situation better than anyone, but he seemed oblivious to the similarities even as he harbored resentment over the pressure placed on him while his wife was bedridden. Instead of sympathizing, he speculated that Victor was frittering away his time, socializing instead of working, and that Eliza was responsible for his behavior. John Woodhouse asked her to consider how "every hour you pass on his knee, is irretrievably gone, as you are not likely to revisit Cuba," and he reminded them both that even as his own wife "was on her death bed not able to turn herself," he was expected to work, and that "she with fortitude and resolution which I had lost, urged me on to my duty with the whole affection and love of her soul." In retrospect, he could only add "*God bless Her*." Ria had not made demands on his time. She had apparently considered his interests thus acting, as he put it, as "only *a wife can*—[68]

Barely six months since burying his wife, John Woodhouse had come round to the view he resented so thoroughly when Ria was dying: illness was no excuse for inaction. But even though his suspicion that the travelers spent a fair amount of time in relative idleness was correct, he might have been more tactful. It was simply impossible for Victor to do much in light of his wife's condition. His mood was gloomy, and he found the scenery as uninspiring as the birds. Indeed, after a month on the island he could promise no more than "if I should shoot anything very curious I will try to bring them to you."[69]

Nor was Maria Martin living up to expectations. She was drying specimens and painting unusual species, but she apologized for doing so little. She wrote John James and Lucy: "I have done nothing since I have been here but enjoy the country, and prepare a few Botanical specimens, and it would require the enthusiasm and zeal of my good friend Mr A—to wade through the red clay to make collections in Nat history."[70] Perhaps too readily accepting blame for disappointing efforts, she attributed her lackluster efforts to having "left home greatly dispirited" by the death of Ria.

Maria was unable to muster interest in painting until March. Six months had elapsed since Ria's death, and she finally felt more like herself. She was pleased to report she was using her paints to draw "a few annuals that I thought pretty," and a week later she was doing even better.[71] They were living with a congenial family on a sugar plantation, and a few days later she painted some of the "rare and beautiful plants" such as those found in the gardens there. But in addition to painting tropical plants such as *Alpinia zerumbet* that grew "in large clusters, about 6 or 8 feet high that would cover the space of our centre bed," she promised to "collect all the little things I can to amuse and interest you all," and she added that she looked forward to examining and discussing her finds with John Bachman when she got home.[72]

By March, Maria Martin's correspondence became noticeably more animated. She reported experiencing "the greatest pleasure yet derived from my rambles in Cuba," and she drew Bachman in, asking him to transplant a number of shrubs and flowers from "our own garden" or from "friends[']" gardens to send to Mr. Burnell, the sugar planter with whom they were staying. She added that he was: "the only kindred spirit, with regard to plants that I have met with on this Island, and [he] has kindly given me seeds of all that he has or can collect, [and] he also intends sending some plants that I expressed a wish to have."[73]

Maria's improved state of mind was obvious in her complimentary view of Burnell, but her good opinion of him also reflected his status as an English émigré. Whereas some people could be very direct in expressing censure, Maria Martin tended to convey negative views through positive commentary. Victor and Eliza, for example, did not hesitate to describe Cubans as déclassé. They had, Eliza wrote, "no taste whatever for the fine arts, but [are willing to] spend thousands in making a display."[74] Maria Martin, on the other hand, signaled contempt by praising those who represented everything the Cubans did not. She wrote about people for whom she had nothing but admiration, for example Mr. and Mrs. Van Rensselaer, residents of New York. Maria made their acquaintance when they happened to stay in the same boarding house in San Pedro, and she approved of them wholeheartedly. Their "plain

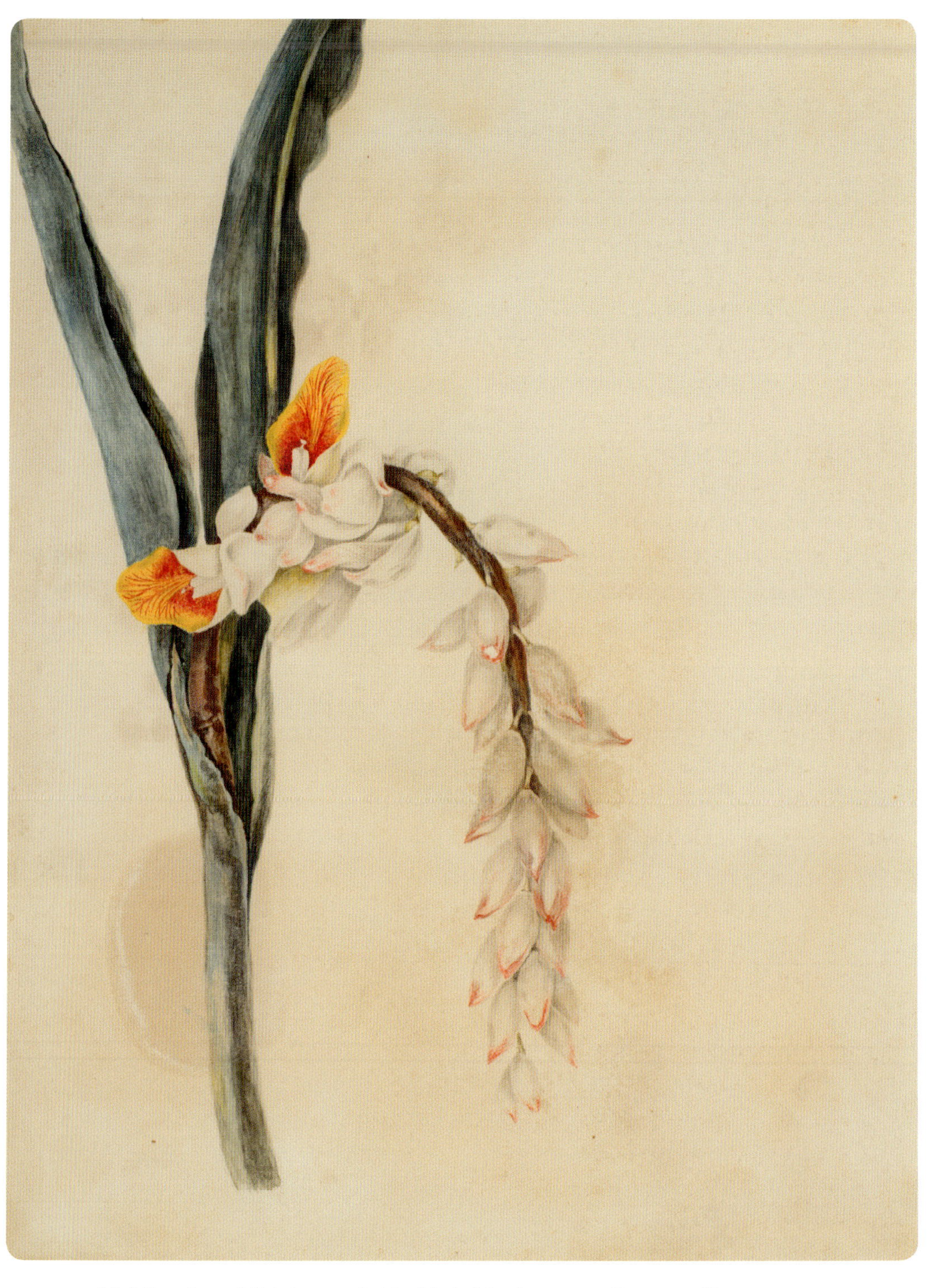

FIGURE 53. Nodding ginger (*Alpinia zerumbet*) by Maria Martin. c. 1841. Courtesy of Jane Grimball Greely.

and unpretending" nature was to her liking, and she believed they would be quite at home in the "plain style" she preferred despite the fact that they were "among the most wealthy, and probably belonging to the fashionable circle of N__Y__." Maria found little to admire in the "disagreeable and proud" wealthy of Charleston with their bad manners, bad habits, and fondness of ostentatious display, but she admired the "simplicity of character" exhibited by her new acquaintances. In fact, she was so sure they would find the Bachman home to their liking that she asked her sister to offer them lodgings as they passed through Charleston on their way north.[75]

It was not that Maria Martin never expressed censure, but she tended to make her preferences known by extolling commendable behavior rather than by pointing out objectionable traits, and she was effusive when it came to Mrs. Rensselaer. She described her as "a beautiful, a finished lady, with the simplicity and artlessness of a village girl. [adding] I have never met her equal, and she seems to me a perfect wonder, when I reflect that she has been [torn] and admired both in Europe & America, is young beautiful & wealthy, and must attract attention where ever she goes, yet has never lost that simplicity of character which is so attractive, nor acquired any of the fashionable follies of the circle in which she is moving, from her earliest years."[76] Less tactful, Victor and Eliza focused their gaze on the Cubans, describing them as common, tawdry, and deceitful. And they were particularly critical of women. Victor described them as immodest and fond of ostentatious display, especially "negroe" and creole women who wore "muslins & silk slippers etc!"[77]

It is possible that Victor held such views because the Cubans were uninterested in his artistic endeavors: he could sell neither subscriptions to *Birds* nor the landscapes he was painting. While Eliza believed the Cubans ignorant, Victor blamed their disinterest in art and science on a preference for bullfights, balls, and banquets. But he was also honest enough to recognize that there was another major impediment: his usual means of selling paintings by raffle was illegal.[78] It was as if the entire population, aside from Burnell, had somehow let them down. The sugar planter was, as Eliza stated, far different from the Cubans who had "not the least taste for natural history and pass by the greatest curiosities, without even noticing them," telling her sister Jane, "Mr Burnell whom Aunt speaks of in her letter, is the only man we have met who seems to take an interest in these things."[79]

While Maria Martin's description of Burnell as the only "kindred spirit" in Cuba was overdramatic and implicitly critical of other people, it was not entirely misplaced. Aside from the fact that local people neither knew nor cared about their natural history proclivities, many were afraid of them. As Victor noted, "there was a great dislike to [*sic*] consumptives" because they believed them contagious, and the Cubans tended to avoid people exhibiting pulmonary symptoms. He reported with disdain that many were actually "so foolish as to deem it necessary to white wash and purify a room in which anyone ill with that disorder has slept or died."[80] It was thus hardly surprising that the only tangible support for natural history came from expatriates, and that only two other residents demonstrated any curiosity about their efforts. Mr. Chartrand, also from Mantanzas, was sufficiently interested to subscribe to the octavo edition, while the [de] Jouve family, coffee planters with a Charleston connection, provided lodgings in a region with some of the most unusual scenery and interesting specimens encountered during their visit.[81]

Chartrand was, Maria Martin reported, "very kind in getting plants for me," and he promised to preserve and send insects to Charleston, but, she added, he was "not so much of a florist" and certainly not in the same league as Burnell.[82] However, as an octavo subscriber, he had endeared himself to the travelers, and, in a brief moment of role reversal, Maria Martin asked Bachman for a favor. She asked him to do what he could to repay Chartrand's kindness. She asked him to forward ornamentals to both Chartrand and Burnell, and as she arranged for the transport of Bachman's plants on vessels to Mantanzas, she went one step further. She plied her brother-in-law (uncharacteristically) with flattery, reminding him that his cooperation would be repaid in full as he and his friends would receive "rare seeds" for their efforts, before adding: "I am glad to find by your last letter that you are again turning florist and hope by the time I return our wilderness will rejoice and blossom as the Rose. Everything will no doubt look delightful to me, for in the midst of enjoyment I cannot forget home, and feel convinced, that in order to value its blessings it is necessary for us sometimes to absent ourselves from it."[83]

The Jouve family was less obviously supportive, but their coffee plantation was ideally located inland from Havana. It was approximately midway between the two coasts, and Victor believed it offered "more picturesque" views than anywhere else in Cuba.[84] As a result, while there he was using his watercolors. So was Maria Martin. She painted a number of pantropicals such as the poinciana shrub (*Caesalpinia pulcherrima*), Bauhinia, lobster claw heliconia (*Heliconia collinsiana*), and Tillandsia, a genus of bromeliads native to the mountainous regions of Central America. Her Cuban sketchbook also contained paintings of some exotic nonindigenous plants, but whether the Schwartzia, native to South America, or the candelabra tree (*Senna didymobotrya*), native to tropical Africa and Asia and a plant in the Capparaceae family were found in Cuba is unknown. She also drew a number of botanicals in pencil, a scene depicting a flat-roofed building, and a palm tree in front of a mountain in the same sketchbook as visual reminders of the trip.[85]

Disappointingly, their sojourn inland produced no measurable improvement in Eliza. Victor's family had advised moving away from the pestilence of the coastal settlements, but doing so did nothing for Eliza's symptoms, and Maria Martin expressed concerns that she normally kept to herself just a few days before their departure from the Jouve plantation. By then, hope that either climate or homeopathy might cure Eliza had vanished, and she was worried that Vanderburgh's advice was ineffectual—or worse, counterproductive. Because Eliza usually read her letters before they were posted, she risked revealing too much when she wrote John Bachman:

> The intervals between some of the prescriptions were longer than they ought probably to have been, and his never having seen Eliza and prescribing according to the knowledge afforded by a description of her care only, was to my idea too much like groping in the dark, and I was not in favour of the use of his medicines while we were traveling, and always felt uneasy about their effects, as we were not near enough for him to judge whether the results were favourable, or such as he wishes them to produce, I thought it would have been the better plan to try the effect of this climate, and if that failed then Dr. Vanderburg's prescriptions would still be left as a resort, and I do most anxiously wish her to give them a fair trial as soon as she returns to New York.[86]

Maria's views were shared by those at home. Both Bachman and Audubon preferred regular physicians, and after receiving her report John James wrote his friend: "I am quite of your opinions respecting the *Homopathean system*, but in Eliza's case it is not imprudent to allow her to have her wishes complied with. We think however that when she is once more with us, that we will soon dissuade her and procure for us an *honest and learned Doctor*!"[87] And yet the homeopaths were not alone in failing Eliza, and Maria Martin was particularly unimpressed with the "learned doctor" Wurdemann. In January, he sent misleading information to Charleston when he claimed that Eliza looked "so much better that he would not have known that she had been sick."[88] This was truly not the case, and Maria Martin set the matter straight in April when

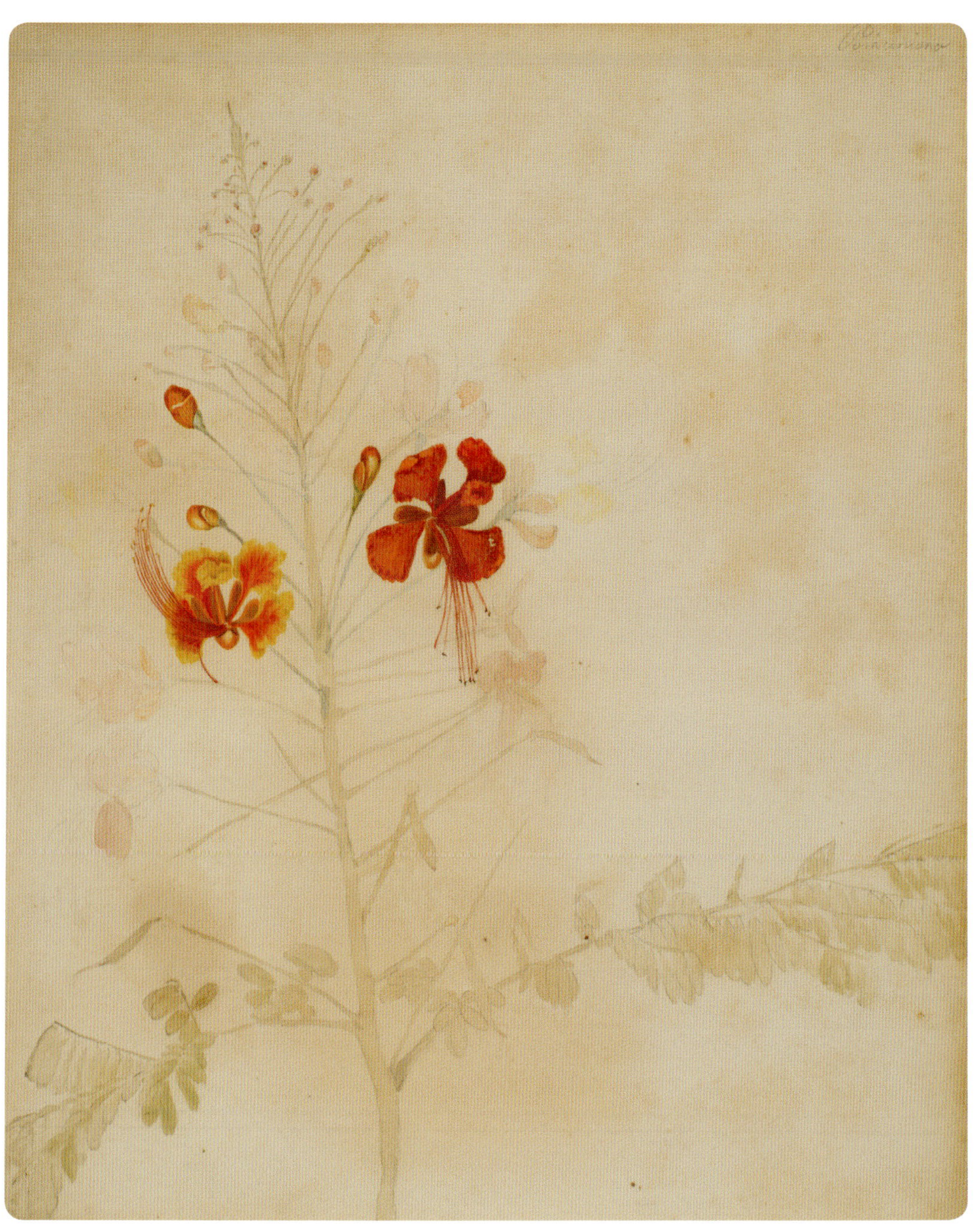

FIGURE 54. Poinciana shrub (*Caesalpinia pulcherrima*) by Maria Martin. c. 1841. Courtesy of Jane Grimball Greely.

she wrote home.[89] But even worse, Wurdemann lent credence to Victor's belief that Eliza was on the verge of being cured. Indeed, Victor was of the view that she would be herself in no time with the assistance of Dr. Vanderburgh.

Victor was determined to get Eliza to New York as quickly as possible, and they stopped just long enough in Charleston to determine who might accompany them north. Maria Martin had been away from home for more than seven months, and it was not clear that she would carry on to New York with them. Much of her secretarial work had been set aside while she was away, and Harriet was so incapacitated by facial spasms that she rarely left her chamber. Maria Martin was needed at home. The problem was that Victor and Eliza could not make the trip alone, and there was no perfect traveling companion among Eliza's sisters: Catherine was only aged ten, Julia and Lynch were adolescents, and Jane, although twenty-three, was visually impaired.

In the end, Jane accompanied Eliza. She was, after all, a devoted daughter who attempted to fill in for her aunt Maria while she was away, but diminished vision imposed limits on what Jane could do. She had not, for example, dealt with either the octavo plates awaiting distribution or the business mail addressed to Victor Audubon.[90] That such work awaited Maria's attention was unsurprising: Jane was frequently reminded to avoid overusing her eyes. However, she had been her mother's steadfast companion, and she was certainly able to sit with Eliza and to report on whether caregivers were doing their job. Of all the Bachman girls, Jane was the least likely to forget her responsibilities, and yet her father reminded her of them as she departed, telling her: "do your duty under all circumstances & to trust in God. Your affections will prompt you to do all that lies in your power to relieve & console your suffering sister & you must direct her to place her trust on him from whom all our alleviations & blessing flow."[91]

Jane's "duty" was of short duration. Eliza Bachman Audubon died on May 21, less than two weeks after arriving in New York, and Jane returned to Charleston three weeks later.[92] By that time, the family had allegedly regrouped after a brief period of mourning, and in *The Pastor of St. John's Lutheran,* Catherine Bachman recalled how Eliza's death was accepted as one of the many trials testing the faithful. And as she described how it affected her father, she articulated principles that had guided her family for longer than she could remember: "Duty has been called '*The stern daughter of the voice of God.*' Yet as she leads forth a bleeding heart to minister to suffering humanity, is she not transformed into an angel, with healing on her wings? Men spoke of the 'large sympathy' of the Pastor of St. John's. Was it not God-given, in the furnace of affliction?"[93] Then, as before, bereavement would precede renewal.

While the following decade had its share of tragedy—two more deaths in the Bachman family and the slow but steady decline of John James as he developed dementia in the years before his death—there was another project in the offing. For Maria Martin, this decade marked a new phase in her natural history endeavors. The frequent, if vague, demands that Audubon made almost from the moment they met seemed to stop once she was home from Cuba. Absorbed in painting figures for *Quadrupeds*, Audubon tended to ignore his Charleston collaborators, and a dramatic change in their relationship occurred.[94] During the 1840s, Bachman assumed a more prominent role in producing *Quadrupeds*, and Maria Martin's scientific expertise served him rather than Audubon.

6

FAMILY AND SCIENCE

Quadrupeds

In December 1841, John Bachman shared a secret with Audubon: he had been approached by the trustees of the College of South Carolina to serve as president but he declined without even informing his family of the offer. The terms were good but, as he put it, "the state of my health & the fatigue attendant on the duties would soon finish me."[1] Moreover, had he accepted, the demands of the position would "have put an end to my amusements in Nat. History" and that was a sacrifice he was not prepared to make. As a result, he specifically kept the news from one person: Maria Martin.

Maria, he explained, disliked city life, and he was sure she would have encouraged him to accept the position because the college was in Columbia, a community less than a fifth the size of Charleston. He could not let such considerations affect his decision, however. His home had a semblance of normalcy not experienced for more than two years, and he and Maria were again devoting time to natural history. Admittedly, there were few references to Maria's efforts other than the secretarial work she performed for John Bachman and Victor Audubon, but she no doubt continued painting for her own edification and amusement. In any event, her brother-in-law was pleased that they had turned to more pleasant matters, and he was not interested in giving up natural history for whatever prestige and status that might have been derived from being president of a college begun just forty years earlier.

In fact, Maria Martin returned to natural history work as soon as she returned from Cuba. After Victor's departure, she assumed his responsibilities for ensuring that local subscribers received plates they had purchased. She oversaw packaging and posting specimens—with the requisite memoranda—to Bachman's collaborators, particularly to John James and to his sons. She was well acquainted with such tasks, and the only difference between 1841 and 1831 was the nature of the specimens: mammalian specimens replaced avian and botanical ones. But more to the point: her role as assistant was essentially unchanged; it was rather oriented to Bachman's benefit. That this was the case was not immediately obvious because when she had painted botanicals for *Birds,* she had aided Bachman's scientific aspirations no less than when she helped him with *Quadrupeds.*

First conceived as a vehicle to allow Audubon's sons to make their mark in the scientific world and to enable them to marry and support a family, by the time John Woodhouse and Victor Gifford were able to turn their attention to *Quadrupeds* they were both widowed, and John Bachman had reimagined the project. He was determined to publish the definitive work on North American mammals, and he assumed control. As a result, his relationship with the men of the Audubon family was tested—several times.

The first intimation that there might be trouble emerged in August 1841, when Bachman sent Audubon a tersely written letter in which he addressed him as if he knew nothing about working in the field or about how to solicit assistance from well-placed individuals.[2] In fact, Audubon had been exchanging information with Spencer Fullerton Baird (1823–1887), the budding naturalist who was to become assistant secretary of the Smithsonian Institution and a recognized expert on mammals (as well as birds), over the previous year. Indeed, Audubon had asked Baird to procure specimens for *Quadrupeds* many times.[3] But Bachman's ignorance of these efforts was hardly sufficient to warrant his censure: he was well aware that Audubon knew from experience just how important collectors and collaborators were to their project. Nonetheless, Bachman addressed him as if he were a novice. He told him rather unceremoniously "to open correspondence with every part of the world," to send requests to military posts, and to have his friend John Kirk Townsend "write to a missionary of his acquaintance near the Columbia River." Wasting no time on niceties, Bachman rattled off instructions entirely unwarranted with an old hand: use plenty of arsenic when preserving skinned specimens and remove skins over the skull; place whole specimens in a solution of "West Indian rum" just strong enough to preserve them intact while avoiding disintegration; construct cages to contain rodents and lagomorphs so as to facilitate observation of seasonal changes (pelage dimorphism) as well as habits; and, of course, obtain specimens unavailable in Charleston. A few months later, Bachman went after Audubon again when he chastised him for disregarding his instructions.

He was, he believed, more concerned about drawing than about "giving true names," and Bachman was unimpressed by his efforts, even though he had close to one hundred figures finished, as well as descriptions for some of the species in their published articles.[4]

In truth, Audubon and his sons were again overextended. The octavo edition of *Birds* was in great demand, and ensuring the distribution of "numbers" kept up with sales required their constant attention. They were also shouldering the financing of *Quadrupeds,* and obtaining subscriptions required travel. John James was often on the road in search of supporters. Last, but not least, both John Woodhouse and Victor Gifford had their share of personal trials. At the same time, Bachman might have taken a less accusatory tone had he considered his own lack of productivity. He was highly critical of their efforts, but he had little to show for himself between 1840 and 1842. Unlike between 1837 and 1839, when he discovered twelve species and sixteen subspecies of lagomorphs, rodents, and soricomorphs (and published corresponding articles), he had added just two species and two subspecies to mammalian orders since. And he had done nothing of note on *Quadrupeds.*

In large measure, Bachman's lackluster productivity was unavoidable. He could only leave Charleston under extraordinary circumstances, and so he was beholden to others for specimens and field descriptions, as well as for scientific publications unavailable locally. And specimens from elsewhere were important. Bachman's most significant and lasting contributions arose from specimens collected in the far west by John Kirk Townsend, specifically: *Thomomys (Megascapheus) townsendii* (Townsend's pocket gopher), *Tamiasciurus douglasii* (Douglas's squirrel), *Glaucomys sabrinus oregonensis* (Oregon flying squirrel), *Urocitellus townsendii* (Townsend's ground squirrel), *Tamais (Neotamias) townsendii* (least chipmunk), and *Scapanus townsendii* (Townsend's mole). Even though unaware that some of the "new" species found closer to home would be later discounted, it was obvious that collections from unexplored areas were essential to making original contributions; but, as a full-time pastor, he had limited time for natural history and was unable to travel. He was frustrated by his inability to make collections himself; however, being a part-time naturalist was only one impediment. Even though not admitting it, he had been affected by the deaths of his two eldest daughters.[5]

Once Bachman was ready to return to natural history, he was impatient to begin, and he needed the kind of complete cooperation that made *Birds* possible. Like John James, he needed assistance, but while Maria Martin did step in to deal with outstanding orders and to ensure specimens were distributed as required, she was less robust than usual. She was so concerned about the state of her health that, despite her misgivings about homeopathy, she consulted Dr. Vanderburgh during the fall and winter of 1841–1842. Initially doctoring by correspondence, it was not long before she questioned whether advice offered from afar was going to do any good. She wondered whether taking salt water baths, adopting a daily exercise regimen, or modifying her diet—that is, foregoing tea, coffee, and chocolate—were sufficient to restore her health in light of a long-distance diagnosis she disambiguated as "my mind has always been too powerful a stimulant to my physical organization."[6] Maria believed she needed to see Vanderburgh in person. She was convinced that more could be done to bring balance to her system, and she was determined to find out what that was. Consequently, as Bachman struggled to accomplish something in mammalogy, Maria contacted Victor Audubon to determine if the invitation extended so many times before was still good. It was.

Maria Martin therefore went to see Vanderburgh in person. So did her sister Harriet. Although travel was entirely out of character for Harriet Bachman, she was increasingly consumptive, and the treatments prescribed by her Charleston physicians for the pain caused by trigeminal neuralgia had not been successful. She wanted to consult Vanderburgh and so, accompanied by her youngest daughter, Catherine, Harriet made the journey to New York in search of relief from the unrelenting throbbing and intense burning she had endured for years.

Harriet also missed her daughter Jane. She had been residing with the Audubon family for weeks while obtaining treatment from Dr. Edward Delafield (1794–1875), a well-known "occulist" who achieved considerable stature as a founder of the New York Eye Infirmary and as a coauthor of *A Synopsis of the Diseases of the Eye.*[7] Jane went to New York time and again, until 1846, when it was determined that any further efforts would diminish rather than improve her vision. But in 1842 she was still optimistic that Delafield might produce some miraculous cure, and so it was that in July, Jane awaited the arrival of her mother, her aunt, and her sister, who arrived as expected along with "a fine lot of ducks & some chickens, geese etc."[8]

On previous visits, Maria Martin roomed at a boarding house because, until 1842, the Audubon family lived in a small rented house on White Street in Manhattan, but they had recently moved to Minnie's Land, the home they had built nine miles north of the city on the Hudson River. Maria, Harriet, and Catherine stayed with them at their estate for more than three months. There, Lucy could accommodate guests, and she embraced the opportunity to

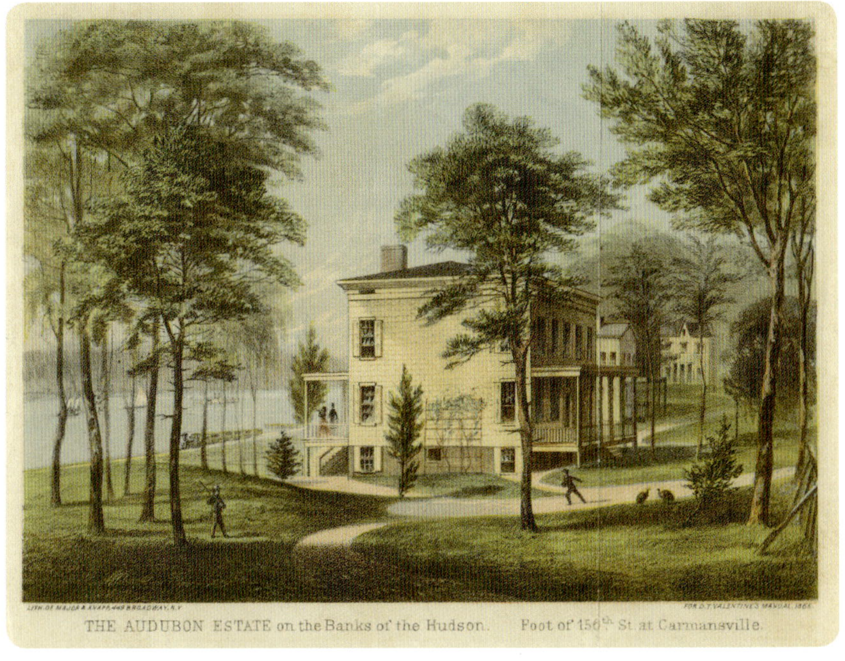

FIGURE 55. Minnie's Land, the Audubon Estate on the banks of the Hudson River, at the foot of 156th Street at Carmansville. From D. T. Valentine's *Manual*, 1865. Lithograph by Major & Knapp. Geographic File, PR-020, NYC, Box 74. Collection of the New-York Historical Society. Digital image created by Oppenheimer Edition.

do so. She could repay those whose hospitality enabled her husband to realize his ambitions, and although described by a New York newspaperman as "simple and unpretending in its architecture," Minnie's Land represented a level of prosperity and middle class respectability that had long eluded her family.[9]

Maria Martin was impressed.[10] Given her preference for country life, she was no doubt pleased to find Minnie's Land so far from the neighborhood where the Audubon family had resided previously, but there was more to admire than the location. There were many similarities between the home she had left and the dwelling before her on the Hudson River. Grand in comparison to most American homes, both were "country" houses with outbuildings, gardens, and a menagerie containing both domesticated and wild animals. Though the kitchen and laundry were on the ground floor of the main house rather than in separate buildings as in Charleston, there were piazzas on two sides of the house and, like the low-country plantations Audubon had visited, the front door faced a river that was one of the main thoroughfares of the state.

Through that door was a center hall and double parlors. The room to the left had northern light, and it was set up as a studio. Just behind the studio was Audubon's library, and both spaces were reminiscent of the "painting room" and ground floor study where Maria Martin had worked with him on *Birds*. Last, but not least, paintings and specimens were everywhere. Parke Godwin (1816–1904), a frequent contributor to the *Evening Post* and the *United States Magazine and Democratic Review*, was so delighted by the curiosities that he saw at Minnie's Land that he described them in *The Homes of American Authors*: "[The left parlor was] evidently a room for work. In one corner stood a painter's easel with a half-finished sketch of a beaver on paper; in the other lay the skin of an American panther. The antlers of elks hung upon the walls, stuffed birds of every description of gay plumage ornamented the mantle-piece; and exquisite drawings of field-mice, orioles, and woodpeckers were scattered promiscuously in other parts of the room, across one end of which a long rude table was stretched to hold artist materials, scraps of drawing paper and immense folio volumes filled with the delicious paintings of birds taken in their haunts."[11] But if the space was a source of wonder to outsiders, it was far less so for Maria Martin. Looking around, she could not but have been reminded of home. Indeed, Minnie's Land bore a striking similarity to the Bachman home, and whether Maria or Harriet would indulge in feeling flattered, they could not but see that this house was a slightly smaller version of the mansion in which they lived.

Being at Minnie's Land was almost like being at home, and while Maria's letters do not say that she picked up a brush, to have done so would have been in character—at least it would have been if John James were in residence. In fact, it is difficult to determine exactly what she did while there, and Bachman complained that she wrote far too seldom and that her letters revealed far too little about her trip.[12] They did not even share much information about the main reason for their journey: medical care. However, one piece of information that did make its way to Charleston was that both Maria and Harriet changed physicians. Never fully committed to homeopathy, they had only been there a month when they began to see Dr. James deBerty Trudeau (1817–1887).

One of Audubon's collector friends, Trudeau was an unusual choice to replace Vanderburgh. His main accomplishments were as a field naturalist, but he was a university-educated physician and, upon examining Harriet Bachman, he did not hesitate to diagnose her condition. Nor was he shy about recommending treatment or offering advice; while the electrical stimulation from the "galvanic apparatus" seemed to provide relief from the facial pain caused by trigeminal neuralgia, the surgical removal of the soft palate, or uvula, was less successful.[13] Trudeau advised this procedure as a means of settling her cough, and he told her that it was a "trifling" operation. Maria Martin wrote home that Trudeau was convincing, and she thought Harriet would have the surgery because his advice had "benefited her so much in one instance, she will be ready to confide in him again, and surely it is worthwhile to make the experiment as her cough is so very annoying." As predicted, Harriet had her palate "clipped off." Unsurprisingly, the procedure did nothing to diminish her cough.

There were, however, more salutary consequences from their consultations with Trudeau. In particular, he convinced Harriet to stand up to her husband. Trudeau clearly made a compelling case: just before leaving New York Harriet informed Bachman that his behavior was counterproductive to her well being. She wrote her husband that Maria and I "are both very sorry that you are so uneasy about our staying so long, but we could not avoid doing so—and I hope you will not say much to us about it when we get home, as we have suffered already enough on that subject. The Dr tells me if I expect to keep well I must not be worried about anything as my complaint is mostly nervous and every excitement will increase it. Therefore all scolding must be put a stop to and I am to be . . . amused."[14]

Though chastised from afar, Bachman was pleased to have his wife, daughter, and sister-in-law home after being separated for more than three months, and he conceded that they were "on the whole, considerably improved."[15] But if Bachman was feeling charitable toward the women in his family when they returned in October, his attitude toward John James was less clear. Indeed, he seldom communicated with his old friend anymore. Aside from one letter sent in May and another sent while Maria and Harriet were at Minnie's Land in August, Bachman had not written Audubon since December 1841, when he berated him for ignoring his advice to examine the volumes in Richard Owen's *Descriptive and illustrated Catalogue of the Physiological Series of Comparative Anatomy* (1833–40).[16] And this reprimand was dispatched just two weeks after another letter accusing him of shoddy work. On November 22, Bachman wrote that he was disappointed by his negligence: Audubon had failed to determine the geographical distribution of a bird when he had the chance to do so, and Bachman described his behavior as inexcusable and unbecoming a naturalist. He belittled him, writing: "I am sorry you cannot do two things at a time. As for me, I can preach, study birds and beasts, write letters, eat fat chick, take snuff, all in one day. But I will drop the subject without referring you to the dictionary for the difference between firmness and obstinacy."[17]

The two men had hardly communicated except through others since June 1840 when Audubon left Charleston under a cloud, and given that Bachman no longer felt like a junior partner in their new venture, there was little likelihood that they would return to the halcyon days when he deferred to Audubon.[18] Indeed, it was only after hearing from Maria that Audubon had been in Upper (Ontario) and Lower (Quebec) Canada that Bachman approached his old friend in a friendlier manner.[19] On the road selling subscriptions, filling orders, and collecting receipts for *Quadrupeds* and *Birds*, Audubon might have species such as the otter, wolf, wolverine, and lemming unavailable farther south, and Bachman wanted to know what he had accomplished in British North America. However, Audubon returned with neither specimens nor paintings. Disappointed that he had not painted the reindeer or moose, Bachman's spirits were nonetheless high and for the first time in a long time he looked forward to seeing Audubon.[20]

Bachman could not have known that in the space of two months a bout of influenza would foil his plans to work on *Quadrupeds*: he was confined to his bed for more than two weeks over the Christmas season. When well enough to leave his sick room Bachman vowed to redouble his efforts, and he informed Audubon that he intended to devote himself to "quadrupeds, which beyond my profession, is the only thing I mean to care about for the next three years if my life is spared so long."[21] As it turned out, Bachman's allusion to death was more than a dramatic flourish. Poor health prevented him from doing much on quadrupeds and while he was indisposed, James [Ellsworth] DeKay's *Mammalia*, or volume one of the scientific findings of the state survey of New York, was published.[22]

The first monograph on mammals to have appeared in more than a decade, DeKay (1792–1851) not only managed to beat Bachman to publish a book on North American mammals but also preempted him methodologically. In deliberately replacing the literary style used previously, for example that found in Audubon's bird biographies, with a more impersonal narrative characterized by quantitative data and thorough citations, both DeKay and Bachman reflected emerging disciplinary dictates, but *Mammalia* deprived Bachman of the distinction of being the first mammalogist to do so in the United States.[23] Instead, he had to reference DeKay alongside eminent naturalists like Linnaeus, Cuvier, Ray, Thomas Pennant (1726–1798), and John Richardson (1796–1852). Bachman had been bested in his plan to pioneer the new approach to taxonomy and systematics in *Quadrupeds*, and he expressed his dismay as he panned the "book that cost $130,000" in a letter to Audubon. He wrote: "The

Lord preserve us from being overwise. All taken from nature & with the camera-lucida. What a lying affair this camera-lucida must be. But the affair is not worth getting into a passion or spitting upon. By George, it is a windy book. The zoology of my dear native state—methinks the very quadrupeds will cry out murder. The oppossum [*sic*] will leap across the Hudson & beg for quarters in the foreign state of New York, & the manatee will rear its head in the rivers of Florida & implore in the name of extra-limital to be let alone. And now after I have blown my nose taken a pinch of snuff & would have pitched the book into my spitting basin if it had not been yours."[24] Bachman found being bested difficult to accept, especially as he believed DeKay should have cited his work more fully than he did, and he never passed up an opportunity to make him "look very foolish" when forced to cite *Mammalia*.[25]

In the meantime, he turned to more pleasant matters. Audubon was planning to undertake an expedition along the route traveled by Meriwether Lewis (1744–1809) and William Clark (1770–1838), and Bachman made a preliminary list of specimens he hoped to receive. Genial, even jovial, he implored John James to collect "everything you can lay your hands on," especially lagomorphs, marmots, wolves, foxes, and wild cats. He also indulged other interests. Although not abandoning natural history entirely, he set aside quadrupeds as he prepared two talks on the benefits of agriculture and became embroiled in a public dispute over a hoax being perpetrated by the Northern fabulist and showman P. T. Barnum (1810–1891). His "Feejee mermaid" was on display at the Masonic Hall in January, and Bachman took exception to the ridiculous claim that it was a "wonder of nature."

The "mermaid" was clearly manufactured from the body of a fish and the head and torso of a monkey, and Bachman was outraged when it was promoted by the Charleston *Courier* as a scientific specimen.[26] The stitched-together oddity had been on display for weeks in New York City where it attracted the gullible and the bemused, and the same was about to happen in the Southern states where it was on tour.[27] Bachman was incensed that the *Courier* pandered to the credulous, taunting them to check out the mermaid in pitches passing as information. According to the editors:

> We, of course, cannot undertake to say whether this seeming wonder of nature be real or not, it not being in our power to apply to it any scientific test of truth; but this we deem it but just to say, that we were permitted to handle and examine it as closely as could be effected by touch and sight, and that if there be any deception, it is beyond the discovery of both those

> senses. The appearance is in every respect that of a natural and not an artificial object—it is certainly no compound or combination, as has been supposed, of ape and fish—but is either altogether nature's handi-work, or altogether the production of art—and if it be indeed artificial, it is the very perfection of art, imitating nature in the closest similitude. We are rather inclined to have faith on the occasion, for the connection, which this curious object establishes between fish and women, is only in analogy with that which every body knows to exist between monkey and man . . .[28]

Leaving aside the highly contentious allusion to evolution, the idea that some might actually believe this "curious object" a real creature was more than Bachman could abide, and when the *Courier* refused to print his comments, he took them to the Charleston *Mercury*.

Infuriated that a reputable scientist could be ignored, he wrote a scathing commentary that insulted many readers. Some offered equally scurrilous counterattacks, but Bachman confided to a friend that he had to speak out as "a naturalist, and [as] an author engaged at the time in preparing a work on the Mammalia." He also stated that he "felt it my duty, to expose this despicable fraud & if possible, drive this man with his vile caricature from our city."[29] He had no regrets, and he would not shirk his responsibility.

Bachman's inability to overlook what he saw as inexcusable ignorance was well known, and it caused him to set aside work on *Quadrupeds* more than once.[30] For example, seven years later he was drawn into a dispute over human origins that resulted in a number of articles and a three hundred-page book. Similarly, in 1845, he took time from *Quadrupeds* to point out the failings of the "uninformed" in botany. The untrained were, he alleged, quite unlike those whose interest in plants was grounded in science, and he took the opportunity afforded by Maria Martin's study of an unusual plant to demonstrate these differences.

In July 1843, Maria Martin was visiting the "Botanic Garden of Mr. Russell" in order to catch the duck plant (*Aristolochia foetida*), a native to Mexico being cultivated there, in flower.[31] The plant's peculiar organs of fructification were highly unusual, and two years after Maria's daily excursions to observe the plant, Bachman published an article accusing the general public of ignorance in the field of botany that was no less egregious than that exhibited when gullible Charlestonians accepted claims that the "Fee-jee mermaid" was a "wonder of nature." In what was an otherwise unembellished article delineating size, shape, and color of external and internal parts, he pointed out—quite gratuitously—how the "uninformed" erroneously interpreted oddities of nature to suit themselves:

> There are many flowers called personate flowers that resemble the countenances of various kinds of animals. The curious and imaginative have seen resemblances in the faces of their domestic cattle to the human countenances. Indeed, the Etrick Shepherd came to the conclusion that by a long association, with his faithful dog, their countenances had gradually put on a similar expression. In all these cases it is evident that a single point of resemblance when the species differ in every other characteristic, does not constitute an affinity. It is not in a mere resemblance of external forms, but in the internal structure, and a similarity in many essential particulars that naturalists seek for evidences of a near approximation of species. Nor should we be misled by the vulgar name given to different species. The so called sea horse sometimes found in our harbor is pretty nearly allied to the shrimp, and generally less in size—the sea lion is a large, ugly seal, and the sea dog is a smaller species of the same genus. Among plants we have the snail flower, the snake plant, the side-saddle flower, the aligator [*sic*] melon, the duck plant, &c., agreeable to this absurd theory there would be a connecting link between the horse and shrimp, the squash and the snake, the aligator and the melon, and our curious Sarraeonia, and the ladies side-saddle. These vulgar names and real or fancied resemblances may mislead the uninformed, but have no effect on the minds of men of science.[32]

This was probably not the best use of his time, but Bachman could not condone contrary views—whether they were anticipated or articulated. At the same time, his behavior might be viewed more charitably as a reflection of how a world defined by illness affected the psyche as well as productivity.

In 1845, both Maria Martin and John Bachman were distracted and anxious. Harriet Bachman had been unusually unwell during the previous two years, and she was so gravely ill in July 1844 that it was feared death was imminent.[33] And things were little better the following year. Bachman wrote Audubon, "We are all in much affliction," especially Harriet, and he asked him to avoid "speak[ing] of her being very low as she always insists on seeing your letters."[34] Hoping that the country air would improve her health, Harriet was staying on the plantation owned by her married daughter Harriet Bachman Haskell, often accompanied by John Bachman, who worked while keeping her company. So focused was he on Harriet's condition that he could not even accompany his daughter Jane, still in need of ophthalmic treatment from Dr. Delafield, and so her sister Julia went with her when she went to New York yet again.

Bachman's efforts in natural history were stalled until late 1845, and he admitted as much. John James returned from the Missouri River region in November 1843 without the lagomorphs, marmots, wolves, foxes, and wild cats Bachman needed, and although this was disappointing, it was not the main cause of his lack of progress on *Quadrupeds*. Likewise, it was frustrating that Audubon had little interest in measuring and describing the various gophers, squirrels and chipmunks that he painted and that all he had to show for eight months work was nine partially finished paintings, one by his assistant Isaac Sprague (1811–1895), a few notes on mammals, and fewer than thirty species skinned by John [Graham] Bell (1812–1899), the taxidermist of the expedition.[35] But Bachman's personal trials and tribulations were of greater consequence to his lack of progress than a lack of western data. Even though Bachman found Audubon's fascination with the Mandan, Assiniboine, "Chippeway," and Peigan they encountered maddening, the fact that John James preferred to record his thoughts on indigenous people was a smaller impediment to work than events taking place in the Bachman residence.[36] In fact, when Bachman went to New York to bring Jane and Julia home in August 1845, he was able to work on *Quadrupeds* for the first time in almost two years.

On route, Bachman stopped in Washington to examine collections deposited there by the Wilkes Expedition, and a month later he was working from four until seven A.M. on descriptions.[37] By the end of October, he was determined to focus on his scientific work, vowing that "nothing but ill health or domestic affliction will keep me back." He worked as he sat next to his invalided wife, and in November he was able to announce that writing had begun on the "very first article" for *Quadrupeds*. He also had a "plan" that would permit him to "finish" three species a week.

More than ten years after conceiving *Quadrupeds*, Bachman was finally in a position to realize their goal, but success was, he stressed, contingent on complete cooperation from everyone.[38] First and foremost, the same specimens must be used whether writing descriptions or preparing plates, and Victor was responsible for conveying both specimens and information collected by his father to Charleston. Bachman also laid out the "arrangement" of the text. The task before him was monumental. Like DeKay before him, he insisted that descriptions reflect emerging taxonomic standards, and he wanted to be able to incorporate Victor's notes into his descriptions "without copying over which is a good fatigue to me."[39] If Victor had any doubts about what he was proposing, he laid it out clearly:

> 1. Class II Order III Family IV Genus so that if the Book is ever arranged regularly it can be done without further labour. We have now arrived to the Genus & I proceed in this manner.
>   1. Genus. Describe the Genus & give the author
>   2. Essential characters
>   3. Synonyms
>   4. Description of form
>   5. Do of colours
>   6. Dimensions—Here you begin & you must give the measurements uniformly thus from head to root of tail—tail vertebrae—end of hair—height from fore shoulder—height of ear particularly—length of head—heel &c this is the usual mode & answers all purposes
>   7. Habits. Here you must not include Geographical distribution but write so carefully—first reading everything on the subject—that the sheets may be inserted without recopying—this includes food—walking—running—sleeping—hibernation—nests &c number of young—time of production &c
>   8. Geographical distribution
>   9. General observations—on the nomenclature—the difficulties of the species—criticism on authors who have given it &c.

With Bachman's guidelines, the assistance of family, and the fact that the research on more than half of the species described had been completed and even partially published, volume one of *The Viviparous Quadrupeds of North America* appeared within a year.

Maria Martin assisted when she could. Bachman needed all sorts of information as he composed descriptions, and she copied borrowed books and Audubon's journals. She packaged specimens and prepared lists. She worked alongside her brother-in-law, describing morphological characteristics, especially the color of organs, and she measured anatomical structures. She also edited drafts of Bachman's descriptions.[40]

Maria Martin sketched as well. She drew, for example, a muskrat foot as they tried to determine whether the anatomical description provided by Victor Audubon was accurate.[41] By 1846, however, her days as a natural history artist were behind her. The injury that paralyzed her right arm by the mid-1850s could not but have an impact on her ability to paint and draw, at least periodically. But that Maria Martin lost some of her former dexterity was in many ways less important than the shift that occurred when Bachman assumed responsibility for *Quadrupeds*. Where Audubon preferred to let images "drawn from nature" relay information on form, function, and purpose, Bachman believed such objectives were best met through description, identification, and classification.[42] He privileged text over art, and so while skills honed under Audubon's tutelage were put to use as Maria Martin swapped her easel and brushes for a desk and pens, during the 1840s Maria worked for Bachman, not Audubon.

Once work began on *Quadrupeds*, her loyalty to Bachman was obvious. He needed her assistance, and she was no longer at Audubon's disposal. It was not so much that she lost interest in botany and painting, but rather that her relationship with John Bachman continued much as it had since he married her sister in 1816, while her relationship with John James changed when her niece Ria married John Woodhouse in 1837. Thereafter, what had been a relationship based on mutual interests in natural history took on religious and legal significance, and her role as botanical illustrator was often trumped by that of dutiful aunt. And when Eliza married Victor Gifford in 1839, Maria Martin's reversion to her traditional role was assured. The marriages that pleased John James and Lucy so much produced a realignment that had a profound impact in the deeply religious and thoroughly Southern household where Maria Martin lived. Admittedly, Maria Martin had always been the self-sacrificing aunt, but as she entered the decade when the Audubon and Bachman families would work together on *Quadrupeds*, the context in which she pursued natural history was firmly situated within a world defined by kinship. And in the South, where "fealty to family was the first law of honor," kinship was stronger than friendship.[43]

As Bachman rushed to get the "letter press" ready, members of his extended family responded admirably. John Woodhouse and Victor Gifford assumed increasingly greater responsibility for painting both figures and backgrounds, eventually replacing their father entirely when both body and mind failed him before *Quadrupeds* was completed, but there were other participants as well. Lynch Bachman translated scientific articles from French to English; John Bachman's son-in-law, William Haskell, and Julia Bachman copied text. Two young women were even hired to dissect specimens. Bachman was interested in the gestational cycle of the opossum (*Didelphis virginiana*), and these women were paid a "trifling" fifty cents per week to extract the fetuses in varying stages of development.[44] If not quite everyone helped out, many were drawn in, and Maria Martin's relationship to John Bachman became even closer when she married him in December 1848.

Bachman predicted their marriage would facilitate work on *Quadrupeds,* and Maria Martin certainly did her part. She worked indefatigably on the manuscript, and her husband described her efforts glowingly. He wrote Victor that she "lops off to the right and the left with your notes and mine; she corrects, criticises, abuses, and praises us by turns."[45] But the concerns that motivated Bachman to issue specific instructions to Victor—namely, that his health might "break down" or some other calamity might occur—conspired against speedy completion. Bachman experienced a number of setbacks before the reconceptualized three-volume set began to emerge in 1851. Moreover, it had long been apparent that John James was not going to see *Quadrupeds* through to completion.

In 1840, Audubon was as optimistic as ever, and with characteristic panache he assured Bachman they could complete *Quadrupeds* in record time. He wrote: "My Hair are grey, and I am growing old, but what of this? My Spirits are as enthusiastical as ever, my legs fully able to carry my body for some Ten Years to come, and in about Two of these I expect to see *the Illustrations* out, and ere the following Twelve Months have elapsed, their Histories studied, their descriptions carefully prepared and the Book printed!"[46] Still full of vim and vigor, he admitted to the limits that human frailty placed on his boundless ambition, but he was undaunted by the prospect of aging. Indeed, he carried on despite poor vision and cognitive impairment, perhaps even incipient dementia, but it was not long after his bravura endorsement of the project that Bachman noticed changes. His memory failed him and, in 1843, for example, Bachman described Audubon as "woolgathering" when his correspondence on a Sciurus specimen was filled with inconsistencies.[47]

Bachman typically commented on Audubon's lapses in jest, but he increasingly corresponded with Victor when he had serious matters to discuss. Through Victor, he also tried to encourage John James to take more interest in their work, but when the elder Audubon did become involved, Bachman found his comments confusing and his painting off. Between receiving garbled information and figures so badly "distorted" that they were worse than useless, Bachman was at his wit's end, and the gravity of the situation was particularly clear in early 1846 when Audubon denied having a lengthy debate with Bachman over the accuracy of DeKay's view that the common grey squirrel with tufted ears (*Sciurus carolinensis*) was a separate species. Audubon even forgot that he had consulted important references and had painted specimens. Bachman was moved to repeat his earlier observation in a letter to Victor. He minimized his concern but conveyed it nonetheless as he reported that his "old friend's memory . . . sometimes goes wool gathering."[48] That anything was accomplished in 1846 was nothing short of astonishing, and the situation worsened the following year.

It would have been entirely plausible to think that 1847 would be better than 1846. Constant worry about Jane, who was undergoing ophthalmic treatment that was doing more harm than good, and coping with the ever-increasing debility of Harriet Bachman dominated the first half of 1846. Both situations affected how people went about their usual affairs, but Jane's absence was especially trying for Harriet. She was accustomed to her daughter's company, and Harriet did not see Jane again before succumbing to consumption in July. The house was yet again in mourning, and a number of the inhabitants were unwell. Even the usually robust Maria Martin was described as "very feeble." A month later, she was "a skeleton" and suffering from "constant headaches with pain in the side & every symptom of a liver affection."[49] Even worse, Julia had developed a "disturbing" cough, and this was a source of great worry since her mother had just died of consumption, as had two older sisters.[50] But for all the trials of 1846, the next year was little better. Bachman began drafting volume two in February, but little progress was made. In addition, to his usual complaints about the "helter skelter" way in which Victor dealt with specimens and information, he developed severe conjunctivitis. He was forced to rest his eyes for more than six weeks.

Maria Martin seldom left his side. She wrote down dictated descriptions and answered correspondence; she also joined him when his third daughter required treatment for consumption.[51] The year was not even half over when she and John Bachman took Julia to Aiken even though the climate there had done nothing to arrest consumptive symptoms in her older sister. Unsurprisingly, a few months later it was clear that going inland was doing little for Julia. More drastic measures were required, and it was decided to go to Red Sulphur Springs, Virginia, where the springs there were reputed to cure pulmonary diseases.

In June, Julia set out for one of the last resorts for consumptives. She was accompanied by Maria Martin, her sister Lynch, and her father. Bachman hoped the trip might benefit his vision as well as Julia's cough; however, his plan to rest his eyes for three to four weeks was set aside.[52] Julia's condition was too delicate for rest. Despite the amenities of the springs, the ministrations of Dr. William Burke, resident physician and author of the *Mineral Springs of West Virginia* (1846), and the untiring efforts of Maria Martin, who was reportedly an excellent "nurse," Julia died on September 7.

Still affected by the loss of his wife to consumption, Victor Audubon also tried to help in those last desperate weeks. He sent a pamphlet by Samuel Sheldon Fitch on curing consumption, but it made little difference.[53] Julia's case was hopeless. To make matters worse, Lynch became ill while at Red Sulphur Springs. She suffered from incessant vomiting that left her so emaciated it was feared she had developed consumption.[54] Although the doctors at the springs attributed her illness "to anxiety of mind," there was certainly justification to think she was following in the path taken by so many in her family. Moreover, she had just spent two months breathing the same air as the "coughers," and bathing in the same mineral waters as those suffering from intestinal tuberculosis; so, despite the prognosis offered by the Virginia physicians, Bachman summoned Doctors Horlbeck and Geddings immediately upon their arrival in Charleston. They followed their normal course of treatment, and Lynch was blistered and bled until she was quite weak.[55] By mid-November, she was still unable to keep food down and was "very much depressed," but it was decided she was suffering from dyspepsia rather than consumption, and their heroic measures were discontinued.

Sufficiently buoyed by the doctors' diagnosis, Bachman prepared to leave for Synod. Before leaving, he wrote Victor and berated him for being slack in organizing and transmitting specimens.[56] He then left the unfinished quadruped business with Maria. A month later, his dependency on her increased further when his eyes, already compromised, were accidently injured. A mixture of gunpowder, sulphur, and lard exploded in his study, and he was subsequently confined to a darkened room with "grated irish potatoe [*sic*] poultices" on his lidless eyes for ten days.[57] Bachman felt he was lucky to have not been blinded, but his eye troubles continued to plague him. The following summer he was unable to write, and Maria Martin took care of his correspondence, including that on quadrupeds. As Bachman was under strict orders to avoid overtaxing his eyes, Maria assumed responsibility for ensuring that Bachman followed his doctor's advice, and she was sufficiently threatening as to intimidate him into writing in secret.[58]

In October, she was still in control. Bachman informed Victor: "Maria promises to write whilst I dictate—you must be patient—you see how I am situated. Your Father began the work before he or I was ready—I have imperative duties—my life is worth something to my children at least—I will aid you all I can but I cannot consent to endanger sight & life to oblige even you."[59] By December, he had to admit defeat. The slightest effort set him back. He had to preach without notes, and he had to avoid reading. Even thirty minutes of reading disrupted his sleep miserably. Indeed, the only way he could proceed with *Quadrupeds* was to turn over the writing to Maria Martin, and he confessed his debility to Victor. But in the same letter, he conveyed some good news: he announced that Maria Martin had not only agreed to serve as his "amanuensis" beginning January 2, 1849, but also that she had agreed to marry him.[60] They were married before the year ended.

It was with relief and pleasure that Victor responded. He wrote Maria Martin Bachman that he was "now more assured of the completion of our hopes and wishes in regard to the letter-press of the 'Quadrupeds' than I have been for months past." He continued: "You will, I know, readily imagine the unpleasant position in which the long delay that has already occurred, has placed us, but I must pass over many things connected with this subject which it would only worry you to no purpose to relate to you. I hope the task of completing the Work will not prove too irksome to you and to our friend your husband."[61] He was, of course, referring to the fact that his father was completely unable to paint or help out in any fashion. No elaboration was needed. A year earlier, John Bachman had visited Minnie's Land, where he witnessed firsthand the dementia only hinted at in his baffling exchanges with John James, and he wrote Maria of the indescribable sadness of seeing "the ruins of a mind once bright & full of imagination."[62]

Victor may have been overoptimistic. In 1849, John Bachman was also laboring under serious impediments, and progress was slow, even with Maria's assistance. Indeed, she was perhaps the overzealous one, and Bachman wrote Victor warning him as much: "Maria has I believe made all manner of promises for me, I fear she has promised too much as my health is extremely uncertain. I have one week of giddiness in the head so much so that my only comfortable position is with my eyes that my head against the wall & my feet on the grate."[63] Three months later, Bachman consented to seek treatment. He and Maria went to Madison Springs, Georgia, with notes and specimens in tow. There, they worked together, integrating information from Victor into descriptions being drafted. Maria took the lead as editor, and as Bachman observed, she "copies better than I write."[64] A month later, Bachman was as hopeful as Victor. He was sure that volume two would soon be completed.[65] It did not appear for another two years though. His eyes were sufficiently healed to begin writing again, but instead of returning to quadrupeds, he began writing a book devoted to disproving claims advanced by Samuel George Morton (1799–1851) on the existence of multiple creations among species.

Within six months, *The Doctrine of the Unity of the Human Race Examined on the Principles of Science* was published. A weighty volume at more than three hundred pages. Bachman spared no effort in supporting his view that there had been but one original couple. Howsoever members of the human race differed from one another, it was not because they had different origins. Drawing on his extensive knowledge of species and hybridization, his approach was disdainful and elicited several retorts from those he attacked.[66] He could not let these rebuttals stand unanswered, and he composed a multipart article for the *Charleston Medical Journal* instead of working on *Quadrupeds*. The dispute was only set aside because Morton died and a temporary truce was invoked, but the debate was revived in 1855 when Bachman published an extensive review of *Types of Mankind* (1854) by Josiah Nott (1804–1873) and George Glidden (1809–1857).[67] By this time, however, Bachman was at liberty to do as he wished. The last volume of *Quadrupeds* had appeared.

By 1855, Bachman worked alone. In fact, even earlier when work began on volume three, Maria Martin was losing the use of her right hand and in pain.[68] As a result, Victor went to Charleston to help Bachman in 1852. Leaving home with snow on the ground, he arrived there as the trees were "coming into leaf—the gardens beginning to look quite pretty and the birds singing delightfully in the mornings" and, in just over two weeks, the descriptions for volume three were written.[69] But Bachman considered the "letter-press" far from finished. He had always believed the flying mammals belonged with quadrupeds, and before Victor left Charleston he convinced him that the last volume should include bats as well as "a synopsis & scientific arrangement of all our American Species, including the Seals, whales & porpoises."[70] In the end, neither bats nor marine mammals made their way into *Quadrupeds*; nor was there a synopsis. Volume three simply adhered to the scheme set out in 1845. There were no concluding or introductory remarks, no acknowledgments, and no mention that one of the authors had died three years previous. Without assistance, Bachman was unable to do more than add thirty-nine brief entries, mostly rodents that had not been figured, and many were erroneously listed as new species.

Far more rigorous and knowledgeable than his collaborators when it came to taxonomy, Bachman benefited from the empirical—even anecdotal—approach Audubon developed during a lifetime spent studying animals in their natural environment. While Bachman never accepted Audubon's views uncritically, their discussions were essential to arriving at the most accurate position possible on many species. But as Audubon became increasingly dysfunctional and difficult to work with, his ability to counter Bachman's autocratic tendencies declined, and the collaboration that was sometimes difficult, but nonetheless fruitful, became impossible. Bachman therefore relied increasingly on Victor Audubon.

John James was puzzled by this turn of events and said so. Bachman felt obliged to respond to his queries and although he sidestepped exactly why he was working with Victor, he revealed much about their new relationship: "When I write to you I write to my equal in some things, my superior in others. In doing so I must stand on my P's & Q'u's. Now on the other hand Victor is a Boy to me & I feel that I can use every manner of freedom. I can order him to copy books, to get specimens, to call on People—I say to him do, & and he doeth it, (not always it is true as quickly as I wish) I can scold him for neglect, & he is too respectful or too good natured to scold back. This writing Books without specimens & without the necessary authorities to consult is no fun. Worrying & bothering, the steam gets up—& it must be blown off or the boiler will burst. Now if I were to blow off my steam on you, there is no [place?] in your house strong enough to hold you."[71] Where John James debated, Victor acquiesced. The tact and diplomacy needed to smooth over disputes about birds and mammals, or about alcohol and tobacco, were unnecessary. Bachman could treat Victor as a "boy" because the younger Audubon always saw him as his father-in-law.

Similarly, Victor saw Maria Martin as his "aunt" first and collaborator second, and she remained "Aunt Maria" to him long after he remarried. Ever respectful, Victor's affectionate designation did not in any way diminish his appreciation of Maria Martin's contributions; however, as *Quadrupeds* approached completion, the woman he regarded so highly was slowly retreating into the background and was clearly unable to perform the role described by descendants as "smoothing the troubled waters" between Audubon and Bachman.[72] Nor could she care for others as she long had.

By the time *Quadrupeds* was finished, it was Maria Martin's turn to be the invalid. She had developed the characteristic symptoms of consumption and could no longer ignore the dislocated elbow that had gone untreated for over a decade.[73] Maria was tormented at night, and the injured arm prevented her from doing activities she enjoyed. John Bachman told Lucy Audubon that he feared the worst as Maria's spirits sank with every passing day:

> Within the last two years she complained of the pains more frequently, for 2 months past, the pain was incessant & the whole hand became perfectly helpless. Drs Horlbeck and Geddings inform me that they had not the shadow of a hope, that the arm could be useful again. The

> bone has enlarged to double its former size, & the pain is such, that she groans nearly all night. To one of her active habits—so fond of sewing & corresponding with her friends, it is a very great deprivation. I have seen her trying to sew with her left hand & making awkward efforts at writing, but she could not succeed with either. It is true Jane & Kate do everything for her & her work is not needed, but she misses the priviledge [*sic*] of occupation. Time hangs heavy on her hands & she seems to regret most that she can now be no longer useful to me & to those around her. To myself her present situation is full of foreboding & terrible anxiety. She has been all to me. A mother to all my children—My adviser—my companion my help in all things. I always relied on her judgment. My house was desolate without her. She was always the same—meek gentle & confiding pious without ostentation, faithful in her friendships & conscientious in the performance of her duties. . . . Please write cheerfully & as far as you can encouraging. She is not naturally of a lively turn of mind, but is well disciplined in the school of trial & adversity.[74]

And things were about to become even worse. Like others of her generation, Maria Martin Bachman was about to witness the South plunge headlong into a war over slavery.

7

FAITH

"Our Trust in God"

Maria Martin spent her entire life in a slave society. Slave labor allowed her to develop her artistic talents. It allowed her to fulfill her Christian duty, but in her reliance on the labor of others, she was far from unique.[1] Northern women with the means to do so also depended on others to lighten their load. Lucy Audubon certainly had servants when finances permitted. There was, of course, a difference between bonded and free labor, and Maria's niece, Eliza, pointed out that difference not long after she moved to New York as a married woman. She wrote home about how in the North maids came and went, often at their own initiative, and they complained about the amount of work expected. They had, Eliza concluded, "notions" unbefitting those who served. She wrote her sister Jane asking her to share her impressions: "Tell dear Mother that since I have been here, I have taken particular notice of the servants or helps as they are erroneously called, and indeed I think she may feel quite contented with those she has for dear Mamma [Lucy Audubon] has trouble enough in this respect. Some of them are so high in their notions that you would really suppose them to be ladies instead of people working for their living. One whom we had yesterday upon trial actually found fault with the house, and said she had never been accustomed to eating in the kitchen, but had always had a room fitted up for the purpose. After this I should not wonder at any thing but it only shows that the obtaining of good servants is a difficulty every where. Mamma soon dispatched the useless ones and in time I hope we shall be well suited."[2] Maria Martin did not disclose her thoughts on the relative merits of "helps versus slaves," although twenty years later, she employed at least one free servant, an Irish maid named Hannah Roddy,[3] who worked alongside five slaves in the Bachman home.[4] This was considerably fewer than in previous years when there were as many as eighteen enslaved men, women, and children, but the number of bonded workers was irrelevant to Maria Martin's views or to her role as a slave owner.[5] She did not question the institution of slavery, and she would not tolerate the impertinence attributed to the Audubon domestics.

As someone who expected obedience from the nieces she raised—let alone the slaves or servants she supervised—Maria Martin dealt expeditiously with anyone having the temerity to complain or voice an opinion on any matter. She could not convey often enough the duty to submit, whether to God or to man. To act otherwise was unacceptable, and her views did not change much over her life. If anything, her views on slavery became more entrenched. As the abolition movement gained support, she became ever more committed to the Southern way of life, and she did so even as the Lutheran Church took an antislavery position during the 1850s.

Opposition to slavery within her church was not new, but it was sometimes a personal affront. As early as 1837, John Bachman felt compelled to defend himself when a Lutheran pastor accused him of profiting "from the sweat and blood of the slave."[6] Whether Lutheran abolitionists were impressed by his claim that he owned slaves by default—having inherited them from his wife—is unlikely, but at the time only the Franckean Synod (New York) took a public position against slavery, and both the charge and the rebuttal faded in the face of other issues.[7] Twenty years later, in 1857, however, opposition to slavery was more widespread and a series of resolutions outlining "the responsibility of the Christian to bear witness against slavery, to exert his influence against it through the ballot box, and to recognize it as a legitimate subject for homilectical presentations" were passed.[8] In this decision, Bachman believed church leaders were in error, and before the year's end his views were published in *The Missionary*.

In his dissenting opinion, he stated that the church was being distracted from its primary purpose of spreading the word of God, and that it was hypocritical to tell pastors they could call for abolition from the pulpit while at the same time telling them to uphold the longstanding policy of abstaining from involvement in politics.[9] As he put it, "the reciprocal duties of masters and servants" were sanctioned in both the Old and New Testament, and as slavery was the law of the land it was ill-advised to weigh in on matters best left to "statesmen." At the same time, Bachman had flirted with politics at least since 1845. He and twenty-three other concerned citizens held a meeting to formulate a plan to disseminate information on the good work being done among the African American population.[10]

Bachman clearly did not see efforts to promote and publicize the "Religious Instruction of Negroes" as political, and his perspective was unsurprising. He was simply following instructions issued in 1814 to actively recruit enslaved "negroes" into the church.[11] The North Carolina Synod mandated this pastoral role, and Bachman took his took his duty to proselytize seriously. Under his ministry, St. John's Lutheran grew significantly: between 1815 and 1857, he increased the number of white congregants by approximately 1,900, and he baptized some 1,700 African Americans.[12] Additionally, in fulfilling the dictates of synod, he was in step with fellow clerics, especially evangelicals from other denominations (who believed it was their duty to convert slaves to Christianity). They believed doing so not only contributed to the spiritual and moral development of enslaved men and women but also conveyed the ideals of obedience and submission that were so crucial to keeping order in a society where as much as half of the population was in bondage.[13]

If Northern Lutherans had previously misunderstood such efforts, Southern clergy did not, and in private Bachman expressed his political views plainly. In 1851, he predicted with remarkable accuracy developments of the next decade. Overoptimistic, he erred in his belief that Northern politicians would uphold constitutional protections as Southerners declared their "independence," but his other predictions were astonishingly accurate. He wrote to Victor Audubon:

> The State secessionists here have I fear a very large majority . . . I confess I am growing every day less attached to the Union as it now exists & if South Carolina declares for secession I will for weal or woe go with her. If we are not to live as equals under the Union I would rather preserve my independence with a crust of bread & be out of it. If such large States as New York & Massachusetts have no power to keep out such men as Seward & Sumner, but send them to Washington to read Abolition petitions & abuse & insult the institutions—the morals & religion of the South—then it is high time to look out for ourselves. All our Southern States except Carolina are disposed to wait a little, but I see none of us have much hope for the preserva[tion of the Uni]on many years longer. . . . Should South Carolina secede she will entail on herself long years of poverty & misery but I feel convinced that from that day the fate of our Union will be sealed. The sending of an army here is nonsense for that would bring from our neighbouring states a hundred thousand volunteers in a week. The shutting up our ports would be a violation of the doctrine

> of state rights advanced by the democracy of every Southern State & many of the democrats of the North. . . . We would be starved & ruined, but the Government would be sure to do justice to the neighbouring states & enter into some permanent arrangement to give security to the property of the south. At present we are under the tyranny of an interested & an unscrupulous majority, & have no security for the future. . . . Love to all.[14]

Victor responded almost immediately. He was not nearly as sanguine about the fate of secessionist South Carolina, and by the end of the decade Maria Martin shared his concern. Not doubting the validity of her husband's position, she worried about the dangers they were facing.

Maria Martin was well aware of current events. Just because some topics were beyond her purview did not mean she was ignorant of them. As Bachman's helpmeet and confident, she was never far from his side, and as Bachman was drawn into the secessionist movement she was privy to conversations that were increasingly belligerent, especially as one of Bachman's closest friends at the time was Edmund Ruffin (1794–1865), an ardent secessionist.[15] It had not been Bachman's practice to be secretive with Maria; when he was riled, she knew it. His antipathy to "black republicans," underground railroads, and "free soilers" was well known, and when he was reveling in the Dred Scott decision and in the pro-Southern platitudes of President Buchanan, she was as well-informed as ever.[16] Maria was further exposed to such views because she often stayed inland with the Gregg family at their home, Kalmia Hill.[17] Like Bachman, William Gregg (1800–1867) was a pro-Union man who chose secession when abolitionist efforts were sanctioned in the 1860 election of Abraham Lincoln. As an owner of one of the largest cotton mills in the state, he saw the economic advantages of remaining in the Union but he was also proslavery and, like Bachman, he moved toward secession as Northern attacks on slavery became increasingly aggressive.[18] By 1860, he had moved entirely toward secession, and he represented his county (Edgefield) at the secessionist convention in Charleston.[19]

As the 1850s drew to a close, Bachman made no effort to hide his political views, and in 1858 he announced his support of secession in church. Two years later, following Lincoln's election, he was even more openly political as he charged his congregation with standing firm against encroachments on their way of life. A month after that, he laid out his views in a lengthy invocation before those assembled to vote on secession at the South Carolina Institute Hall. Devoted to the advance of the arts, agriculture, and manufacturing, the building where Carolinians were about to chart a course much feared by Maria

Martin was built on the very ground where her mother had operated a mantua-making business almost a century earlier, but standing before those assembled there, John Bachman was convinced he was speaking for all present. He prayed:

> O thou Creator of men, our heavenly Father, who art the eternal, Immortal, & Invisible, the only wise God; we humbly approach Thee in the attitude of supplicant at the footstool, beseeching Thee for thy guidance, thy protection, & for thy divine interposition, & thy blessing on the deliberations and acts of thy servants, who are now assembled before thee.
>
> We acknowledge that through our transgressions, we are justly exposed to thy displeasure. But we beseech Thee to restrain thy righteous indignation; & to remember us in mercy.
>
> We thank Thee for the blessings which Thou hast poured out on our land, through several generations of men; and; now, when a long fanaticism, injustice, & oppression, have estranged us from those, who by the ties of nature, & by the laws of justice, were bound to us as brethren—now, when we are about to sever the bonds by which we have hitherto been united, & to form a government more in accordance with our rights & our duties, we beseech thee, to give us that wisdom from on high, which will render the acts of this Convocation, a blessing to our own dear Southern land, through unborn generations.
>
> In thine Almighty wisdom enable us to protect & bless the humble race, that has been confided to our care; so that we may save them from corruption & ruin, so that while we teach them duty to those who are their protectors, we may also train them up under all the hallowed influences of the religion of thy dead Son, our Savior.
>
> Grant O God! That this division of the government in our land, may under the influence of thy sustaining power, be effected in peace. O Gracious Father restrain, we humbly beseech Thee, the efforts of our enemies, & save us from the perils & evils of war; so that our Southern Union may not be cemented by the blood of those who were once our brethren.
>
> But, shouldest Thou, to whom vengeance belongeth, permit these trials to befall us, we beseech Thee, Gracious Father, to spread thine arms of protection over those who are contending for these liberties, their institutions, & their chartered rights in their own soil in defence of their firesides & their altars.
>
> When these trials are over then, we pray Thee, give prosperity to our

> Southern land—May the sails of our commerce whiten every sea, may our agriculture & our manufactures be prosperied,[sic] & may the religions of our Redeemer restrain the passions of men and under us a righteous & a virtuous people who by their industry, their temperance, their justice, & their religion, shall become a name & a praise in the whole earth.
>
> Again we ask Thee, O God, to direct & bless us. We ask in the name of Jesus Christ our Savior. Amen.[20]

While the views expressed in Bachman's invocation were shared by most Southerners, they were not held unanimously, and one Lutheran clergyman spoke out. More than an ordinary pastor, Dr. James Brown (1821–1882) was the president of the Theological Seminary at Newberry, and Bachman could not overlook his criticisms. While admitting that he was a "faithful teacher & an upright man" and that his wife a "pure, intelligent, pious woman—a pattern of a clergyman's wife," Brown held Unionist sympathies, which presented a problem. Indeed, even after Brown was forced to leave Newberry in secrecy, Bachman could not let well enough alone, and just two months before shots were fired at Fort Sumter he wrote Brown. In this letter, he confessed to being "one of those who rejoice that this union is overthrown," and he expressed his views on the future. He stated that he was "confident there will be no reconstruction of the union—that the south has resolved to govern the South & will do so in peace if she is let alone—but if our northern oppressors insist on coercing us, we will meet them as brave men. To conquer the South they must murder every man woman & child on Southern soil."[21]

As Bachman saw it, women were going to suffer no less than men in the forthcoming conflict, and he clearly believed they agreed with the men who spoke on their behalf. No doubt his assumption was confirmed when he looked to Maria Martin. She accepted that men spoke for her. While she could not conceive of a role for women in public life, she believed they had a part to play in the secession movement, and she conveyed this view in a letter to her niece Catherine. As she described the sermon delivered by Bachman on the occasion of Lincoln's election, Maria Martin left no doubt as to her sympathies:

> We were not surprised at your enthusiasm at the stirring events of the day as they are calculated to raise into action the most weak and quiet spirit, even *yours*, and although it is not our province to *act like men*, we can feel with them, and unite our prayer for them in this their time of trial, not of physical courage, but of moral strength, and cheer them on, by encouraging them in the path of duty and honour, not shackling their

> manly efforts, by our foolish fears, but by setting an example of dignified firmness to our households, and showing to them, that we in a quiet way are ready to meet difficulties if they come, or to make sacrifices for the honour and prosperity of our Southern land. The topic is too absorbing now to turn the mind to any other, and even our ministers are addressing their prayers to the God of Nations for aid in behalf of our Southern land. Yesterday your father preached a very eloquent sermon, on the duty of the Christian to his country the text was, from 137 Psalm. If I forget thee O Jerusalem &c—There was a singular coincidence, the Citadel Cadets making their appearance in the gallery, and the sermon was quite appropriate to them particularly—Of course he avoided the political questions of the day as much as he possibly could in a discourse of such a character enjoining on his people the necessity of firmness decision, & dignity, and moderation at a time when he believed that secession was inevitable, and that as truth and justice were on our side, we must put our trust in God, do our duty as men and citizens, and all would be well—He gave the ladies good advice and ended with the same to our coloured brethren. The day was bright and beautiful, and I never saw a more attentive and interested congregation (which was unusually large). I am perhaps not a proper judge and might be too much interested individually, but to me it was a solemn and impresse [*sic*] appeal to all our feelings of patriotism, full of eloquence.[22]

A week later, Maria Martin revisited the topic of politics as she discussed recent developments. Uncharacteristically candid about a topic she believed best left to men, she relayed news about secessionist activities in Charleston. Not quite as pessimistic as Victor Audubon, she was nevertheless concerned about what would happen if Southerners beyond her home state were less enthusiastic about secession than those hoisting the Liberty pole. She worried about the consequences of anything less than a united front:

> Jane & myself are deeply interested in passing events but see very little of the demonstrations that are made in our City by night & day. Your Father visited Mr Ruffin at the Hotel on Saturday and witnessed the inauguration of the Liberty pole, which he said was one of the most imposing ceremonies he has witnessed [in] many a day—all here is enthusiasm, and the spir[it of] 76 seems to animate every son and daughter of Caroline, I wish that I could be assured that it is burning as brightly in all our sister states, but they seem to lack the ardour that we feel, and

> yet to halt between two opinions. Those who ought to know best say all will go right *if we lead*, but I see so many political changes that although I would not have my little state recede one step, I tremble for the result, not that I dread pecuniary sacrifices, but that she may not be able to sustain the position she has so nobly assumed, and I could not stand the scorn and contempt of the North if she is forced to brave the storm alone, this is all that distresses or gives me one anxious thought about it. But we pray that such a result may not follow the patriotic efforts of those who are so bravely battling in our sacred cause.[23]

Four months later, she waited anxiously as those charged with preserving what she called "the honor and prosperity of our Southern land" fired the first shots on Fort Sumter. Unlike other Charlestonians who went to the Battery to watch the spectacle, Maria Martin remained at home. She and her niece Catherine sat "with clasped hands & blanched cheeks, awaiting the issue."[24] They were apprised of events by visitors who dropped off messages at the door, and when the fort surrendered after three days of shelling, there was jubilation and prayers of thanks all round.

Maria Martin did not live to see her worst fears realized. Neither did Victor Audubon. He died on August 17, 1860, from back injuries sustained several years earlier.[25] John Woodhouse was typically less inclined to correspond than others in his family, and his views on the Civil War can only be surmised. In any event, he, too, died before seeing the devastation inflicted on his families. He succumbed to a cold on February 21, 1862, because, his daughter claimed, he was: "Worn out in body and spirit, overburdened with anxieties, [and] saddened by the condition of the country."[26] Of the original Northern participants in *Birds* and *Quadrupeds,* only Lucy Audubon survived the war.

Left to fend for herself yet again, Lucy Audubon continued teaching youngsters in the neighborhood. Her financial situation was, however, tenuous. She had loaned her sons $6,000 against homes they built on Minnie's Land, and because they died before settling their debts, her situation was dire. Indeed, it was far worse than she knew. Her sons had remortgaged their properties (twice), and she was presented with a demand for payment just two months after the death of John Woodhouse. She tried to settle their debts by selling her copies of *Birds* and Audubon's original paintings, but times were tough. She was unable to find buyers and was reduced to begging for assistance. Just two weeks away from the deadline to pay the interest on her sons' loan, she offered Edward Harris (1799–1863), a long-time supporter and friend, any painting he liked. She had nowhere else to turn. She wrote: "oh Mr. Harris this is a hard world and I feel it sorely. This horrid war is partly the cause and I can have no communication with either Charleston or New Orleans."[27]

Edward Harris forwarded the requested relief, but within months Lucy was contemplating selling Minnie's Land. She could not afford to live there. After repaying her sons' loans she believed she could manage with the funds left over for another five or six years, but this plan did not work out. By the end of August, Lucy was actively looking for a buyer for the original paintings, which, according to Robert Havell, were worth more than $60,000. She was, however, unable to find anyone to purchase the 430 paintings in the United States, and so she looked to Britain for potential buyers. She hoped the British Museum would be interested, and she engaged two men to oversee the transaction, but this plan also failed. When the paintings had not been sold by October, Lucy was worried about repaying Harris and her other creditors, and she informed Mrs. Harris she would sell the paintings "for what I can get, and the copper plates by weight as old copper!"[28] Six months later, the New-York Historical Society announced it would purchase, by subscription, Audubon's paintings, and fundraising began to raise the $4,000 agreed to by Lucy Audubon.[29]

Lucy was no longer in communication with Audubon's Charleston collaborators, and so they were ignorant of her sad plight. Nor were they aware of the fate of the paintings Maria Martin had helped create, but, by 1862 when Lucy was trying to dispose of the paintings, Maria Martin would not have much cared about such matters. She had painted botanicals and whatever else Audubon needed without regard for compensation or acknowledgment, and by the time the New-York Historical Society had agreed to the transaction, such matters were of little significance. She was increasingly consumptive and distressed by the effect of the war on family and friends. In fact, her husband detected the unfortunate impact that the "alarming state of the country" had on her health a year earlier, and as she contemplated the death and destruction around her, the importance of material possessions receded.[30] Even though Maria Martin was relatively affluent and accustomed to caring for her assets—even protecting them in a prenuptial agreement when she married John Bachman—she was emphatic that she preferred to see her possessions destroyed rather than be "polluted by contact with any of the vile invaders who are bent on our subjugation."[31]

That same month, fully two years before she died of consumption in

1863, Maria Martin believed that her fate would be much like that of the other women in her family. Separated from her niece Catherine for some time, she warned her that if they were to meet again "[you would] realize how weak and frail I am [and] surely you would not hesitate to place me on the list of the helpless ones, that had better be out of the way." She elaborated: "I have had a very severe attack not unlike the pneumonia that prostrated me so long 3 years ago, and although there is not the same indication of congestion of the lungs as there was at that time, my chest seems to be the seat of my present malady. The cough is almost incessant and expectoration such as to confirm the opinion that I have long entertained, that I am now the subject of chronic consumption, which is incurable & will end my conflict here, long before peace is restored to our distracted country. . . . I pray for submission to the will of God and will try to be reconciled to my lot let it be good or evil—and bear it as a christian should."[32]

As Maria Martin described her situation, she no doubt assumed her husband was at home preparing for Synod. He had done so every year since 1814, but this was not a normal year. In 1861, the annual meeting was rescheduled. The differences between Northern and Southern synods had become irreconcilable, and in January 1862, Southern clergy met in Newberry for the purpose of forming a General Synod of the Confederate States.[33] Within a few months, the first meeting of the Southern Synod was convened, and in May, John Bachman was elected president of the General Synod of the Evangelical Lutheran Church in the Confederate States of America.

By the time Bachman was elevated to this new role, Maria Martin had been in Columbia for a year. She relocated there along with Catherine and the four Haskell children who had been living with them since their mother, Harriet, had died in 1858.[34] It was considered too dangerous to stay in Charleston, and Maria Martin returned only once. Although unfit to travel, she went to Charleston in August 1863 when some parishioners found John Bachman comatose, but as soon as he was ambulatory she returned to Columbia.[35] By Christmas Eve, when Bachman joined his family in the state capital, Maria was in the final stages of pulmonary failure. She died three days later.

Not long after, her family discovered a poem written as she awaited death. Precisely when the poem that conveyed her fears and her faith so poignantly was composed is unclear, but as her family understood, provenance was irrelevant. Her poem embodied beliefs held dear her entire life:

Man's Only Refuge

Infirm, desponding and dismayed,
My faith cast down, my hope grown dim,
I seek for light; but human aid
Can shed no light on doubts within.
Around my path dark shadows fall,
And gloomy visions crowd my way,
While clouds, like a funereal pall,
Obscure the cheerful light of day.

When foes invade, and dread alarms
Are pressing sore on ev'ry side,
E'en life has nearly lost its charms
As war rolls on its crimson tide.
Where shall I flee? To whom apply
Or look for help? To God alone!
For He will hear my humble cry,
And raise me to His heav'nly throne.

God's promises were freely giv'n
To me, as to the saints of old,
Then, why should I by doubts be driv'n,
Oh teach me, Lord, to watch and pray
For light and comfort from above;
To ask for faith's illuminating ray,
To fill me with a Saviour's love.

This alone the gloom dispel,
Which darkens life at this sad hour,
And break the with'ring dreary spell,
Which bends me down with magic pow'r.
In ecstacy of faith and love,
All gloom and doubt shall flee away,
And angels welcome me above
To realms of everlasting day. M.B.

ABBREVIATIONS

Persons

MM	Maria Martin
JJA	John James Audubon
JWA	John Woodhouse Audubon
VGA	Victor Gifford Audubon
LBA	Lucy Bakewell Audubon
MRA	Maria Rebecca Audubon
JB	John Bachman
CLB	Catherine L. Bachman
MRB(A)	Maria Rebecca Bachman (Audubon)
EB(A)	Mary Eliza Bachman (Audubon)
ARC	Annie Roulhac Coffin

Archives

ADA-HDC	Alabama Department of Archives, Historical Digital Collections, Montgomery
APSL, B Au 25	John James Audubon Papers, American Philosophical Society Library, Philadelphia
BRBML, GEN MSS 85	Morris Tyler Family Collection of John James Audubon, General Collection, Beinecke Rare Book and Manuscript Library, Yale University
CLS	Charleston Library Society
CL-USC	Caroliniana Library, University of South Carolina
CM, SC/A/1.	South Carolina Collection, Letters and Diaries, Audubon and Bachman Families, Charleston Museum Library
HL, bMS Am 1492	John James Audubon Collection, Houghton Library, Harvard University

JRCA-LTSS	James R. Crumley Jr. Archives, Lineberger Memorial Library, Lutheran Theological Southern Seminary, Lenoir-Rhyne University, Columbia, S.C.
MNAL, MS 66	Jay Shuler Papers, Marlene and Nathan Addlestone Library, College of Charleston
PHS	Pennsylvania Historical Society, Philadelphia
PU, C0006	John James Audubon Collection, Princeton University
SCDAH	South Carolina Department of Archives and History, Columbia
WL-JDCA	Winterthur Library, Joseph Downs Collection and Archives

Journals

AEH	Anglican and Episcopal History
AHR	American Historical Review
AJMS	American Journal of the Medical Sciences
AJS	American Journal of Sociology
AQR	American Quarterly Review
ANH	Archives of Natural History
AM	Audubon Magazine
AJPH	Australian Journal of Politics and History
BSNH	Boston Society of Natural History
BMJ	British Medical Journal
BHM	Bulletin of the History of Medicine
CHIQ	Concordia Historical Institute Quarterly
ENPJ	Edinburgh New Philosophical Journal
FJHP	Flinders Journal of History & Politics
GH	Gender & History
GHQ	Georgia Historical Quarterly
GSIJ	Grainger Studies: An Interdisciplinary Journal
GPQ	Great Plains Quarterly
HEQ	History of Education Quarterly
ISR	Interdisciplinary Science Reviews
JAH	Journal of American History

JER Journal of the Early Republic

JFH Journal of Family History

JHB Journal of the History of Biology

JIH Journal of Interdisciplinary History

JMF Journal of Marriage and Family

JSH Journal of Southern History

LMNH Loudon's Magazine of Natural History and Journal of Zoology, Botany, Mineralogy, Geology, and Meteorology

LQ Lutheran Quarterly

MAJGNS Monthly American Journal of Geology and Natural Science

N-YHSQ New-York Historical Society Quarterly

PP Preservation Progress

PAPS Proceedings of the American Philosophical Society

PSCHA Proceedings, South Carolina Historical Association

PHG Progress in Human Geography

SAM South Atlantic Monthly

SCHM South Carolina Historical Magazine

SCHGM South Carolina Historical and Genealogical Magazine

TAPL Transactions, American Philosophical Library

WMQ William and Mary Quarterly

NOTES

Preface

1. MM was acknowledged in four of five volumes of JJA's *Ornithological Biography*, but her contributions have since been recognized more fully. A volume compiled by Marshall B. Davidson identified twenty-two folio plates in *Birds of America* containing her work in *The Original Water-Color Paintings by John James Audubon for* The Birds of America, *Reproduced in Color from the Collection at the New-York Historical Society* (1966; repr., New York: American Heritage Press/Bonanza Books, 1985), n.p., and her efforts have been noted more fully by Roberta J. M. Olson in *Audubon's Aviary; The Original Watercolors for* The Birds of America, (New York: New-York Historical Society and Skira Rizzoli Pubs., 2012). For a detailed list of contributors to the original paintings that became folio plates, see "Listing of Audubon's Bird Watercolors in the New-York Historical Society," compiled with the assistance of Alexandra Mazzitelli, 410–31. For specific reference to MM's work: John James Audubon, *Ornithological Biography, or An account of the habits of the birds of the United States of America*: accompanied by descriptions of the objects represented in the work entitled *The Birds of America*, and interspersed with delineations of American scenery and manners, 5 vols., with William McGillivray (Edinburgh: Adam and Charles Black, 1831–1839), 2:482–83, 564, 566; 3:177; 4:xiv, 14, 293, 479, 556; 5:57, 152, 181.

2. JJA, *Ornithological Biography*, 4:xiv.

3. Phebe A. Hanaford, *Women of the Century* (Boston: B. B. Russell, 1877), Chapter 9, "Women-Scientists," 223–38, and Chapter 10, "Women Artists," 239–71. When it came to women artists, her entries did not stray far from those in Elizabeth Ellet, *Women Artists in All Ages and Countries* (New York: Harper and Brothers, 1859), 301–12, 342–44. Also, Obituary, Phebe A. Hanaford, *New York Times*, June 3, 1921.

4. In chronological order, publications on Audubon that ignore MM: Robert Buchanan, *The Life and Adventures of John James Audubon the Naturalist*, edited, from materials supplied by his widow (London: Sampson, Son, Low & Marston, 1868); Lucy Audubon, *The Life of John James Audubon, the Naturalist*, intro. by Jas. Grant Wilson (New York: Putnam & Sons, 1869); Maria Rebecca Audubon (1843–1925), "Reminiscences of Audubon (By A Granddaughter)," *Scribner's Monthly Magazine* 12, no. 3 (July 1876): 333–36 and "Audubon's Story of His Youth: 'Myself,'" *Scribner's Monthly Magazine* 13, no. 3 (March 1893): 267–89; R. W. Schufeldt and Maria Rebecca Audubon, "The Last Portrait of Audubon, Together with a Letter to his Son," *Auk* 11 (1894): 309–13; Maria Rebecca Audubon, *Audubon and His Journals*, with Zoological and other notes by Elliott Coues, 2 vols. (New York: Scribner's Sons, 1897). Herrick published

The American Lobster: A Study of its Habits and Development (Washington: Bulletin of the U.S. Fish Commission, 1895) and *The American Eagle: A Study in Natural and Civil History* (New York: D. Appleton-Century, 1934), among others.

5. Francis Hobart Herrick, *Audubon the Naturalist: A History of his Life and Time*, 2 vols. (New York: Appleton, 1917), 2: 6, 32, 61, 65, 156, 281, 283.

6. LBA, *Audubon*, 382, 400, 416 and Buchanan, *Audubon*, 284, 300, 312.

7. Smithsonian scientist Spencer Fullerton Baird (1823–1887) described *Quadrupeds* as the "crowning work" of their labors in *The Mammals of North America: The Descriptions of Species Based Chiefly on the Collections in the Museum of the Smithsonian Institution* (Philadelphia: J. B. Lippincott, 1859), xiii.

8. Ford provides an abbreviated but close account of Coffin's version of the day in 1831 when MM met JJA, and she acknowledges Coffin's assistance in preparing her book. See, Alice Ford, *Audubon's Butterflies, Moths and other Studies* (New York: Studio Pub. in assoc. with Thomas Y. Crowell Co., 1952), 5, 81–83. Ford also references MM's work for Holbrook, 96, 103. For Coffin's description of their meeting, see, "The Amiable Miss Martin: A Record of a Woman and Her Times," unpub mss, CM, SC/A/1.

9. George C. Groce and David H. Wallace, *The New-York Historical Society's Dictionary of Artists in America, 1564–1860* (New Haven, CT: Yale University Press, 1957), xx.

10. Ibid., 426.

11. Ford, *Audubon's Butterflies*, 81.

12. [E.] Buckner Hollingsworth, *Her Garden Was Her Delight* (New York: Macmillan, 1962), 163.

13. Annie Roulhac Coffin, "Maria Martin (1796–1863)," *AQ* (1960): 281–300; and "Audubon's Friend—Maria Martin," *N-YHSQ* 49, no. 1 (1965): 29–51.

14. Edward T. James and Janet Wilson James, eds., "Preface," *Notable American Women, 1607–1950: A Biographical Dictionary*, with Paul S. Boyer, 3 vols. (Cambridge, MA: Belknap Press of Harvard University Press, 1971), 1:xi.

15. There were more than two-dozen exhibitions of JJA's work between 1930 and 1965. A list is available in Series VIII. Exhibitions: Catalogues and other Miscellany in the Guide to the Waldemar H. Fries Audubon Research Papers, 1805–1980. Collection Number: 3427, Division of Rare and Manuscript Collections, Cornell University Library.

16. For information on Davidson's career: "Marshall B. Davidson; Culture Writer Was 82," *New York Times*, August 11, 1989; on his earlier work, see, Groce and Wallace, *Dictionary of Artists*, xxiii.

17. Edward H. Dwight, *Audubon: Watercolors and Drawings* (New York: Munson-Williams-Proctor Institute and the Pierpont Morgan Library, 1965), 44, 46. His papers are at the Archives of American Art, Smithsonian Institution.

18. These exhibitions are referenced in ARC, "Audubon's Friend—Maria Martin," 29, and W. O. Freeland, Maria Martin Exhibition, May 3–31, 1964.

19. In 1971, ARC and Dwight met in Charleston, where they examined paintings

subsequently attributed to Maria Martin. ARC to William C. Coleman, 14 June 1971, MNAL, MS 66.

20. Albert E. Sanders and Warren Ripley, eds., *Audubon: The Charleston Connection*, with a foreword by John Henry Dick and photographs by William A. Jordan. From the Charleston Museum Collection, September 8–November 17, 1985; contributions from the Charleston Museum, XVI (Charleston, SC: the Charleston Museum, 1986), 77.

21. Ibid., xi. Mrs. John (Jane Grimball) Greely has supplied much information on recent family history. Also, Roberta Smith, "Anne Coffin Hanson, 82, Yale Professor of Art History, Dies," *New York Times*, September 4, 2004.

22. ARC, "The Amiable Miss Martin: A Record of a Woman and Her Times," unpub ms., CM, SC/A/1. Information regarding how she devoted her life to this project came from Mrs. John (Jane Grimball) Greely, her niece. For correspondence with William C. Coleman and publisher Devin A. Garrity detailing the difficulties of finding a publisher: Garrity to ARC, March 31, 1971; ARC to Coleman, June 11 and June 4, 1971; Coleman to ARC, June 4, 1971, MNAL, MS 66.

23. Chloe Ward, "Biography, History, Agency: Where Have All the 'Great Men' Gone?" *FJHP* 28 (2012): 84–86 and Susan Ware, "Writing Women's Lives: One Historian's Perspective," *JIH* 40, no. 3 (2010): 414–16.

24. In her manuscript, ARC describes Audubon as "very generous in his praise," but short on formal "Commendation." However, by the time she published parts of the manuscript in an article, half of which was devoted to plates illustrating MM's botanical and entomological contributions, ARC's criticisms were tempered. JJA was described as "vague in his attributions," and MM's obscurity was blamed on an ignorant public unfamiliar "with the naturalist's techniques." Oversight, confusion, and misunderstanding replaced deliberate silencing as Martin moved from the background to the foreground. ARC, "The Amiable Miss Martin," CM, SC/A/1, Chap III, p. 8; "Audubon's Friend—Maria Martin," 38 and 41.

25. Some biographical information is in the Finding Aid of the Shuler Papers, MNAL, MS 66. In addition to writing two books on Badlands National Park, he published *South Carolina Birds of the Foothills* (Greenville, SC: Visulearn, 1966); (with A. E. Sanders) "A New Look at the Type Locality of the Bachman's Warbler," *The Chat* (Winter 1977): 12–13; "Clutch Size and Onset of Laying in Bachman's Warbler," *The Chat* (Spring 1979): 27–29; and *Snakes in the Outhouse and Other Causes for Wonder* (McClellanville, SC: Arts Council, 1994). Correspondence with a descendant of Christopher Happoldt (1823–1878), one of JB's theological protégés, suggests Jay Shuler had been collecting material since the 1970s. Claude H. Neuffer (1911–1984) to J. Shuler, November 15, 1979, MNAL, MS 66.

26. Jay Shuler, *"Had I the Wings": The Friendship of Bachman and Audubon* (Athens: University of Georgia Press, 1995) and "Maria Martin, Audubon's Sweetheart," in Marcia Myers Bonta, *Women in the Field: America's Pioneering Women Naturalists* (College Station: Texas A & M Press, 1991), 9–13. She is also discussed a dozen times in

Lester D. Stephens, *Science, Race, and Religion in the American South: John Bachman and the Charleston Circle of Naturalists, 1815–1895* (Chapel Hill: University of North Carolina Press, 2000). Interestingly, a few years later, both MM and JB are mentioned only briefly in Richard Rhodes, *John James Audubon: The Making of an American* (New York: Alfred A. Knopf, 2005).

27. Olson, *Audubon's Aviary*, 26; Olson and Mazzitelli, "Listing of Audubon's Bird Watercolors," 418–20, 424, 426–30.

28. Cassandra A. Good, "Friendly Relations: Situating Friendship of Males and Females in the Early American Republic, 1780–1830," *GH* 24, no. 1 (2012): 29.

29. Robin Fleming, "Writing Biography on the Edge of History," *AHR* 114 (2009): 606. Also see commentary preceding papers based on a roundtable hosted by the American Historical Society. David Nasaw, "Introduction," *AHR* 114, no. 3 (2009): 573–78, and Nigel Hamilton, *Biography: A Brief History* (Cambridge, MA: Harvard University Press, 2007), 279–90. It might be argued that *Maria Martin's World* has as much in common with ethnohistory as with biography. Jennifer S. H. Brown and Elizabeth Vibert have captured the essence of how ethnohistorians reconstruct the history of largely oral cultures in a collection of essays gathered in an aptly named volume—*Reading Beyond Words: Contexts for Native History* (Peterborough, Ontario: Broadview, 1996).

30. A recent collection of essays edited by Hans Renders and Binne de Haan provides an overview of these debates. See, *Theoretical Discussions of Biography: Approaches from History, Microhistory, and Life Writing*, foreword by Nigel Hamilton (Lewiston, NY: Edwin Mellen Press, 2013). Similar discussions may be found in journals such as *Biography*, *Biography: An Interdisciplinary Quarterly*, the *Journal of Historical Biography*, and in any of several magazines devoted to history and biography. In *How to Do Biography: A Primer* (Cambridge, MA: Harvard University Press, 2009), Nigel Hamilton provides a less academic but influential treatment, 22–46.

31. Robert I. Rotberg, "Biography and Historiography: Mutual Evidentiary and Interdisciplinary Considerations," *JIH*, 40, no. 3 (2010): 306, 309–17, 324.

32. Ibid., 322.

33. Edward T. James and Janet Wilson James, eds., "Preface," *Notable American Women, 1607–1950: A Biographical Dictionary*, with Paul S. Boyer, 3 vols. (Cambridge, MA: Belknap Press of Harvard University Press, 1971), 1: ix–xii. The problems of short biographical entries are still plaguing scholars. See, Michael Piggotti, "Brief Biography and the 'All-Round Man,'" *GSIJ* 1 (2011): 5–20.

34. Susan Ware, "Writing Women's History: One Historian's Perspective," *JIH* 40, no. 3 (2010), 423. Alice Kessler-Harris also argued for historicized biography when she claimed that "larger cultural and social and even political processes of a moment in time" can be understood through the individual. Alice Kessler-Harris, "Why Biography?" *AHR* 114, no. 3 (2009): 626.

Introduction

1. There are several Bachman genealogies. For the most accurate, Joseph Douglas Cawley, *From Herrstein to South Carolina: Reverend John Nicholas Martin, 1724–1795: Pastor, Patriot and Some of his Children and Grandchildren*, Number Two in the J. D. Cawley Ancestor Series (Centennial, CO: J and J Publishers, 2003), 235–36. Like others in her family, Maria contracted the tubercle bacilli (*Mycobacterium tuberculosis*) from John Bachman, who initially went to Charleston in search of a climate more amenable to his condition. Without the added strain of childbearing or chronic illness, Maria was a latent consumptive who suffered from reactivated tuberculosis; she admitted to having full-blown consumption in 1861. See MM to CLB, Nov. 16 1861, CM, SC/A/1. It should be noted that while tuberculosis and consumption are caused by the same microbe, they are not, according to Katherine Ott, the same disease. See *Fevered Lives: Tuberculosis in American Culture since 1870* (Cambridge, MA : Harvard University Press, 1996), 1–8. On the accident that eventually paralyzed MM's arm: JB to LBA, Mar 30, 1856, CM, SC/A/1. This letter has also been edited and reprinted, in part, in Catherine L. Bachman, *John Bachman: The Pastor of St. John's Lutheran Church, Charleston* (Charleston, SC: Walker, Evans & Cogswell, 1888), 332–34. The published letters often differ significantly from the originals.

2. JB to LBA, Mar 30, 1856, CM, SC/A/1. CLB, *Pastor of St. John's Lutheran*, 332–34.

3. For a detailed list of the paintings and who contributed to them, see Olson and Mazzitelli, "Listing of Audubon's Bird Watercolors," 410–31. Olson contends that there are probably thirty folio plates bearing Maria Martin's work even though only twenty-two can be authenticated with absolute certainty. "A Biographical Sketch of an American Icon," 26.

4. Ann Shelby Blum, *Picturing Nature: American Nineteenth-Century Zoological Illustration* (Princeton, NJ: Princeton University Press, 1993), 3–18, 121, 160, 344–45. Karen Reeds also points out that drawing is/was both a means of learning about plants and a vehicle to disseminate knowledge in her analysis of Linnaeus's preference for descriptive botany. He could not draw, and his ineptitude—when it came to anything other than technical diagrams—was a serious impediment. Karen Reeds, "When the botanist can't draw: The case of Linnaeus," *ISR* 29, no. 3 (2004): 248–58.

5. JB to Edmund Ruffin, Nov 15, 1864, CM, SC/A/1.

6. For the best account of the meeting and collaboration of JJA and JB: Shuler, *Had I the Wings*, 4–7, *passim*. Their meeting is also mentioned in Stephens, *Science, Race and Religion*, 17. CLB's biography of her father contains reprinted letters with information on efforts by JB and MM, but letters of different dates are often combined without indication. On MM specifically, see articles by JB's great granddaughter, ARC, "Maria Martin (1796–1863)," 281–300; "Audubon's Friend—Maria Martin," 29–51; and "Maria Martin (July 3, 1796–Dec. 27, 1863)," *Notable American Women*, 2:505–06.

7. LBA claimed her husband was as at home among the rich and famous as he was in the great outdoors; however, her comments were in response to a bowdlerized biography published the previous year. The publisher to whom she had submitted her manuscript employed Robert Buchanan, a professional editor, to rework her text, and he prepared a biography that she considered unflattering. See, Herrick, *Audubon*, 1:22. For more recent depictions of Audubon as a dashing adventurer, sometimes a bit of a rogue, and indifferent to those who did not see his work as important: Shirley Streshinsky, *Audubon: Life and Art in the American Wilderness* (Athens: University of Georgia Press, 1995); and Richard Rhodes, *John James Audubon: The Making of an American* (New York: Alfred A. Knopf, 2005). For a synopsis of his journey south: Kathryn Hall Proby, *Audubon in Florida, with Selections from the Writings of John James Audubon* (Coral Gables, Fl: University of Miami Press, 1974), 13–14.

8. JJA reported they prepared 280 skins while in Charleston. JJA to LBA, Nov 7 and Dec 8, 1831 in Ben Forkner, ed., *John James Audubon: Selected Journals and other Writings* (New York: Penguin, 1996), 165–66; 176–7. The letter written in November is also reprinted in Howard Corning, ed., *Letters of John James Audubon, 1826–1840*, 2 vols. (1930; repr. New York: Kraus Reprint, 1969), 1:147–49. Also, JB, "Retrospective Criticism," *LMNH* 7 (1834): 167.

9. For references to the location and former use of the painting room: CLB, *Pastor of St. John's*, 367 and EB(A) to Harriet Bachman, Dec 11, 1838, CM, SC/A/1.

10. Gene Waddell provides descriptions of the architecture that distinguished Charleston homes and gardens. He also provides statistical information on the location and styles of single houses in the eighteenth and nineteenth centuries: *Charleston Architecture, 1670–1860*, 2 vols. (Charleston, SC: Wyrick, 2003), 1:67–78, 257–60, 266, and "A Companion Guide to Charleston House Types," *PP* 49, no. 2 (2005): 10–11. Also, William H. Pease and Jane H. Pease, *The Web of Progress: Private Values and Public Styles in Boston and Charleston, 1828–1843* (New York: Oxford University Press, 1985), 126.

11. For recollections from the nineteenth century: Jennie Haskell Rose [Jane Bachman Haskell Rose, 1856–1935], "John Bachman at Home," read before the Lutheran Church, April 17, 1927, CM, SC/A/1 and "John Bachman's Home on Rutledge Avenue, Charleston, S.C.," *Charleston Courier* [1921]. Also, JJA to VGA, Dec 24, 1833, Herrick, *Audubon*, 2:55. Invited time and again to stay with the Bachman family, JJA may have actually influenced decorative purchases, as an objet d'art consisting of stuffed birds posed on an artificial tree encased in a glass globe graced a table near the piano in 1832. See, Daniel Alexander Payne, D.D., LL.D. Senior Bishop of the African Methodist Episcopal Church, *Recollections of Seventy Years*, intro. by Rev. F. J. Grimke, A. M., D. D. Compiled and arranged by Sarah C. Bierce Scarborough, edited by Rev. C. S. Smith (Nashville, TN: Publishing House of the A.M.E. Sunday School Union, 1888), 24.

12. JJA to LBA, Oct 23, 1831, Corning, *Letters*, 1:142–44.

13. JJA to LBA, Oct 30, 1831, Corning, *Letters*, 1:145–46.

14. JJA to LBA, Nov 7, 1831, Corning, *Letters*, 1:147–49.

15. JB to VGA, Aug 5, 1843, CM, SC/A/1.

16. JB to JJA, Sept 22, 1833, BRBML, GEN MSS 85. On JB's planter connections: Claude Henry Neuffer, ed., introduction to *The Christopher Happoldt Journal: His European Tour with the Rev. John Bachman (June–December, 1838)*. Contributions from the Charleston Museum XIII (Charleston, SC: Charleston Museum, 1960), 91.

17. JB to Jane Bachman, July 18, 1846, CM, SC/A/1. In South Carolina, parents were provided a catechism based on Reverend Mayer's Instruction in the Principles and Duties of the Christian Religion for Children and Youth in 1827. On this and Lutheran women, see Raymond M. Bost, *A History of the Lutheran Church in South Carolina* (Columbia: South Carolina Synod of the Lutheran Church in America, 1971), 228. On Lutheran women more generally: Steven Ozment, *Protestants: The Birth of a Revolution* (New York: Doubleday, 1992), 165–66.

18. For example, Anne Firor Scott, *The Southern Lady: From Pedestal to Politics, 1830–1930* (Chicago: University of Chicago Press, 1970); Catherine Clinton, *The Plantation Mistress: Woman's World in the Old South* (New York: Pantheon Books, 1982); Elizabeth Fox-Genovese, *Within the Plantation Household: Black and White Women of the Old South* (Chapel Hill: University of North Carolina Press, 1988); Sally G. McMillen, *Motherhood in the Old South: Pregnancy, Childbirth, and Infant Rearing* (Baton Rouge: Louisiana State University Press, 1990) and *Southern Women: Black and White in the Old South* (Arlington Heights, IL: Harlan Division, 1992); Jane H. Pease and William H. Pease, *Ladies, Women and Wenches: Choice and Constraint in Antebellum Charleston and Boston* (Chapel Hill: University of North Carolina Press, 1990); Carol Bleser, ed., *In Joy and Sorrow: Women, Family and Marriage in the Victorian South, 1830–1900* (Oxford, UK: Oxford University Press, 1991); Victoria E. Bynum, *Unruly Women: The Politics of Social and Sexual Control in the Old South* (Chapel Hill: University of North Carolina Press, 1992); and Marli Weiner, *Mistresses and Slaves: Plantation Women in South Carolina, 1830–80* (Chicago: University of Illinois Press, 1998).

19. There is a detailed list of the men and women owned by Rebecca Martin; however, the Bachman slaves are less easily identified. An aged nurse, Mary Ann, and a "faithful servant," Caroline, are mentioned in family records, and Jennie Haskell Rose identifies a number of enslaved men and women in her presentation to the congregation of St. John's Lutheran. There are bills of sale for Thomas and William Skining, one a "mulatto" carpenter slave. The death notices of four slaves may be found in records of the Health Department, and eight slaves are enumerated anonymously in the 1830 Census. Population Schedules, Fifth Census, Charleston, 1830, Reel 170, p. 140. Also, Bills of Sale, May 19 and Sept 22, 1831, Secretary of State, Miscellaneous Records, 1741–1843, S213003, pp. 430 and 491, and Charleston County Records, Inventories, Appraisements and Sales, Vol. A, 1839–1844, Appraisement of Goods and Chattels of Mrs. Rebecca Martin, July 13, 1840, SCDAH. Also, George K. Bennoitt, *City of Charleston, Health Department Death Records* (Charleston, SC: Historical

Committee, St. John's Lutheran Church, 1997), June 1821 through December 1828, p. 4, 1829–1837, January 1846–December 1852, p. 3; Rose, "John Bachman at Home," CM, SC/A/1; CLB, *Pastor of St. John's*, 38–39; and, Kate [CLB] Bachman, Leaves from a Notebook; Civil War Reminiscences, 1862–1865, p. 49, CLS, 51–236. For the impact of a home laboratory: JB to VGA, Feb 18, 1846, CM, SC/A/1. It was noted that cockroaches ate the labels off the stored specimens.

20. Countless studies have shown that scientific work usually took place in masculine spaces: Sandra Harding and Jean F. O'Barr, eds., *Sex and Scientific Inquiry* (Chicago : University of Chicago Press, 1987); Evelyn Fox Keller, *Reflections on Gender and Science* (New Haven, CT: Yale University Press, 1985); Margaret W. Rossiter, *Women Scientists in America: Struggles and Strategies to 1940* (Baltimore, MD: John Hopkins University Press, 1982); Londa Schiebinger, *The Mind Has No Sex?: Women in the Origins of Modern Science* (Cambridge, MA: Harvard University Press, 1989); and David F. Noble, *A World Without Women: The Christian Clerical Culture of Western Science* (New York: Oxford University Press, 1992). A slightly different view of discrimination, science, and domesticity is provided by David N. Livingstone in *Putting Science in its Place: Geographies of Scientific Knowledge* (Chicago: University of Chicago Press, 2003), 22–24, and other historians have found examples of a more inclusive domestic science: Pnina G. Abir-am and Dorinda Outram, eds., *Uneasy Careers and Intimate Lives, Women in Science, 1789–1979*, foreword by Margaret Rossiter (New Brunswick, NJ: Rutgers University Press, 1989); Helena M. Pycior, Nancy G. Slack, and Pnina Abir-Am, eds., *Creative Couples in the Sciences*, (New Brunswick, NJ: Rutgers University Press, 1996); Ann B. Shteir, *Cultivating Women, Cultivating Science: Flora's Daughters and Botany in England, 1760–1860* (Baltimore, MD: John Hopkins University Press, 1996); Debra Lindsay, "Intimate Inmates: Scientific Wives and Households in Nineteenth Century America," *Isis* 90, no. 4 (1998): 631–52; Deborah R. Coen, "A Lens of Many Facets: Science through a Family's Eyes," *Isis* 97, no. 3 (2006): 395–419; Tina Gianquitto, *"Good Observers of Nature": American Women and the Scientific Study of the Natural World, 1820–1885* (Athens: University of Georgia Press, 2007); and Annette Lykknes, Donald L. Opitz, and Brigitte van Tiggelen, eds., *For Better or For Worse? Collaborative Couples in the Sciences* (New York: Birhäuse, 2012).

21. Lester D. Stephens, "The Literary and Philosophical Society of South Carolina: A Forum for Intellectual Progress in Antebellum Charleston," *SCHM* 104, no. 3 (July 2003): 162–65. Also, Albert E. Sanders and William D. Anderson Jr., *Natural History Investigations in South Carolina: From Colonial Times to the Present* (Columbia: University of South Carolina Press, 1999), 21–61.

22. In fulfilling her religious convictions, MM was receiving intangible compensation in return for providing her expertise as an artist and assistant. As a result, she was part of the "asymmetrical relationship" that prevails within families. See, John N. Edwards, "Familial Behavior as Social Exchange," *JMF* 31, no. 3 (1969): 518–26, especially, 518–21. With a vast body of literature on social exchange, much of it quantitative

and contemporary rather than qualitative and historical, see two publications for an overview: Linda D. Molm, "The Social Exchange Framework," in *Contemporary Social Psychological Theories*, ed. Peter James Burke (Redwood City, CA: Stanford University Press, 2006), 24–45, and Linda D. Molm, Jessica L. Collett, and David R. Schaefer, "Building Solidarity through Generalized Exchange: A Theory of Reciprocity," *AJS* 113, no. 1, (2007): 205–42. Lastly, because this is a historical situation and because sociological approaches are "not historically grounded" see, Allan Silver, "Friendship in Commercial Society: Eighteenth-Century Social and Modern Sociology," *AJS* 95, no. 6 (1990): 1474–1504, specifically, 1496. Work by Bertram Wyatt-Brown and Elizabeth Fox-Genovese are also relevant: Wyatt-Brown argues that the ideal Southern woman was to carry out her proscribed duties "with grace, courage and silence," and Fox-Genovese highlights the differences between the North and the South in terms of the value placed on individualism within patriarchy. See, Wyatt-Brown, *Southern Honor: Ethics and Behavior in the Old South*, 25th Anniversary Ed. (New York: Oxford University Press, 2007), 234–35, and Fox-Genovese, *Within the Plantation Household*, 63.

23. MM to JJA, October 28, 1836, CLB, Pastor of St. John's, 143–44.

24. There are many sources on the making of *The Birds of America*, beginning in 1937: Stanley Clisby Arthur, *Audubon: An Intimate Life of the American Woodsman* (1937; repr., Gretna, LA: Pelican Pub., 2000); Dwight, *Audubon: Watercolors and Drawings* (1965); Waldemar H. Fries, *The Double Elephant Folio: The Story of Audubon's Birds of America* (Chicago: American Library Association, 1973); Lois Elmer Bannon and Taylor Clark, *Handbook of Audubon Prints* (Gretna, LA: Pelican Pub., 1980); Susanne M. Low, *An Index and Guide to Audubon's Birds of America: A Study of the Double-Elephant Folio of John James Audubon's Birds of America as engraved by William H. Lizars and Robert Havell*. The American Museum of Natural History (New York: Abbeville Press, 1988); Ron Tyler, *Nature's Classics: John James Audubon's Birds and Animals* (Orange, TX: Stark Museum of Art, 1992), 6–39; Annette Blaugrund and Theodore E. Stebbins Jr., eds., *John James Audubon: The Watercolors for* The Birds of America (New York: Villard Books, 1993); Annette Blaugrund, "John James Audubon: Producer, Promoter and Publisher," *Imprint: Journal of the American Historical Print Collectors Society* 21 (1996): 10–19; Linda Dugan Partridge, "By the Book: Audubon and the Tradition of Ornithological Illustration," *Huntington Library Quarterly* 59, no. 2/3 (1996): 269–301; Amy R. W. Meyers, ed., *Art and Science in America: Issues of Representation* (San Marino, CA: Huntington Library, 1998), 97–129; Ella M. Foshay, *John James Audubon* (New York: Harry N. Abrams, 1997); Duff Hart-Davis, *Audubon's Elephant: America's Greatest Naturalist and the Making of* The Birds of America (New York: Henry Holt, 2004); William Souder, *Under A Wild Sky: John James Audubon and the Making of* The Birds of America (New York: North Point Press, 2004); and *Audubon's Aviary*.

25. Low, *Index and Guide*, 11, 186–191. Illustrations of the original painting as compared to the Havell plates are provided in Part III, where she specifically focuses on the folio plates depicting multiple species. Fries states that the work generated by *Birds*

necessitated another engraver and as many as fifty colorists. *Double Elephant Folio*, 84–85.

26. The replacement of Lehman by MM and JWA has also been noted by Shuler, *Had I the Wings*, 95. Robert McCracken Peck, "Audubon and Bachman: A Collaboration in Science," in *John James Audubon in the West: The Last Expedition*, ed. Sarah E. Boehme, Buffalo Bill Historical Center (New York: Harry N. Abrams, 2000), 101.

27. JJA to LBA, Feb 1, 1832, in Forkner, *Audubon*, 185–87.

28. Pierre Belon (1517–1564) and the Comte de Buffon, George-Louis Leclerc (1707–1788), for example, took credit for work done by anonymous artists, as did masters such as Peter Paul Rubens. See, Gloria K. Fiero, "Audubon the Artist," in *Audubon: A Retrospective*, ed. James H. Dorman (Lafayette: University of Southwestern Louisiana, 1990), 38; and Lois E. Bannon, "The Audubon Prints," in *Audubon: A Retrospective*, 62. On the Audubon-Mason dispute: Arthur, *American Woodsman*, 273–76.

29. Analyses of contributions to *The Birds of America* began long ago with Irving T. Richards (in consultation with Stanley C. Arthur): "Audubon, Joseph R. Mason, and John Neal," *American Literature* 6, no. 2 (May 1934), 129–30, fn. 30. Building on Richards's work, Marshall B. Davidson identifies contributions by other artists in *Original Watercolor Paintings* (1985). About a decade later, Theodore Stebbins Jr. points out that Audubon only acknowledged Joseph Mason's work in two plates (Northern Parula; Pine Warbler), although Mason claimed that he "made between 150 and 200 plant and flower drawings for Audubon" and that Havell was not treated any better. He also stated that Audubon was only slightly more generous in acknowledging the efforts of his sons and George Lehman. See, "Audubon's Drawings of American Birds, 1805–38," in Blaugrund and Stebbins Jr., *Audubon: Watercolors*, 14 and 19 (on Lehman). For a much-needed update and detailed list of the original paintings and who contributed to them: Olson and Mazzitelli, "Listing of Audubon's Bird Watercolors," 410–31.

30. JJA, *Ornithological Biography*, 1832, 3: 177.

31. MM's artistic efforts do not fit existing analyses of how her middle class contemporaries endeavored to professionalize. See, for example, Laura R. Prieto, *At Home in the Studio: The Professionalization of Women Artists in America* (Cambridge, MA: Harvard University Press, 2001) and April F. Masten, *Art Work: Women Artists and Democracy in Mid-Nineteenth-Century New York* (Philadelphia: University of Pennsylvania Press, 2008).

32. JJA's visits of October 19, 1831, March 14, 1832, June 6, 1832, October 26,1833, November 19, 1836, and June 10, 1837 were noted in the *Charleston Courier*. See, Anna Wells Rutledge, *Artists in the Life of Charleston: Through Colony and State, from Restoration to Reconstruction* 39, Part 2, *TAPL* (Philadelphia: APS, 1949), 184–85. Also see, Herrick, *Audubon* 2: 156–57.

33. It has often been stated (or implied) that MM was an accomplished artist prior to meeting JJA. Described as a "thirty-five year old artist and helpmeet" when she met JJA in 1831 (Rhodes, *Making of an American*, 352), this description is not without precursors, especially ARC and Freeland in his introduction to "A Survey Exhibition

in Memory of Maria Martin, May 3–31, 1964," Columbia Museum of Art, Columbia South Carolina. There are two notable exceptions to this view: In the 1960s, E. Buckner Hollingsworth advanced more modest claims when she observed that "Audubon would awaken in her a talent she didn't know she possessed," and over thirty years later, Shuler described Maria's pre-1831 "experiences as an artist" as "limited." See, Hollingsworth, "Maria Martin," *AM* (July–August, 1962): 197 and Shuler, *Had I the Wings*, 16.

34. JB to JJA, Dec 23 1831, CLB, *Pastor of St. John's*, 99–102.

35. There is a reference to JB's visit in LBA to VGA, May 19, 1833, BRBML, GEN MSS 85 and JJA to VGA, Sept 9, 1833, in George Bird Grinnell (1849–1938), "Some Audubon Letters," *The Auk* 33 (1916): 124–30.

36. JB to JJA, Sept 14, 1833, CLB, *Pastor St. John's*, 135–37.

37. In 1833, JJA wrote LBA that Reverend Bachman is "the *only parson on Earth* for me!" See, JJA to LBA, May 28, 1833, BRBML, GEN MSS 85. Later in life, he occasionally mentioned missing church, but did so without remorse. He never quite got past the cynicism of his youth. In 1820, for example, he stated: "I confess I never think of churches without feeling sick at heart at the sham and show of their professors. To repay evil with kindness is the religion I was taught to practice, and this will forever be my rule." *Audubon, By Himself: A Profile of John James Audubon*, from writings selected, arranged and edited by Alice Ford (Garden City, NY: Natural History Press, 1969), 133.

38. JJA to LBA, Nov 7, 1831 and Dec 8, 1831, Forkner, *Audubon*, 165–66 and 176–79; JJA to LBA, Oct 23, 1831, Corning, *Letters*, 1: 142–44. For a list of JB's articles and monographs, see, Gene Waddell, *John Bachman: Selected Writings on Science, Race and Religion* (Athens: University of Georgia Press, 2011), 359–69 and Stephens, *Science, Race and Religion*, 307–09. Raymond Bost mentions JB's early activities in "John Bachman: Man of Faith, Man of Science," *LQ* 2, no. 2 (1988): 216, but there is little evidence of scientific activity prior to 1831. His publications appeared between 1836 and 1854 when the final volume of the imperial edition of *The Quadrupeds of North America* was published. For JB's contributions to the *Charleston Medical Journal and Review* and his role in the founding of the Elliot Society of Natural History—activities postdating Audubon: Thomas Cary Johnson Jr., *Scientific Interests in the Old South* (New York: D. Appleton-Century, 1936), 87, 138–40, 142–43, 149; and Ronald L. Numbers and Janet S. Numbers. See, "Science in the Old South: A Reappraisal, *JSH* 48, no. 2 (1982): 163–84.

39. Rose, "John Bachman at Home," CM, SC/A/1. Rose refers to being four years old when Fort Sumter was surrendered to the Confederacy. She was the daughter of Harriet Eva Bachman and William Elnathan Haskell. See Haskell genealogy typescript, Mrs. John (Jane Grimball) Greely and Cawley, *Herrstein to South Carolina,* 236.

40. Specimens turned within twenty-four hours, except in the coldest winter months. For the speed of "putridity" in Charleston: "No.1 Letter from Audubon to the Editor [George W. Featherstonhaugh]," *MAJGNS* 1 (1832): 362.

41. JB noted the efforts of one of his slaves in particular. He wrote that "my man,

Thomas" was employed in taxidermy. JB to JJA, Dec 23, 1831, CLB, *Pastor of St. John's*, 101. For reference to the lynx: John James Audubon and John Bachman, *The Quadrupeds of North America* (New York: V.G. Audubon, 1851), 1:13.

42. Arthur, *American Woodsman*, 88, 266 and Caroline E. DeLatte, *Lucy Audubon: A Biography*, foreword by Christoph Irmscher (Baton Rouge: Louisiana State University Press, 2008), 170–71, 178–79, 185–90, 192, 208.

43. Beginning with Fries, it has been commonplace to state that *Birds* was a family project. However, even Fries, who wrote that the third volume became "a family project at the Bachman home," did not link Audubon's transition from depending on paid employees to using family with his first sojourn in the Bachman home. See, "Winter at Charleston, 1833–34," in Fries, *Double Elephant Folio*, 79. For quotation: JJA to LBA, Dec 5, 1831, Forkner, *Audubon*, 173–76.

44. Bost, *History of the Lutheran Church in South Carolina*, 211, 323–24; "John Bachman and the Development of Southern Lutheranism" (PhD dissertation, Yale University, 1963), 124–31; and "Bachman: Man of Faith, Man of Science," 211–14. Many of JB's religious writings are available online.

45. CLB was a staunch Confederate who spoke publicly and proudly as late as 1898 of her father's bravery and her family's forbearance during "The War between the States." See, paper read before the Daughters of the Confederacy to commemorate the Birthday of Jefferson Davis, June 1898, CLS, 51–236 and CLB, *Pastor of St. John's*, 366–67.

46. For CLB's role as her father's assistant: baptisms, confirmations, deaths, 1822–1917, St John Lutheran Church Records, Sworn oath by Catherine Bachman, June 29, 1897, CL-USC, I & O, pp. 6–7; and diary entries, 1863–1864; and 1865 in "Leaves from a Notebook," CLS, 51–236.

47. For the best account of the meeting and subsequent collaboration: Shuler, *Had I the Wings*, 4–7; quotation 79. Also, Stephens, *Science, Race and Religion*, 17, and ARC, "Audubon's Friend—Maria Martin," 29–30.

48. LBA attributed many of his personality traits to his "race," as did his more folksy confreres. According to Dr. Arthur T. Lincoln, his father, Tom Lincoln, one of Audubon's companions on the Labrador expedition in 1833, described him as "Frenchy as thunder." LBA, *Audubon*, 197, and Charles W. Townsend, "A Visit to Tom Lincoln's House with some Auduboniana," *The Auk* 41, no. 2 (1924): 240–41.

Chapter 1

1. See Charleston newspapers for descriptions of the damage, specifically an excerpt from the *City Gazette* in Daniel J. Crooks Jr., *Charleston is Burning! Two Centuries of Fire and Flames* (Charleston, SC: History Press, 2009), 30. Also, Waddell, *Charleston Architecture*, Appendix 3: House Statistics, 1: 266; Charles Fraser (1782–1860), *Reminiscences of Charleston, Lately Published in the Charleston Courier* (Charleston, SC: John Russell, 1854), 33; and Jeanne A. Calhoun, Elizabeth J. Reitz, Michael B. Trinkley,

Martha A. Zierden, *Meat in Due Season: Preliminary Investigations of Marketing Practices in Colonial Charleston*, Archaeological Contributions 9 (Charleston, SC: Charleston Museum, 1984), 25.

2. The experiences of the thrice-married Rebecca Martin reflect those found among other members of the artisanal community during the construction boom. See, Emma Hart, *Building Charleston: Town and Society in the Eighteenth-Century British Atlantic World* (Charlottesville: University of Virginia Press, 2010), 98–113.

3. Waddell, *Architecture*, 1: 266.

4. On South Carolina Hall, the Circular Church, and construction materials: Waddell, *Charleston Architecture*, 1:133–34, fn. 1, 142–43, 150–54; and Jonathan H. Poston, *The Buildings of Charleston: A Guide to the City's Architecture* (Columbia: University of South Carolina Press, 1997), 123–24, 166–67, 169, 182.

5. For Rebecca Martin's real estate holdings: Charleston County, Inventory Book A 1783–1787 for the "Lease and Release" title transfer registered in the Register of Mesne Conveyances, Charleston District, 1785, Conveyance Book M–5, pp. 25–29 [Family History Library, Salt Lake City, Film # 1,429,863]. Inventory submitted to the Probate Court in 1786 as part of the decision of Probate Judge, W. E. Vincent, making Mrs. Rebecca Solzar the Administrix of the estates of John Duvall and Jacob Solzar, June 16, 1786, in Charleston County, Letters of Administration, 1785–1791, pp. 35–36 [Family History Library, Salt Lake City, Film # 0,194,686 and # 0,194,638]; Marriage Settlement of Rebecca Solzar and Jacob Martin, Nov 3, 1789, Columbia, South Carolina, no. 1, 1785–1792, pp. 452–55 [Family History Library, Salt Lake City, Film # 0,022,513]; and "Distribution of Real and Personal Property of John Jacob Martin, June 18, 1813," Historical Commission, Columbia South Carolina, Book 4-G, p. 115 in Cawley, *From Herrstein to South Carolina*, 126, 130–31, 176–79, 180–82. Cawley's reference to the Meeting Street property as a "lease" is misleading. The term "lease and release" referred to a specific manner of title transfer from one owner to another. See, Hart, *Building Charleston*, 70–72. Of the five properties deeded to Rebecca Martin in 1813, that located south of the Circular Church cemetery is mentioned twice, and it was deeded to her in perpetuity, regardless of marital status, presumably because it was part of the property protected by her "Marriage Settlement." For further confirmation of the location of the Martin home: Jeanne A. Calhoun, Martha A. Zierden and Elizabeth A. Paysinger, "The Geographic Spread of Charleston's Mercantile Community, 1732–1767," *SCHM* 86, no. 3 (1985): 187, 219. Using information from city directories, petitions, and the *South Carolina Gazette*, they indicate that Duvall was both a stay maker and merchant on Meeting Street from 1762 to 1767.

6. Benjamin N. Martin (1816–1883), "Rev. John N. Martin," in *American Lutheran Biographies, or Historical Notices of Over Three Hundred and Fifty Leading Men of the American Lutheran Church, From its Establishment to the Year 1890*, historical intro., numerous portrait engravings, and ed. Rev. J. C. Jensson (Milwaukee, WI: A. Houtkamp & Son, 1890), 504.

7. The size and location of the Martin home has been arrived at using both primary and secondary sources. See, inventory appended to the decision of probate judge, W. E. Vincent, making Mrs. Rebecca Solzar the administrix of the estates of John Duvall and Jacob Solzar, June 16, 1786, in which it is stated that the property purchased in 1784 by her second husband, Jacob Solzar, was valued at £1000, and the property purchased by her first husband, John Duvall, was valued at £800; and there was a "lease and release" title transfer registered in the Register of Mesne Conveyances, Charleston District, 1785. For the site and dimensions of the Meeting Street properties: "Distribution of Real and Personal Property of John Jacob Martin, 18 June 1813," Cawley, *Herrstein to South Carolina*, 126–31, 180–82. For secondary sources: Lee Soltow, "Socioeconomic Classes in South Carolina and Massachusetts in the 1790s and the Observations of John Drayton," *SCHM* 81, no. 4 (1980), 301–02; Waddell, *Charleston Architecture*, 1:67–78, 257–60; Waddell, "Companion Guide to Charleston House Types," 10–11; Poston, *Buildings of Charleston*, 67–195, 213, 232–35, 244, 260, 265, 282–84, 288, 530, 573–74, 634; James D. Kornwolf, *Architecture and Town Planning in Colonial North America*, with the assistance of Georgiana W. Kornwolf, 2 vols. (Baltimore, MD: Johns Hopkins University Press, 2002), 2:851–94; and Maurie D. McInnis, *The Politics of Taste in Antebellum Charleston* (Chapel Hill: University of North Carolina Press, 2005), 36–46. Soltow notes that during the 1790s, there were 1,157 dwellings valued between $1,000 and $2,999, 204 dwellings valued between $3,000 and $5,999, and 45 dwellings worth in excess of $6,000. While many assume substantial, even luxurious, homes were the prerogative of the elite, the artisans and tradespeople, as well as shopkeepers—or the carpenters, cabinetmakers, butchers, tanners, silversmiths, jewellers, gunsmiths, tinsmiths, bakers, milliners, tailors, grocers, and chandlers—also built such homes. Hart, *Building Charleston*, 92–113.

8. According to city directories, petitions, and the *South Carolina Gazette*, John Duvall, stay maker (1767), was one of the few merchants conducting business on Meeting Street between 1732 and 1767. By 1790, Meeting Street was more commercial, but with sixty-seven businesses it was still far behind King Street and East Bay. See, "Distribution of Merchants and Appended information," in Calhoun, Zierden, and Paysinger, "Geographic Spread of Charleston's Mercantile Community, 1732–1767," 187, 219, and "Distribution of commercial premises in Charleston's major thoroughfares, 1790" in Hart, *Building Charleston*, 206.

9. Despite a paucity of sources on both the cost of building and real estate transactions, Soltow has found that about 22% of free white men over the age of 26 owned property. Of those, 75% held real estate worth less than $1,000 (or £250) in the 1790s. See, "Socioeconomic Classes in South Carolina and Massachusetts in the 1790s," 301–02. By comparison, Jacob Martin's father owned a small farm on the outskirts of Charleston valued at £495. In addition to a two-storied house and the usual outbuildings, he had a stable and a fowl house. See, "Nicholas Martin for Sundry houses, outhouses, boards, etc burned by order of Governor Rutledge in May 1779," Packet in the

Name of John Nicholas Martin, Accts Audited AA 4809, RW 2779, South Carolina Historical Commission, Cawley, *Herrstein to South Carolina*, 92–94, 96B. Lastly, Alice R[avenel] Huger Smith (1876–1958) and D[aniel] E[lliott] Huger Smith (1846–1932) provide information on the homes of the Charleston elite: the Middleton-Pinckney mansion was valued at $53,800 (or approximately £13,450) in 1796; the William Washington house was purchased in 1785 for £4,460; the William Gibbes mansion was "conveyed" to a new owner in 1794 for £2,500; the Miles Brewton property and mansion was valued at £8,000 in 1769; and a "large brick mansion" on Hassell Street near the Martin property was worth £3,000 in 1788. See, *The Dwellings of Charleston, South Carolina* (Philadelphia: J.B. Lippincott, 1917), 132–33, 187–90, 208–09, 272–73, 373. The Martin home was better than average.

10. Waddell, *Architecture*, 1:1, 69.

11. In 1786, Rebecca owned three enslaved women and one man according to inventories submitted to the Probate Court [Court of Ordinary] and Letters of Administration, 1785–1792, Charleston County. See, Cawley, *Herrstein to South Carolina*, 127–31. In the 1790 federal census, Rebecca Martin is listed as the head of household; Jacob is not listed by name but rather as a white man over the age of sixteen. Three slaves, two women and one man, are also listed. See, First Census of the United States taken in the year 1790, South Carolina, Part Two, Heads of Families, Department of Commerce and Labor, Bureau of the Census, S.N.D. North, Director (Washington, 1908), 40. In 1813, when Rebecca and Jacob Martin parted company, there were twenty-seven enslaved men and women in their household. Twenty-four were sold at the time of their separation. See, "Distribution of Real and Personal Property of John Jacob Martin, 18 June 1813," Cawley, *Herrstein to South Carolina*, 181. Nothing more is known about the enslaved men and women of the Martin household. For documents detailing slave sales: Miscellaneous Records (Main Series), SCDAH, specifically, S213003: V005W, p. 247 and 005W, p. 263 and V005W, p. 525.

12. For information on household goods: Inventory accompanying Letters of Administration, June 16, 1786, and the Marriage Settlement of Rebecca Solzar and Jacob Martin, Nov 3, 1789, in Cawley, *Herrstein to South Carolina*: 130–31, 176–79. For inventories detailing household possessions owned by wealthy Charlestonians: E. Milby Burton, *Charleston Furniture, 1700–1825*, contributions from the Charleston Museum XII (Charleston, SC: Charleston Museum, 1955), 11–12. For an idea of how the Martin family possessions differed in value from those who could afford imported English furniture or that manufactured locally by master cabinetmaker, Thomas Elfe Jr.: M. Allison Carrill, "An Assessment of English Furniture Imports into Charleston, 1760–1800," *Journal of Early Southern Decorative Arts* 11, no. 2 (1985): 4, 14. A dozen plain mahogany side chairs from England were worth approximately £2 more than those listed in Rebecca Solzar Martin's inventories of 1786, and the cost of a mahogany bedstead from Elfe Jr. was £25–35, considerably more than the £8 assigned the same item in the inventory of goods inherited as the widow of Jacob Solzar. For additional

information on household goods: J. W. Joseph, *"Of Sterling Worth and Good Qualities": Status and Domesticity in Nineteenth-Century Middle Class Charleston*, Archaeological Investigations at Site 38CH1871, Final Report August 30, 2004, Marlene and Nathan Addlestone Library, College of Charleston (Charleston, SC, 2004), 198–202.

13. For a negative assessment of urban Charleston: "Ebenezer Kellogg's [1789–1846] Visit to Charleston, 1817," ed. Sidney Walter Martin *SCHGM* 49, no.1 (1948): 4–5. When observers focused on slavery, observations shifted from buildings, roads, and the natural surroundings to human activity in a city where curfews were strictly enforced and working slaves everywhere. See, Thomas D Clark, *South Carolina: The Grand Tour, 1780–1865* (Columbia: University of South Carolina Press, 1973), 103, fn. 27. For other relevant excerpts in this volume: Basil Hall (1788–1844), *Travels in North America, in the Years 1827 and 1828*, 3 vols. (Edinburgh, 1829), 113–34; and Karl Bernhard, Duke of Saxe-Weimer-Eisenbach, *Travels Through North America, During the Years 1825 and 1826*, 2 vols. (Philadelphia, 1828), 88–112.

14. Martin Strobel, "An Exposition of the Relationship Existing Between Jacob Martin, Formerly of South Carolina, and Elizabeth Pennington, Residing Together in Philadelphia," PHS, Biog .M381s 1825, p. 4. [also in Cawley, *Herrstein to South Carolina*, 168–75]. Rebecca Martin's life is only somewhat reflected in studies by Mary Beth Norton and Cynthia A. Kierner. Norton focuses on the elite, the poor, and the enslaved rather than on the world inhabited by women who were wealthy but not from the elite. See, Norton, *Liberty's Daughters: The Revolutionary Experience of American Women, 1750–1800* (Boston: Little, Brown and Co., 1980), 3–9, 26–33; and Kierner, *Beyond the Household: Women's Place in the Early South, 1700–1835* (Ithaca, NY: Cornell University Press, 1998), 19–23, 109.

15. For Rebecca's apprenticeship and marital status, 1781–83: "Will of John Murray," Charleston County, South Carolina, Record of Wills, 1771–1774, p. 517 [Family History Library, Salt Lake City, Film # 0.023, 461]; Cawley, *Herrstein to South Carolina*, 125–26.

16. On eighteenth-century apprenticeships in Charleston, specifically milliners and mantua-makers: Mary Ferrari, "'Obliged to Earn Subsistence for Themselves': Women Artisans in Charleston, South Carolina, 1763–1808," *SCHM* 106, no. 4 (2005): 240–41. When describing the basic tasks of running a business, Ferrari draws on the unpublished work of Amy Simon, specifically: "'She is so neat and sits so well': Garment Construction and the Millinery Business of Eliza Dodds, 1821–1833" (master's thesis, University of Delaware, 1993). Interestingly, Appendix Two, "Charleston's Women Artisans, 1763–1808," lists Rebecca Duvall, Eliza Murray, and Mrs. Solzar as mantua-makers. All three entries refer to one woman: Rebecca Murray Duvall Solzar Martin. Rebecca Martin is strangely absent, but she might have sold the business once Jacob Martin became a successful investor. See, Ferrari, "'Obliged to Earn Subsistence,'" 253–55, fn. 72, p. 251. For experiences more closely resembling those of Rebecca Martin: Emma Hart, "Work, Family, and the Eighteenth-Century History of a Middle Class in the American South," *JSH* 78, no. 3 (2012): 551–78.

17. Letters of Administration, June 16, 1786, Cawley, *Herrstein to South Carolina*,

127–30. In a comparison of women's economic roles in Newport, Rhode Island, and Charleston, South Carolina, it has been stated: "as shoppers and provisioners, urban women were ideally positioned to reap the benefits of an expanded [eighteenth century] material life." However, discussions of women's roles as executors or administrators tend to emphasize discharging outstanding debts and obtaining credit rather than collecting monies or as creditors. Ellen Hartigan-O'Connor, *The Ties that Buy: Women and Commerce in Revolutionary America* (Philadelphia: University of Pennsylvania Press, 2009), 4, 90–96.

18. Gail Gibson, "Costume and Fashion in Charleston, 1769–1782," *SCHM* 82, no. 3 (1981): 227.

19. See fn. 14 in Gibson, "Costume and Fashion in Charleston," 230. Her information on the Watteau gown comes from R. Turner Wilcox, *The Mode in Costume* (New York, 1958), 196, as well as from pictorial representations, namely, *Monument du Costume*, "Goodbyes," engraving by Robert Delaunay after Jean Michel Moreau de Jeune (Neuwied, West German, 1777), #40–80–57; "Fashion Plate: Modes and Manners," exhibit, Museum of Art, Philadelphia, September 1979.

20. Gibson, "Costume and Fashion," 228, 246.

21. Letters of Administration, June 16, 1786, Cawley, *Herrstein to South Carolina*, 127–30. Cawley states "because of her wealth received from her two deceased husbands, John Duvall and Jacob Solzar, it was necessary to draft what was known as a 'Marriage Settlement' prior to her marriage to Jacob Martin." It could also be argued that her decision to protect her inheritance was more than simply necessary or, as Cawley implies, inevitable, because of the extent of her inheritance. Widowed women had "first claim to administer intestate estates," and many did because doing so protected both personal and institutionalized privileges bestowed by property. See, Kirsten E. Wood, *Masterful Women: Slaveholding Widows from the American Revolution through the Civil War* (Chapel Hill: University of North Carolina Press, 2004), 11, 15. Indeed, Rebecca Martin's "Last Will and Testament" also suggests she made a calculated decision as she provided specifically for female descendants. Cawley is no doubt correct in stating that her will reflected the fact that she was abandoned by her husband but her actions are equally indicative of her experience with *femme covert*. See, "Will of Rebecca Martin," Probate Court, Charleston County, South Carolina vol. 42, Will Book St 0529 (1839–1845) 137–38, SCDAH; and Cawley, *Herrstein to South Carolina*, 133–34. For the classic analysis of this topic: Marylynn Salmon, "Women and Property in South Carolina: The Evidence from Marriage Settlements, 1730 to 1830," *WMQ* 39, no. 4 (1982): 655–85. Lastly, A. G. Roeber states that transplanted German women were predisposed toward prenuptial agreements (in South Carolina), and that they "closely approximated Ulm and eastern Swabian custom." See *Palatines, Liberty and Property: German Lutherans in Colonial British America* (Baltimore, MD: Johns Hopkins University Press, 1993), 225.

22. Marriage Settlement of Rebecca Solzar and Jacob Martin, Nov 3, 1789; Cawley, *Herrstein to South Carolina*, 176–79.

23. Whether Rebecca Solzar is indicative of trends among post-Revolutionary women is unclear. She left no documentation suggesting she wanted recognition and compensation for her efforts at home or in public, but her actions reflect some knowledge of the law. On women and "equity," see Kierner, *Beyond the Household*, 124–29. On Rebecca's property, in particular the three enslaved women and one man she owned: Inventory submitted in 1786 to the Court of Ordinary (Probate Court), Letters of Administration, June 16, 1786; Cawley, *Herrstein to South Carolina*, 130–31.

24. On eighteenth-century women and religion: Norton, *Liberty's Daughters*, 126; Kierner, *Beyond the Household*, 5–6, 30–32, 43.

25. The marriage record for Rebecca Murray and John Duvall (October 7, 1781) is in *Register of St. Philip's Parish, Charles Town or Charleston, 1754–1810*, ed. D. E. Huger Smith and A. S. Salley Jr. (1927; repr. Columbia: University of South Carolina Press, 1971), 212, cited in Cawley, *Herrstein to South Carolina*, 124. Having a somewhat chequered career, Reverend Robert Cooper served the parishes of Prince William's Sheldon (1758–1759) and St. Michael's, Charleston (1761–1776) before being dismissed. See, Theo. D. Jervey, "Reverend Robert Cooper," *SCHGM* 38, no. 4 (Oct 1937): 120–25, as well as George W. Williams and Gene Waddell, eds. "Letters from the Clergy of the Anglican Church in South Carolina, c.1696–1775," List of South Carolina Clergy, 12–15. College of Charleston Faculty Manuscript Collection, Lowcountry Digital Library. St. Philip's Church was "an evocative symbol" denoting "social position." See, McInnis, *Politics of Taste in Antebellum Charleston*, 110–13, and Poston, *Buildings of Charleston*, 87–88.

26. David L. Danner, "The Parting of the Ways for Lutherans and Episcopalians: The Movement from Eucharistic Hospitality to Mutual Isolation in the Nineteenth Century," *AEH* 68, no. 2 (1999): 174–76, and Richard B. Baumann, "Lutherans and Anglican-Episcopal Conformity, 1565–1957: Called to Common Mission," *AEH* 73, no. 4 (2004): 447–50. The topic of interdenominational cooperation has been revisited in Andrew H. M. Stern, *Southern Crucifix, Southern Cross: Catholic-Protestant Relations in the Old South*, Religion and American Culture (Tuscaloosa: University of Alabama Press, 2012).

27. For details of Martin's pastoral assignments: Cawley, *Herrstein to South Carolina*, 40–42, 57–60, 76–77. For comments on Martin's ordination: Gotthardt Bernheim, *History of the German Settlements and Lutheran Church in North and South Carolina* (Philadelphia: The Lutheran Bookstore, 1872), 208. He states that Martin was "said to have been ordained by the Salzberg pastors in Georgia." For the origins and activities of the various Lutheran settlements, including Ebenezer and the village at the forks of the Broad and Saluda where John Nicholas Martin owned land: Roeber, *Palatines, Liberty, and Property*, 206, 211–13.

28. In an effort to ensure that congregations had pastors when none meeting the educational standards of the church was available, the American Lutheran Church chose to "license" theological students, usually annually, rather than ordain untrained

men. See, Bost, *Lutheran Church in South Carolina*, 160, fn. 21. On curricula and the establishment of public schools in post-Reformation Germany, see, Gerald Strauss, "The Social Function of Schools in the Lutheran Reformation in Germany," *HEQ* 28, no. 2 (1988): 195–97; Christopher R. Friedrichs, "Whose House of Learning? Some Thoughts on German Schools in Post-Reformation Germany," *HEQ* 22, no. 3 (1982): 371–77; and Lowell Green, "The Education of Women in the Reformation," *HEQ* 19, no. 1 (1979): 93–116.

29. See entries between October and December 1774 in *The Journals of Henry Melchior Muhlenberg*, 3 vols., trans. and ed. Theodore G. Tappert and John W. Doberstein (Philadelphia: Evangelical Lutheran Ministerium of Pennsylvania and Adjacent States and the Muhlenberg Press, 1946), 2:571, 576, 581, 594, 651. On Lutheran clergy in eighteenth-century America: Theodore G. Tappert, "The Church's Infancy, 1650–1790," in *The Lutherans in North America*, ed. E. Clifford Nelson (Philadelphia: Fortress Press, 1975), 44–49.

30. The German Friendly Society was founded in 1766 to provide philanthropic, social, and educational assistance to Charlestonians of German ancestry; members promised to abide by "parliamentary-style rules" and avoid "cursing, inebriety, gaming, [and] dancing at meetings." See, Helene M. Riley, "Michael Kalteisen and the Founding of the German Friendly Society in Charleston," *SCHM* 100 (1999): 40–42.

31. Jacob Martin is listed as a merchant in the "Marriage Settlement" he signed in 1789, but where he was employed in that capacity is unknown. He is also listed as a merchant in 1790 in *The Charleston Directory*, but he is listed as a clerk at the South Carolina Bank in the 1796 Directory. He is not listed in the 1801 Directory, but listed as a bookkeeper at the South Carolina Bank in the Directories for 1802, 1803, 1806, 1807, 1809, and 1813. See, James W. Hagy, *People and Professions of Charleston, South Carolina, 1782–1802* (Baltimore, MD: Clearfield Co., 1992), 17; and Hagy, *City Directories for Charleston, South Carolina for years 1803, 1806, 1807, 1809, and 1813* (Baltimore, MD: Clearfield Co., 1995), 14, 43, 77, 119, 153.

32. First Census of the United States, 1790, South Carolina, 37.

33. A curio cabinet attributed to him is among memorabilia owned by a descendant, Mrs. John (Jane Grimball) Greely, Charleston, South Carolina.

34. For observations on merchants: Charles Fraser, Robert Gourdin, and Harriet Horry Ravenel, as summarized in a perceptive, if dated, book. See, Rosser H. Taylor, *Ante-Bellum South Carolina: A Social and Cultural History*. Albert Ray Newsome et al., eds. The James Sprout Studies in History and Political Science 25, no. 2 (Chapel Hill: University of North Carolina Press, 1942): 41, 44. For more recent analyses echoing Taylor: Richard Waterhouse, "Development of Elite Culture in the Colonial American South: A Study of Charles Towne, 1670–1770," *AJPH* 28, no. 3 (1982): 391–404; and Pease and Pease, *Web of Progress*, 9, 13–15, 18–19. For a list of successful import-export merchants: Stuart O. Stumpt, "South Carolina Importers of General Merchandise, 1735–1765," *SCHM* 84, no.1 (1983): 3–10. For information on the incomes of merchants:

Soltow, "Socioeconomic Classes," 289–94. A more recent restating of earlier views of merchants, with quantification for the late antebellum period: John P. Radford, "Model of the Pre-Industrial City: Charleston, South Carolina," *Transactions of the Institute of British Geographers*, New Ser. 4, no. 3 (1979): 396–97.

35. Strobel, "Exposition of the Relationship Between Jacob Martin, and Elizabeth Pennington," PHS, Biog .M381s 1825, p. 4.

36. On the genealogy and occupations of the Martin and Schmidt families: Cawley, *Herrstein to South Carolina*, 2–3, 10, 45. Nicholas Martin received lands open to immigrants, purchased others, and sold land between 1762 and 1778. His holdings included over five hundred acres of farmland with a house and outbuildings twenty miles northwest of Columbia. These were obtained as bounty lands from the British. He was among the "foreign Protestants" strategically located between the coast and the interior so as to create a defensive perimeter. He also had a "little farm" of just over two acres slightly beyond the Charleston city limits. For South Carolina Deed Abstracts: Cawley, *Herrstein to South Carolina*, 64–68. Martin acquired these lands even though he was a poorly paid pastor. On clerical remuneration: Roeber, *Palatines, Liberty and Property*, 212–13, 233; Bost, *Lutheran Church in South Carolina*, 211, 323–24; and H. George Anderson, "Early National Period, 1790–1840," in *Lutherans in North America*, 61–62.

37. Will of John Nicholas Martin, Office of Judge of Probate, Book of Wills (C), 1793–1800 [Family History Library, Salt Lake City, #0023481, v. 27, Will Book C, 1793–1800, pp. 728–30], Cawley, *Herrstein to South Carolina*, 165–67.

38. Nicholas Martin's farm was appraised in 1786 in order to compensate him for damages incurred during the Revolution. "Nicholas Martin for Sundry houses, outhouses, boards, etc burned by order of Governor Rutledge in May 1779," Cawley, *Herrstein to South Carolina*, 92–94, 96B.

39. The only indication that Jacob participated in Rebecca's mantua-making business comes from a court record detailing a successful suit filed in 1798 against the estate of a former client for money owed to Jacob Solzar. See, Claim against Edward Perry, the executor of John Sommer's estate, Judgments Roll, Charleston County, 1798, SCDAH, L10018, Item 1029A.

40. This turn of events has been attributed to an uncanny, but undocumented, financial acuity that allowed Jacob Martin to "nurse" his wife's "nest egg" into a "fortune." See, Shuler, *Had I the Wings*, 37.

41. W[illiam] L[ee] Trenholm [1836–1901], Centennial Address before the Charleston Chamber of Commerce, February 11, 1884, p. 27 in Taylor, *Ante-Bellum South Carolina*, 44. For the financial status of planters: Michael P. Johnson, "Planters and Patriarchy: Charleston, 1800–1860," *JSH* 46, no. 1 (1980): 52–54. While most of Johnson's data pertains to accumulated wealth in 1860, Jacob Martin would still qualify as one of those individuals who managed to acquire the wealth, if not the status and prestige, requisite to the title of "planter." This is the case even if cited property values were

reduced by half. Also: Lawrence H. Officer and Samuel H. Williamson, "Purchasing Power of Money in the United States from 1774 to 2005," MeasuringWorth.com, August 2006.

42. Strobel, "Exposition of the Relationship Between Jacob Martin and Elizabeth Pennington," PHS, Biog .M381s 1825, p. 9.

43. For information on Jacob Martin's property, see the legal document stipulating what properties Rebecca was to receive when they separated. Jacob may have had other holdings, but none has been discovered in the Charleston Directories, and he departed Charleston for Philadelphia in 1813. Had the entirety of Jacob's holdings been distributed to his wife and children, he would have been considered a wealthy man; however, he may have had an even larger estate as he was off to a new life in Philadelphia, where living according to the standards to which he had become accustomed would be impossible without means. See, "Distribution of Real and Personal Property of John Jacob Martin, 18 June 1813," Cawley, *Herrstein to South Carolina*, 180–82.

44. Martin Strobel, "A Short Memoir of Martin Strobel Esq of Charleston, So Caro," MS [c1838], CL-USC, P8288.

45. There are numerous studies of post-Revolutionary Southern women, although most do not focus on those whose experiences differed from those of the planter elites or the enslaved population. See, Clinton, *The Plantation Mistress* (1982); Fox-Genovese, *Within the Plantation Household* (1988); McMillen, *Motherhood in the Old South* (1990) and *Southern Women: Black and White in the Old South* (1992); Bleser, *In Joy and Sorrow* (1991); Bynum, *Unruly Women* (1992); and Katy Simpson Smith, *We Have Raised All of You: Motherhood in the South, 1750–1835* (Baton Rouge: Louisiana State Press, 2013). Focusing more specifically on South Carolina or Charleston: Jane H. Pease and William H. Pease, *Ladies, Women and Wenches: Choice and Constraint in Antebellum Charleston and Boston* (Chapel Hill: University of North Carolina Press, 1990); Kierner, *Beyond the Household* (1998); and Weiner, *Mistresses and Slaves* (1998).

46. Strobel, "Exposition of the Relationship Between Jacob Martin and Elizabeth Pennington," PHS, Biog .M381s 1825, pp. 5–6, 9.

47. Ibid., p. 6.

48. Ibid., p.11.

49. Minutes, Vestry Meeting, St. John's Lutheran Church, July 15, 1817, Lutheran Church, Charleston County, CL-USC, I &O.

50. A facsimile of an "Appraisal of Personal Property of John Nicholas Martin," Sept 13, 1800, lists the enslaved men and women, valued at $2,475, as part of Martin's estate; also, "Nicholas Martin for Sundry houses, outhouses, boards, etc burned by order of Governor Rutledge in May 1779," Cawley, *Herrstein to South Carolina*, 92–94, 167.

51. A letter (in private hands) written in 1850 by Reverend Philip A. Strobel (1812–1882) describes his ancestor's love of flowers. Cawley, *Herrstein to South Carolina*, 160, and Strobel, "Exposition of the Relationship Between Jacob Martin and Elizabeth Pennington," PHS, Biog .M381s 1825, p. 9.

52. MM to EB(A), Aug 1,1839, CM, SC/A/1.

53. CLB, *Pastor of St. John's*, 186.

54. John Bachman, *Defence of Luther and the Reformation, against the charges of John D. Bellinger and others, to which are appended communications of other Protestant and Roman Catholic Writers who engaged in the Controversy* (Charleston, SC: William Y. Paxton, 1853). This episode is examined in a scientific context in Stephens, *Science, Race and Religion*, 213–14.

55. JB, *Defence of Luther*, 204, 210, 227, 244.

56. CLB, *Pastor of St. John's*, 186.

Chapter 2

1. MM to Julia Bachman, June 5, 1845, CM, SC/A/1.

2. Bost, *Lutheran Church in South Carolina*, 228. Bost remains the expert on Lutheranism in South Carolina; however, a very brief article on this topic has since been published. See, Mary Havens, "The Liturgical Traditions II: Lutherans," in *Religion in South Carolina*, ed. Charles H. Lippy (Columbia: University of South Carolina Press, 1993), 59–66. On education, Strauss, "Social Function of Schools," 201. For a more general discussion of the role of Southern women in educating children: Smith, *We Have Raised All of You*, 117–33. For an even more general discussion: Ozment, *Birth of a Revolution*, 165.

3. Benjamin N. Martin, "Rev. John N. Martin," in *American Lutheran Biographies*, 501–05.

4. Susan C. Karant-Nunn and Merry Wiesner-Hanks argue that Luther's view on women and marriage shaped attitudes for some four hundred years. See, *Luther on Women: A Sourcebook* (Cambridge, UK: Cambridge University Press, 2003), 1–14. Susan M. Johnson extends that influence by another seventy-five years, arguing: "Luther's catechisms, his prescription for household management and child rearing, still [in 1992] form a part of Lutheran doctrine. . . . The family unit was recognized as patriarchal, but the patriarch was to rule with gentleness as well as strictness." See, "Luther's Reformation and (Un)Holy Matrimony," *JFH* 17, no. 3 (1992): 276. Also, Kirsi Stjerna, *Women and the Reformation* (Malden, MA: Blackwell Pub., 2009) and Lyndal Roper, *The Holy Household: Women and Morals in Reformation Augsburg* (Oxford: Clarendon Press, 1989). While agreeing that Lutheranism changed the lives of girls and women, the pioneering work of Steven Ozment offers a much more positive view of the Reformation than the above-cited studies. See, *When Fathers Ruled: Family Life in Reformation Europe* (Cambridge, MA: Harvard University Press, 1983).

5. Frederick Maroni Cawley, "Our Ancestors and Kindred," Typescript, 1950, p. 103, Cawley, *Herrstein to South Carolina*, 136.

6. MM to Julia Bachman, June 5,1845, CM, SC/A/1.

7. CLB, *Pastor of St. John's*, 216.

8. JB to Mrs. H [a parishioner], Jan 1852, CLB, *Pastor of St. John's*, 283–87. JB's views regarding education for women are noted in Pease and Pease, *Ladies, Women and Wenches*, 78. For discussions of women and marriage in the Lutheran tradition, see fn. 5.

9. On pietism: Joanna Bowen Gillespie, "'The Clear Leadings of Providence': Pious Memoirs and the Problems of Self-Realization for Women in the Early Nineteenth Century," *JER* 5, no. 2 (1985): 205–06; and Benjamin A. Kolodziej, "Pietism and Rationalism: A Dichotomy of Resemblance," *CHIQ* 77, no.1 (2004): 35–54. On the catechism: Strauss, "Social Function of Schools," 191–206.

10. JB to Jane Bachman, March 8, 1846, CM, SC/A/1.

11. JB to Jane Bachman, July 18, 1846, CM, SC/A/1.

12. JB to Jane Bachman, March 8, 1846, CM, SC/A/1.

13. In this, Lutherans were no different than other denominations. Philip Greven points out that there was a general belief—at least as early as the seventeenth century—that what happened in early childhood was key to the development of character and temperament in later life. Interestingly, he does not include Lutheranism in his analysis of American Protestantism, although there are some references to Martin Luther. *The Protestant Temperament: Patterns of Child Rearing, Religious Experience, and the Self in Early America* (Chicago: University of Chicago Press, 1977), 15–16. Also, Gillespie, "'Clear Leadings of Providence,'" 205–06.

14. JB to VGA, Sept 8, 1847, CM, SC/A/1.

15. JB to his children, Sept 6, 1847 CLB, *Pastor of St. John's*, 234–35. Note: The reprinted letter differs from the original.

16. JB to VGA, Sept 8, 1847, CM, SC/A/1.

17. CLB, *Pastor of St. John's*, 237.

18. Tappert, "The Church's Infancy, 1650–1790," 71–72. Gillespie's analyses of an earlier period are also instructive. She states that narratives detailing dying moments employ a "language of exuberance," and that many such stories were written to "comfort" the mourners, especially the families of deceased children, rather than to offer "spiritual insight." See, "'Clear Leadings of Providence,'" 209, 213. That Julia's deathbed story was part of a larger work, and that she was the daughter of a pastor, suggests her story had both institutional and familial significance. The experience of Southern Lutheran evangelicals seems to have been overlooked by scholars, for example: Scott Stephan, *Reforming the Southern Family: Evangelical Women and Domestic Devotion in the Antebellum South* (Athens: University of Georgia Press, 2008), 185–200, 202–10.

19. Kolodziej, "Pietism and Rationalism," 43. For a discussion of *Sola fide* in Lutheranism: Peter L. Berger, "On Lutheran Identity in America," *LQ* 20 (2006): 345–47.

20. JB to Jane Bachman, 10 Sept 1847, CLB, *Pastor of St. John's*, 239–40. On JB and emotionalism, see, Bost, "John Bachman and the Development of Southern Lutheranism," 352–53.

21. CLB, *Pastor of St. John's*, 240.

22. JB to Mrs H [a parishioner], Jan 1852, CLB, *Pastor of St. John's*, 285. For JB's views on death: "Fifty-Fifth Anniversary Sermon," *Charleston Daily Courier*, January 10, 1870.

23. JB to Jane Bachman, Sept 10, 1847, CLB, *Pastor of St. John's*, 239.

24. CLB, *Pastor of St. John's*, 188.

25. Patriarchy was the norm in most homes in the nineteenth century; however, Southern women and Lutheranism has been little studied. For example, in *Religion in the American South: Protestants and Others in History and Culture*, ed. Beth Barton Shweiger and Donald G. Mathews (Chapel Hill: University of North Carolina Press, 2004), it is stated that Lutheran, Mormon, Presbyterian, and Jewish women have been understudied. See, Lynn Lyerly, "Women and Southern Religion," 279–80, fn. 109. For quotation: CLB, *Pastor of St. John's*, 237.

26. MM to CLB, Mar 14, 1841, CM, SC/A/1.

27. Ibid.

28. Gillespie, "'Clear Leadings of Providence,'" 217.

29. Bost comments on the reprinted articles of the *Unio Ecclesiastica*. See, *Lutheran Church in South Carolina*, 114–27; 123–24 for quotation.

30. On this aspect of being a pastor's wife: Stjerna, *Women and the Reformation*, 35–37. For a discussion of why women chose to marry pastors and how they were viewed by the church and by outsiders: Marjorie Elizabeth Plummer, "'Partner in his Calamities': Pastors' Wives, Married Nuns and the Experience of Clerical Marriage in the Early German Reformation," *GH* 20, no. 2 (2008): 207–27. Interestingly, Plummer's analysis questions the idyllic picture of early marriage described by Bachman as he defended Luther against attacks by local Catholics.

31. Tertullian, Chapter XIII, "It is Not Enough that God Know Us to Be Chaste: We Must Seem So Before Men. Especially in These Times of Persecution We Must Inure Our Bodies to the Hardships Which They May Not Improbably Be Called to Suffer," Book II, *De cultu feminarum*, English trans. Sidney Thelwall, *Ante-Nicene Christian Library* (ANCL) 11 (1869), 304–22; reprinted *ANF* [Ante-Nicene Fathers] 4 (1885), 14–25. Avail: [accessed: February 2013] For the modernized version: The Gatherer (regular feature), "Recipe for a Lady's Dress," *The Mirror of Literature, Amusement and Instruction* 23 (April 5, 1823), 367. The Gatherer specifically noted that the poem was based on Tertullian.

32. George Lochman, *History, Doctrine and Discipline of the Evangelical Lutheran Church* (Harrisburg, PA: John Wyeth, 1818), 156.

33. John Bellinger to the editor of the *Charleston Evening News*, April 22, 1852, in JB, *Defence of Luther*, 39. Correspondence between the debaters, as well as letters and excerpts from the local press and interested commentators, are reprinted.

34. See, specifically, Articles XI and XVIII, *Unio Ecclesistica*. Bost, *Lutheran Church in South Carolina*, 123, 126. Waddell contextualizes JB's *Defence of Luther* and provides a twelve-page excerpt in *Bachman, Writings*, 263–66.

35. JB became embroiled in a doctrinal controversy with the Catholic Bishop, Reverend John England, in 1841. Bost, "John Bachman and the Development of Southern Lutheranism," 299–304.

36. Advertisement: "Popish Confession and Priesthood Exposed," *Charleston Evening News*, March 13, 1852; JB, *Defence of Luther*, 1.

37. "The Press of Charleston," *Catholic Miscellany* (March 1852); JB, *Defence of Luther*, 9.

38. JB, *Lutheran Observer* 21, no. 17 (April 22, 1853) in Bost, "John Bachman and the Development of Southern Lutheranism," 263–64.

39. JB is quoting from Luther's correspondence. *Defence of Luther*, 86. There are numerous studies of Luther's views of women and marriage, most focusing to a greater or lesser extent on Katharina von Bora. See, Charmarie Jenkins Blaisdell, "The Matrix of Reform: Women in the Lutheran and Calvinist Movements," in *Triumph over Silence: Women in Protestant History*, ed. Richard L. Greaves Contributions to the Study of Religion, No.15 (Westport, CT: Greenwood Press, 1985), 13–23; Steven Ozment, "Re-Inventing Family Life," *Christian History* 12, no. 3 (1993): 22–25; Martin Treu, "Katharina von Bora, the Woman at Luther's Side," *LQ* 13 (1999): 157–78; Scott Hendrix, "Luther on Marriage," *LQ* 14, no. 3 (2000): 335–50; Mickey L. Mattox, "Luther on Eve, Women and the Church," *LQ* 17 (2003): 456–74; and Trevor O'Reggio, "Martin Luther: Marriage and the Family as a Remedy for Sin," *Andrews University Seminary Studies* 51, no. 1 (2013): 1–29.

40. JB's discussion of Rosa Madiai appears in an "Address to the Protestant Public given in response to a letter from "A Charlestonian" [October/November 1852] entitled "The Rev. John Bachman and the Irish Catholics, *Defence of Luther*, 398. Rosa and Francesco Madiai are again referred to in a "Letter to the Roman Catholic Bishop of Charleston," [Right Rev. Ignatius Reynolds, D.D.], 457–58.

41. JB, *Defence of Luther*, 90.

42. Quoting Luther as found in the twenty-four volumes compiled by Johann Georg Walch (1740–1752). Ibid., 204.

43. HB to JB, May 24, 1846, CM, SC/A/1.

44. JB to VGA, Dec 18, 1848, CM, SC/A/1. This event was also noted by Jacob Schirmer who recorded that they were married by Dr. Hazelius in a "private" ceremony at St. John's Lutheran Church on December 28, 1848. See, "Schmirer Diary," *SCHM* 81, no. 1 (January 1980): 93. At this time, church weddings were still uncommon.

45. Journal of John Bachman, August 9–September 25, 1827, including an Account of a Trip to the North and Copies of Letters written while there. Facsimile based on original owned by Harriet B. Coffin, CM, SC/A/1.

46. JB to Harriet Bachman [June 27 or 28, 1827], CM, SC/A/1.

Chapter 3

1. Elizabeth Kent, "Art. VII. Considerations of Botany, as a Study for Young People, intended as an Introduction to a Series of Papers Illustrative of the Linnaean

System of Plants," *Magazine of Natural History* 1 (1829): 126. Interestingly, Kent's essay appeared in the same issue as did ornithologist William Swainson's positive review of *Birds of America*. For Swainson's review, 43–52. On Elizabeth Kent and the impediments to scientific study: Shteir, *Cultivating Women, Cultivating Science*, 135–46, 233–37.

2. Many articles and books attest to the difficulties encountered by women, and while impossible to sum up the message in one sentence, Shteir states: "For both daughters and sons, nieces and nephews, scientific interests could develop within a family context, but the public expression of these interests shows more among sons than daughters." See, "Botany in the Breakfast Room," *Uneasy Careers and Intimate Lives*, 36. For a more recent examination of the same themes, but in the Canadian context: Kimberlie M. Robert, "Women's Botanical Illustration in Canada: Its Gendered, Colonial and Garden Histories" (master's thesis, Concordia, 2008). For studies that identify female gains in science more generally and in the United States: Noble, *World Without Women*, 244–78, and Rossiter, *Women Scientists in America to 1940*, passim, xv–xviii.

3. Rutledge, "Artists in the Life of Charleston," specifically Appendices: "Artists' Advertisements," 183–228, and "Classified Lists of Artists–Drawing Masters and Mistresses," 232–33.

4. Marjorie Shelley, "Drawing Birds: Audubon's Artistic Practices," in Olson, *Audubon's Aviary*, 116.

5. MM to JJA, July 12, 1832, BRBML, GEN MSS 85. For dates of JJA's paintings: Olson and Mazzitelli, "Listing of Audubon's Bird Watercolors," 410–19.

6. JB to LBA, Nov 15, 1831, CLB, *Pastor of St. John's*, 95–97.

7. JB to JJA, Dec 23, 1831; CLB, *Pastor of St. John's*, 99–102.

8. JJA returned to Charleston from Florida March 10, 1832, and then went south again on April 18. JJA to LBA, Apr 18, 1832, APSL, B Au25 and letters dated March 13 and April 15, 1832 in Corning, *Letters*, 1:184–87, 193–95. Also: JB to LBA Apr 21, 1832, CL-USC, Pob.

9. JB to JJA, July 21, 1832; Ruthven Deane, "Some Letters of Bachman to Audubon," *The Auk* 46, no. 2 (1929): 177–79.

10. JB to JJA, Oct 20, 1832, CLB, *Pastor of St. John's*, 102–03.

11. JB to JJA, Nov 11, 1832, CLB, *Pastor of St. John's*, 105–08.

12. Herrick, *Audubon*, 2:29–44.

13. Almost without exception, studies of JJA mention LBA—and none more eloquently than Robert Cushman Murphy. He wrote: "For 38 years she was his inspiration, and for 34 of them his constant helpmate, both in America and abroad." Murphy, "John James: An Evaluation of the Man and His Works," *N-YHSQ* (1955–1956): 350. Also: introduction by Christoph Irsmscher to *Lucy Audubon* (DeLatte). Although Irsmscher points out the gaps in DeLatte's retelling, specifically LBA's years as a widow, in fact, the gaps are more profound. There is little about LBA's life after 1830.

14. LBA to JJA, Mar 19, 1832, BRBML, GEN MSS 85.

15. Three days later, LBA wrote Robert Havell, Audubon's London engraver, to chastise him for plates of inferior quality. She assured him that she and her husband were "of one mind," and that "he would thank me for pointing out to you those things which have and on which his success and reputation so much depend." LBA to Robert Havell, Mar 22, 1832, HL, bMS Am1492.

16. Information on JJA's travels in June comes from several sources. He left Indian Key on May 31, 1832, according to Proby, *Audubon in Florida*, 4. For his Savannah business and arrival in Philadelphia: Herrick, *Audubon*, 2:25–26. For the details of his journey: JJA to JB, July 1, 1832, Corning, *Letters*, 1:195–96. Based on an account written by JB and published in the Charleston *Courier*, June 6, 1832, Shuler describes Audubon's cargo as consisting of "shells, corals, boxes of seeds, roots of plants, amphibious animals, mammals, and upwards of five hundred and fifty birds, principally of the larger species." *Had I the Wings*, 87, 91. Because the date of June 25, 1832, is penciled on plate 363, Shuler states that JJA was still in Charleston; however, that claim is countered by correspondence and by Herrick's reconstruction. He would have had to leave Charleston no later than June 3 to arrive in Philadelphia when he did.

17. JB to JJA, Mar 27, 1833, Deane, "Letters Bachman to Audubon," 182–85.

18. JB to JJA, Nov 11, 1832, CLB, *Pastor of St. John's*, 105–08; Also, Olson, *Audubon's Aviary*, 428.

19. JB to JJA, Mar 27, 1833, Deane, "Letters Bachman to Audubon," 182–85.

20. For the most recent examination of JJA's painting: Olson, "Audubon's Innovations and the Traditions of Ornithological Illustration," 41–106; and Shelley, "Drawing Birds," 109–31. Olson claims that he had "a possible awareness of works by other artists, such as Dutch still-life painters and draftsmen like the German Albrecht Durer" by 1820, and she illustrates the influence of artists such as Jean-Baptiste Oudry (1686–1755) and Jacques-Louis David (1748–1825). Although most of her comparisons focus on ornithological illustrators, artists such as Frans Synder and Edwin Henry Landseer are also discussed. Also, Partridge, "Audubon and the Tradition of Ornithological Illustration," 97–129; Stebbins Jr., "Audubon's Drawings," 3–26; and Blum, *Picturing Nature*, 88–118.

21. JJA's journal contains references to this letter of introduction and to a letter Sully wrote directly to Lawrence on his behalf. See, entry, Dec 18, 1826, and letters to LBA, Dec 22, 1826, and Thomas Sully, Dec 20, 1826 in *The 1826 Journal of John James Audubon*, transcribed and intro. by Alice Ford [from original in collection of Henry Bradley Martin] (Norman: University of Oklahoma Press, 1967), 295, 352–54, 355–57. More generally, the events of this period were reconstructed using documents supplied by MRA in Herrick, *Audubon*, 1:377–80; 393–95. Also: Buchanan, *Audubon*, 128–31 and LBA, *Audubon*, 149–53.

22. JJA to VGA, Oct 29, 1826; Ford, *1826 Journal*, 341–45; and JJA, Feb 24, 1828, "European Journals," MRA, *Journals*, 1:284. On Lawrence and learning to paint oils: JJA, July 24, 1826, "European Journals," MRA, *Journals*, 1:101.

23. Buchanan, *Audubon*, 129; and LBA, *Audubon*, 150. JJA wrote that he heard Lawrence dissuaded the British Museum from purchasing *Birds*, and regardless of the veracity of that rumor, it is true that Lawrence did not subscribe. See, "Original Subscription List" and "Final Lists of Subscribers," Fries, *Double Elephant Folio*, 140–50, 162–71. Less charitably, an early biographer wrote: "Audubon reverenced the great. He had a habit of fawning on those who had achieved fame in their presence . . . he usually put them in a less flattering light when he discussed them in his journal at night!" See, Arthur, *American Woodsman*, 271.

24. JJA, Dec 5, 1826; Ford, *1826 Journal*, 275. For a slightly different version: "European Journals," MRA, *Journals*, 1: 175.

25. JJA, Jan 11 and Feb 10, 1827, "European Journals," MRA, *Journals*, 1: 204 and 210. These criticisms are explored in Edward H. Dwight, "Audubon's Oils," *Art in America* 51, no. 2 (1963): 77–79. For a slightly more positive interpretation of JJA's impressions: Olson, "Audubon's Innovations," 48–50. For a decidedly more positive interpretation: Annette Blaugrund, "'My Style of Drawing': Audubon and His Artistic Milieu," in *John James Audubon in the West*, 18–19.

26. Lists of officials and members in *The Royal Scottish Academy, 1826–1917: A Complete List of the Works Exhibited by Raeburn and by Academicians, Associates and Hon. Members, giving details of those Works in Public Galleries, with a Historical Narrative of the Origins and Development of the Royal Scottish Academy by W.D. McKay, R.S.A., Preceded by an Essay on Academies and Art by Frank Rinder* (Glasgow: James Maclehose and Sons, 1917), xli, cxxv; on Reynolds and the Academy: xxi–xxv. At Dalmohay, the estate of George Douglas, 16th Earl of Morton, he examined works of art completely unfamiliar to someone of his modest background. See, JJA, Dec 27 1826; Ford, *1826 Journal*, 309, and Dec 27, 1826, MRA, *Journals*, 1:195–200.

27. JJA, July 29, 1826, "European Journal," MRA, *Journals*, 105.

28. Martin Hardie, *Watercolour Painting in Britain, III: The Victorian Period*, ed. Dudley Snelgrove with Jonathan Mayne and Basil Taylor, 3 vols. (London: B.T. Batsford, 1971), 3:104–09, and Scott Wilcox and Christopher Newall, *Victorian Landscape Watercolors*, Yale Center for British Art, Cleveland Museum of Art, Birmingham Museums and Art Gallery (New York: Hudson Hills Press, 1992), 17–19.

29. JJA to LBA, Nov 25, 1827, Corning, *Letters*, 1:43–54.

30. Arthur, *American Woodsman*, 336, 356, 402; and Olson, *Audubon's Aviary*, 180, 204, 434. Audubon's oils are referred to as "potboilers," and Kidd's role discussed in reference to certain original paintings is in *Audubon's Aviary*.

31. It has been pointed out that watercolor produced the realistic images Audubon created better than oil. See, Marjorie Shelley, "The Craft of American Drawing: Early Eighteenth to Late Nineteenth Century," in *American Drawings and Watercolors in the Metropolitan Museum of Art: A Catalogue of Works by Artists before 1835*, vol. 1, ed. Kevin J. Avery (New York: Metropolitan Museum of Art, 2001), 70–71; and "Drawing

Birds," 116. Also: Blum, *Picturing Nature*, 88–118; and Olson, "Audubon's Innovations," Figs. 22, 27, 31, 54b, 61. On Kidd: George Featherstonhaugh, "Audubon, Author of: 'The Birds of America' and 'Ornithological Biography,'" *MAJGNS* 1 (1831): 467; and Herrick, *Audubon*, 1:446–47.

32. While Olson refers to JJA's awareness of his amateur status as an ornithologist, his inability in oil was also problematic. Elisabeth Hardouin-Fugier, for example, argues that Pierre-Joseph Redouté's legacy as a watercolorist and a teacher is obscure because of his preference for watercolor in an artistic milieu that preferred oil. She states: "In France, watercolour painting was very much looked down upon at the time, and oil paintings hold pride of place at the Salons, treated as a *parent pauvre*." See, *The Pupils of Redouté* (Leigh-on-Sea, UK: F. Lewis Pubs., 1981), 19; also: Shelley, "Drawing Birds," 116. In a recent study of "American" painting techniques before 1860, watercolors are mentioned briefly and only in reference to their use with oils; Audubon is not mentioned. See, Lance Mayer and Gay Myers, *American Painters on Technique: The Colonial Period to 1860* (Los Angeles: J. Paul Getty Museum, 2011). On watercolorists: Hazel Harrison, *Master Strokes: Watercolor, A Step-by-Step Guide to Using the Techniques of the Masters* (New York: Sterling Pub., 2005), 10–11, 19–23, 28–31, 36–39.

33. In a manuscript prepared in 1851, Sully appended a letter written in 1820 by Thomas Lawrence that recommended students read Reynolds's treatises. See, *Hints to Young Painters, and the Process of Portrait-Painting as Practiced by the Late Thomas Sully* (Philadelphia: J.M. Stoddart and Co., 1873), 50–55. Moreover, Reynolds treatises were highly regarded and popular in America, where "almost every private library that contained works on fine arts included the artist's writings." See, Lillian B. Miller, *Patrons and Patriotism: The Encouragement of the Fine Arts in the United States, 1790–1860* (Chicago: University of Chicago Press, 1966), 17. Lastly, Reynolds was held in high regard by George Brookshaw, whose *Groups of Flowers* was among the possessions retained by Maria Martin's descendants (Mrs. John Greely). See, "Advertisement," in *Groups of Flowers, Drawn and Accurately Coloured after nature, with Full Directions for the Young Artist; Designed as a Companion to the Treatise of Flower Painting* (London: Longman, Hurst, Rees, Orme and Brown, 1817), n.p.

34. JJA believed Reynolds over-used glaze to the detriment of his paintings: it made them more vulnerable to deterioration. Jan 30, 1827, "European Journals," MRA, *Audubon Journals*, 1:208–09.

35. Mark Hallett, "Reynolds, Celebrity and the Exhibition Space," in *Joshua Reynolds: The Creation of Celebrity*, ed. Martin Postle (London: Tate Pub., 2005), 35–48, refers to Reynolds as a seeker and creator of celebrity. This theme is explored by other contributors, especially Martin Postle: "The Life and Art of Joshua Reynolds," 275. Quotations from Reynolds in the order of their appearance: *Seven Discourses delivered in the Royal Academy by the President* (London: T. Cadell, 1778), 53 [Second Discourse, Dec 11, 1769]; 19 [First Discourse, Jan 2, 1769]; and 24 [First Discourse].

36. Reynolds, *Seven Discourses*, 22 [First Discourse] as compared to: "Art. IX. —Account of the Method of Drawing Birds employed by J. J. Audubon, Esq. F.R.S.E. In a Letter to a Friend," *Edinburgh Journal of Science* 8, no.1 (1828): 52.

37. Reynolds, *Seven Discourses*, 90 [Third Discourse, 14 Dec 1770] as compared to: JJA, "Method of Drawing Birds," 52.

38. JJA, "Method of Drawing Birds," 53.

39. The German Friendly Society library grew largely through bequest, especially after 1823, and a catalogue was prepared in 1842. See, George J. Gongaware [1866–1951], *The History of the German Friendly Society of Charleston, South Carolina, 1766–1916* (Richmond, VA: Garrett and Massie, Pubs., 1935), 93, 103–25. On the Charleston Library Society: Minute Book of the Membership, 1815–87, Charleston Library Society, Microfilm D4733; Accession Book, Charleston Library Society, 1798–1805 [hard copy]; and Catalogues [1811, 1813, 1816, 1818 Supplement, 1826], CLS, Microfilms D4746, D4747.

40. Miller, *Patrons and Patriotism*, 17.

41. On *Les Liliacées* (and more generally): Martyn and Alison Rix, *The Redouté Album* (London: Studio Editions, 1990), 26–28. Also: Frans A. Stafleu, "Redouté and his Circle," in *Bibliography and Natural History*: Essays presented at a conference in June 1964 by Thomas R. Buckman (Lawrence: University of Kansas Libraries, 1966), 46–65. Unfortunately, the only full-scale English biography is not referenced and imputes dialogue to individuals in the narrative. Even though it is based on archival research and includes a chapter on Audubon's meeting with Redouté, it is not as useful as it might be. Antoina Ridge, *The Man Who Painted Roses: The Story of Pierre-Joseph Redouté* (London: Faber and Faber, 1974).

42. JJA, Sept 20, 1828, "European Journals," MRA, *Journals*, 1:321.

43. MM to JJA, July 12, 1832, BRBML, GEN MSS 85.

44. See, Sept 5, 6, 9, 10, 18, 19, 21, 26 and Oct 4, 5, 1828, JJA, "European Journals," MRA, *Journals*, 1:307–08, 312–13, 320–21, 325, 332. According to the official website of Muséum National d'Histoire Naturelle, the works of the following zoological and botanical painters were housed there: Jean Joubert (1643–1707); Claude Aubriet (c. 1665–1742); Madeleine-Francois Basseporte (1701–1780); Gerard van Spaëndonck; Nicolas Maréchal (d. 1803); Jean-Pierre Redouté; and Henri-Joseph Redouté (1766–1852). Avail: mussi.mnhn.fr/webcontent
/viewer/viewer.asp?INSTANCE=INCIPIO&EXTERNALID=WBCTDOC_451

45. JJA, Oct 14, 1828, "European Journals," MRA, *Journals*, 1:335.

46. On purchasing *Birds*: "Balances 27 feby 1834," VGA to JJA, BRBML, GEN MSS 85. Redouté had on account, 77£ 14p. On the trade: JJA, 27 Sept 1828, "European Journals," MRA, *Journals*, 1:326.

47. Hardouin-Fugier, *Pupils of Redouté*, 15 and Rix, *Redouté Album*, 94. Specifically: P-J Redouté, *Choix des plus belles fleurs et des plus beaux fruits* (Paris: Ernest Panckoucke, 1827), n.p. It is stated in the Introduction: "C'est pour encourager les nombreux

disciplines, les maîtres qui se present à son Cours, que M. Redouté a composé ces brillans modèles." Redouté' benefited from the teachings of Gerard van Spaëndonck, his predecessor at the Muséum National d'histoire Naturelle, and Francesco Bartolozzi (1727–1815), whose stippling technique was so vastly superior to the line process used by most engravers that he produced more than two thousand plates for the best artists of his generation (including Joshua Reynolds and Thomas Lawrence). Bartolozzi, in turn, shared his expertise. On Redouté's training, career, and accomplishments: Wilfrid Blunt, *The Art of Botanical Illustration* (London: Collins, 1967), 173–82; Eva Mannering, Introduction to *The Best of Redouté's Roses* (London: Ariel Press, 1959), iii–v; Madeleine Pinault, *The Painter as Naturalist: from Dürer to Redouté*, trans. Philip Sturgess (Paris: Flammarion, 1991), 24–26, 119–20, 136, 154–59. More generally, Pinault states that artists kept numerous plates and books as references when painting (p. 10). Also: Kärin Nickelson, "Draughtsmen, Botanists, and Nature: Constructing Eighteenth-Century Botanical Illustrations," *Studies in History and Philosophy of Biology and Biomedical Sciences* 37 (2006): 1–25. On Bartolozzi, see, J. T. Herbert Baily, *Francesco Bartolozzi: A Biographical Essay* (London: Otto, 1907), xxviii, 74–78.

48. VGA to JJA, July 3, 1834, BRBML, GEN MSS 85.

49. JJA to JB, Feb 19, 1833, Corning, *Letters*, 1:197.

50. Although this plant is generally referred to as a wild orange, it is depicted with characteristic features (e.g., thorns and "golf-ball sized" fruits) of *Citrus trifoliate* or what is commonly called the trifoliate, Chinese bitter, winder hardy bitter lemon, or mock orange. It was introduced to America in the early 1800s, was eventually naturalized, and is now common in the southeast. See, G. L. Nesom, "*Citrus trifoliata* (Rutaceae): Review of Biology and Distribution in the USA," *Phytoneuron* 46 (2014): 1.

51. According to Olson and Mazzitelli, Lehman added botanicals to the following plates: Plate 115—Swamp Honeysuckle Azalea (*Rhododendron viscosum*); Plate 122—Dog-wood (*Cornus florida*); Plate 123—Flowering Rasp-berry (*Rubus odoratus*); Plate 136—Gerardia flava (smooth false foxglove/*Aureolaria virginica*); Plate 156—Black Walnut (*Juglans nigra*); Plate 162–Anona (*Annona*); Plate 163—Wild Orange (*Citrus trifoliata*); Plate 170—Agati grandiflora (hummingbird tree/*Sesbania grandiflora*); Plate 177—Geiger Tree (*Cordia sebestena*); Plate 178—Vaccinium; Plate 182–Wild Orange (*Citrus trifoliata*); Plate 183—Hardy Canna (*Thalia dealbata*). See, Olson and Mazzitelli, Listing of Audubon's Watercolors," 416–19.

52. For JJA's promise to send volume one and MM's plans to copy: JB to JJA, Dec 23, 1831, CLB, *Pastor of St. John's*, 99–102. For a reference to how *Birds of America* made its way to JB: JJA to a "Dear Friend," Apr 6, 1834, HL, bMS Am 1482.

53. JB to JJA, July 21, 1832; Deane, "Letters Bachman to Audubon," 177–79.

54. The species of *Cleome* has been identified in *Audubon: Beyond Birds, Plant Portraits and Conservation Heritage of John James Audubon*, ed. Ernest Small, Paul M. Catling, Jacques Cayouette, and Brenda Brookes (Ottawa: NRC-CNRC Research Press, 2009), xiii.

55. The original study in the archives of the New-York Historical Society has just three flowers whereas the Havell edition has five. See, 1863.17.393 in Olson, *Audubon's Aviary*, 402.

56. JJA, "Method of Drawing Birds," 49–51, 53.

57. "My Style of Drawing Birds" (c.1838), MRA, *Journals*, 2: 527.

58. JJA, Oct 14, 1828, "European Journals," MRA, *Journals*, 1: 335.

59. In 1902, a description of Audubon's method of mounting birds was recorded by William Ingalls, one of his assistants on his trip to Labrador in 1833. It was published by Ruthven Deane in 1910 in *The Auk*. Olson, *Audubon's Aviary*, 55.

60. For Audubon's supplies: "Articles recommended by J. J. Audubon for the South Sea Exploring Expedition, (27 October 1836)" included in a letter from Charles Pickering, a naturalist associated with the Academy of Natural Science in Philadelphia, to Mahlon Dickerson, Secretary of the Navy, October 29, 1836, in House Documents, 25th Congress, 2nd Session, House of Representatives, Executive Documents, Doc. No. 147 [South Seas] Exploring Expedition, 135–37. There are also many letters regarding paints, brushes, and paper supplies for Charleston; however, the information is not specific. For example: LBA mentioned sending MM a "Box of Colours" in a letter to her husband (31 May 1833, BRBML, GEN MSS 85), for which she was thanked by John Bachman who informed her that Maria "had been making good use of them." JB to LBA, Sept 4, 1833, BRBML, GEN MSS 85.

61. On American paper: Howard Corning, ed., *Journal of John James Audubon, Made while Obtaining Subscriptions to his "Birds of America," 1840–1843*, foreword Francis H. Herrick (Cambridge, MA: Club of Odd Volumes and Business Historical Society, 1929), 60. JJA specifically requested "French water colour brushes of assorted sizes made in Paris" by "Vial Lebault, successor de Cherion, Fabricant de Pinceaus No 61" in JJA to VGA, Sept 9, 1833, Grinnell, "Some Audubon Letters," 124–30. On British products: "British artists' suppliers, 1650–1950," National Portrait Gallery. www.npg.org.uk/research/programmes/directory-of-suppliers/b/british-artists-suppliers-1650–1950-br.php For references to Arzoni, see family correspondence, for example, LBA to Robert Havell, Oct 4, 1835, HL, bMS Am 1482. On Arzoni family deaths: John Wilson, "Peculiar Symptoms Affecting an Entire Family, and Terminating in Death [May 10, 1842] *Medico-Chirurgical Trans* 25 (1842): 74–90; "Peculiar Symptoms Affecting an Entire Family, and Terminating in Death [May 10, 1842] *Royal Medico-Chirurgical Trans* 4, no. 87 (1842): 153–54; and "Peculiar Symptoms Affecting an Entire Family, and Terminating in Death [May 10, 1842] *The Chemist* 3 (1842): 190–92. Speculation about poisoning as the cause of death, specifically its relation to the production of ultramarine, appeared in *The Chemist*, 191. On American suppliers: Marian Sadtler Carson, "Early American Water Color Painting, *Antiques* 59, no. 1 (1951): 54, and Shelley, "Craft of American Drawing," 64–76. By 1841, pigments of similar quality were available in the United States.

62. In criticizing Lawrence, JJA stated his preference for northern light. The long

side of the Bachman home had a north-south orientation, permitting the light he preferred. For the pigments used on the original paintings: Shelley, "Drawing Birds," *Audubon's Aviary*, 117. For information on the Havell colors: Cathleen A. Baker, "Audubon's *The Birds of America*: A Technical Examination and Condition Survey of the Four-Volume Folio Set Belonging to Syracuse University," M. Fine Arts, Syracuse, 1985. Baker cites analysis in Neil Adair and Gregory Young, "The Analysis of Watercolour Pigments from Audubon's The Birds of America, Vol.1," *Journal of International Institute for Conservation-Canadian Group* 6 (Spring 1981): 15.

63. There are many instructional guides available on botanical painting. Most helpful: Siriol Sherlock, *Botanical Illustration: Painting with Watercolours* (London: B.T. Batsford, 2007); and *Exploring Flowers in Watercolour: Techniques and Images* (London: B.T. Batsford, 2000); and Margaret Stevens, *The Botanical Palette: Color for the Botanical Painter*, in association with the Society of Botanical Artists (New York: Harper Collins, 2007), 11, 14–20, 78, 84–90.

64. For positive assessments: Shuler, *Had I the Wings*, 144; Fries, *Elephant Folio*, 107–08.

65. For some idea of the profusion of plants in the Bachman garden: a list provided by John Bachman in *An Address Delivered Before the Horticultural Society of Charleston*, at the Anniversary Meeting, July 10, 1833 (Charleston: the Society, 1833); Waddell, *Bachman, Writings*, 41–69; a manuscript by Jennie Haskell Rose, "John Bachman at Home," in the possession of Mrs. John (Jane Grimball) Greely; and a letter written by MM to JB, Mar 11, 1841, CM, SC/A/1.

66. MM's painting of the Cherokee rose accompanies JJA's Townsend's Bunting, 1863.18.13, Audubon Collection, New-York Historical Society. Olson, *Audubon's Aviary*, 406.

67. JJA to JB, Apr 5, 1834, HL, bMS Am 1482.

68. According to Dwight, subscribers were demanding the finished sets they had been promised and, as Audubon's "work neared completion he had less and less time to spend on his drawings." See, *Audubon Watercolors and Drawings*, 44.

69. JJA to JB, Dec 27, 1835, Corning, *Letters*, 2:108–09.

70. Prospectus of "The Birds of America," as issued in 1828, when ten numbers of the original folio were engraved," Herrick, *Audubon the Naturalist*, 2: 386–88. Although the wording varied slightly when appended to the first volume of *Ornithological Biography*, the message was unchanged.

71. JJA to MM, [postscript in letter to JB] Jan 22, 1836, HL, bMS Am 1482. This letter appears in Corning without the postscript. JJA to JB, Jan 22, 1836, Corning, *Letters*, 2:109–14.

72. JJA to JB, Oct 20 and Dec 1, 1835, Corning, *Letters*, 2:96–100.

73. JJA to LBA, May 26, 1833, copied in a letter from LBA to VGA, June 9, 1833, BRBML, GEN MSS 85.

74. LBA to VGA, Dec 15, 1833, BRBML, GEN MSS 85.

75. MRA, "Reminiscences of Audubon," 336.

76. Prospectus, "The Birds of America," (1828), Herrick, *Audubon*, 2:387.

77. JB to JJA, Jan 22, 1836, BRBML, GEN MSS 85.

78. JJA to JB, March 7, 1836, Corning, *Letters*, 2:114–16.

79. JJA to JB, June 12, 1836, HL, bMS Am 1482.

80. Audubon inscribed this token of his affection as follows: "To Miss Maria Martin from her sincerely attached Friend & Servant, John J. Audubon, London, July 31st 1836." The book was Arthur Parsey, *The Art of Miniature Painting on Ivory* (London: Longman, Rees, Brown and Green, 1831). See, Mrs AG Rose to Ruthven Deane, Oct 7, 1916, CM, SC/A/1.

81. MM to JJA, Oct 28, 1836, CLB, *Pastor of St. John's*, 143–44.

82. Herrick, *Audubon*, 2:149–56 and JJA to JB Sept 10 1836, Oct 2 and 23, 1836, Corning, *Letters*, 2:130–37. A year later, JJA noted that there were only "8 species . . . as yet unknown." JJA to [JB], Oct 4, 1837, Corning, *Letters*, 2:180–85.

83. There are several references to Nuttall's specimens in contemporary monographs. On *Cleome serrulata,* see John Torrey (1796–1873), "Some account of a collection of plants made during a journey to and from the Rocky Mountains in summer of 1820, by Edwin P. James [1797–1861], M.D., Assistant Surgeon, U.S. Army," in *Annals of the Lyceum of Natural History of New York*, March 1826 (New York: James Seymore, 1828), 2:162, 167, and John Torrey and Asa Gray, *Flora of North America*; *containing abridged descriptions of all the known indigenous and naturalized plants growing north of Mexico, arranged according to the Natural System*, 2 vols. (New York: Wiley and Putnam, 1838–40), 1:ix, 121–22. On *Crataegus rivularis,* see *Flora of North America*, 1:464. The species of Cleome has been identified in *Audubon: Beyond Birds*, xiii.

84. For acknowledgement: JJA, *Ornithological Biography*, 4:xiv. ARC suggests MM's efforts were greatly underacknowledged in both the last volume of the elephant folio and in the octavo edition. See, "Audubon's Friend—Maria Martin," 29–51. Other plates that might contain work by MM and/or JWA are: 378 (Northern Hawk Owl/*Surnia ulula*); 380 (Boreal Owl/*Aegolius funereus*); 383 (Long-eared Owl/*Asio otus*); 388 (Bullock's Owl/*Icterus bullockii*, Tricolored Blackbird/*Agelaius tricolor*, Yellow-headed Blackbird/*Xanthocephalus xanthocephalus*); 389 (Red-cockaded Woodpecker/ *Leuconotopicus borealis*); 392 (Harris's Hawk/*Parabuteo unicinctus*); 400 (Smith's Longspur/*Calcarius pictus*, Lesser Goldfinch/*Spinus psaltria*, Black-headed Siskin/*Spinus notatus*, Western Tanager/*Piranga ludoviciana*, Hoary Redpoll/*Acanthis hornemanni*, Townsend's Bunting/*Emberiza townsendii*); 417 (Hairy Woodpecker/ *Leuconotopicus villosus*–subspecies *audubonii* and *harrisi*, American Three-toed Woodpecker/*Picoides dorsalis*); 420 (Red-winged Blackbird/*Agelaius phoeniceus*); 422 (Rough-legged Hawk/*Buteo lagopus*); 424 (House Finch/*Haemorhous mexicanus*, Gray-crowned Rosy-Finch/*Leucosticte tephrocotis*, Lazuli Bunting/*Passerina amoena*, Brown-headed Cowbird/*Molothrus ater*, Evening Grosbeak/*Coccothraustes vespertinus*, Fox Sparrow/*Passerella iliaca*); 426 (California Condor/*Gymnogyps califorianus*); 432 (Burrowing Owl/*Athene*

cunicularia, Little Owl/*Athene noctua*, Northern Pygmy-Owl/*Glaucidium gnoma*, Short-eared Owl/*Asio flammeus*); and 434 (Red-eyed Vireo/*Vireo olivaceus*, Least Flycatcher/*Empidonax minimus*, Small-headed Flycatcher/??, Black Phoebe/*Sayornis nigricans*, Blue Mountain Warbler/??, Western Wood-Peewee/*Contopus sordidulus*). JJA also glossed over who painted the botanicals in some eight plates pieced together in 1837 by Havell, specifically: plate 380 (Boreal owl/*Aegolius funereus*); plate 383 (Long-eared owl/*Asio otus*); plate 389 (Red-cockaded Woodpecker/*Leuconotopicus borealis*); plate 392 (Harris's hawk/*Parabuteo unicinctus*); plate 420 (Red-winged Blackbird/*Agelaius phoeniceus*); plate 422 (Rough-legged Hawk/*Buteo lagopus*); plate 424 (House Finch/ *Haemorhous mexicanus*, Gray-crowned Rosy-Finch/*Leucosticte tephrocotis*, Lazuli Bunting/*Passerina amoena*, Brown-headed Cowbird/*Molothrus ater*, Fox Sparrow/*Passerella iliaca*); and plate 426 (California Condor/*Gymnogyps californianus*). For updated nomenclature: Olson and Mazzitelli, "Listing of Audubon's Watercolors," 427–30.

85. JWA was only twice acknowledged formally for his artistic contributions: for painting the American bittern that appears in folio plate 337 and for the western duck that appears in folio plate 430. VGA is acknowledged but once for placing JJA's figure of the rock wren (*Salpinctes obsoletus*) in plate 360. See, JJA, *Ornithological Biography*, 4:298 and 443, and 5:253. The most recent assessment of their artistic role identifies VGA as contributing to a dozen original paintings and JWA to twenty-six originals. Olson and Mazzitelli, "Listing of Audubon's Watercolors," 419–30.

86. JJA to VGA, Nov 10, 1828, Corning, *Letters*, 1:70–73.

87. JJA to VGA, Nov 24, 1833, Corning, *Letters*, 1:268–70.

88. On colorists, in reference to Audubon and *Birds*: Christine E. Jackson, "The Painting of Hand-Coloured Zoological Illustrations," *Archives of Natural History* 38, no. 1 (2011): 42–43; and "The Materials and Methods of Hand-Colouring Zoological Illustrations," *ANH* 38, no. 1 (2011): 60–61.

89. JJA to JB, Nov 5, 1834, Corning, *Letters*, 2:47–49.

90. CLB, "Leaves from a Note-book" containing Civil War reminiscences, CLS, 51–236. Unpublished sketches depicting subjects from Say's *North American Entomology* are in the Charleston Museum Library. To compare MM's paintings with the originals, see, Thomas Say, *American Entomology or Descriptions of the Insects of North America*, illustrated by Coloured Figures from Original Drawings executed from Nature (Philadelphia: Samuel Augustus Mitchell, 1825), n.p. The descriptions in *American Entomology* were based on Say's journal, which was also published as the appendix in volume two of *A Narrative of an Expedition to the Source of St. Peter's River, Lake Winnepeek* [*Winnipeg*], *Lake of the Woods, &c., &c., performed in the year 1823*, by order of the Honorable J. C. Calhoun, Secretary of War, under the command of Stephen H. Long, Major, U.S.T.E., compiled from the Notes of Major Long, Messrs. Say, Keating and Calhoun, by William H. Keating (Philadelphia: H.C. Carey and I. Lea, 1824). For three pages on Maria Martin's role in painting for Audubon: Ford,

Audubon's Butterflies, 81–84. There is, however, an erroneously labeled tag accompanying her painting of the snout butterfly (*Libythea bachmani*; Kirtland, 1852). See, Herman Strecker, *Complete Synonymical Catalogue of Macrolepidopter with a full Bibliography* (Reading, PA: B. F. Owen, 1878), 105. Strecker's taxonomy gives priority to Kirtland's article in *Silliman's Journal of Science* 2 ed. XIII (1852), 336. On early entomology and illustration, specifically Thomas Say and his artists: Blum, *Picturing Nature*, 55–59, 78–79, 140–47, and 355–56, fn. 21; and Margaret Welch, *The Book of Nature: Natural History in the United States, 1825–1875* (Boston: Northeastern University Press, 1998), 20–21, 58–60. On European entomological illustration: David Knight, *Zoological Illustration, an essay towards a history of printed zoological pictures* (Folkestone, UK: Dawson Pubs., 1977), 118–25. On Titian Peale: Charlotte M. Porter, "The Lifework of Titian Ramsay Peale," *PAPS* 129, no. 3 (1985): 300–12.

91. On JJA's views of Peale's paintings and abilities: Brian W. Edington, *Charles Waterton: A Biography* (Cambridge: Lutterworth Press, 1996), 101. For JJA's view of Peale's ornithological paintings for Charles Lucien Bonaparte's *American Ornithology* (1825–1833): Herrick, *Audubon*, 1:329–330.

92. Charles Waterton, *Wanderings in South America, the North-West of the United States and the Antilles in the years 1812, 1816, 1820, and 1824* (London: J. Mawman, 1825). See pages 15, 113, 186, 187 and 258–59 on the aforementioned bug. For JJA's comment: Sept 17, 1826, Ford, *1826 Journal*, 150.

93. Neither Davidson nor Olson identifies entomological species, but they do both point out that the beetle added to plate 352 was removed prior to engraving. *Original Water-color Paintings*, n.p. and *Audubon's Aviary*, 410–31. For quotation: JJA to VGA, Dec 24, 1833, Herrick, *Audubon*, 2:61.

94. Jeannette E. Graustein, *Thomas Nuttall, Naturalist: Explorations in America, 1808–1841* (Cambridge, MA: Harvard University Press, 1967), 322; Herrick, *Audubon*, 2:149–55; Fries, *Double Elephant Folio*, 99; and Shuler, *Had I the Wings*, 142–43.

95. Evidence that Audubon painted the sheep moths is from a letter from T. W. Harris to E. Doubleday, Sept 27, 1840, in "Entomological Correspondence of Thaddeus William Harris," ed. Samuel H. Scudder, *Occasional Papers of the Boston Natural History Society* (Boston, 1869), 149–52. In it, he states: "As I was accidentally turning over the fourth volume of Audubon's Birds of America, a little while ago, I saw on plate 359 a figure of your *Hera chrysocarena*, together with another moth marked exactly like it, but of a rich ochre or Indian yellow color, and which I suspect is the other sex. Audubon was here at the time, and I asked him about these insects. He told me that he received them from Nuttall; and that those on plate 359, which we reëxamined together, were taken by Nuttall near or among the Rocky Mountains. Audubon further said that as soon as he had drawn and colored them he gave the original specimens to Mr. Bachman." (p. 149)

96. JB to LBA, Sept 4, 1833, BRBML, GEN MSS 85.

97. Edward Donovan, *Instructions for Collecting and Preserving Various Subjects of*

Natural History, as Quadrupeds, Birds, Reptiles, Fishes, Shells, Corals, Plants, Etc., together with a Treatise on the Management of Insects in their several states, selected from the best authorities (London: F.C. and J. Rivington, 1805), 37–38, 43. This book is listed in the 1811 Catalogue of the Library Society. CLS, Microfilm # D4746/D 4747.

98. Blum, *Picturing Nature*, 56.

99. Although justifiably criticized by Vladimir Nabokov (in "A World of Butterflies," December 28, 1952, *New York Times*) for missing John Abbot's contributions to American entomology, Ford provides useful information on his interactions in entomology. See, *Audubon's Butterflies*, 45–94.

100. JJA to JB, Apr 20, 1835, Corning, *Letters*, 2:63–71.

101. There is little information on André Melly. Audubon states that he married into the Rathbone family, and that is how he came to know him, but his name appears only sporadically in nineteenth-century entomological publications, and not as an author. He is mentioned as a prosperous merchant and father of George Melly, whose papers are in the Liverpool Record Office and Local History Service (Reference: 920 MEL), and there is an obituary in the *Courier*, Hobart, Tasmania August 20, 1851. National Library of Australia. Avail: nla.gov.au/nla.news-article2960360. On Audubon and Melly: Ford, *1826 Journal*, fn. 7, 58, 77, 112, 114–17, 120, 125, 127–28, 138, 146.

102. JB, "Address Delivered Before the Horticultural Society of Charleston at the Anniversary Meeting, July 10th, 1833," Waddell, *Bachman: Writings*, 54–56.

103. John Bachman, "Art. V.—The Insect World: Morals of Entomology etc" ("On the habits of Insects," *Southern Literary Journal* 2 [August 1836]:, 409–27) in William Gilmore Simms, *The Charleston Book: A Miscellany in Prose and Vers*e (Charleston, SC: Samuel Hart, Sen., 1845), 32. This article was published a number of times. See, for example, *De Bow's Review of Agricultural, Commercial, Industrial Progress and Resources*, 2nd n.s. 1, no. 4 (October 1858): 430–35.

104. JB, "Morals of Entomology," 36.

105. Ibid., 33–34, 39–40. Thomson's Seasons [Winter, Spring, Summer, and Autumn] were first published between 1726 and 1730, but they were reprinted many times, and Bachman could have read the American edition. See, *The Works of [William] Cowper and [James] Thomson, Letters and Poems never before published in this country of the Life of Thomson*, complete in one volume (Philadelphia: J. Grigg, 1832). Also, Thomas Seccombe, "James Thomson (1700–1748)," *Dictionary of National Biography* 56 (1885–1900).

106. Samuel Gaillard Stoney, ed., "Memoirs of Frederick Adolphus Porcher," *SCHM* 47 (1946): 218–19. For other evidence of Bachman's intemperate behavior regarding opposition to his word: "The Diary of John Hamilton Cornish, 1846–1860," R. Conover Bartram ed., *SCHM* 64 (1963): 78.

Chapter 4

1. According to geographers, place determines behavior no less than societal norms and expectations. That the Audubon-Bachman relationship impinged on the lives

of the women and children, especially in a context of domestic science, should not be surprising. See, Doreen Massey, *Space, Place and Gender* (Minneapolis: University of Minnesota Press, 1994), 166–71, 179–80, 249–69. Also, Gillian Rose, "Progress in Geography and Gender, Or Something Else," *PHG* 17, no. 4 (1993): 531–37; and "Engendering and Degendering," *PHG* 18, no. 4 (1994): 507–15; Linda McDowell, "Space, Place and Gender Relations: Part I: Feminist Empiricism and the Geography of Social Relations," *Progress in Human Geography* 17, no. 2 (1993): 157–79; and "Space, Place and Gender Relations: Part II. Identity, Difference, Feminist Geometries and Geographies," *PHG* 17, no. 3 (1993): 305–18; Kirsten Simonsen, "What Kind of Space in What Kind of Social Theory?" *PHG* 20, no. 4 (1996): 494–512; and Alison Blunt, "Cultural Geography: Cultural Geographies of Home," *PHG* 29, no. 4 (2005): 505–15. For a more historical approach: Alison Blunt and Gillian Rose, eds., *Writing Women and Space: Colonial and Postcolonial Geographies* (New York: Guilford Press, 1994); Lise Nelson and Joni Seager, eds., *A Companion to Feminist Geography* (Oxford: Blackwell Pub., 2005); and Deborah L. Rotman and Ellen-Rose Savulis, eds., *Shared Spaces and Divided Places: Material Dimensions of Gender relations and the American Historical Landscape* (Knoxville: University of Tennessee Press, 2003). For historical analyses of scientific work within a domestic context: Coen, "A Lens of Many Facets," 395–419; Livingstone, *Putting Science in its Place*, 21–24; Lindsay, "Intimate Inmates," 631–52; Shteir, *Cultivating Women, Cultivating Science*; and Shuler, *Had I the Wings*, 19–30, 131.

2. JB to JJA, Sept 14, 1833, CLB, *Pastor of Saint John's*, 135. Family members were aware of his feelings on this issue; his youngest daughter, Catherine [CLB], noted that he viewed emotional forms of worship as "not in accordance with Lutheran teaching and usage," and he even frowned on grieving. CLB, *Pastor of Saint John's*, 351–52, and letters JB to Jane Bachman in 1846, 196–97, 222–23. Also: Bost, *Lutheran Church in South Carolina*, 149, and "John Bachman and the Development of Southern Lutheranism," 347–53.

3. MM did not even repeat the most innocuous neighborhood gossip, and compared those who tended to engage in neighborhood chit-chat to the fictionalized Pringle family correspondence serialized in *Blackwood's Edinburgh Magazine* during the 1820s. MM to VGA, [Apr 22/28, 1840], WL-JDCA, Col. 170. For an essay on the author of "The Ayrshire Legatees; or, the correspondence of the Pringle family," see, Ian Duncan, "Altered States: Galt, Serial Fiction and the Romantic Miscellany," in *John Galt: Observations and Conjectures in Literature, History and Society*, ed. Regina Hewitt (Washington, DC: Lexington Books, 2012), 53–72.

4. CLB, *Pastor of St. John's*, 78–80.

5. JB to JJA, Sept 22, 1833, BRBML, GEN MSS 85.

6. JB, "Address at the Opening of the Synod of the Lutheran Church at Lexington Village, November 16, 1833," in Extract from the Minutes of the Tenth Session of the Evangelical Lutheran Synod of South Carolina and Adjacent States, November 17, 1833, and "Address of the President Delivered at the Opening of the Synod"

[Justification for founding the Southern Seminary, Thursday 20 November 1828] delivered at St. John's Church, Charleston, from the S.C. Synod Proceedings, 1828, p.17, JRCA-LTSS. On accomplishments and responsibilities: Bost, *Lutheran Church in South Carolina*, 181, 196; and "John Bachman and the Development of Southern Lutheranism," 207–08. Also: H. George Anderson, "Early National Period, 1790–1840," 112–14; 124–27; and August R. Suelflow and E. Clifford Nelson, "Following the Frontier, 1840–1875," in *Lutherans in North America*, 204. The theological seminary established in Pomaria, South Carolina, was relocated several times. Absences from synod were permitted only in cases of "urgent necessity," and JB would not have considered missing synod—even to talk birds with Audubon. For ministerial responsibilities and the constitution: Ernest L. Hazelius, *History of the American Lutheran Church, from its commencement in the year of our Lord 1685, to the year 1842* (Zanesville, OH: Edwin C. Church, 1846), 261–65, 296–300.

7. CLB, *Pastor of St. John's*, 90–91, and Shuler, *Had I the Wings*, 119. On Hazelius: J. C. Jensson, *American Lutheran Biographies; or, Historical Notices of over Three Hundred and Fifty leading men of the American Lutheran Church, from its establishment to the year 1890* (Milwaukee, WI: A. Houtkamp and Son, 1890), 320–23.

8. JB to JJA, Oct 15, 1833, BRBML, GEN MSS 85.

9. Ibid.

10. For the trials and tribulations of the journey to Charleston: Buchanan, *Audubon*, 313. On the arrival of JWA: Shuler, *Had I the Wings*, 117.

11. LBA to VGA, Nov 8, 1833, BRBML, GEN MSS 85.

12. Ibid. The Bachman household listed eight slaves in the 1830 census. A decade later, the Last Will and Testament drafted by Rebecca Martin listed sixteen enslaved men and women, and the Slave Schedules from the 1850 U.S. Census listed six slaves owned by John Bachman and ten slaves owned by Catherine Bachman. When these slaves were acquired is unclear. Some predated the arrival of the Audubon family in October 1833: Fifth Census of the United States taken in the year 1830, South Carolina Population Schedules, Reel 170, p. 140; "Appraisement of the Goods and Chattels of Mrs. Rebeca Martin," July 13, 1840, Charleston County Records, Inventories, Appraisements and Sales, vol. A, 1839–44, SCDAH; and Seventh Census of the United States taken in the year 1850, South Carolina, Slave Schedule, Dec 3–4, 1850, pp. 718 and 893. On recollections: Rose, "John Bachman at Home," April 17, 1927, CM, SC/A/1 and CLB, *Pastor of St. John's*, 356, 359. CLB states: "When the property of Mrs. Bachman's mother, Mrs. Martin, was divided among her children, the slaves, according to custom, selected their owners in the family." Also: JB to Rev JD, 1837, in which Bachman states: "My wife brought into my family four of her domestics, who were attached to her from infancy; they are her private property, are still with us, and are without exception, communicants of the Church."

13. JJA to W Swainson, Aug 22, 1830, and W Swainson to JJA, Aug 24 and 28, 1830, Herrick, *Audubon*, 2:101–03, 103–05.

14. Rose, "John Bachman at Home," CM, SC/A/1.

15. CLB, *Pastor of St. John's*, 186.

16. In 1827, Bachman described his wife as "one of the most fond and affectionate of wives," whose "life had been devoted to me" CLB, *Pastor of St. John's*, 56, and John Bachman's Journal, August 9–September 25, 1827, CM, SC/A/1. Details of their northern journey are also in his 1827 journal.

17. Writing VGA, he refers to finishing volume two on Nov 4, 1833, and mentions drawings in preparation as well as being "weakened & fatigued" in Nov 24, 1833. Corning, *Letters*, 1:263–67; 268–70.

18. JJA to R Havell, Nov 24, 1833, Corning, *Letters*, 1:263–67, 268–70 and 2:267–68.

19. JJA to VGA, Dec 7, 1833, Corning, *Letters*, 1:271–72.

20. Ibid., and Herrick, *Audubon*, 2:55–62. The transcription in Herrick is considerably longer than that in Corning, who added a notation saying the "letter ends abruptly as above without signature." For reference to MM: Herrick, *Audubon*, 2:61.

21. JJA to VGA, Dec 7, 1833, Corning, *Letters*, 1:271–72. The sedge wren (*Cistothorus platensis*) Audubon named Nuttall's short-billed marsh wren (plate 175) was the same species identified and classified by John Latham several decades earlier, and the seaside sparrow (*Ammodramus maritimus*) referred to as MacGillivray's finch (plate 355) had been identified and named by Alexander Wilson in 1811.

22. JJA to VGA, Dec 21, 1833, Corning, *Letters*, 1:272–77.

23. JJA to VGA, Dec 24, 1833, Herrick, *Audubon*, 2:55–62, specifically 2:61.

24. LBA to VGA, Dec 15, 1833, BRBML, GEN MSS 85.

25. JWA to JJA and LBA, Oct 21, 1834, BRBML, GEN MSS 85.

26. JB to JJA, Oct 20, 1832, CLB, *Pastor of St. John's*, 102–03 and JB to JJA, Mar 27, 1833, Deane, "Letters Bachman to Audubon," 182–85. The green-winged teal is depicted in folio plate 228; however, it was painted in 1822. Olson, *Audubon's Aviary*, 421. MM's painting of the green-winged teal is in private hands.

27. The Audubon-Waterton dispute has been described many times, but the most comprehensive is: Herrick, *Audubon*, 2:67–92, 142. Also: Shuler, *Had I the Wings*, 122–27; Stephens, *Science, Race and Religion*, 19–20; Fiero, "Audubon the Artist," 44–45; Dwight, *Audubon: Watercolors and Drawings*, 44; Streshinsky, *Audubon*, 288–89, 292–93. For a description of the experiments on whether turkey vultures detect prey by sight or smell: JJA, *Ornithological Biography*, 2:33–50.

28. Waterton, "On the 'Biography of Birds' of J. J. Audubon," *LMNH* 6 (1833): 215–18.

29. Waterton, "On the Faculty of Scent in the Vulture" *LMNH* 5 (1832): 233–41; "The Habits of the Carrion Crow" *LMNH* 6 (1833): 208–14; and "On the 'Biography of Birds' of J. J. Audubon," 215–18. On Rennie: Frederick G. Page, "James Rennie (1787–1867): Author, Naturalist and Lecturer," *ANH* 35, no.1 (2008): 128–42.

30. Waterton, "Remarks on Professor Rennie's Edition of Montagu's *Ornithological Dictionary*" *LMNH* 4 (1831): 516–20, was a critique of Audubon and his "Account of the Habits of the Turkey Buzzard (*Vultur aura*), particularly with the view of exploding the

opinion generally entertained of its extraordinary power of Smelling" *ENPJ* 2 (October–April 1826–1827), 172–84. James Rennie, *Ornithological Dictionary of British Birds by Colonel G. Montagu*, 2nd ed. with A Plan of Study, and Many New Articles and Original Observations (London: Hurst, Chance and Co., 1831), vii and lviii. Brian W. Edington notes how Rennie's omission rankled, and he discusses briefly the Rennie-Waterton dispute: *Charles Waterton: A Biography* (Cambridge, UK: Lutterworth Press, 1996), 124. Similarly, an earlier biography intimates the depth of antipathy between the two men, although with less focus on the issues: Julia Blackburn, *Charles Waterton, 1782–1865: Traveler and Conservationist* (London: Bodley Head, 1989), 108–10, 182.

31. Quoted phrases reflect general views. See, Waterton to George Ord, July 3, 1835, in Charles Waterton, *Essays on Natural History*, ed. with a life of the author by Norman Moore (New York: Scribner, Welford and Armstrong, 1871), 551–54. Letters to Ord spanning a thirty-year period are reprinted in the 1871 edition. Waterton, "On the 'Biography of Birds' of J. J. Audubon," 215.

32. Waterton, "Retrospective Criticism: The Gland on the Rump of Birds," *LMNH* 6 (1833): 276–77.

33. Waterton, "Retrospective Criticism," *LMNH* 6 (1833): 465.

34. VGA, "Retrospective Criticism: Mr. Audubon, Jun., in Reply to Mr. Waterton's Remarks (p. 215) on Audubon's Biography of Birds," *LMNH* 6 (1833): 369.

35. Waterton, "Retrospective Criticism," *LMNH* 6 (1833): 465.

36. VGA, "Retrospective Criticism," *LMNH* 6 (1833): 552.

37. Waterton, "Retrospective Criticism," *LMNH* 7 (1834): 66–74. See 69 and 71.

38. James Simson, *Charles Waterton: Naturalist* (Edinburgh: MacLahlan and Stewart; London: Ballière, Tyndall and Co., 1880), 7–8. [William] Perceval Hunter, "The Means by which the Vulture (*Vúltur Aúra* L.) traces its Food," *LMNH* 6 (1833), 83–84. For Waterton's response: "The Means by which the Turkey Buzzard (*Vúltur Aúra* L.) traces its Food," *LMNH* 6 (1833), 162–63; "Retrospective Criticism," *LMNH* 6 (1833): 464–68; and "Retrospective Criticism," *LMNH* 7 (1834), 66–71. On Hunter: H. S. Torrens, "William Perceval Hunter (1812–1878), forgotten English student of dinosaurs-to-be and of Wealden Rocks," in *Dinosaurs and Other Extinct Saurians: A Historical Perspective*, ed. R. T. J. Moody, E. Buffetant, D. Naish, and D. M. Martill, Geological Society Special Publication 343 (London: Geological Society, 2010), 31–47.

39. JJA to VGA, Dec 21, 1833, Corning, *Letters*, 2:272–77.

40. LBA to VGA, Dec 15, 1833, BRBML, GEN MSS 85.

41. JJA to VGA, Dec 21, 1833, Corning, *Letters*, 1:272–77.

42. Simson, *Charles Waterton*, 11.

43. See, JB, "Retrospective Criticism: "Remarks in Defence of [Mr. Audubon] the Author of the '[Biography of the] Birds of America," [VII. 66] by the Rev. John Bachman, Charleston, South Carolina" *LMNH* 7 (1834): 164–75, and "Remarks in Defence of the Author of the 'Birds of America." By the Rev. John Bachman, Charleston, South Carolina, Read before the Boston Society of Natural History, Feb. 5, 1834.," *BSNH* 1,

no. 1 (1834): 15–31. For reference to the Academy of Natural Sciences reading: JJA to VGA, Mar 9, 1834, Corning, *Letters*, 2:10–13. For a popular account of their experiment and others on the ability of vultures to identify prey with their olfactory organs, see Noah Striker, "The Buzzard's Nostril: Sniffing out a Turkey Vulture's Talents," in *The Thing with Feathers: The Surprising Lives of Birds and What They Reveal About Being Human* (New York: Riverhead Books, 2014), 53–57. Lastly, it is important to note that scientists still debate the issue of functionality in avian olfaction; however, electrophysiological experimentation has provided insights not available through behavioral studies. Bernice M. Wenzel, "Avian olfaction: then and now," *Journal of Ornithology* 148, Suppl 2 (June 14, 2007), doi.10.1007/s10336–007–0147-z

44. Waterton, "Retrospective Criticism: The Vulture's Nose (March 6 1834); Audubon's Claim to the Authorship of the Biography of Birds; Audubon and his Ornithology (January 19 1834)," *LMNH* 7 (1834): 276–83.

45. JB, "Retrospective Criticism," *LMNH* 7 (1834): 167–68.

46. In addition to the published account of the buzzard experiment: JB, "Notes on some Experiments made on the Buzzards of Carolina–*Cathartes aura* [Turkey Vulture] and [*Coragyps*] *C. atratus* [Black Vulture]," original manuscript in the papers of G. E. Manigault, Museum of Natural History, Charleston, CML, SC/A/1.

47. JJA to VGA, Dec 21, 1833, Corning, *Letters*, 2:272–77. For Waterton's criticism: "Gland on the Rump of Birds," 276. His view stood until Laurence Monroe Klauber, a twentieth-century herpetologist, credited Audubon with being the first to report rattlesnakes sometimes swallow their prey tail first. *Rattlesnakes: Their Habits, Life Histories and Influence on Mankind*, 2 vols. with a foreword by Henry W. Greene, 2nd. ed. (Berkeley: University of California Press, 1997), 1:657. At the same time, Klauber is less charitable when it comes to Audubon's other claims, specifically, his drawing of the rattlesnake with recurved fangs and his repetition of the "boot" myth in which subsequent wearers of a boot with a fang embedded in the leather die from a scratch from the fang. See 1:493–95.

48. Theodore Gill, "Biographical Memoir of John Edwards Holbrook, 1794–1871," Read before the National Academy of Science, April 22, 1903, 54. From 1826 until he died in 1837, J. Sera was an artist for Holbrook. See, Blum, *Picturing Nature*, 147–50.

49. *Lampropeltis elapsoides* (Holbrook, 1838) recognized by P. Uetz , TIGR Reptile Database in the Catalogue of Life Partnership: Catalogue of Life. Avail: www.gbif.org

50. JB to JJA, Jan 22, 1836, BRBML, GEN MSS 85. MM was credited with painting two snakes, the first—*Coluber elapsoides* (*Lampropeltis elapsoides*, Holbrook, 1838)—appeared as Fig. 28 in vol. 2, *North American Herpetology or a Description of the Reptiles Inhabiting the United States* 3 vols. (Philadelphia: J Dobson, 1838), 122; the second—*Coluber constrictor* (Lin.)—appeared in the second edition of Holbrook's revised series. Fig. 11, *North American Herpetology*, 5 vols. (Philadelphia: J. Dobson, 1842), 3:54.

51. JB, "Remarks in Defence of [Mr. Audubon]," 164.

52. Mark Catesby, *The Natural History of Carolina, Florida and the Bahama Islands*:

containing the figures of birds, beasts, fishes, serpents, insects, and plants: particularly, the forest-trees, shrubs, and other plants, not hitherto described, or very incorrectly figured by authors: together with their descriptions in English and French: to which, are added observations on the air, soil, and waters: with remarks upon agriculture, grain, pulse, roots, &c : to the whole, is prefixed a new and correct map of the countries (London, 1743), 3: 41, 42. On Catesby: Christoph Irmscher, *The Poetics of Natural History: From John Bartram to William James* (New Brunswick, NJ: Rutgers University Press, 1999), 163–65.

53. Waterton, "Retrospective Criticism," *LMNH* 7 (1834): 68.

54. For reference to LBA's role: JB to JJA, Mar 26, 1834, Stark Museum of Art (Orange, TX), Audubon Collection, 11.102/1.

55. LBA's educational background was unusual for women in the eighteenth century but her English father was a Unitarian dissenter with progressive ideas. Although some branches of the Bakewell family were Presbyterian, LBA's father counted dissenters among his closest friends, and he was buried in a Unitarian cemetery near Philadelphia. B. G. Bakewell, compiler, *The Family Book of Bakewell, Page Campbell* (Pittsburgh, PA: Wm. G. Johnston and Co., Printers and Stationers, 1896), 26–27. Also: DeLatte, *Lucy Audubon*, 152.

56. JB believed that the children of the elite were too self-indulgent and frivolous and would be a bad influence on his daughters. JB to VGA, Aug 5, 1843, CM, SC/A/1. For a list of works suggesting "that southerners in the 1830s had little faith in the efficacy of educating women": Anya Jabour, "'Grown Girls, Highly Cultivated': Female Education in an Antebellum Southern Family," *JSH* 64, no.1 (1998): 25–26. Also: Kim Tolley, "Science for Ladies, Classics for Gentlemen: A Comparative Analysis of Scientific Subjects in the Curricula of Boys' and Girls' Secondary Schools in the United States, 1794–1850," *HEQ* 36, no. 2 (1996): 133–37, 142–44.

57. For reference to stuffed and posed birds, pressed plants and insects, as well as garden curiosities in 1832: Payne, *Recollections of Seventy Years*, 24.

58. The German Friendly Society School opened during a period when similar schools were being founded in northern states; however, the latter took in paying students only. Students without means were apparently uncommon attendees in the north. J. M. Opal, "Exciting Emulation: Academies and the Transformation of the Rural North, 1780s–1820s," *JAH* 91, no. 2 (2004): 445–70. Although there were two men named Jacob Martin, the man who belonged in 1803 must have been Maria's father, as he was born in 1763; the other Jacob Martin was born in 1785. For the membership list, the school in general, and the girl's school: Gongaware, *German Friendly Society*, 59–63; Report of School Committee, April 3 and Dec 18, 1822, and JB, Report of Committee on the Female School, July 1, 1829, German Friendly Society Records, Collection # 0019, MNAL.

59. JB, Address Before the Horticultural Society of Charleston, July 1833, Waddell, *Bachman: Writings*, 58.

60. JB to LBA, Aug 26, 1835, BRBML, GEN MSS 85; JB to JJA, Oct 2, 1837, CM, SC/A/1; and JB to JJA, Aug 16, 1837, CLB, *Pastor of St. John's*, 152–53.

61. *Southern Agriculturalist and Register of Rural Affairs* [1828–1839] 8, no. 4 (April 1835): 189–96 and 8, no. 6 (June 1835): 286–91. CLB claimed this "was really the joint work of all the elder members of the family" in "Leaves from a Notebook: Civil War Reminiscences, 1862–65," CLS, 51–236. For further confirmation: "Catalogue of Phaenogamous Plants and ferns native or naturalized found growing in the vicinity of Charleston, (S.C.)," *Southern Agriculturalist and Register of Rural Affairs* [1828–1839] 8 (April 1835): 189; and "Vindication of Rev. Dr. John Bachman, of Charleston, S.C. in Answer to Rev. E. Hutter, in Regard to an Article Published in the 'Lutheran and Missionary,' of the 27th of July, 1865, Published by a Personal Friend, 1868, 300–16," Waddell, *Bachman: Writings*, 312.

62. JJA to MM, Apr 6, 1834, Corning, *Letters*, 2: 21–25. Southern women lived in a world dominated by men. The extent to which women participated in that world varied according to time, place, and class. For most of them, life was dull, whether from the planter elite or the professional classes. See, Virginia Gearhart Gray, "Activities of Southern Women: 1840–1860," *SAM* 27 (1928): 264–79; Julia Cherry Spruill, "'Conjugal Felicity' and Domestic Discord," in *Women's Life and Work in the Southern Colonies* (Chapel Hill: University of North Carolina Press, 1938), 163–84; Guion Griffis Johnson, "Family Life," in *Ante-bellum North Carolina: A Social History* (Chapel Hill: University of North Carolina Press, 1937) all reprinted in *Unheard Voices: The First Historians of Southern Women*, ed. Anne Firor Scott (Charlottesville: University of Virginia Press, 1993). By contrast, LBA enjoyed her independence, and said so. In 1829, she offered to give it up if her husband could assure her that he did not need her financial assistance. She proposed selling one of her pianos, which would not be needed if she joined him in England rather than teaching students at $12.50 per month, but she begged him to quit vacillating between having her company or having her income. LBA to JJA, Sept 27, 1829, BRBML, GEN MSS 85, and DeLatte, *Lucy Audubon*, 91.

63. Comments in correspondence and information on reading materials suggest familiarity with the classics, and this is unsurprising as the Bachman girls attended the German Friendly Society School where such books were available. Gongaware, *German Friendly Society*, 109. For references to Rhea, Mentor, and others: MM to Julia Bachman, June 5, 1845, CM, SC/A/1 and EB(A) to JWA and MB(A), [March 1840?], BRBML, GEN MSS 85. MM owned a copy of *Calliope: A Collection of Poems, Legendary and Pathetic by various authors* (Baltimore, MD: Edward J. Coke, 1814), CML, SC/A/.

64. Friendly Repository and Keepsake of Mary Eliza Bachman, WL-JDCA, Doc.722, and Jane Bachman's Keepsake Album, c. 1832–1836, Private Collection, Harlan Greene, Charleston, S.C.

65. Grinnell, "Recollections of Audubon Park," 373.

66. Ibid.

67. MM recounts observing herons and ibises in a secluded pond in: MM to JJA, July 12, 1832, BRBML, GEN MSS 85.

68. *Essays on School Keeping: Comprising Observations on the Qualifications of Teachers, on School Government, and the Most Approved Methods of Instruction in the Various branches of a Useful Education*, by an experienced teacher [Allison Wrifford] (Philadelphia, PA: John Grigg, 1831), 78.

69. Sally Gregory Kohlstedt, *Teaching Children Science: Hands-On Nature Study in North America, 1890–1930* (Chicago: University of Chicago Press, 2010), 13–27.

70. For references to memorized "speeches and dialogues" in scholars' examinations at the German Friendly Society school: Minutes, 1822–29, MNAL, Collection 0019, Mss 0151, Box 4. For pedagogical preferences at the seminary begun by JB: Stephen S. Hahn, "Lexington's Theological Library, 1832–1859," *SCHM* 80, no.1 (1979): 39. LBA mentions working in the parlor with five young people in: LBA to VGA, Jan 26, 1834, BRBML, GEN MSS 85. For the role of parlors: Sally Gregory Kohlstedt, "Parlors, Primers, and Public Schooling: Education for Science in Nineteenth-Century America," *Isis* 81 (1990): 425–34.

71. In 1845, the Bachman children were using books from [Lyman] Cobb's School Book series and the Grimshaw history series; however, these authors did not write texts on natural history. MM to Harriet Bachman Haskell, May 27, 1845, CM, SC/A/1.

72. Wrifford, *Essays on School Keeping*, 35–39.

73. The first issue of *Parley's Magazine for Children and Youth* (Boston: Lilly, Wait and Co.) appeared in March 1833, and JJA was in an article on the passenger pigeon in one of the May issues. See p. 94. While most of the poetry found in the girl's "Keepsake albums" can be easily identified as written by major poets of the seventeenth to nineteenth centuries, there are a number of poems and narrative excerpts that only appeared in popular magazines, and they were published without attribution. For example: "The Tomb of a Woman" and "Affection–Her Smile and Her Tear" from the *American Farmer* (1826) appear in Eliza Bachman's Keepsake Album; and "Song" from *The Juvenile Keepsake* (1829) and "Love Stanzas" from the *Monthly Traveler, or Spirit of the Periodical Press* (183) appear in Jane Bachman's Keepsake Album. See, Friendly Repository and Keepsake of Mary Eliza Bachman," WL-JDCA, Doc.722 and Jane Bachman's Keepsake Album, c. 1832–1836, Private Collection, Harlan Greene, Charleston, SC.

74. Sanders and Anderson Jr., *Natural History Investigations*, 36–45.

75. Stephen Elliott, *A Sketch of the Botany of South Carolina and Georgia*, 2 vols. (Charleston, SC: J. R. Schenck, 1821 and 1824). The second volume covers flowering plants, whereas volume one is devoted mainly to grasses and trees. For a brief reference to the format of Elliott's book: George A. Rogers, Vivian Rogers-Price, and Daniel V. Hagan, "André Michaux's Influence on Stephen Elliott's *A Sketch of the Botany of South Carolina and Georgia*," *Castanea* 69 (2004): 218–19.

76. Friendly Repository and Keepsake of Mary Eliza Bachman, WL-JDCA, Doc. 722, 9.

77. JJA to JB, Mar 13, 1834, PU, C0006. On drawing and botany: Blum, *Picturing Nature*, 3–18, 121, 160, 344–45.

78. JJA to MM, Apr 6, 1834, Corning, *Letters*, 2:21–25.

79. JJA to JB, 25 Aug 1834, in *John James Audubon: Writings and Drawings*, intro. by Christoph Irmscher (New York: Library of America, 1999), 825–29.

80. Pages detailing how to paint moss rose buds and the dog rose (as well as illustrations) are among the memorabilia owned by Mrs. John (Jane Grimball) Greely, Charleston.

81. JB to JJA, Oct 2, 1837 and MM to JB, Mar 11, 1841, CM, SC/A/1; JJA to JB, Oct 31, 1837, Corning, *Letters*, 2:187–89.

82. JB to Lewis Gibbes, June 30, 1834, CM, SC/A/1.

83. For reference to the girls' role in making the herbarium: "Vindication of Rev. Dr. John Bachman, of Charleston, S.C. in Answer to Rev. E.W. Hutter," Waddell, *Bachman: Writings*, 312, and Mary Eliza Bachman Audubon, Keepsake Book. There is a pressed and labeled sprig of wintergreen (*Chimaphila*) preserved in her book. WL-JDCA, Doc. 722, 81.

84. JB to JJA, Jan 15, 1835, BRBML, GEN MSS 85.

85. The volumes by Bewick and Yarrell were in the package containing Brookshaw's manual. Volume two of the *Ornithological Biography* was added to their collection by the end of 1834. JJA to JB, Nov 19 and Dec 3, 1834, Corning, *Letters*, 2:49–52 and 52–55.

86. JB to JWA, Aug 1837, CLB, *Pastor of St. John's*, 151–52.

87. JB to Mrs. H [a parishioner], Jan 1852, CLB, *Pastor of St. John's*, 283–87.

88. MM to VGA, Apr 9, 1852, CM, SC/A/1.

89. MM to CLB, Mar 11, 1841, CM, SC/A/1.

90. JB, *An Address on Education*, delivered on the Day of the Laying of the Corner-Stone of Newberry College, July 15, 1857 (Charleston, SC: James & Williams, 1857), 280–98; Waddell, *Bachman: Writings*, 291.

91. JJA to JB, Sept 15, 1835, Corning, *Letters*, 2:84–90. JJA notes that Maria Rebecca had written John Woodhouse fifty-two times since their departure from Charleston. These letters have not been found.

92. LBA to JJA, Nov 8, 1831, and LBA to VGA, Dec 15, 1833, BRBML, GEN MSS 85.

93. As Wyatt-Brown points out, marriage was a means to improve or at least maintain social status among wealthy Southerners, and many parents preferred that their children marry cousins rather than take a chance with outsiders. The marriages of the Bachman girls and the Audubon boys did conform to Southern patterns in one way though. It was common for sisters from one family to marry brothers of another. Wyatt-Brown, *Southern Honor*, 217–19.

94. JJA to LBA, May 28, 1833, BRBML, GEN MSS 85.

95. In 1820, he stated, "I confess I never think of churches without feeling sick at heart at the sham and show of their professors. To repay evil with kindness is the

religion I was taught to practice, and this will forever be my rule." Ford, *Audubon, By Himself*, 133. His baptism is noted in Ford, *Audubon*, 424. On Audubon's Philadelphia experiences: Buchanan, *Audubon*, 10; Rhodes, *Making of an American*, 6–7.

96. LBA to JJA, Mar 22, 1829, and LBA to VGA and JWA, May 15, 1830, BRBML, GEN MSS 85.

97. JB to JJA, Oct 15, 1833, BRBML, GEN MSS 85.

98. JB to LBA, Aug 26, 1835, BRBML, GEN MSS 85.

99. JB was an avid nature lover, collecting all kinds of specimens from an early age. However, when he became seriously committed to original research is less easy to determine. In retrospect, he claimed an affinity for natural history even as a child, but his actual record of accomplishment was meagre until after Audubon. Increasingly productive, most of his articles and monographs appeared between 1836 and 1854. In 1854, the final volume of the imperial edition of *The Quadrupeds of North America* appeared. Johnson, *Scientific Interests in the Old South*, 87, 138–140, 142–143, 149; Numbers and Numbers, "Science in the Old South," 161–84; Bost, "John Bachman: Man of Faith, Man of Science," *LQ* 2, no.2 (1988): 216; Stephens, *Science, Race and Religion*, 18–38, 307–09; Waddell, *Bachman: Writings*, 359–69.

100. JWA to VGA, Apr 6, 1834, BRBML, GEN MSS 85.

101. JJA to JB, July 20, 1835, Corning, *Letters*, 2:75–81.

102. Ibid., and Dec 1, 1835, Corning, *Letters*, 2:75–81; 102–06.

103. JJA to JB, Dec 27, 1835, Corning, *Letters*, 2:108–09.

104. JJA to JB, Mar 9, 1836, Corning, *Letters*, 2: 117–19.

105. Their trip is mentioned in JJA to JB, Mar 9 and June 12, 1836, Corning, *Letters*, 2: 117–19; 121–25. Their activities are described in VGA and JWA to LBA and JJA, Apr 25 and 30, 1836, BRBML, GEN MSS 85.

106. These views on marriage were expressed by Martin Luther in *That Parents Should Neither Compel Nor Hinder the Marriage of Their Children and That Children Should not become Engaged without their Parents' Consent* (April 1524). See, Martin Brecht, *Martin Luther: Shaping and Defining the Reformation, 1521–1532* (Stuttgart: Calwer Verlag, 1986; Minneapolis: Augsburg Fortress, 1994), 92–93.

107. JB to JJA, Oct 22, 1836, BRBML, GEN MSS 85.

108. JWA to VGA, Feb 17, 1837, BRBML, GEN MSS 85.

109. JJA to JB, Mar 3, 1837, Corning, *Letters*, 2:148–51; JB to JJA, Apr 8 and 24, 1837, BRBML, GEN MSS 85; and JB to JJA May 14, 1837, CLB, *Pastor of St. John's*, 148–49.

110. MM to JJA, Oct 28, 1836, CLB, *Pastor of St. John's*, 143–44.

111. Within months of his departure, JJA suggested MM assist collecting and preserving ornithological specimens. JJA to JB, Nov 5, 1834, Corning, *Letters*, 2:47–49. On other activities: JJA to JB, Feb 24, 1837, Corning, *Letters*, 2:145–48.

112. These sketches belong to Mrs. John (Jane Grimball) Greely. On the verso of one is a pencil drawing of a hacienda visited while in Cuba.

113. JB to JJA, Apr 16, 1838, MNAL, MSS 66. There is a photocopy of the original letter and a transcription; I have been unable to determine which repository holds the original.

114. JB refers to causing offense by "smelling too strong of the creature" in: JB to JJA and JWA, Apr 8, 1837, BRBML, GEN MSS 85.

115. The drawings appear in "Description of a New Species of Hare Found in South Carolina," and "Some Remarks on the Genus *Sorex* [Shrews], with a Monograph of the North American Species," *Journal of the Academy of Natural Sciences of Philadelphia*, 7, pt. 2 (1837), 282–361, pls 15, 16; 362–402, and pl. 23. The article was "read" on May 10, 1836. For sketch of the muskrat foot: JB to VGA, Feb 7, 1846, BRBML, GEN MSS 85. The best Bachman could muster when it came to drawing were stick men: JB to JJA, Apr 16, 1838, typescript, MNAL, MS 66.

116. JB to JJA, Sept 30, 1836, CLB, *Pastor of St. John's*, 142–43.

Chapter 5

1. MM to Mary Elizabeth and Amelia Davis, July 23, 1839, CM, SC/A/1. Shuler, *Had I the Wings*, 170–71.

2. Thomas H. Keels, *Philadelphia Graveyards and Cemeteries* (Charleston, SC: Arcadia Pub., 2004), 21–34.

3. MM to EB(A), Aug 1, 1839, CM, SC/A/1.

4. There are many references to such afflictions in family correspondence. For information on common diseases in the antebellum South: Peter McCandless, *Slavery, Disease, and Suffering in the Southern Lowcountry* (Cambridge: Cambridge University Press, 2011), 1–148; K. David Paterson, "Disease Environments of the Antebellum South," in *Science and Medicine in the Old South*, ed. Ronald L. Numbers and Todd L. Savitt (Baton Rouge: Louisiana State University Press, 1989), 152–65; and Joseph Ioor Waring, *A History of Medicine in South Carolina, 1825–1900* (Columbia: South Carolina Medical Association, 1967), 30–58.

5. Harriet Bachman to JB, Aug 8, 1827, CM, SC/A/1.

6. Harriet Bachman to Jane Bachman, May 24, 1846, CM, SC/A/1.

7. Shuler, *Had I the Wings*, 138.

8. JB to JJA, Oct 17, 1839, BRBML, GEN MSS 85.

9. MM to Mary Elizabeth Davis, July 23, 1839, CM, SC/A/1.

10. MM to EB(A), Apr 24, 1840, CM, SC/A/1.

11. VGA to JJA, Dec 14, 1839, BRBML, GEN MSS 85.

12. JJA to MM, Apr 6, 1834, Corning, *Letters*, 2:21–25.

13. LBA to VGA and JWA, June 30, 1839, (from Edinburgh), PU, C0006.

14. VGA to JJA, May 2, 1831 and LBA to JJA and JWA, October 9, 1836, BRBML, GEN MSS 85. Also: Ford, *Audubon*, 338, 344, 350.

15. LBA to JJA and JWA, Oct 9, 1836, BRBML, GEN MSS 85; Ford, *Audubon*, 338, 344, 350.

16. JJA and LBA [in a postscript] to Benjamin Phillips, June 23, 1839, PU, C0006 .

17. The Audubon home was located south of Canal Street between Broadway and Lafayette. See, "Schirmer Diary," *SCHM* 69, no. 4 (October 1968): 266; and VGA to JJA, Dec 14, 1839, BRBML, GEN MSS 85.

18. On JB: CLB, *Pastor of St. John's*, 26. On Eliza: VGA to JJA, Mar 2, 1840 and VGA to JWA, Mar 2/Apr 7, 1840, BRBML, GEN MSS 85. On physicians: Amory Coffin and W. H. Geddings, *Aiken; or Climatic Cure* (Charleston, SC: Walker, Evans and Cogswell, 1869), 46–47.

19. EB(A) to Mary Elizabeth Davis, Jan 21, 1840, CM, SC/A/1. For observations made six months earlier: MM to Mary Elizabeth Davis, July 23, 1839, CM, SC/A/1.

20. Baby Harriet remained with Lucy Audubon in New York. For references to familial arrangements: *MRB*(A) to VGA, May 4, 1840, APSL, B Au 25. For quoted passage: LBA to the Phillips family Mar 9, 1840, PU, C0006.

21. JJA to VGA Feb 23 1840, Corning, *Letters*, 2: 233–36. On her treatment: LBA to JWA and *MRB*(A), Apr 18, 1840, BRBML, GEN MSS 85; JB to VGA, May 8, 1840, CM, SC/A/1; VGA to JWA June 16, 1840 and JWA to family in New York, July 1, 1840, BRBML, GEN MSS 85.

22. Coffin and Geddings, *Climatic Cure*, 8–9; 24–32. Coffin and Geddings identify three climatic variables affecting consumptives: temperature, "hygrometric condition" or dryness/wetness, and sudden change in barometric pressure. JJA to VGA, Apr 28, 1840, WL-JDCA, Col. 170.

23. JB to VGA, May 8, 1840, CM, SC/A/1.

24. JJA to VGA, May 7, 1840, Corning, *Letters*, 2:269–71.

25. MM to EB(A), Apr 24, 1840, CM, SC/A/1.

26. James Ewell, *The Medical Companion or Family Physician*: Treating the Diseases of the United States, with their symptoms, causes, cure, and means of prevention: Common cases in surgery, as Fractures, Dislocations, etc, the Management and Diseases of Women and Children, A Dispensatory for Preparing Family Medicines, and a Glossary Explaining Technical Terms, 7th ed. (Washington, 1827), 755–69. On dietary suggestions for the sick: 769–78. Quoted passage: 756. Ewell's particular melding of religion and medicine is discussed in Claire Hoertz Badaracco, *Prescribing Faith: Medicine, Media, and Religion in American Culture* (Waco, TX: Baylor University Press, 2007), 30–35.

27. Shuler provides an excellent account of the winter of 1840, but interprets "operations" as indicative of bleeding rather than bowel movements, even though her physicians referred to ulcerations of the bowel and the fact that the tubercle bacilli affect the bowel as well as the lungs. *Had I the Wings*, 175–80. See, Roger S. Mitchell and Leonard J. Bristol, "Intestinal Tuberculosis: An Analysis of 346 Cases Diagnosed by Routine Intestinal Radiography on 5,529 Admissions for Pulmonary Tuberculosis, 1929–49," *AJMS* 227, no. 3 (1954): 241–49 and G. J. Burke and S. A. Zafar, "Problems in Distinguishing Tuberculosis of Bowel from Crohn's Disease in Asians," *BMJ* 4 (July

1975): 395–97. For a less technical overview: Mark Caldwell, *The Last Crusade: The War on Consumption, 1862–1954* (New York: Atheneum, 1988), 7–9.

28. MM to EB(A), Apr 24, 1840, CM, SC/A/1.

29. JB to VGA, May 8, 1840, CM, SC/A/1.

30. JB to VGA, May 10, 1840, CM, SC/A/1.

31. JB to VGA, June 6, 1840, CM, SC/A/1. During this period, most people died at home, and Maria Martin and her female kin were as familiar as any with what that meant. For example, John Bachman's mother spent her last years with her son before dying in February 1838. Her death is noted in "The [Jacob Frederic] Schirmer Diary," *SCHM* 69, no. 3 (July 1968): 204. On this topic more generally: Emily K. Abel, *The Inevitable Hour: A History of Caring for Dying Patients in America* (Baltimore, MD: Johns Hopkins Press, 2013), 8–21.

32. He arrived on April 21. MM to EB(A), Apr 24, 1840, CM, SC/A/1. Audubon left Charleston on June 6, 1840, according to a letter owned by the William Coleman Family. See, Shuler, *Had I the Wings*, 180.

33. Shuler, *Had I the Wings*, 168–69. JJA to JB, Jan 2, 1840, Corning, *Letters*, 2:228–31.

34. JB to JJA, Jan 13, 1840, CLB, *Pastor of St. John's*, 181–82.

35. JJA to JB, Feb 15, 1840, Corning, *Letters*, 2:231–33.

36. JJA to VGA, May 10, 1840, CM, SC/A/1.

37. JB to VGA, June 25, 1840. This letter is from a private collection. Belonging to the William Coleman Family (Charleston), the only copy available is a transcript made by Jay Shuler. MNAL, MSS 66.

38. VGA, LBA, and EB(A) to JWA, Apr 23, 1840, BRBML, GEN MSS 85. In this letter, there is a reference to four previous letters in which the same request was made. For reference to the nurse: LBA to JWA, July 8, 1840, BRBML, GEN MSS 85.

39. LBA to JJA, Mar 22, 1837, BRBML, GEN MSS 85.

40. On MM and probating her mother's will: JB to VGA, June 6, 1840, CM, SC/A/1. Will of Rebecca Martin, probated May 25, 1840, St 0529, Probate Court, Charleston County Will Books, Vol. 42, pp. 137–38; Appraisement of the Goods and Chattels of Mrs. Rebecca Martin, July 13, 1840, Charleston County Records, Vol. A, 1839–44; Bills of Sale, Samuel Wilson, executor for Rebecca Martin, [ten slaves] Miscellaneous Records, S 213003, v. 005W, p. 247, 263, and 525. SCDHA.

41. VGA to JWA, Aug 23, 1840, BRBML, GEN MSS 85.

42. VGA and LBA to JWA, July 8, 1840; JJA and LBA to JWA, July 12, 1840; LBA and VGA to JWA, Aug 2, 1840, BRBML, GEN MSS 85.

43. LBA to JWA, July 31, 1840, BRBML, GEN MSS 85.

44. Waring, *History of Medicine*, 235–38, 246–47.

45. It has been argued that Southern physicians continued to prescribe calomel for a longer period and to a greater degree than northern doctors. John Harley Warner, "The Idea of Southern Medical Distinctiveness: Medical Knowledge and Practice in

the Old South," in *Science and Medicine in the Old South*, 181–82. Mercury was viewed positively by professors in Charleston: Henry R. Frost advised it for several conditions, saying it was particularly efficacious for "pulmonic affectations," and "useful in the diseases of children." Henry R. Frost, *Syllabus of A Course of Lectures on the Materia Medica, delivered in the Medical College of the State of South Carolina* (Charleston: Daniel J. Dowling, 1834), 19. On Ria's reaction to mercury: JWA to VGA, July 1, 1840, and VGA to JJA, July 20, 1840, BRBML, GEN MSS 85.

46. On the blue pills: LBA to JWA, June 14, 1840, BRBML, GEN MSS 85. Known as *Pilulae hydrargyri*, the Edinburgh College made them to a specific formula, differing from those made elsewhere. James Rennie, *A New Supplement to the latest Pharmacopoeias of London, Edinburgh, Dublin, and Paris*, forming a complete Dispensatory, Conspectus, and Dictionary of Medical Chemistry, giving all the old and new names, including the new French and American medicines, and Poisons; with Symptoms, Treatments and Tests . . . 4th ed. (London: Baldwin and Cradock, 1837), 320.

47. LBA to JWA, Aug 10, 1840; VGA to JWA, Aug 12, 1840; BRBML, GEN MSS 85. For the medical attributes of benne leaf and directions for making a "waistcoat" with cinchona: Ewell, *Medical Companion or Family Physician*, 220, 643.

48. EB(A) to JWA and *MRB*(A), Aug 12, 1840, BRBML, GEN MSS 85.

49. VGA to JWA, Aug 17, 1840 and JWA to VGA, Sept 2 and 9, 1840, BRBML, GEN MSS 85.

50. For the gendered nature of choices made by consumptives seeking treatment, namely, that men tended to travel while women stayed home: Sheila M. Rothman *Living in the Shadow of Death: Tuberculosis and the Social Experience of Illness in American History* (New York: Basic Books, 1994). Rothman states: "Unlike male invalids of her social class and background, Deborah [Fiske] did not undertake a long voyage for health; instead, throughout her adult life she took her cure at home" (107). Also: Jeanne Abrams, "On the Road Again: Consumptives Traveling for Health in the American West, 1840–1925," *GPQ* (2010): 271–85.

51. There are few studies of Harlan, but Herrick discusses his relationship with JJA in a few places, while Lester Stephens does the same for Harlan and JB. Some of Harlan's contributions to natural history are listed in Elliott Coues and Joel Asaph Allen, *Material for a Bibliography of North American Mammals* prepared by Theodore Gill and Elliott Coues, Extracted from the 11th volume of the Final Reports of the [United States Geological and Geographical] Survey, Appendix B of the Monographs of North American Rodents (Washington: Government Printing Office, 1877), 985–86. See specifically: "Art. III Audubon's Ornithology," *AQR* 18 (1835): 38–62. Also: Herrick, *Audubon*, 1:328–29; Stephens, *Science, Race and Religion*, 25, 58; and Shuler, *Had I the Wings*, 63, 112.

52. VGA to JJA, Sept 19, 1840, BRBML, GEN MSS 85.

53. Mrs. M.H. Harlan to LBA, Apr 23, 1838, BRBML, GEN MSS 85.

54. Shuler, *Had I the Wings*, 128–30, 137–38.

55. JB to VGA, MM, and EB(A), Oct 27, 1840, CM, SC/A/1.

56. VGA to JWA, Nov 7, 1840, BRBML, GEN MSS 85. On Vanderburgh: William Harvey King, *History of Homoeopathy and Its Institutions in America*, Their Founders, Benefactors, Faculties, Officers, Hospitals, Alumni, etc., with a Record of Achievements of its Representatives in the World of Medicine (New York: Lewis Pub. Co., 1905), 79–84. Although Vanderburgh became the president of the Homeopathic Society in 1865, he does not figure in Haller's books on homeopathy or in Rothstein's study of nineteenth-century medical practitioners. J. S. Haller Jr., *The History of American Homeopathy: The Academic Years, 1820–1935* (New York: Haworth Press, 2005) and *The History of American Homeopathy: From Rational Medicine to Holistic Health Care* (New Brunswick, NJ: Rutgers University Press, 2009); William G. Rothstein, *American Physicians in the Nineteenth Century: From Sects to Science* (Baltimore, MD: Johns Hopkins University Press, 1972).

57. JWA to VGA, Dec 13, 1840. On examinations: LBA to EB(A), Jan 31, 1841, BRBML, GEN MSS 85.

58. VGA to JWA and LBA, Jan 9 and 24, 1841, BRBML, GEN MSS 85.

59. LBA to VGA, Feb 24, 1841, BRBML, GEN MSS 85. [J. G. F. Wurdemann], *Notes on Cuba*, Containing An Account of Its Discovery and Early History; A Description of the Face of the Country, Its Population, Resources, and Wealth; Its Institutions, and the Manners and Customs of its Inhabitants, With Directions to Travelers Visiting the Island by a Physician (Boston: James Munroe and Co., 1844), 124. For a short note on Wurdemann: Waring, *A History of Medicine in South Carolina*, 318.

60. JWA to VGA and EB(A)/MM, Mar 10, 1841, BRBML, GEN MSS 85.

61. VGA to LBA and JWA, Dec 23, 1840; VGA to LBA and JWA, Jan 17, 1841; VGA to JWA and LBA, Jan 24, 1841, BRBML, GEN MSS 85. On the contents of elixirs: J. U. Lloyd, *Elixirs, Their History, Formulae, and Methods of Preparation*, 2nd ed. (Cincinnati, OH: Robert Clarke and Co., 1883), 166–68. On lycopodium (club moss) and bryonia (wild hops): Edward Hamilton, *The Flora Homoeopathica; or Illustrations and Descriptions of the Medicinal Plants used as Homoeopathic Remedies*, 2 vols. (London: H. Bailliere, 1852), 1:99–109, 2:28–32.

62. VGA to JWA and LBA, Nov 20 and 28, 1840, BRBML, GEN MSS 85.

63. JJA to VGA, Feb 24, 1841, BRBML, GEN MSS 85.

64. JB to MM, Oct 27, 1840, CM, SC/A/1.

65. JJA to VGA, Jan 7, 1841, APSL, B Au25.

66. VGA to Audubon family, Jan 17, 1841, BRBML, GEN MSS 85.

67. JWA to VGA, Feb 7, 1841, BRBML, GEN MSS 85.

68. Ibid.

69. VGA to JJA, Feb 12, 1841, BRBML, GEN MSS 85.

70. MM to JJA and LBA, Feb 12, 1841, BRBML, GEN MSS 85.

71. MM to JJA, Mar 4, 1841, BRBML, GEN MSS 85.

72. MM to JB, Mar 11, 1841, CM, SC/A/1.

73. Ibid. The "Mr. Burnell" described by MM may have been a partner in George and Burnell. David Trumbull, *Travels in the West: Cuba, With Notices of Porto Rico and the Slave Trade* (London: Longman, Orme, Brown, Green and Longmans, 1840), 219.

74. EB(A) to LBA, Jan 9, 1841, BRBML, GEN MSS 85.

75. MM to Harriet Bachman, Feb 13, 1841, CM, SC/A/1. For MM's opinion of the Charleston elite: MM to Harriet Bachman, July 24, 1827, CM, SC/A/1.

76. MM to Harriet Bachman, Feb 13, 1841, CM, SC/A/1.

77. VGA to LBA [and Friends], Dec 23, 1840. BRBML, GEB MSS 85.

78. VGA to LBA [dear Friends], Jan 3, 1841, BRBML, GEN MSS 85.

79. EB(A) to Jenny [Jane] Bachman, Mar 14, 1841, CM, SC/A/1.

80. VGA to Audubon family, Jan 17, 1841, BRBML, GEN MSS 85. For similar views in other correspondence: Rothman, *Living in the Shadow of Death*, 55. Rothman specifically attributed the idea of contagion to the Spanish physicians there. The experience of musician Frédéric Chopin in Spain attests to her point. Thomas M. Daniel points out: "George Sand was indignant that Frédéric Chopin's tuberculosis was considered contagious by the residents of Mallorca." *Captain of Death: The Story of Tuberculosis* (1997; repr. Rochester, NY: University of Rochester Press, 1999), 69, 121.

81. MM mentions two family members by name: Adolphus Jouve and Zepherina Jouve. Adolphus was a medical student at the University of Pennsylvania in 1829, and Zepherina (b. 1825, Cuba) married into the Heyward family. *Catalogue of the Trustees, Officers and Students of the University of Pennsylvania and the Officers of the Grammar and Charity Schools* (Philadelphia, 1829), 15; and James B. Heyward, "The Heyward Family of South Carolina," *SCHM* 59, no. 4 (1958): 207, 213 and Heyward Family Genealogy.

82. MM to JB, Mar 11, 1841, CM, SC/A/1. On his subscription to octavo *Birds*: JWA to VGA, Mar 10, 1841, BRBML, GEN MSS 85.

83. MM to JB, Mar 11, 1841, CM, SC/A/1.

84. VGA to Audubon family, Mar 16, 1841, BRBML, GEN MSS 85.

85. MM's sketchbook is in the private collection of Mrs. John (Jane Grimball) Greely. Some of the botanicals have been framed, and those not in the Greely collection belong to Mrs. Haskell Carr of Charleston. Both are descendants of the Bachman family.

86. MM to JB, Mar 11, 1841, CM, SC/A/1.

87. JJA to JB, Apr 23, 1841, APSL, B Au25.

88. In her letter dated Apr 3, 1841, MM referred to information conveyed by Wurdemann to JB in January and repeated in JB to JWA, Jan 24, 1841, CM, SC/A/1.

89. MM to JB, Apr 3, 1841, CM, SC/A/1.

90. JB to Jane Bachman, May 11, 1841, CM, SC/A/1.

91. Ibid.

92. VGA to Audubon family, May 5, 1841 and JWA to JJA and LBA, June 12, 1841, BRBML, GEN MSS 85; Schirmer Diary, *SCHM* 70, no. 2 (April 1969): 123.

93. CLB, *Pastor of St. John's*, 198.

94. In August 1841, JJA stated he had painted one hundred figures of quadrupeds. JJA to W. O. Ayers, Aug 15, 1841, Herrick, *Audubon*, 2:229–30. Also: Alice Ford, *John James Audubon* (Norman: University of Oklahoma Press, 1964), 379–80.

Chapter 6

1. JB to JJA, Dec 7, 1841, CM, SC/A/1.

2. JB to JJA, Aug 5, 1841, CM, SC/A/1.

3. JJA to Spencer Fullerton Baird, June 13, June 22, Dec 25, 1840, and July 29, 1841, Herrick, *Audubon*, 2: 219–23, 226–27.

4. JB to JJA, Nov 22, 1841, MNAL, MSS 66. Their different approaches to *Quadrupeds* have been noted previously, specifically: "the Audubons viewed the book primarily as a work of art and as a source of revenue, while Bachman envisioned it as a scientific treatise in which the description advanced knowledge of mammals and the drawings gave form and substance to the information provided." Stephens, *Science, Race and Religion*, 42–43. Also: Peck, "Audubon and Bachman: A Collaboration in Science," 71–115.

5. CLB, *Pastor of St. John's*, 188. For JB's views on death: "Fifty-Fifth Anniversary Sermon," *Charleston Daily Courier*, January 10, 1870. Tyler also notes that his work, family, and health interfered with *Quadrupeds*. Ron Tyler, "The Publication of *The Viviparous Quadrupeds of North America*," 121.

6. MM to VGA, June 2, 1842, CM, SC/A/1.

7. LBA to Mrs. Phillips, [Apr/May 1842], PU, C0006. See, Delafield and Benjamin Travers, *A Synopsis of the Diseases of the Eye, and Their Treatment*, to which are prefixed a short anatomical description and a sketch of the physiology of that organ (New York: E. Bliss and E. White, 1825). There are several letters on the operations Jane endured, particularly by Delafield, but also by Trudeau. Exactly what procedures were used is unclear, but she apparently lost most of her vision in both eyes. JB to VGA, Aug 15 and Sept 19, 1846, BRBML, GEN MSS 85.

8. VGA to JJA, July 21, 1842, BRBML, GEN MSS 85.

9. Parke Godwin, *Little Journeys to Homes of American Authors* (New York: G.P. Putnam's Sons, 1896), 241.

10. VGA to JJA, July 21, 1842, BRBML, GEN MSS 85.

11. Godwin published his description of Minnie's Land several times. See, *The Houses of American Authors* (1853; 1870), 89–110 and "John J. Audubon," in *Little Journeys to Homes of American Authors,* 239–43. Godwin is quoted in Herrick, *Audubon*, 2:237. Godwin notes visiting JJA the year before he went on his Missouri River Expedition in *Little Journeys*, 245.

12. JB to VGA, Sept 8, 1842, CM, SC/A/1.

13. George E. Gifford Jr., "James de Berty Trudeau: Physician-Naturalist," *BHM* 54 (1908); 78–94. MM to Mary Eliza Davis, Aug 21, 1842, CM, SC/A/1. VGA to JJA, Aug 25, 1842, BRBML, GEN MSS 85.

14. Harriet Bachman to JB, Oct 9, 1842, CM, SC/A/1.

15. JB to JJA, Oct 21, 1842, BRBML, GEN MSS 85.

16. These letters have not survived. One is mentioned in MM to VGA, June 2, 1842, CM, SC/A/1 and the letter of August 8, 1842 is referred to in his journal. See, Howard Corning, ed. *Journal of John James Audubon, Made while Obtaining Subscriptions to his "Birds of America," 1840–1843*, foreword Francis H. Herrick (Cambridge, MA: Club of Odd Volumes and Business Historical Society, 1929), 83–84. Information on his whereabouts in 1842 is also contained in this journal. See, JB to JJA, Dec 7, 1841, CM, SC/A/1. With regard to Richard Owen, Bachman was referring to the volumes published in the 1830s under the auspices of the Royal College of Surgeons of England on comparative anatomy and physiology.

17. JB to JJA, Nov 22, 1841, MNAL, MS 66.

18. This letter has not survived. It is mentioned in MM to VGA, June 2, 1842, CM, SC/A/1.

19. MM to Mary Eliza Davis, Aug 21, 1842 and MM to JB, Oct 5, 1842, CM, SC/A/1.

20. JB to JJA, Oct 21, 1842, BRBML, GEN MSS 85.

21. JB to JJA, Jan 15, 1843, BRBML, GEN MSS 85.

22. James E. DeKay, *Zoology of New York, or the New-York Fauna*; Part I: Mammalia (Albany, NY: W. & A. White and J. Visscher, 1842) in *Natural History of New York* (New York: Appleton & Co., 1842).

23. Welch, *Book of Nature*, 54–57.

24. JB to JJA, Jan 15, 1843, BRBML, GEN MSS 85.

25. JB's disputes with DeKay revolved around the eastern chipmunk (*Tamias striatus*) and the grey rabbit (*Lepus nanus*) in particular. JB to VGA, Nov 29, 1845, CM, SC/A/1 and Dec 10, 1845, BRBML, GEN MSS 85.

26. Lester D. Stephens, "The Mermaid Hoax: Indications of Scientific Thought of Charleston, South Carolina, in the 1840s," *PSCHA* 5, no.1 (1983): 45–55; and Kenneth S. Greenberg, "The Nose, the Lie, and the Duel in the Antebellum South," *AHR* 95 (1990): 59–65.

27. Jan Bondeson, *The FeeJee Mermaid and other Essays in Natural and Unnatural History* (Ithaca, NY: Cornell University Press, 1999), 49–54; Neil Harris, *Humbug: The Art of P.T. Barnum* (Boston: Little, Brown and Co., 1971), 65–66.

28. "The Exhibition at the Masonic Hall," *Charleston Courier*, January 21, 1843. Fee-Jee Mermaid Archive, The Lost Museum, American Social History Project/Center for Media and Learning, Graduate Center, City University of New York in collaboration with Center for History and New Media, George Mason University. Avail: chnm.gmu.edu/lostmuseum/mermaid/ Accessed: 22 Nov 2014.

29. JB to unknown recipient, May 8, 1843, CM, SC/A/1. It has been argued that JB and other local scientists had personal reasons for revealing the mermaid as a hoax. According to Irmscher, they believed ignoring it would jeopardize their reputations as serious scientists; according to Greenberg, it was a question of Southern honor. See, Irmscher, *Poetics of Natural History*, 141, and Greenberg, "The Nose, the Lie, and the Duel, 59–63.

30. Stoney, "Memoirs of Frederick Augustus Porcher," 218–19.

31. LBA to JJA, July 23, 1843, BRBML, GEN MSS 85.

32. John Bachman, "The Duck Plant," *Edgefield Advertiser* August 20, 1845.

33. VGA to JJA, July 15, 1844, BRBML, GEN MSS 85.

34. JB to JJA, Mar 24, 1845, CM, SC/A/1.

35. For information on paintings: Boehme, *Audubon in the West*, 47, 50, 63, 64, 81, 97, 115, 154, 177. On the skinned specimens and JB's disappointment: Peck, "Audubon and Bachman: A Collaboration in Science," 86–87. For a list of specimens collected: *Up the Missouri with Audubon: The Journal of Edward Harris*, ed. John Francis McDermott (Norman: University of Oklahoma Press, 1951), Appendix IV, Skins and Specimens Collected on the Missouri, 207–13. It is unclear how many mammals Sprague painted. The journal he kept indicates he painted several: a wolf, buffalo, deer, and antelope. "Isaac Sprague Diary, 1843, covering his trip to the Missouri River in the party with James Audubon," Boston Athenaeum, Mss S68.

36. Audubon's Missouri Journal is filled with detailed ethnographic information. MRA, *Journals*, 1:447–532; 2:1–195.

37. JB to JJA, Aug 1 and JB to JJA, Oct 31, 1845, CM, SC/A/1.

38. JB to VGA, Nov 24, 1845, CM, SC/A/1.

39. JB to VGA, Nov 27, 1845, CM, SC/A/1.

40. CLB, *Pastor of St. John's*, 268.

41. JB to VGA, Feb 7, 1846, BRBML, GEN MSS 85.

42. On JB's approach to mammalogy: Stephens, *Science, Race, and Religion*, 42–51.

43. In Bertram Wyatt-Brown's study of Southern society, he emphasizes the importance of family, stating that once established, kinship bonds were unbreakable. *Southern Honor*, 55.

44. JB to VGA, Jan 17, 1846, MNAL, MSS 66. Also: JB to VGA, Mar 22, 1846, CM, SC/A/1.

45. JB to VGA, June 30, 1849, CLB, *Pastor of St. John's*, 270–72.

46. JJA to JB, Jan 2, 1840, Corning, *Letters*, 2:228–31.

47. JB to JJA, Jan 15, 1843, BRBML, GEN MSS 85.

48. JB to VGA Jan 17, 1846, MNAL, MSS 66.

49. JB to VGA, July 25, 1846, CM, SC/A/1; JB to VGA, Aug 15, 1846, BRBML, GEN MSS 85.

50. JB to VGA, Aug 12, 1846, BRBML, GEN MSS 85.

51. JB to VGA, Feb 10, 1847, BRBML, GEN MSS 85; JB to VGA, June 19, 1847, CM, SC/A/1.

52. JB to VGA, June 19, 1847, CM, SC/A/1.

53. JB to Audubon family, Aug 29, 1847, CM, SC/A/1. VGA forwarded a copy of *Six Lectures on the uses of lungs; and causes, prevention, and cure of pulmonary consumption, asthma, and disease of the heart; on the laws of longevity; and on the mode of preserving male and female health to an hundred years* (New York: H. Carlisle, 1847). VGA to JB, July 14, 1847, HL, bMS Am 1482.

54. JB to VGA, Oct 28, 1847, CM, SC/A/1.

55. Ibid.

56. JB to VGA, Nov 18, 1847, CM, SC/A/1.

57. JB to VGA, Dec 14, 1847, CM, SC/A/1.

58. JB to VGA, Sept 16, 1848, CM, SC/A/1.

59. JB to VGA, Oct 20, 1848, CM, SC/A/1.

60. JB to VGA, Dec 18, 1848, CM, SC/A/1.

61. VGA to MM, Jan 28, 1849, CM, SC/A/1.

62. JB to MM, May 11, 1848, CM, SC/A/1.

63. JB to VGA, Mar 30, 1849, BRBML, GEN MSS 85.

64. JB to VGA, June 30, 1849, CM, SC/A/1. This letter was posted in Madison Springs, Georgia, a resort for invalids and tourists. See, E. Merton Coulter, "Madison Springs, Georgia Watering Place," *GHQ* 47, no. 4 (1963): 375–407. Shuler also contends that MM played a key role in preparing this volume, stating: "Editing material Victor had sent, as well as script Bachman provided, she shaped the book." *Had I the Wings*, 209.

65. JB to VGA, Aug 24, 1849, CLB, *Pastor of St. John's*, 274.

66. Stephens, *Science, Race and Religion*, 173–94, 195–211; Brad D. Hume, "Quantifying Characters: Polygenist Anthropologists and the Hardening of Heredity," *JHB* 41 (2008): 124–27, 135–38, 142–43; and Peter McCandless, "The Political Evolution of John Bachman: From New York Yankee to South Carolina Secessionist," *SCHM* 108, no. 1 (2007): 20–23.

67. Stephens, *Science, Race and Religion*, 194.

68. JB and MM to VGA, Apr 9, 1852, CM, SC/A/1.

69. VGA to LBA, Feb 26, 1852, BRBML, GEN MSS 85.

70. JB to Edward Harris, Mar 13, 1852, CM, SC/A/1.

71. JB to JJA, Dec 23, 1846, BRBML, GEN MSS 85.

72. ARC, "The Amiable Miss Martin," Chap 6, p. 11, CM, SC/A/1.

73. MM to VGA, Apr 14, 1856, CM, SC/A/1.

74. JB to LBA, Mar 30, 1856, CM, SC/A/1.

Chapter 7

1. Rebecca Fraser, *Gender, Race and Family in Nineteenth Century America: From Northern Women to Plantation Mistress* (New York: Palgrave Macmillan, 2012),

especially 35–40; and Tiffany K. Wayne, *Women's Roles in Nineteenth-Century America* (Westport, CT: Greenwood Pub., 2007), 29–31, 40. Still important: Catherine E. Kelly, *Reshaping Women's Lives in the Nineteenth Century* (Ithaca, NY: Cornell University Press, 1999), and Faye E. Dudden, *Serving Women: Household Service in Nineteenth Century America* (Middletown, CT: Wesleyan University Press, 1983).

2. For quotation: EBA to Jane Bachman, Mar 22, 1840, CM, SC/A/1. On the "servant" questions: MM to EBA, Feb 24, 1840, CM, SC/A/1 and LBA to JJA, July 27, 1840, BRBML, GEN MSS 85.

3. She also "hired" a girl in 1845, but it there is no evidence to suggest it was not an enslaved woman. MM to Harriet Bachman, Mar 14, 1845, CM, SC/A/1. The Irish maid is listed in the 1860 South Carolina Federal Population Census Schedules, Charleston District, City of Charleston, Wards 1–8, "Free Inhabitants of the Sixth Ward, Charleston," 88.

4. Eighth Census of the United States, Population Schedules, Slave Schedule, Ward 6, 25 June 1860, 19. Two of the slaves were aged sixty, and at least one, Caroline, came with Rebecca Martin when she joined the household. Caroline is named in the Will of Rebecca Martin, probated May 25, 1840; Bills of Sale, Samuel Wilson, executor for Rebecca Martin, [ten slaves] Miscellaneous Records, S 213003, v. 005W, pp. 247, 263, and 525. SCDHA. Caroline is also mentioned in a presentation by Kate Bachman (CLB) to the Daughters of the Confederacy, June 1898, CLS, 51–236.

5. A slave named Kitty was identified specifically in the "Marriage Settlement between Rev. John Bachman and Maria Martin," Columbia, South Carolina Marriage Settlements, No. 17, 1848–53, pp. 77–82, Cawley, *Herrstein to South Carolina*, 191–93. Also: Seventh Census of the United States, Population Schedules, Slave Schedule, December 3–4, 1850, pp.718, 893, and List of the Taxpayers of the City of Charleston for 1860 (Charleston, SC: Steam-power presses of Evans and Cogswell, 1861), 12. In 1860, John and Maria Bachman paid taxes on six slaves.

6. McCandless, "Political Evolution of John Bachman," 9, 13–15, 24. For a detailed discussion of Bachman's defense of the morality of slavery within the Lutheran Church: Bost, "John Bachman and the Development of Southern Lutheranism," 408–25. The role of politics in the slave question factored prominently in this debate.

7. Bost, "John Bachman and the Development of Southern Lutheranism," 409. On the Franckean abolitionist Lutherans: Clinton Daggan, "The New York Lutheran Churches and the Question of Slavery," *CHIQ* 78 (2005): 33–36, and Paul P. Kuenning, "New York Lutheran Abolitionists: Seeking a Solution to a Historical Enigma," *Church History* 58, no. 1 (1989): 52–65. Kuenning argues that while most northern Lutherans may have supported abolition, they subverted those beliefs to maintaining "unity" among American Lutherans.

8. Bost, "John Bachman and the Development of Southern Lutheranism," 422.

9. John Bachman, *The Missionary* 2, no. 46 (December 19, 1857), in Bost, "John Bachman and the Development of Southern Lutheranism," 422–24.

10. Circular announcing a meeting in the Depository, May 13, 1845, in *Proceedings of the meetings in Charleston, May 13–15 1845, on the Religious Instruction of the Negroes, Together with the Report of the Committee and the Address to the Public* (Charleston, SC: B. Jenkins, 1845), 13–15.

11. At this time, Charleston was still under the auspices of the Synod of North Carolina, which instructed pastors to baptize slaves with the permission of their masters. Bost, "John Bachman and the Development of Southern Lutheranism," 175, and Douglas C. Strange, "Our Duty to Preach the Gospel to Negroes: Southern Lutherans and American Slavery," *CHIQ* 42 (1969): 173–75.

12. Before 1857, Bachman baptized 1,864 whites and 1,551 blacks; in 1857, he baptized eighty-two whites and 109 blacks; in total, between 1824 and 1871, he baptized 2,608 whites and 2,065 blacks. It should be noted that during the last decade there were fewer than 140 blacks baptized, forty-nine after the Civil War. Bost, "John Bachman and the Development of Southern Lutheranism," 124–26.

13. Blake Touchstone, "Planters and Slave Religion in the Deep South," in *Masters and Slaves in the House of the Lord: Race and Religion in the American South, 1740–1870*, ed. John B. Boles (Lexington: University of Kentucky Press, 1988), 103–04, 108, 111–12, 121. Also: Boles, "Introduction," 11.

14. JB to VGA, Sept 11, 1851, CM, SC/A/1.

15. McCandless, "Political Evolution of John Bachman," 24–26.

16. JB wrote VGA just three days after the Dred Scott decision expressing the opinion that it should "bring the people of the U. States to their senses." JB to VGA, Mar 9, 1857 and JB to VGA, Jan 30, 1857, CM, SC/A/1.

17. JB to VGA, Aug 15, 1857, CM, SC/A/1; JB to Henry Summer, Nov 12, 1861, CL-USC, Pob; MM Bachman to CLB, Nov 16, 1861, and Jane Bachman to CLB, Dec 17, 1861, CM, SC/A/1.

18. Gregg, like Ruffin and Bachman, published advice on how to improve Southern agriculture. Equally important, he was a temperance man. Tom Downey, *Planting a Capitalist South: Masters, Merchants and Manufacturers, 1790–1860* (Baton Rouge: Louisiana State University Press, 2006), 131, 206–08, 224. For Gregg's views on secession: Broadus Mitchell, *William Gregg: Factory Master of the Old South* (Chapel Hill: University of North Carolina Press, 1928), 166, 202–04.

19. MM Bachman to CLB, Nov 12, 1860, CM, SC/A/1 and McCandless, "Political Evolution of John Bachman," 28–29.

20. For the (previously unpublished) text of the prayer preceding the Ordinance of Secession, Dec 20, 1860: CLB, "Leaves from a Notebook, Civil War Reminiscences," CLS, 51–236, pp. 6–9. On the South Carolina Institute Hall: "A Sketch of Charleston," in *Premium List of the South Carolina Institute, Incorporated in 1850 for the Promotion and Encouragement of the Arts, Agriculture, Ingenuity, Mechanics, Manufacturing, and a General Development of Industry* (Charleston, SC: Walker, Evans and Cogswell, 1870), 41–42.

21. JB to JA Brown, Feb 13, 1861, CM, SC/A/1. On the situation at Newberry College: Charles William Heathcote, *The Lutheran Church and the Civil War* (New York: Fleming H. Revell Co., 1919), 124–25, and correspondence from JB to Brown, Feb 13 and 14, 1861, CM, SC/A/1.

22. MM Bachman to CLB, Nov 12, 1860, CM, SC/A/1.

23. MM Bachman to CLB, Nov 19, 1860, CM, SC/A/1.

24. CLB, "Leaves from a Notebook, Civil War Reminiscences," CLS, 51–236, p. 16.

25. John Woodhouse Audubon, *Audubon's Western Journey: 1849–1850*, Being the MS. Record of a Trip from New York to Texas, and an overland journey through Mexico and Arizona to the Gold Fields of California, with biographical memoir by his daughter, Maria Rebecca Audubon, and Introduction, Notes and Index by Frank Heywood Hodder (Cleveland, OH: Arthur H. Clark Co., 1906), 36.

26. MRA, Biographical Memoir, *Audubon's Western Journey*, 37–38.

27. LBA to Edward Harris, Apr 14, 1862, Edward Harris Papers, ADA-HDC, LPR98, Box 2, F. 7, Q22590–Q22593.

28. LBA to Mrs. Harris, Oct 16, 1862, and for the sequence of events: LBA to Mrs. Edward Harris, June 6, 1862 and LBA to Edward Harris, Aug 29, 1862, ADA-HDC, LPR98, Box 2, F. 7, Q22578–Q22581.

29. Olson, "Biographical Sketch of an American Icon," 34 and 38, fn. 56.

30. JB to Henry Summer, Nov 12, 1861, CL-USC, Pob.

31. MM Bachman to CLB, Nov 16, 1861, CM, SC/A/1. See, "Marriage Settlement between Rev. John Bachman and Maria Martin," Cawley, *Herrstein to South Carolina*, 191–93.

32. MM Bachman to CLB, Nov 16, 1861, CM, SC/A/1.

33. Heathcote, *Lutheran Church and the Civil War*, 91, 93–95.

34. CLB, "Leaves from a Notebook, Civil War Reminiscences," CLS, 51–236, p. 30 and *Pastor of St. John's*, 367.

35. CLB, *Pastor of St. John's*, 369.

BIBLIOGRAPHY

Abel, Emily K. *The Inevitable Hour: A History of Caring for Dying Patients in America.* Baltimore, MD: Johns Hopkins Press, 2013.

Abrams, Jeanne. "On the Road Again: Consumptives Traveling for Health in the American West, 1840–1925." *Great Plains Quarterly* (2010): 271–85.

Arthur, Stanley Clisby. *Audubon: An Intimate Life of the American Woodsman*, 1937; Gretna, LA: Pelican Pub., 2000. Citations refer to the Pelican edition.

Audubon, John James. "Account of the Habits of the Turkey Buzzard (*Vultur aura*), particularly with the view of exploding the opinion generally entertained of its extraordinary power of Smelling" *Edinburgh New Philosophical Journal* 2 (October–April 1826–1827): 172–84.

———. "Art. IX. M—Account of the Method of Drawing Birds employed by J. J. Audubon, Esq. F. R. S. E. In a Letter to a Friend" *Edinburgh Journal of Science* 8, no.1 (1828): 48–54.

———. "No.1 Letter [7 Dec. 1831] from Audubon to the editor [George W. Featherstonhaugh]." *Monthly American Journal of Geology and Natural Science* 1 (1832): 358–63.

———. *Ornithological Biography*, or An account of the habits of the birds of the United States of America: accompanied by descriptions of the objects represented in the work entitled *The Birds of America*, and interspersed with delineations of American scenery and manners. With William McGillivray. 5 vols. Edinburgh: Adam and Charles Black, 1831–1839.

Audubon, John James and John Bachman. *The [Viviparous] Quadrupeds of North America*. 3 vols. New York: V. G. Audubon, 1846–1854.

Audubon, John Woodhouse. *Audubon's Western Journey: 1849–1850*, Being the MS. Record of a Trip from New York to Texas, and an overland journey through Mexico and Arizona to the Gold Fields of California. Biographical memoir by his daughter, Maria Rebecca Audubon. Introduction, Notes and Index by Frank Heywood Hodder. Cleveland, OH: Arthur H. Clark Co., 1906.

Audubon, Lucy. *The Life of John James Audubon, the Naturalist.* Introduction by Jas. Grant Wilson. New York: Putnam & Sons, 1869.

Audubon, Maria Rebecca. "Audubon's Story of His Youth: 'Myself,'" *Scribner's Monthly Magazine* 13, no. 3 (March 1893): 267–89.

———. ed. *Audubon and His Journals.* Zoological and other notes by Elliott Coues. 2 vols. New York: Charles Scribner's Sons, 1897.

———. "Reminiscences of Audubon (By a Granddaughter)." *Scribner's Monthly Magazine* 12, no. 3 (July 1876): 333–36.

Audubon, Victor Gifford. "Retrospective Criticism: Mr. Audubon, Jun., in Reply to Mr. Waterton's Remarks (p. 215) on Audubon's Biography of Birds." *Loudon's Magazine of Natural History and Journal of Zoology, Botany, Mineralogy, Geology, and Meteorology* 6 (June 7, 1833): 369–72.

———. "Retrospective Criticism." *Loudon's Magazine of Natural History and Journal of Zoology, Botany, Mineralogy, Geology, and Meteorology* 6 (1833): 550–53

Bachman, Catherine L. *John Bachman: The Pastor of St. John's Lutheran Church, Charleston*. Charleston, SC: Walker, Evans & Cogswell Co., 1888.

Bachman, John. *An Address Delivered Before the Horticultural Society of Charleston*, at the Anniversary Meeting, July 10th, 1833. Charleston, SC: the Society, 1833.

———. *An Address on Education*, delivered on the Day of the Laying of the Corner-Stone of Newberry College, July 15, 1857. Charleston: James & Williams, 1857.

———. "Art. V.—The Insect World: Morals of Entomology etc," ["On the habits of Insects," *Southern Literary Journal* 2 (August 1836), 409–27]: 30–40. In William Gilmore Simms, *The Charleston Book: A Miscellany in Prose and Verse*. Charleston, SC: Samuel Hart, Sen., 1845 and in *De Bow's Review of Agricultural, Commercial, Industrial Progress and Resources*, 2nd n.s. 1, no. 4 (October 1858): 430–35.

———. *Defence of Luther and the Reformation, against the charges of John D. Bellinger and others, to which are appended communications of other Protestant and Roman Catholic Writers who engaged in the Controversy*. Charleston, SC: William Y. Paxton, 1853.

———. "Description of a New Species of Hare Found in South Carolina." *Journal of the Academy of Natural Sciences of Philadelphia*, 7, pt. 1 (1836): 194–99; pt. 2 (1837): 282–361.

———. "Remarks in Defence of the Author of the 'Birds of America.' By the Rev. John Bachman, Charleston, South Carolina Read before the Boston Society of Natural History, Feb. 5, 1834." *Boston Society of Natural History* 1, no. 1 (1834): 15–31.

———. "Retrospective Criticism: "Remarks in Defence of [Mr. Audubon] the Author of the '[Biography of the] Birds of America,' [VII. 66] by the Rev. John Bachman, Charleston, South Carolina." *Loudon's Magazine of Natural History and Journal of Zoology, Botany, Mineralogy, Geology, and Meteorology* 7 (1834): 164–75.

———. "Some Remarks on the Genus *Sorex* [Shrews], with a Monograph of the North American Species." *Journal of the Academy of Natural Sciences of Philadelphia*, 7, pt. 2 (1837): 362–402.

Badaracco, Claire Hoertz. *Prescribing Faith: Medicine, Media, and Religion in American Culture*. Waco, TX: Baylor University Press, 2007.

Baily, J. T. Herbert. *Francesco Bartolozzi: A Biographical Essay*. London: Otto, 1907.

Baird, Spencer Fullerton. *The Mammals of North America: The Descriptions of Species Based Chiefly on the Collections in the Museum of the Smithsonian Institution*. Philadelphia, PA: J. B. Lippincott, 1859.

Baker, Cathleen A. "Audubon's *The Birds of America*: A Technical Examination and Condition Survey of the Four-Volume Folio Set Belonging to Syracuse University." M. Fine Arts, Syracuse University, 1985.

Bakewell, B. G. *The Family Book of Bakewell. Page Campbell.* Pittsburgh, PA: Wm. G. Johnston and Co., Printers and Stationers, 1896.

Bannon, Lois Elmer, and Taylor Clark. *Handbook of Audubon Prints.* Gretna, LA: Pelican Pub., 1980.

Bartram, R. Conover, ed. "The Diary of John Hamilton Cornish, 1846–1860." *South Carolina Historical Magazine* 64, no. 2 (1963): 73–85.

Baumann, Richard B. "Lutherans and Anglican–Episcopal Conformity, 1565–1957: Called to Common Mission." *Anglican and Episcopal History* 73, no. 4 (2004): 434–65.

Berger, Peter L. "On Lutheran Identity in America." *Lutheran Quarterly* 20 (2006): 337–47.

Bernheim, Gotthardt. *History of the German Settlements and Lutheran Church in North and South Carolina.* Philadelphia: The Lutheran Bookstore, 1872.

Blackburn, Julia. *Charles Waterton, 1782–1865: Traveler and Conservationist.* London: Bodley Head, 1989.

Blaisdell, Charmarie Jenkins. "The Matrix of Reform: Women in the Lutheran and Calvinist Movements." In *Triumph over Silence: Women in Protestant History*, edited by Richard L. Greaves, 13–44. Contributions to the Study of Religion, no. 15. Westport, CT: Greenwood Press, 1985.

Blaugrund, Annette. "John James Audubon: Producer, Promoter and Publisher." *Imprint: Journal of the American Historical Print Collectors Society* 21 (1996): 10–19.

———. "'My Style of Drawing': Audubon and His Artistic Milieu." In *John James Audubon in the West: The Last Expedition, Mammals of North America,* edited by Sarah E. Boehme, 11–30. New York: Harry N. Abrams, 2000.

Blaugrund, Annette, and Theodore E Stebbins Jr., eds. *John James Audubon: The Watercolors for The Birds of America.* New York: Villard Books, 1993.

Blum, Ann Shelby. *Picturing Nature: American Nineteenth-Century Zoological Illustration.* Princeton, NJ: Princeton University Press, 1993.

Blunt, Wilfrid. *The Art of Botanical Illustration.* London: Collins, 1967.

Bondeson, Jan. *The FeeJee Mermaid and other Essays in Natural and Unnatural History.* Ithaca, NY: Cornell University Press, 1999.

Bonta, Marcia Myers. *Women in the Field: America's Pioneering Women Naturalists.* College Station: Texas A & M Press, 1991.

Bost, Raymond M. *A History of the Lutheran Church in South Carolina.* Columbia: South Carolina Synod of the Lutheran Church in America, 1971.

———. "John Bachman and the Development of Southern Lutheranism." PhD diss. Yale University, 1963.

———. "John Bachman, Man of Faith, Man of Science." *Lutheran Quarterly* 2, no. 2 (1988): 209–26.

Brecht, Martin. *Martin Luther: Shaping and Defining the Reformation, 1521–1532.* Stuttgart: Calwer Verlag, 1986; Minneapolis: Augsburg Fortress, 1994.

Brookshaw, George. *Groups of Flowers, Drawn and Accurately Coloured after nature, with Full Directions for the Young Artist; Designed as a Companion to the Treatise of Flower Painting*. London: Longman, Hurst, Rees, Orme and Brown, 1817.

Brown, Jennifer S. H., and Elizabeth Vibert. *Reading Beyond Words: Contexts for Native History*. Peterborough, Ontario: Broadview, 1996.

Buchanan, Robert. *The Life and Adventures of John James Audubon the Naturalist*, edited from materials supplied by his widow. London: Sampson, Son Low & Marston, 1868.

Burke, G. J., and S. A. Zafar. "Problems in Distinguishing Tuberculosis of Bowel from Crohn's Disease in Asians." *British Medical Journal* 4 (July 1975): 395–97.

Burton, E. Milby. *Charleston Furniture, 1700–1825*. Contributions from the Charleston Museum XII. Charleston, SC: Charleston Museum, 1955.

Caldwell, Mark. *The Last Crusade: The War on Consumption, 1862–1954*. New York: Atheneum, 1988.

Calhoun, Jeanne A., Elizabeth J. Reitz, Michael B. Trinkley, and Martha A. Zierden. *Meat in Due Season: Preliminary Investigations of Marketing Practices in Colonial Charleston*. Archaeological Contributions 9. Charleston, SC: Charleston Museum, 1984.

Calhoun, Jeanne A., Martha A. Zierden, and Elizabeth A Paysinger. "The Geographic Spread of Charleston's Mercantile Community, 1732–1767." *South Carolina Historical Magazine* 86, no. 3 (1985): 182–220.

Carrill, M. Allison. "An Assessment of English Furniture Imports into Charleston, 1760–1800." *Journal of Early Southern Decorative Arts* 11, no. 2 (1985): 1–18.

Carson, Marian Sadtler. "Early American Water Color Painting, *Antiques* 59, no. 1 (1951): 54–56.

Catalogue of the Trustees, Officers and Students of the University of Pennsylvania and the Officers of the Grammar and Charity Schools. Philadelphia, 1829.

Cawley, Joseph Douglas. *From Herrstein to South Carolina: Reverend John Nicholas Martin, 1724–1795: Pastor, Patriot and Some of his Children and Grandchildren*. Number Two in the J. D. Cawley Ancestor Series. Centennial, Colorado: J and J Publishers, 2003.

Clark, Thomas D. *South Carolina: The Grand Tour, 1780–1865*. Columbia: University of South Carolina Press, 1973.

Coen, Deborah R. "A Lens of Many Facets: Science through a Family's Eyes." *Isis* 97, no. 3 (2006): 395–419.

Coues, Elliott, and Joel Asaph Allen. *Material for a Bibliography of North American Mammals* prepared by Theodore Gill and Elliott Coues, Extracted from the Eleventh Volume of the Final Reports of the [United States Geological and Geographical] Survey. Washington: Government Printing Office, 1877.

Coffin, Amory, and W. H. Geddings. *Aiken; or Climatic Cure*. Charleston, SC: Walker, Evans and Cogswell, 1869.

Coffin, Annie Roulhac. "Audubon's Friend—Maria Martin." *New-York Historical Society Quarterly* 49, no. 1 (1965): 29–51.

———. "Maria Martin (1796–1863)." *Art Quarterly* (Autumn 1960): 281–300.

———. "Maria Martin (July 3, 1796–Dec. 27, 1863)." In *Notable American Women: A Biographical Dictionary.* 3 vols, edited by Edward T. James, II, 505–06 Cambridge, MA: Belknap Press of Harvard University Press, 1971.

Corning, Howard, ed. *Journal of John James Audubon, Made while Obtaining Subscriptions to his "Birds of America," 1840–1843.* Foreword by Francis H. Herrick. Cambridge, MA: Club of Odd Volumes and Business Historical Society, 1929.

———, ed. *Letters of John James Audubon, 1826–1840.* 2 vols. 1930; New York: Kraus Reprint Co., 1969.

Coulter, E. Merton. "Madison Springs, Georgia Watering Place." *Georgia Historical Quarterly* 47, no. 4 (1963): 375–407.

Groce, George C., and David H. Wallace. *The New-York Historical Society's Dictionary of Artists in America, 1564–1860.* New Haven, CT: Yale University Press, 1957.

Crooks, Jr., Daniel J. *Charleston is Burning! Two Centuries of Fire and Flames.* Charleston, SC: History Press, 2009.

Daggan, Clinton. "The New York Lutheran Churches and the Question of Slavery." *Concordia Historical Institute Quarterly* 78 (2005): 28–45.

Daniel, Thomas M. *Captain of Death: The Story of Tuberculosis.* Rochester, NY: University of Rochester Press, 1999.

Danner, David L. "The Parting of the Ways for Lutherans and Episcopalians: The Movement from Eucharistic Hospitality to Mutual Isolation in the Nineteenth Century." *Anglican and Episcopal History* 68, no. 2 (1999): 158–87.

Davidson, Marshall B. *The Original Water-Color Paintings by John James Audubon for the Birds of America,* Reproduced in Color from the Collection at the New-York Historical Society 1966; New York: American Heritage Press Inc./Bonanza Books, 1985.

Deane, Ruthven. "Some Letters of Bachman to Audubon." *The Auk* 46, no. 2 (1929): 177–85.

DeKay, James E. *Zoology of New York, or the New-York Fauna*; Part I: Mammalia. Albany: W. & A. White and J. Visscher, 1842. In the *Natural History of New York.* New York: Appleton & Co., and Wiley and Putnam; Boston: Gould, Kendall and Lincoln; Albany: Thurlow Weed, 1842.

DeLatte, Caroline E. *Lucy Audubon: A Biography.* Updated ed. with foreword by Christoph Irmscher, 1982; Baton Rouge: Louisiana State University Press, 2008.

Donovan, Edward. *Instructions for Collecting and Preserving Various Subjects of Natural History, as Quadrupeds, Birds, Reptiles, Fishes, Shells, Corals, Plants, Etc., together with a Treatise on the Management of Insects in their several states, selected from the best authorities.* London: F. C. and J. Rivington, 1805.

Downey, Tom. *Planting a Capitalist South: Masters, Merchants and Manufacturers, 1790–1860.* Baton Rouge: Louisiana State University Press, 2006.

Dudden, Faye E. *Serving Women: Household Service in Nineteenth Century America.* Middletown, CT: Wesleyan University Press, 1983.

Duncan, Ian. "Altered States: Galt, Serial Fiction and the Romantic Miscellany." In *John Galt: Observations and Conjectures in Literature, History and Society*, edited by Regina Hewitt, 53–72. Washington, DC: Lexington Books, 2012.

Dwight, Edward H. "Audubon's Oils." *Art in America* 51, no. 2 (1963): 76–80.

———. *Audubon: Watercolors and Drawings.* Utica, NY: Munson-Williams-Proctor Institute and Pierpont Morgan Library, 1965.

Edington, Brian W. *Charles Waterton: A Biography.* Cambridge, UK: Lutterworth Press, 1996.

Edwards, John N. "Familial Behavior as Social Exchange." *Journal of Marriage and Family* 31, no. 3 (1969): 518–26.

Ellet, Elizabeth. *Women Artists in All Ages and Countries.* New York: Harper and Brothers Pubs., 1859.

Elliott, Stephen. *A Sketch of the Botany of South Carolina and Georgia.* 2 vols. Charleston, SC: J. R. Schenck, 1821 and 1824.

Ewell, James. *The Medical Companion or Family Physician*: Treating the Diseases of the United States, with their symptoms, causes, cure, and means of prevention: Common cases in surgery, as Fractures, Dislocations, etc, the Management and Diseases of Women and Children, A Dispensatory for Preparing Family Medicines, and a Glossary Explaining Technical Terms. 7th ed. Washington, 1827.

"Fashion Plate: Modes and Manners." Exhibit, Museum of Art, Philadelphia, September 1979.

Featherstonhaugh, George. "Audubon, Author of 'The Birds of America' and 'Ornithological Biography.'" *Monthly American Journal of Geology and Natural Science* 1 (1831): 456–68.

Ferrari, Mary. "'Obliged to Earn Subsistence for Themselves': Women Artisans in Charleston, South Carolina, 1763–1808." *South Carolina Historical Magazine* 106, no. 4 (2005): 235–55.

Fiero, Gloria K. "Audubon the Artist." In *Audubon: A Retrospective*, edited by James H. Dorman. 34–60. Lafayette: University of Southwestern Louisiana, 1990.

Fitch, Samuel Sheldon. *Six Lectures on the uses of lungs; and causes, prevention, and cure of pulmonary consumption, asthma, and disease of the heart*; on the laws of longevity; and on the mode of preserving male and female health to an hundred years. New York: H. Carlisle, 1847.

Fleming, Robin. "Writing Biography on the Edge of History." *American Historical Review* 114 (2009): 606–14.

Ford, Alice, ed. *The 1826 Journal of John James Audubon.* [from original in collection of Henry Bradley Martin]. Norman: University of Oklahoma Press, 1967.

———. *Audubon's Butterflies, Moths, and other Studies.* New York: Studio Pubs., in assoc. with Thomas Y. Crowell Co., 1952.

———ed. *Audubon, By Himself: A Profile of John James Audubon*. Garden City, NY: Natural History Press, 1969.

———. *John James Audubon*. Norman: University of Oklahoma Press, 1964.

Forkner, Ben, ed. *John James Audubon: Selected Journals and other Writings*. New York: Penguin, 1996.

Foshay, Ella M. *John James Audubon*. New York: Harry N. Abrams, 1997.

Fox-Genovese, Elizabeth. *Within the Plantation Household: Black and White Women of the Old South*. Chapel Hill: University of North Carolina Press, 1988.

Fraser, Charles. *Reminiscences of Charleston, Lately Published in the Charleston Courier*. Charleston, SC: John Russell, 1854.

Fraser, Rebecca. *Gender, Race and Family in Nineteenth Century America: From Northern Women to Plantation Mistress*. New York: Palgrave Macmillan, 2012.

Freeland, W. O. "A Survey Exhibition in Memory of Maria Martin, May 3–31, 1964." Columbia Museum of Art, Columbia, South Carolina.

Friedrichs, Christopher R. "Whose House of Learning? Some Thoughts on German Schools in Post-Reformation Germany." *History of Education Quarterly* 22, no. 3 (1982): 371–77.

Fries, Waldemar H. *The Double Elephant Folio: The Story of Audubon's Birds of America*. Chicago: American Library Association, 1973.

Frost, Henry R. *Syllabus of A Course of Lectures on the Materia Medica, delivered in the Medical College of the State of South Carolina*. Charleston, SC: Daniel J. Dowling, 1834.

Gibson, Gail. "Costume and Fashion in Charleston, 1769–1782." *South Carolina Historical Magazine* 82, no. 3 (1981): 225–47.

Gifford, Jr., George E. "James de Berty Trudeau: Physician-Naturalist." *Bulletin of the History of Medicine* 54 (1908): 78–94.

Gill, Theodore. "Biographical Memoir of John Edwards Holbrook, 1794–1871." Read before the National Academy of Science, April 22, 1903.

Gillespie, Joanna Bowen. "'The Clear Leadings of Providence': Pious Memoirs and the Problems of Self-Realization for Women in the Early Nineteenth Century." *Journal of the Early Republic* 5, no. 2 (1985): 191–221.

Godwin, Parke. *Little Journeys to Homes of American Authors*. New York: G. P. Putnam's Sons, 1896.

Gongaware, George J. *The History of the German Friendly Society of Charleston, South Carolina, 1766–1916*. Richmond, VA: Garrett and Massie, 1935.

Good, Cassandra A. "Friendly Relations: Situating Friendship of Males and Females in the Early American Republic, 1780–1830," *Gender & History* 24, no.1 (2012): 18–34.

Graustein, Jeannette E. *Thomas Nuttall, Naturalist: Explorations in America, 1808–1841*. Cambridge, MA: Harvard University Press, 1967.

Gray, Virginia Gearhart. "Activities of Southern Women: 1840–1860." *South Atlantic Monthly* 27 (1928): 264–79.

Green, Lowell. "The Education of Women in the Reformation." *History of Education Quarterly* 19, no. 1 (1979): 93–116.

Greenberg, Kenneth S. "The Nose, the Lie, and the Duel in the Antebellum South." *American Historical Review* 95 (1990): 57–74.

Greven, Philip. *The Protestant Temperament: Patterns of Child Rearing, Religious Experience, and the Self in Early America*. Chicago: University of Chicago Press, 1977.

Grinnell, George Bird. "Some Audubon Letters." *The Auk* 33 (1916): 119–30.

———. "Recollections of Audubon Park." *The Auk* 37, no. 3 (July 1920): 372–80.

Hagy, James W. *People and Professions of Charleston, South Carolina, 1782–1802*. Baltimore, MD: Clearfield, 1992.

Hagy, James W. *City Directories for Charleston, South Carolina for years 1803, 1806, 1807, 1809, and 1813*. Baltimore, MD: Clearfield, 1995.

Hahn, Stephen S. "Lexington's Theological Library, 1832–1859." *South Carolina Historical Magazine* 80, no. 1 (1979): 36–49.

Haller Jr., J. S. *The History of American Homeopathy: The Academic Years, 1820–1935*. New York: Haworth Press, 2005.

———. *The History of American Homeopathy: From Rational Medicine to Holistic Health Care*. New Brunswick, NJ: Rutgers University Press, 2009.

Hallett, Mark. "Reynolds, Celebrity and the Exhibition Space." In *Joshua Reynolds: The Creation of Celebrity*, edited by Martin Postle. 35–48. London: Tate Pub., 2005.

Hamilton, Edward. *The Flora Homoeopathica; or Illustrations and Descriptions of the Medicinal Plants used as Homoeopathic Remedies*. 2 vols. London: H. Bailliere, 1852.

Hamilton, Nigel. *Biography: A Brief History*. Cambridge, MA: Harvard University Press, 2007.

———. *How to Do Biography: A Primer*. Cambridge, MA: Harvard University Press, 2009.

Hanaford, Phebe A. *Women of the Century*. Boston: B. B. Russell, 1877.

Hardie, Martin. *Watercolour Painting in Britain, III: The Victorian Period*, edited by Dudley Snelgrove with Jonathan Mayne and Basil Taylor. London: B. T. Batsford, 1971.

Hardouin-Fugier, Elisabeth. *The Pupils of Redouté*. Leigh-on-Sea: F. Lewis Pubs., 1981.

Harlan, Richard. "Art. III Audubon's Ornithology." *American Quarterly Review* 18 (1835): 38–62.

Harris, Neil. *Humbug: The Art of P.T. Barnum*. Boston: Little, Brown and Co., 1971.

Harrison, Hazel. *Master Strokes: Watercolor, A Step-by-Step Guide to Using the Techniques of the Masters*. New York: Sterling Pub. Co., 2005.

Hart, Emma. *Building Charleston: Town and Society in the Eighteenth-Century British Atlantic World*. Charlottesville: University of Virginia Press, 2010.

———. "Work, Family and the Eighteenth-Century History of a Middle Class in the American South." *Journal of Southern History* 78, no. 3 (2012): 551–78.

Hart-Davis, Duff. *Audubon's Elephant: America's Greatest Naturalist and the Making of the Birds of America*. New York: Henry Holt and Co., 2004.

Hartigan-O'Connor, Ellen. *The Ties that Buy: Women and Commerce in Revolutionary America*. Philadelphia: University of Pennsylvania Press, 2009.

Havens, Mary. "The Liturgical Traditions II: Lutherans." In *Religion in South Carolina*, edited by Charless H. Lippy, 59–66. Columbia: University of South Carolina Press, 1993.

Hazelius, Ernest L. *History of the American Lutheran Church, from its commencement in the year of our Lord 1685, to the year 1842*. Zanesville, OH: Edwin C. Church, 1846.

Heathcote, Charles William. *The Lutheran Church and the Civil War*. Chicago: Fleming H. Revell Co., 1919.

Hendrix, Scott. "Luther on Marriage." *Lutheran Quarterly* 14, no. 3 (2000): 335–50.

Herrick, Francis Hobart. *Audubon, The Naturalist: A History of his Life and Time*. 2 vols. 1917; 1938; repr. New York: Dover Pub., 1968.

Heyward, James B. "The Heyward Family of South Carolina." *South Carolina Historical Magazine* 59, no. 4 (1958): 206–23.

Holbrook, John Edwards. *North American Herpetology or a Description of the Reptiles Inhabiting the United States*. 5 vols. Philadelphia: J. Dobson, 1842.

Hollingsworth, E. Buckner. *Her Garden Was Her Delight*. New York: Macmillan Co., 1962.

———. "Maria Martin." *Audubon Magazine* (July–August/ Sept–Oct 1962): 197–99; 266–69.

Hume, Brad D. "Quantifying Characters: Polygenist Anthropologists and the Hardening of Heredity." *Journal History of Biology* 41, no. 1 (2008): 119–58.

Hunter, Perceval. "The Means by which the Vulture (Vúltur Aúra L.) traces its Food." *Loudon's Magazine of Natural History and Journal of Zoology, Botany, Mineralogy, Geology, and Meteorology* 6 (1833): 83–84.

Irmscher, Christoph, ed. *John James Audubon: Writings and Drawings*. New York: Library of America, 1999.

———. *The Poetics of Natural History: From John Bartram to William James*. New Brunswick, NJ: Rutgers University Press, 1999.

Jabour, Anya. "'Grown Girls, Highly Cultivated': Female Education in an Antebellum Southern Family." *Journal of Southern History* 64, no. 1 (1998): 23–64.

Jackson, Christine E. "The Materials and Methods of Hand- Colouring Zoological Illustrations," *Archives of Natural History* 38, no. 1 (2011): 53–64.

———. "The Painting of Hand-Coloured Zoological Illustrations." *Archives of Natural History* 38, no.1 (2011): 36–52.

James, Edward T., and Janet Wilson James, eds. *Notable American Women, 1607–1950: A Biographical Dictionary*. With Paul S. Boyer. 3 vols. Cambridge, MA: Belknap Press of Harvard University Press, 1971.

Jensson, J. C. *American Lutheran Biographies; or, Historical Notices of over Three Hundred and Fifty Leading Men of the American Lutheran Church, from its establishment to the year 1890*. Milwaukee, WI: A. Houtkamp and Son, 1890.

Jervey, Theo. D. "Reverend Robert Cooper." *South Carolina Historical and Genealogical Magazine* 38, no. 4 (October 1937): 120–25.

Johnson, Michael P. "Planters and Patriarchy: Charleston, 1800–1860." *Journal of Southern History* 46, no. 1 (1980): 45–72.

Johnson, Susan M. "Luther's Reformation and (Un)Holy Matrimony." *Journal of Family History* 17, no. 3 (1992): 271–88.

Johnson Jr., Thomas Cary. *Scientific Interests in the Old South.* New York: D. Appleton-Century Co., 1936.

Joseph, J. W. *"Of Sterling Worth and Good Qualities": Status and Domesticity in Nineteenth-Century Middle Class Charleston.* Archaeological Investigations at Site 38CH1871, Final Report August 30, 2004. Marlene and Nathan Addlestone Library, College of Charleston, 2004.

Karant-Nunn, Susan C., and Merry Wiesner-Hanks, eds. *Luther on Women: A Sourcebook.* Cambridge, UK: Cambridge University Press, 2003.

Keating, William H., ed. *A Narrative of an Expedition to the Source of St. Peter's River, Lake Winnepeek [Winnipeg], Lake of the Woods, &c., &c., performed in the year 1823,* by order of the Honorable J.C. Calhoun, Secretary of War, under the command of Stephen H. Long, Major, U.S.T.E., compiled from the Notes of Major Long, Messrs. Say, Keating and Calhoun. Philadelphia: H. C. Carey and I. Lea, 1824.

Keels, Thomas H. *Philadelphia Graveyards and Cemeteries.* Charleston, SC: Arcadia Pub., 2004.

Kelly, Catherine E. *Reshaping Women's Lives in the Nineteenth Century.* Ithaca, NY: Cornell University Press, 1999.

Kent, Elizabeth. "Art. VII. Considerations of Botany, as a Study for Young People, intended as an Introduction to a Series of Papers Illustrative of the Linnaean System of Plants." *Magazine of Natural History* 1 (1829): 124–35.

Kessler-Harris, Alice. "Why Biography?" *American Historical Review* 114, no. 3 (2009): 625–30.

Kierner, Cynthia A. *Beyond the Household: Women's Place in the Early South, 1700–1835.* Ithaca, NY: Cornell University Press, 1998.

King, William Harvey. *History of Homoeopathy and Its Institutions in America*: Their Founders, Benefactors, Faculties, Officers, Hospitals, Alumni, etc., with a Record of Achievements of its Representatives in the World of Medicine. 4 vols. New York: Lewis Pub. Co., 1905.

Klauber, Laurence Monroe. *Rattlesnakes: Their Habits, Life Histories and Influence on Mankind.* 2 vols. Foreword by Henry W. Greene, 2nd ed. Berkeley: University of California Press, 1997.

Knight, David. *Zoological Illustration, an essay towards a history of printed zoological pictures.* Folkestone, UK: Dawson Pubs., 1977.

Kohlstedt, Sally Gregory. "Parlors, Primers, and Public Schooling: Education for Science in Nineteenth-Century America." *Isis* 81 (1990): 425–45.

Kohlstedt, Sally Gregory. *Teaching Children Science: Hands-On Nature Study in North America, 1890–1930*. Chicago: University of Chicago Press, 2010.

Kolodziej, Benjamin A. "Pietism and Rationalism: A Dichotomy of Resemblance." *Concordia Historical Institute Quarterly* 77, no.1 (2004): 35–54.

Kornwolf, James D. *Architecture and Town Planning in Colonial North America*. With the assistance of Georgiana W. Kornwolf. 2 vols. Baltimore, MD: Johns Hopkins University Press, 2002.

Kuenning, Paul P. "New York Lutheran Abolitionists: Seeking a Solution to a Historical Enigma." *Church History* 58, no. 1 (1989): 52–65.

Lindsay, Debra. "Intimate Inmates: Scientific Wives and Households in nineteenth century America." *Isis* 90, no. 4 (1998): 631–52.

Lloyd, J. U. *Elixirs, Their History, Formulae, and Methods of Preparation*. 2nd ed. Cincinnati, OH: Robert Clarke and Co., 1883.

Lochman, George. *History, Doctrine and Discipline of the Evangelical Lutheran Church*. Harrisburgh, PA: John Wyeth, 1818.

Low, Susanne M. *An Index and Guide to Audubon's Birds of America: A Study of the Double-Elephant Folio of John James Audubon's Birds of America as engraved by William H. Lizars and Robert Havell*. American Museum of Natural History. New York: Abbeville Press, 1988.

Lyerly, Lynn. "Women and Southern Religion." In *Religion in the American South: Protestants and Others in History and Culture*, edited by Beth Barton Shweiger and Donald G. Mathews, 247–81. Chapel Hill: University of North Carolina Press, 2004.

Mannering, Eva. Introduction to *The Best of Redouté's Roses*. London: Ariel Press, 1959.

Martin, Benjamin N. "Rev. John N. Martin." In *American Lutheran Biographies, or Historical Notices of Over Three Hundred and Fifty Leading Men of the American Lutheran Church, From its Establishment to the Year 1890*, edited by Rev. J.C. Jensson, with a Historical Introduction and Numerous Portrait Engravings, 501–05. Milwaukee, WI: A. Houtkamp & Son, 1890.

Martin, Sidney Walter, ed. "Ebenezer Kellogg's Visit to Charleston, 1817." *South Carolina Historical and Genealogical Magazine* 49, no. 1 (1948): 1–14.

Massey, Doreen. *Space, Place and Gender*. Minneapolis: University of Minnesota Press, 1994.

Masten, April F. *Art Work: Women Artists and Democracy in Mid-Nineteenth-Century New York*. Philadelphia: University of Pennsylvania Press, 2008.

Mattox, Mickey L. "Luther on Eve, Women and the Church." *Lutheran Quarterly* 17 (2003): 456–74.

Mayer, Lance, and Gay Myers. *American Painters on Technique: The Colonial Period to 1860*. Los Angeles: J. Paul Getty Museum, 2011.

Mazzitelli, Alexandra. "Listing of Audubon's Bird Watercolors in the New York Historical Society." In Roberta J. M. Olson, *Audubon's Aviary; The Original Watercolors for the Birds of America*, 410–31. New York: New-York Historical Society and Skira Rizzoli Pubs., 2012.

McCandless, Peter. "The Political Evolution of John Bachman: From New York Yankee to South Carolina Secessionist." *South Carolina Historical Magazine* 108, no.1 (2007): 6–31.

———. *Slavery, Disease, and Suffering in the Southern Lowcountry*. Cambridge, UK: Cambridge University Press, 2011.

McDermott, John Francis, ed. *Up the Missouri with Audubon: The Journal of Edward Harris*. Norman: University of Oklahoma Press, 1951.

McInnis, Maurie D. *The Politics of Taste in Antebellum Charleston*. Chapel Hill: University of North Carolina Press, 2005.

McKay, W. D., and Frank Rinder. *The Royal Scottish Academy, 1826–1916: A Complete List of the Works Exhibited by Raeburn and by Academicians, Associates and Hon. Members, giving details of those Works in Public Galleries, with a Historical Narrative of the Origins and Development of the Royal Scottish Academy*. Glasgow, UK: James Maclehose and Sons, 1917.

Miller, Lillian B. *Patrons and Patriotism: The Encouragement of the Fine Arts in the United States, 1790–1860*. Chicago: University of Chicago Press, 1966.

Mitchell, Broadus. *William Gregg: Factory Master of the Old South*. Chapel Hill: University of North Carolina Press, 1928.

Mitchell, Roger S., and Leonard J. Bristol. "Intestinal Tuberculosis: An Analysis of 346 Cases Diagnosed by Routine Intestinal Radiography on 5,529 Admissions for Pulmonary Tuberculosis, 1929–49." *American Journal of the Medical Sciences* 227, no. 3 (1954): 241–49.

Molm, Linda D. "The Social Exchange Framework." In *Contemporary Social Psychological Theories*, edited by Peter James Burke, 24–45. Redwood City, CA: Stanford University Press, 2006.

Molm, Linda D., Jessica L. Collett, and David R. Schaefer. "Building Solidarity through Generalized Exchange: A Theory of Reciprocity." *American Journal of Sociology* 113, no. 1, (2007): 205–42.

Moody, R. T. J., E. Buffetant, D. Naish, and D. M. Martill, eds. *Dinosaurs and Other Extinct Saurians: A Historical Perspective*. Geological Society Special Publication 343. London: Geological Society, 2010.

Murphy, Robert Cushman. "John James: An Evaluation of the Man and His Works." *New-York Historical Society Quarterly* 39–40 (1955–1956): 315–50.

Nasaw, David. "Introduction to AHR Roundtable: Historians and Biography." *American Historical Review* 114, no. 3 (2009): 573–78.

Nesom, G. L. "*Citrus trifoliata* (Rutaceae): Review of biology and distribution in the USA." *Phytoneuron* 46 (2014): 1–14.

Neuffer, Claude Henry, ed. *The Christopher Happoldt Journal: His European Tour with the Rev. John Bachman (June–December, 1838)*. Contributions from the Charleston Museum, XIII. Charleston, SC: Charleston Museum, 1960.

Nickelson, Kärin. "Draughtsmen, Botanists, and Nature: Constructing Eighteenth-Century Botanical Illustrations." *Studies in History and Philosophy of Biology and Biomedical Sciences* 37 (2006): 1–25.

Noble, David F. *A World Without Women: The Christian Clerical Culture of Western Science*. Oxford: Oxford University Press, 1992.

Norton, Mary Beth. *Liberty's Daughters: The Revolutionary Experience of American Women, 1750–1800*. Boston: Little, Brown and Co., 1980.

Numbers, Ronald L. and Janet S. Numbers. "Science in the Old South: A Reappraisal." *Journal of Southern History* 48, no. 2 (1982): 163–84.

Officer, Lawrence H., and Samuel H. Williamson. "Purchasing Power of Money in the United States from 1774 to 2005." MeasuringWorth.com

Olson, Roberta J. M. *Audubon's Aviary; The Original Watercolors for the Birds of America*. New York: New-York Historical Society and Skira Rizzoli Pubs., 2012.

———. "Audubon's Innovations and the Traditions of Ornithological Illustration," In Roberta J. M. Olson, *Audubon's Aviary; The Original Watercolors for the Birds of America*, 40–106. New York: New-York Historical Society and Skira Rizzoli Pubs. 2012.

Opal, J. M. "Exciting Emulation: Academies and the Transformation of the Rural North, 1780s–1820s." *Journal of American History* 91, no. 2 (2004): 445–70.

O'Reggio, Trevor. "Martin Luther: Marriage and the Family as a Remedy for Sin." *Andrews University Seminary Studies* 51, no. 1 (2013): 1–29.

Ott, Katherine. *Fevered Lives: Tuberculosis in American Culture since 1870*. Cambridge, MA: Harvard University Press, 1996.

Ozment, Steven. *Protestants: The Birth of a Revolution*. New York: Doubleday, 1992.

———. "Re-Inventing Family Life." *Christian History* 12, no. 3 (1993): 22–26.

———. *When Fathers Ruled: Family Life in Reformation Europe*. Cambridge, MA: Harvard University Press, 1983.

Page, Frederick G. "James Rennie (1787–1867): Author, Naturalist and Lecturer." *Archives of Natural History* 35, no. 1 (2008): 128–42.

Partridge, Linda Dugan. "By the Book: Audubon and the Tradition of Ornithological Illustration." In *Art and Science in America: Issues of Representation*, edited by Amy R. W. Meyers, 97–129. San Marino, CA: Huntington Library, 1998.

Paterson, K. David. "Disease Environments of the Antebellum South." In *Science and Medicine in the Old South*, edited by Ronald L. Numbers and Todd L. Savitt, 152–65. Baton Rouge: Louisiana State University Press, 1989.

Payne, Daniel Alexander. *Recollections of Seventy Years*, edited by Rev. C. S. Smith with an Introduction by Rev. F. J. Grimke, A. M., D. D., Compiled and arranged by Sarah C. Bierce Scarborough. Nashville, TN: Publishing House of the A.M.E. Sunday School Union, 1888.

Pease, Jane H., and William H. Pease. *Ladies, Women and Wenches: Choice and Constraint in Antebellum Charleston and Boston*. Chapel Hill: University of North Carolina Press, 1990.

———. *The Web of Progress: Private Values and Public Styles in Boston and Charleston, 1828–1843*. Oxford: Oxford University Press, 1985.

Peck, Robert McCracken. "Audubon and Bachman: A Collaboration in Science." In *John James Audubon in the West: The Last Expedition*, edited by Sarah E. Boehme, Buffalo Bill Historical Center, 71–115. New York: Harry N. Abrams Pubs., 2000.

Piggotti, Michael. "Brief Biography and the 'All-Round Man.'" *Grainger Studies: An Interdisciplinary Journal* 1 (2011): 5–20.

Pinault, Madeleine. *The Painter as Naturalist: from Dürer to Redouté*, translated by Philip Sturgess. Paris: Flammarion, 1991.

Plummer, Marjorie Elizabeth. "'Partner in his Calamities': Pastors' Wives, Married Nuns and the Experience of Clerical Marriage in the Early German Reformation." *Gender & History* 20, no. 2 (2008): 207–27.

Porter, Charlotte M. "The Lifework of Titian Ramsay Peale." *Proceedings of the American Philosophical Society* 129, no. 3 (1985): 300–12.

Postle, Martin. "The Life and Art of Joshua Reynolds." In *Joshua Reynolds: The Creation of Celebrity*, edited by Martin Postle, 271–79. London: Tate Pub., 2005.

Poston, Jonathan H. *The Buildings of Charleston: A Guide to the City's Architecture*. Columbia: University of South Carolina Press, 1997.

Premium List of the South Carolina Institute, Incorporated in 1850 for the Promotion and Encouragement of the Arts, Agriculture, Ingenuity, Mechanics, Manufacturing, and a General Development of Industry. Charleston, SC: Walker, Evans and Cogswell, 1870.

Prieto, Laura R. *At Home in the Studio: The Professionalization of Women Artists in America*. Cambridge, MA: Harvard University Press, 2001.

Proby, Kathryn Hall. *Audubon in Florida*. With Selections from the Writings of John James Audubon. Coral Gables, FL: University of Miami Press, 1974.

Proceedings of the meetings in Charleston, May 13–15 1845, on the Religious Instruction of the Negroes, Together with the Report of the Committee and the Address to the Public. Charleston, SC: B. Jenkins, 1845.

Radford, John P. "Model of the Pre-Industrial City: Charleston, South Carolina." *Transactions of the Institute of British Geographers* New Ser. 4, no. 3 (1979): 392–410.

Redouté, P-J. *Choix des plus belles fleurs et des plus beaux fruits*. Paris: Ernest Panckoucke, 1827.

Reeds, Karen. "When the botanist can't draw: The case of Linnaeus." *Interdisciplinary Science Reviews* 29, no. 3 (2004): 248–58.

Renders, Hans and Binne de Haan, eds. *Theoretical Discussions of Biography: Approaches from History, Microhistory, and Life Writing*. foreword by Nigel Hamilton. Lewiston, NY: Edwin Mellen Press, 2013.

Rennie, James. *A New Supplement to the latest Pharmacopoeias of London, Edinburgh, Dublin, and Paris*, forming a complete Dispensatory, Conspectus, and Dictionary of Medical Chemistry, giving all the old and new names, including the new French and American medicines, and Poisons; with Symptoms, Treatments and Tests . . . 4th. ed. London: Baldwin and Cradock, 1837.

———. *Ornithological Dictionary of British Birds by Colonel G. Montagu*. 2nd ed. With a Plan of Study, and Many New Articles and Original Observations. London: Hurst, Chance and Co., 1831.

Reynolds, Joshua. *Seven Discourses delivered in the Royal Academy by the President*. London: T. Cadell, 1778.

Rhodes, Richard. *John James Audubon: The Making of an American*. New York: Alfred A. Knopf, 2005.

Richards, Irving T. "Audubon, Joseph R. Mason, and John Neal." *American Literature* 6, no. 2 (May 1934), 122–40.

Ridge, Antoina. *The Man Who Painted Roses: The Story of Pierre-Joseph Redouté*. London: Faber and Faber, 1974.

Riley, Helene M. "Michael Kalteisen and the Founding of the German Friendly Society in Charleston." *South Carolina Historical Magazine* 100 (1999): 29–48.

Rix, Martyn, and Alison Rix. *The Redouté Album*. London: Studio Editions, 1990.

Robert, Kimberlie M. "Women's Botanical Illustration in Canada: Its Gendered, Colonial and Garden Histories." Master's thesis, Concordia University, Ottawa, 2008.

Roeber, A. G. *Palatines, Liberty and Property: German Lutherans in Colonial British America*. Baltimore, MD: Johns Hopkins University Press, 1993.

Rogers, George A., Vivian Rogers-Price, and Daniel V. Hagan. "André Michaux's Influence on Stephen Elliott's *A Sketch of the Botany of South Carolina and Georgia*." *Castanea* 69 (2004): 217–22.

Roper, Lyndal. *The Holy Household: Women and Morals in Reformation Augsburg*. Oxford: Clarendon Press, 1989.

Rossiter, Margaret W. *Women Scientists in America: Struggles and Strategies to 1940*. Baltimore, MD: John Hopkins University Press, 1982.

Rotberg, Robert I. "Biography and Historiography: Mutual Evidentiary and Interdisciplinary Considerations." *Journal of Interdisciplinary History* 40, no. 3 (2010), 305–324.

Rothman, Sheila M. *Living in the Shadow of Death: Tuberculosis and the Social Experience of Illness in American History*. New York: Basic Books, 1994.

Rothstein, William G. *American Physicians in the Nineteenth Century: From Sects to Science*. Baltimore, MD: Johns Hopkins University Press, 1972.

Rutledge, Anna Wells. "Artists in the Life of Charleston: Through Colony and State, from Restoration to Reconstruction." *Transactions of the American Philosophical Society*. New Ser. 39, no. 2 (1949): 101–250.

Salmon, Marylynn. "Women and Property in South Carolina: The Evidence from

Marriage Settlements, 1730 to 1830." *William and Mary Quarterly* 39, no. 4 (1982): 655–85.

Sanders, Albert E., and Warren Ripley, eds. *Audubon: The Charleston Connection.* Foreword by John Henry Dick and Photographs by William A. Jordan. From the Charleston Museum Collection, 8 September–17 November 1985. Contributions from the Charleston Museum, XVI. Charleston, SC: Charleston Museum, 1986.

Sanders, Albert E., and William D. Anderson Jr. *Natural History Investigations in South Carolina: From Colonial Times to the Present.* Columbia: University of South Carolina Press, 1999.

Say, Thomas. *American Entomology or Descriptions of the Insects of North America.* Illustrated by Coloured Figures from Original Drawings executed from Nature. Philadelphia: Samuel Augustus Mitchell, 1825.

Schufeldt, R. W., and Maria Rebecca Audubon. "The Last Portrait of Audubon, Together with a Letter to his Son." *The Auk* 11 (1894): 309–13.

Scudder, Samuel H., ed. *Entomological Correspondence of Thaddeus William Harris, M. D.* Boston: Boston Society of Natural History, 1869.

Shweiger, Beth Barton, and Donald G. Mathews, eds. *Religion in the American South: Protestants and Others in History and Culture.* Chapel Hill: University of North Carolina Press, 2004.

Seccombe, Thomas. "James Thomson (1700–1748)." *Dictionary of National Biography*, 56 (1885–1900).

Shelley, Marjorie. "The Craft of American Drawing: Early Eighteenth to Late Nineteenth Century." In *American Drawings and Watercolors in the Metropolitan Museum of Art: A Catalogue of Works by Artists before 1835*, edited by Kevin J. Avery, 1:28–78. New York: Metropolitan Museum of Art, 2001.

———. "Drawing Birds: Audubon's Artistic Practices." In Roberta J. M. Olson, *Audubon's Aviary; The Original Watercolors for the Birds of America*, 108–31. New York: New-York Historical Society and Skira Rizzoli Pubs., 2012.

Sherlock, Siriol. *Botanical Illustration: Painting with Watercolours.* London: B. T. Batsford, 2007.

———. *Exploring Flowers in Watercolour: Techniques and Images.* London: B. T. Batsford, 2000.

Shteir, Ann B. "Botany in the Breakfast Room." In *Uneasy Careers and Intimate Lives: Women in Science, 1789–1979*, edited by Pnina G. Abir-Am and Dorinda Outram, 31–43. New Brunswick, NJ: Rutgers University Press, 1989.

———. *Cultivating Women, Cultivating Science: Flora's Daughters and Botany in England, 1760–1860.* Baltimore, MD: John Hopkins University Press, 1996.

Shuler, Jay. *"Had I the Wings": The Friendship of Bachman and Audubon.* Athens: University of Georgia Press, 1995.

Silver, Allan. "Friendship in Commercial Society: Eighteenth-Century Social Theory and Modern Sociology." *American Journal of Sociology* 95, no. 6 (1990): 1474–1504.

Simson, James. *Charles Waterton: Naturalist.* New York: James Miller Pub.; Edinburgh: MacLahlan and Stewart; London: Baillière, Tyndall and Co., 1880.

Small, Ernest, Paul M. Catling, Jacques Cayouette, and Brenda Brookes, eds. *Audubon: Beyond Birds, Plant Portraits and Conservation Heritage of John James Audubon.* Ottawa: NRC-CNRC Research Press, 2009.

Smith, Alice R. Huger, and D. E. Huger Smith. *The Dwellings of Charleston, South Carolina.* Philadelphia: J. B. Lippincott Co., 1917.

Smith, D. E. Huger, and A. S. Salley Jr., eds. *Register of St. Philip's Parish, Charles Town or Charleston, 1754–1810.* 1927; Repr. Columbia: University of South Carolina Press, 1971.

Smith, Katy Simpson. *We Have Raised All of You: Motherhood in the South, 1750–1835.* Baton Rouge: Louisiana State Press, 2013.

Smith, Pamela H. "Art, Science, and Visual Culture in Early Modern Europe." *Isis* 97 (2006): 83–100.

Soltow, Lee. "Socioeconomic Classes in South Carolina and Massachusetts in the 1790s and the Observations of John Drayton." *South Carolina Historical Magazine* 81, no. 4 (1980): 283–305.

Souder, William. *Under A Wild Sky: John James Audubon and the Making of the Birds of America.* New York: North Point Press, 2004.

Spruill, Julia Cherry. "'Conjugal Felicity' and Domestic Discord." In *Women's Life and Work in the Southern Colonies*, edited by Julia Cherry Spruill, 163–84. Chapel Hill: University of North Carolina Press, 1938.

Stafleu, Frans A., ed. "Redouté and his Circle." In *Bibliography and Natural History*: Essays presented at a conference in June 1964 by Thomas R. Buckman, 46–65. Lawrence: University of Kansas Libraries, 1966.

Stephan, Scott. *Reforming the Southern Family: Evangelical Women and Domestic Devotion in the Antebellum South.* Athens: University of Georgia Press, 2008.

Stephens, Lester D. "The Literary and Philosophical Society of South Carolina: A Forum for Intellectual Progress in Antebellum Charleston." *South Carolina Historical Magazine* 104, no. 3 (July 2003): 154–75.

———. "The Mermaid Hoax: Indications of Scientific Thought of Charleston, South Carolina, in the 1840s." *Proceedings*, South Carolina Historical Association 5, no. 1 (1983), 45–55.

———. *Science, Race and Religion in the American South: John Bachman and the Charleston Circle of Naturalists, 1815–1895.* Chapel Hill: University of North Carolina Press, 2000.

Stern, Andrew H. M. *Southern Crucifix, Southern Cross: Catholic-Protestant Relations in the Old South*, Religion and American Culture. Tuscaloosa: University of Alabama Press, 2012.

Stevens, Margaret. *The Botanical Palette: Color for the Botanical Painter.* In association with the Society of Botanical Artists. New York: Harper Collins, 2007.

Stjerna, Kirsi. *Women and the Reformation*. Malden, MA: Blackwell Pub., 2009.

Stoney, Samuel Gaillard, ed. "Memoirs of Frederick Adolphus Porcher." *South Carolina Historical Magazine* 47 (1946): 214–27.

Strange, Douglas C. "Our Duty to Preach the Gospel to Negroes: Southern Lutherans and American Slavery." *Concordia Historical Institute Quarterly* 42 (1969): 171–82.

Strauss, Gerald. "The Social Function of Schools in the Lutheran Reformation in Germany." *History of Education Quarterly* 28, no. 2 (1988): 191–206.

Strecker, Herman. *Complete Synonymical Catalogue of Macrolepidopter with a full Bibliography*. Reading, PA: B. F. Owen, 1878.

Streshinsky, Shirley. *Audubon: Life and Art in the American Wilderness*. Athens: University of Georgia Press, 1995.

Striker, Noah. *The Thing with Feathers: The Surprising Lives of Birds and What They Reveal About Being Human*. New York: Riverhead Books, 2014.

Stumpt, Stuart O. "South Carolina Importers of General Merchandise, 1735–1765." *South Carolina Historical Magazine* 84, no.1 (1983): 1–10.

Suelflow, August R., and E. Clifford Nelson. "Following the Frontier, 1840–1875." In *The Lutherans in North America*, edited by E. Clifford Nelson, 147–254. Philadelphia: Fortress Press, 1975.

Sully, Thomas. *Hints to Young Painters, and the Process of Portrait-Painting as Practiced by the Late Thomas Sully*. Philadelphia: J. M. Stoddart and Co., 1873.

Tappert, Theodore G., and John W. Doberstein, eds. *The Journals of Henry Melchior Muhlenberg*. 3 vols. Philadelphia: Evangelical Lutheran Ministerium of Pennsylvania and Adjacent States and the Muhlenberg Press, 1946.

Tappert, Theodore G. "The Church's Infancy, 1650–1790." In *The Lutherans in North America*, edited by E. Clifford Nelson, 3–77. Philadelphia: Fortress Press, 1975.

Taylor, Rosser H. *Ante-Bellum South Carolina: A Social and Cultural History*. The James Sprout Studies in History and Political Science, 25, no. 2, edited by Albert Ray Newsome et al. Chapel Hill: University of North Carolina Press, 1942.

Teal, Harvey S. *Partners in the Sun: South Carolina Photographers, 1840–1940*. Columbia: University of South Carolina Press, 2001.

Tertullian. "It is Not Enough that God Know Us to Be Chaste: We Must Seem So Before Men. Especially in These Times of Persecution We Must Inure Our Bodies to the Hardships Which They May Not Improbably Be Called to Suffer." Book II, *De cultu feminarum*, translated by Sidney Thelwall, English Trans. *Ante-Nicene Christian Library* (ANCL) 11 (1869): 304–322. Reprinted *ANF* [Ante-Nicene Fathers] 4 (1885): 14–25.

Tolley, Kim. "Science for Ladies, Classics for Gentlemen: A Comparative Analysis of Scientific Subjects in the Curricula of Boys' and Girls' Secondary Schools in the United States, 1794–1850." *History of Education Quarterly* 36, no. 2 (1996): 129–53.

Torrens, H. S. "William Perceval Hunter (1812–1878), forgotten English student of dinosaurs-to-be and of Wealden Rocks." In *Dinosaurs and Other Extinct Saurians:*

A Historical Perspective, edited by R. T. J Moody, E. Buffetant, D. Naish, and D. M. Martill, 31–47. Geological Society Special Publication 343. London: Geological Society, 2010.

Torrey, John. "Some account of a collection of plants made during a journey to and from the Rocky Mountains in summer of 1820, by Edwin P. James, M.D., Assistant Surgeon, U.S. Army." In *Annals of the Lyceum of Natural History of New York*, March 1826, 161–97. New York: James Seymore, 1828.

Torrey, John, and Asa Gray. *Flora of North America; containing abridged descriptions of all the known indigenous and naturalized plants growing north of Mexico, arranged according to the Natural System*. 2 vols. New York: Wiley and Putnam, 1838–40.

Touchstone, Blake. "Planters and Slave Religion in the Deep South." In *Masters and Slaves in the House of the Lord: Race and Religion in the American South, 1740–1870*, edited by John B. Boles, 99–126. Lexington: University of Kentucky Press, 1988.

Townsend, Charles W. "A Visit to Tom Lincoln's House with some Auduboniana." *The Auk* 41, no. 2 (1924): 237–42.

Travers, Benjamin, and Edward Delafield. *A Synopsis of the Diseases of the Eye, and Their Treatment*, to which are prefixed a short anatomical description and a sketch of the physiology of that organ. New York: E. Bliss and E. White, 1825.

Treu, Martin. "Katharina von Bora, the Woman at Luther's Side." *Lutheran Quarterly* 13 (1999): 157–78.

Trumbull, David. *Travels in the West: Cuba, With Notices of Porto Rico and the Slave Trade*. London: Longman, Orme, Brown, Green and Longmans, 1840.

Tyler, Ron. *Nature's Classics: John James Audubon's Birds and Animals*. Orange, TX: Stark Museum of Art, 1992.

Waddell, Gene. *Charleston Architecture, 1670–1860*. 2 vols. Charleston, SC: Wyrick and Co., 2003.

———. "A Companion Guide to Charleston House Types." *Preservation Progress* 49, no. 2 (2005): 10–11.

———. *John Bachman: Selected Writings on Science, Race and Religion*. Athens: University of Georgia Press, 2011.

Ward, Chloe. "Biography, history, agency: where have all the 'great men' gone?" *Flinders Journal of History & Politics* 28 (2012): 77–97.

Ware, Susan. "Writing Women's History: One Historian's Perspective." *Journal of Interdisciplinary History* 40, no. 3 (2010): 413–35.

Waring, Joseph Ioor. *A History of Medicine in South Carolina, 1825–1900*. Columbia: South Carolina Medical Association, 1967.

Warner, John Harley. "The Idea of Southern Medical Distinctiveness: Medical Knowledge and Practice in the Old South." In *Science and Medicine in the Old South*, edited by Ronald L. Numbers and Todd L. Savitt, 179–205. Baton Rouge: Louisiana State University Press, 1989.

Waterhouse, Richard. "Development of Elite Culture in the Colonial American

South: A Study of Charles Towne, 1670–1770." *Australian Journal of Politics and History* 28, no.3 (1982): 391–404.

Waterton, Charles. "Art. III. On the Faculty of Scent in the Vulture." *Loudon's Magazine of Natural History and Journal of Zoology, Botany, Mineralogy, Geology, and Meteorology* 5 (1832): 233–41.

———. "Art. IV. The Habits of the Carrion Crow." *Loudon's Magazine of Natural History and Journal of Zoology, Botany, Mineralogy, Geology, and Meteorology* 6 (1833): 208–18.

———. "Art. V. On the 'Biography of Birds' of J. J. Audubon." *Loudon's Magazine of Natural History and Journal of Zoology, Botany, Mineralogy, Geology, and Meteorology* 6 (1833): 215–18.

———. "Art.IX. Remarks on Professor Rennie's Edition of Montagu's *Ornithological Dictionary*." *Loudon's Magazine of Natural History and Journal of Zoology, Botany, Mineralogy, Geology, and Meteorology* 4 (1831): 516–20.

———. "Audubon's Claim to the Authorship of the Biography of Birds; Audubon and his Ornithology." *Loudon's Magazine of Natural History and Journal of Zoology, Botany, Mineralogy, Geology, and Meteorology* 7 (1834): 276–78.

———. *Essays on Natural History*, edited with a life of the author by Norman Moore. London: Frederick Warne and Co.; New York: Scribner, Welford and Armstrong, 1871.

———. "The Means by which the Turkey Buzzard (Vúltur Aúra L.) traces its Food." *Loudon's Magazine of Natural History and Journal of Zoology, Botany, Mineralogy, Geology, and Meteorology* 6 (1833): 162–63.

———. "Retrospective Criticism: The Gland on the Rump of Birds." *Loudon's Magazine of Natural History and Journal of Zoology, Botany, Mineralogy, Geology, and Meteorology* 6 (1833): 274–77.

———. "Retrospective Criticism." *Loudon's Magazine of Natural History and Journal of Zoology, Botany, Mineralogy, Geology, and Meteorology* 6 (1833): 464–68.

———. "Retrospective Criticism." *Loudon's Magazine of Natural History and Journal of Zoology, Botany, Mineralogy, Geology, and Meteorology* 7 (1834): 66–74.

———. "Retrospective Criticism: The Vulture's Nose." *Loudon's Magazine of Natural History and Journal of Zoology, Botany, Mineralogy, Geology, and Meteorology* 7 (1834): 278–83.

———. *Wanderings in South America, the North-West of the United States and the Antilles in the years 1812, 1816, 1820, and 1824*. London: J. Mawman, 1825.

Wayne, Tiffany K. *Women's Roles in Nineteenth-Century America*. Santa Barbara, CA: Greenwood Pub. Group, 2007.

Welch, Margaret. *The Book of Nature: Natural History in the United States, 1825–1875*. Boston: Northeastern University Press, 1998.

Wenzel, Bernice M. "Avian Olfaction: Then and Now." *Journal of Ornithology* 148, supplement 2 (June 14, 2007): S191–S194. doi.10.1007/s10336–007–0147-z

Wilcox, R. Turner. *The Mode in Costume*. New York, 1958.

Wilcox, Scott, and Christopher Newall. *Victorian Landscape Watercolors*. Yale Center for British Art, Cleveland Museum of Art, Birmingham Museums and Art Gallery. New York: Hudson Hills Press, 1992.

Wilson, John. "Peculiar Symptoms Affecting an Entire Family, and Terminating in Death." *Medico-Chirurgical Transactions* 25 (1842): 74–90.

———. "Peculiar Symptoms Affecting an Entire Family, and Terminating in Death." *Royal Medico-Chirurgical Transactions* 4, no. 87 (1842): 153–54.

———. "Peculiar Symptoms Affecting an Entire Family, and Terminating in Death." *The Chemist* 3 (1842): 190–92.

Williams, George W., and Gene Waddell, eds. "Letters from the Clergy of the Anglican Church in South Carolina, c.1696–1775." List of South Carolina Clergy, 12–15. College of Charleston Faculty Manuscript Collection, Lowcountry Digital Library.

Wood, Kirsten E. *Masterful Women: Slaveholding Widows from the American Revolution through the Civil War*. Chapel Hill: University of North Carolina Press, 2004.

Works of [William] Cowper and [James] Thomson, Letters and Poems never before published in this country of the Life of Thomson. Complete in one volume. Philadelphia: J. Grigg, 1832.

Wrifford, Allison. *Essays on School Keeping: Comprising Observations on the Qualifications of Teachers, on School Government, and the Most Approved Methods of Instruction in the Various Branches of a Useful Education* By an experienced teacher. Philadelphia: John Grigg, 1831.

Wurdemann, J. G. F. *Notes on Cuba*, Containing An Account of Its Discovery and Early History; A Description of the Face of the Country, Its Population, Resources, and Wealth; Its Institutions, and the Manners and Customs of its Inhabitants, With Directions to Travelers Visiting the Island by a Physician. Boston: James Munroe and Co., 1844.

Wyatt-Brown, Bertram. *Southern Honor: Ethics and Behavior in the Old South*. 25th Anniversary ed. Oxford: Oxford University Press, 2007.

INDEX